I0891837

Ancient Christian Texts

Incomplete Commentary on Matthew

(*Opus imperfectum*)

Volume 1

Translated with an Introduction and Notes by

James A. Kellerman

Edited by

Thomas C. Oden

Series Editors

Thomas C. Oden and Gerald L. Bray

IVP Academic

An imprint of InterVarsity Press
Downers Grove, Illinois

InterVarsity Press
P.O. Box 1400, Downers Grove, IL 60515-1426
World Wide Web: www.ivpress.com
E-mail: email@ivpress.com

©2010 by James A. Kellerman, Thomas C. Oden, Gerald L. Bray, Michael Glerup and the Institute for Classical Christian Studies

All rights reserved. No part of this book may be reproduced in any form without written permission from InterVarsity Press.

InterVarsity Press® is the book-publishing division of InterVarsity Christian Fellowship/USA®, a movement of students and faculty active on campus at hundreds of universities, colleges and schools of nursing in the United States of America, and a member movement of the International Fellowship of Evangelical Students. For information about local and regional activities, write Public Relations Dept., InterVarsity Christian Fellowship/USA, 6400 Schroeder Rd., P.O. Box 7895, Madison, WI 53707-7895, or visit the IVCF website at <www.intervarsity.org>.

The Scripture quotations quoted herein are from the Revised Standard Version of the Bible, copyright 1946, 1952, 1971 by the Division of Christian Education of the National Council of the Churches of Christ in the U.S.A. Used by permission. All rights reserved.

Design: Cindy Kiple

ISBN 978-0-8308-2901-9

Printed in the United States of America ∞

InterVarsity Press is committed to protecting the environment and to the responsible use of natural resources. As a member of Green Press Initiative we use recycled paper whenever possible. To learn more about the Green Press Initiative, visit <www.greenpressinitiative.org>.

Library of Congress Cataloging-in-Publication Data

Opus imperfectum in Matthaeum. English.
Incomplete commentary on Matthew/translated with an introduction and notes by James A. Kellerman; editd by Thomas C. Oden.
p. cm.—(Ancient Christian texts)
Translation of: Opus imperfectum in Matthaeum.
includes bibliographical references and index.
ISBN 0-978-8308-2901-9 (cloth: alk. paper)
1. Bible. N.T. Matthew—Sermons. 2. Sermons, Latin—Translations into English. I. Kellerman, James A., 1962- II. Oden, Thomas C. III. Title
BS2575.54.O6813 2010
226.2'0609015—dc22

2010000190

P 24 23 22 21 20 19 18 17 16 15 14 13 12 11 10 9 8 7 6 5 4 3 2 1
Y 31 30 29 28 27 26 25 24 23 22 21 20 19 18 17 16 15 14 13 12 11 10

CONTENTS

General Introduction / PAGE VII

Abbreviations / PAGE XV

Translator's Introduction / PAGE XVII

Incomplete Commentary on Matthew
(*Opus imperfectum*) / PAGE 1

Prologue / PAGE 1

The First Homily: *On Matthew 1* / PAGE 2

The Second Homily: *On Matthew 2* / PAGE 30

The Third Homily: *On Matthew 3* / PAGE 43

The Fouth Homily: *On Matthew 3* / PAGE 55

The Fifth Homily: *On Matthew 4* / PAGE 61

The Sixth Homily: *On Matthew 4* / PAGE 73

The Seventh Homily: *On Matthew 4* / PAGE 77

The Eighth Homily: *On Matthew 4* / PAGE 80

The Ninth Homily: *On Matthew 5* / PAGE 83

The Tenth Homily: *On Matthew 5* / PAGE 89

The Eleventh Homily: *On Matthew 5* / PAGE 94

The Twelfth Homily: *On Matthew 5* / PAGE 100

The Thirteenth Homily: *On Matthew 5 and 6* / PAGE 110

The Fourteenth Homily: *On Matthew 6* / PAGE 121

THE FIFTEENTH HOMILY: *ON MATTHEW 6* / PAGE 126

THE SIXTEENTH HOMILY: *ON MATTHEW 6* / PAGE 135

THE SEVENTEENTH HOMILY: *ON MATTHEW 7* / PAGE 138

THE EIGHTEENTH HOMILY: *ON MATTHEW 7* / PAGE 144

THE NINETEENTH HOMILY: *ON MATTHEW 7* / PAGE 152

THE TWENTIETH HOMILY: *ON MATTHEW 7* / PAGE 160

THE TWENTY-FIRST HOMILY: *ON MATTHEW 8* / PAGE 165

THE TWENTY-SECOND HOMILY: *ON MATTHEW 8* / PAGE 169

THE TWENTY-THIRD HOMILY: *ON MATTHEW 10* / PAGE 173

THE TWENTY-FOURTH HOMILY: *ON MATTHEW 10* / PAGE 181

THE TWENTY-FIFTH HOMILY: *ON MATTHEW 10 AND 11* / PAGE 189

THE TWENTY-SIXTH HOMILY: *ON MATTHEW 11* / PAGE 195

THE TWENTY-SEVENTH HOMILY: *ON MATTHEW 11* / PAGE 203

SCRIPTURE INDEX / PAGE 210

GENERAL INTRODUCTION

Ancient Christian Texts (hereafter ACT) presents the full text of ancient Christian commentaries on Scripture that have remained so unnoticed that they have not yet been translated into English.

The patristic period (A.D. 95-750) is the time of the fathers of the church, when the exegesis of Scripture texts was in its primitive formation. This period spans from Clement of Rome to John of Damascus, embracing seven centuries of biblical interpretation, from the end of the New Testament to the mid-eighth century, including the Venerable Bede.

This series extends but does not reduplicate texts of the Ancient Christian Commentary on Scripture (ACCS). It presents full-length translations of texts that appear only as brief extracts in the ACCS. The ACCS began years ago authorizing full-length translations of key patristic texts on Scripture in order to provide fresh sources of valuable commentary that previously were not available in English. It is from these translations that the ACT series has emerged.

A multiyear project such as this requires a well-defined objective. The task is straightforward: *to introduce full-length translations of key texts of early Christian teaching, homilies and commentaries on a particular book of Scripture.* These are seminal documents that have decisively shaped the entire subsequent history of biblical exegesis, but in our time have been largely ignored.

To carry out this mission each volume of the Ancient Christian Texts series has four aspirations:

1. To show the approach of one of the early Christian writers in dealing with the problems of understanding, reading and conveying the meaning of a particular book of Scripture.

2. To make more fully available the whole argument of the ancient Christian interpreter of Scripture to all who wish to think with the early church about a particular canonical text.

3. To broaden the base of the biblical studies, Christian teaching and preaching to include classical Christian exegesis.

4. To stimulate Christian historical, biblical, theological and pastoral scholarship toward deeper inquiry into early classic practitioners of scriptural interpretation.

For Whom Is This Series Designed?

We have selected and translated these texts primarily for general and nonprofessional use by an audience of persons who study the Bible regularly.

In varied cultural settings around the world, contemporary readers are asking how they might grasp the meaning of sacred texts under the instruction of the great minds of the ancient church. They often study books of the Bible verse by verse, book by book, in groups and workshops, sometimes with a modern commentary in hand. But many who study the Bible intensively hunger to have available as well the thoughts of a reliable classic Christian commentator on this same text. This series will give the modern commentators a classical text for comparison and amplification. Readers will judge for themselves as to how valuable or complementary are their insights and guidance.

The classic texts we are translating were originally written for anyone (lay or clergy, believers or seekers) who wished to reflect and meditate with the great minds of the early church. They sought to illuminate the plain sense, theological wisdom, and moral and spiritual meaning of an individual book of Scripture. They were not written for an academic audience, but for a community of faith shaped by the sacred text.

Yet in serving this general audience, the editors remain determined not to neglect the rigorous requirements and needs of academic readers who until recently have had few full translations available to them in the history of exegesis. So this series is designed also to serve public libraries, universities, academic classes, homiletic preparation and historical interests worldwide in Christian scholarship and interpretation.

Hence our expected audience is not limited to the highly technical and specialized scholarly field of patristic studies, with its strong bent toward detailed word studies and explorations of cultural contexts. Though all of our editors and translators are patristic and linguistic scholars, they also are scholars who search for the meanings and implications of the texts. The audience is not primarily the university scholar concentrating on the study of the history of the transmission of the text or those with highly focused interests in textual morphology or historical-critical issues. If we succeed in serving our wider readers practically and well, we hope to serve as well college and seminary courses in Bible, church history, historical theology, hermeneutics and homiletics. These texts have not until now been available to these classes.

Readiness for Classic Spiritual Formation

Today global Christians are being steadily drawn toward these biblical and patristic sources for daily meditation and spiritual formation. They are on the outlook for primary classic sources of spiritual formation and biblical interpretation, presented in accessible form and grounded in reliable scholarship.

These crucial texts have had an extended epoch of sustained influence on Scripture interpretation, but virtually no influence in the modern period. They also deserve a hearing among modern readers and scholars. There is a growing awareness of the speculative excesses and spiritual and homiletic limitations of much post-Enlightenment criticism. Meanwhile the motifs, methods and approaches of ancient exegetes have remained unfamiliar not only to historians but to otherwise highly literate biblical scholars, trained exhaustively in the methods of historical and scientific criticism.

It is ironic that our times, which claim to be so fully furnished with historical insight and research methods, have neglected these texts more than scholars in previous centuries who could read them in their original languages.

This series provides indisputable evidence of the modern neglect of classic Christian exegesis: it remains a fact that extensive and once authoritative classic commentaries on Scripture still remain untranslated into any modern language. Even in China such a high level of neglect has not befallen classic Buddhist, Taoist and Confucian commentaries.

Ecumenical Scholarship

This series, like its two companion series, the ACCS and Ancient Christian Doctrine (ACD), are expressions of unceasing ecumenical efforts that have enjoyed the wide cooperation of distinguished scholars of many differing academic communities. Under this classic textual umbrella, it has brought together in common spirit Christians who have long distanced themselves from each other by competing church memories. But all of these traditions have an equal right to appeal to the early history of Christian exegesis. All of these traditions can, without a sacrifice of principle or intellect, come together to study texts common to them all. This is its ecumenical significance.

This series of translations is respectful of a distinctively theological reading of Scripture that cannot be reduced to historical, philosophical, scientific, or sociological insights or methods alone. It takes seriously the venerable tradition of ecumenical reflection concerning the premises of revelation, providence, apostolicity, canon and consensuality. A high respect is here granted, despite modern assumptions, to uniquely Christian theological forms of reasoning, such as classical consensual christological and triune reasoning, as distinguishing premises of classic Christian textual interpretation. These cannot be acquired by empirical methods alone. This approach does not pit theology against critical theory; instead, it incorporates critical historical methods and brings them into coordinate accountability within its larger purpose of listening to Scripture.

The internationally diverse character of our editors and translators corresponds with the global range of our audience, which bridges many major communions of Christianity. We have sought to bring together a distinguished international network of Protestant, Catholic and Orthodox scholars, editors and translators of the highest quality and reputation to accomplish this design.

But why just now at this historical moment is this need for patristic wisdom felt particularly by so many readers of Scripture? Part of the reason is that these readers have been longer deprived of significant contact with many of these vital sources of classic Christian exegesis.

The Ancient Commentary Tradition

This series focuses on texts that comment on Scripture and teach its meaning. We define a commentary in its plain-sense definition as a series of illustrative or explanatory notes on any work of enduring significance. The word *commentary* is an Anglicized form of the Latin *commentarius* (or "annotation" or "memoranda" on a subject, text or series of events). In its theological meaning it is a work that explains, analyzes or expounds a biblical book or portion of Scripture. Tertullian, Origen, John Chrysostom, Jerome, Augustine and Clement of Alexandria all revealed their familiarity with both the secular and religious commentators available to them as they unpacked the meanings of the sacred text at hand.

The commentary in ancient times typically began with a general introduction covering such questions as authorship, date, purpose and audience. It commented as needed on grammatical or lexical problems in the text and provided explanations of difficulties in the text. It typically moved verse by verse through a Scripture text, seeking to make its meaning clear and its import understood.

The general western literary genre of commentary has been definitively shaped by the history of early Christian commentaries on Scripture. It is from Origen, Hilary, the *Opus imperfectum in Matthaeum*, John Chrysostom and Cyril of Alexandria that we learn what a commentary is—far more so than in the case of classic medical, philosophical or poetic commentaries. It leaves too much unsaid simply to assume that the Christian biblical commentary took a previously extant literary genre and reshaped it for Christian texts. Rather it is more accurate to say that *the Western literary genre of the commentary (and especially the biblical commentary) has patristic commentaries as its decisive pattern and prototype.*

It is only in the last two centuries, since the development of modern historicist methods of criticism, that modern writers have sought more strictly to delimit the definition of a commentary so as to include only certain limited interests focusing largely on historical-critical method, philological and grammatical observations, literary analysis, and socio-political or economic circumstances impinging on the text. While respecting all these approaches, the ACT editors do not hesitate to use the classic word *commentary* to define more broadly the genre of this series. These are commentaries in their classic sense.

The ACT editors freely take the assumption that the Christian canon is to be respected as the church's sacred text. The reading and preaching of Scripture are vital to religious life. The central hope of this endeavor is that it might contribute in some small way to the revitalization of religious faith and community through a renewed discovery of the earliest readings of the church's Scriptures.

An Appeal to Allow the Text to Speak for Itself

This prompts two appeals:

1. For those who begin by assuming as normative for a commentary only the norms considered typical for modern expressions of what a commentary is, we ask: Please allow the ancient commentators to define *commentarius* according to their own lights. Those who assume the preemptive authority and truthfulness of modern critical methods alone will always tend to view the classic Christian exegetes as dated, quaint, premodern, hence inadequate, and in some instances comic or even mean-spirited, prejudiced, unjust and oppressive. So in the interest of hermeneutical fairness, it is recommended that the modern reader not impose upon ancient Christian exegetes modern assumptions about valid readings of Scripture. The ancient Christian writers constantly challenge these unspoken, hidden and indeed often camouflaged assumptions that have become commonplace in our time.

We leave it to others to discuss the merits of ancient versus modern methods of exegesis. But even this cannot be done honestly without a serious examination of the texts of ancient exegesis. Ancient commentaries may be disqualified as commentaries by modern standards. But they remain commentaries by the standards of those who anteceded and formed the basis of the modern commentary.

The attempt to read a Scripture text while ruling out all theological and moral assumptions—as well as ecclesial, sacramental and dogmatic assumptions that have prevailed generally in the community of faith out of which it emerged—is a very thin enterprise indeed. Those who tendentiously may read a single page of patristic exegesis, gasp and toss it away because it does not conform adequately to the canons of modern exegesis and historicist commentary are surely not exhibiting a valid model for critical inquiry today.

2. In ancient Christian exegesis, chains of biblical references were often very important in thinking about the text in relation to the whole testimony of sacred Scripture, by the analogy of faith, comparing text with text, on the premise that *scripturam ex scriptura explicandam esse*. When ancient exegesis weaves many Scripture texts together, it does not limit its focus to a single text as much modern exegesis prefers, but constantly relates them to other texts, by analogy, intensively using typological reasoning, as did the rabbinic tradition.

Since the principle prevails in ancient Christian exegesis that each text is illumined by other texts and by the whole narrative of the history of revelation, we find in patristic comments on a given text many other subtexts interwoven in order to illumine that text. In these ways the models of exegesis often do not correspond with modern commentary assumptions, which tend to resist or rule out chains of scriptural reference. We implore the reader not to force the assumptions of twentieth-century hermeneutics upon the ancient Christian writers, who themselves knew nothing of what we now call hermeneutics.

The Complementarity of Research Methods in this Series

The Ancient Christian Texts series will employ several interrelated methods of research, which the editors and translators seek to bring together in a working integration. Principal among these methods are the following:

1. The editors, translators and annotators will bring to bear the best resources of *textual criticism* in preparation for their volumes. This series is not intended to produce a new critical edition of the original-language text. The best urtext in the original language will be used. Significant variants in the earliest manuscript sources of the text may be commented upon as needed in the annotations. But it will be assumed that the editors and translators will be familiar with the textual ambiguities of a particular text and be able to state their conclusions about significant differences among scholars. Since we are working with ancient texts that have, in some cases, problematic or ambiguous passages, we are obliged to employ all methods of historical, philological and textual inquiry appropriate to the study of ancient texts. To that end, we will appeal to the most reliable text-critical scholarship of both biblical and patristic studies. We will assume that our editors and translators have reviewed the international literature of textual critics regarding their text so as to provide the reader with a translation of the most authoritative and reliable form of the ancient text. We will leave it to the volume editors and translators, under the supervision of the general editors, to make these assessments. This will include the challenge of considering which variants within the biblical text itself might impinge upon the patristic text, and which forms or stemma of the biblical text the patristic writer was employing. The annotator will supply explanatory footnotes where these textual challenges may raise potential confusions for the reader.

2. Our editors and translators will seek to understand the *historical context* (including socioeconomic, political and psychological aspects as needed) of the text. These understandings are often vital to right discernment of the writer's intention. Yet we do not see our primary mission as that of discussing in detail these contexts. They are to be factored into the translation and commented on as needed in the annotations, but are not to become the primary focus of this series. Our central interest is less in the social location of the text or the philological history of particular words than in authorial intent and accurate translation. Assuming a proper social-historical contextualization of the text, the main focus of this series will be upon a dispassionate and fair translation and analysis of the text itself.

3. The main task is to set forth the meaning of the biblical text itself as understood by the patristic writer. The intention of our volume editors and translators is to help the reader see clearly into the meanings which patristic commentators have discovered in the biblical text. *Exegesis* in its classic sense implies an effort to explain, interpret and comment upon a text, its meaning, its sources and its connections with other texts. It implies

a close reading of the text, utilizing whatever linguistic, historical, literary or theological resources are available to explain the text. It is contrasted with *eisegesis*, which implies that interpreters have imposed their own personal opinions or assumptions upon the text. The patristic writers actively practiced intratextual exegesis, which seeks to define and identify the exact wording of the text, its grammatical structure and the interconnectedness of its parts. They also practiced extratextual exegesis, seeking to discern the geographical, historical or cultural context in which the text was written. Our editors and annotators will also be attentive as needed to the ways in which the ancient Christian writer described his own interpreting process or hermeneutic assumptions.

4. The underlying philosophy of translation that we employ in this series is, like the Ancient Christian Commentary on Scripture, termed *dynamic equivalency*. We wish to avoid the pitfalls of either too loose a paraphrase or too rigid a literal translation. We seek language that is literary but not purely literal. Whenever possible we have opted for the metaphors and terms that are normally in use in everyday English-speaking culture. Our purpose is to allow the ancient Christian writers to speak for themselves to ordinary readers in the present generation. We want to make it easier for the Bible reader to gain ready access to the deepest reflection of the ancient Christian community of faith on a particular book of Scripture. We seek a thought-for-thought translation rather than a formal equivalence or word-for-word style. This requires the words to be first translated accurately and then rendered in understandable idiom. We seek to present the same thoughts, feelings, connotations and effects of the original text in everyday English language. We have used vocabulary and language structures commonly used by the average person. We do not leave the quality of translation only to the primary translator, but pass it through several levels of editorial review before confirming it.

The Function of the ACT Introductions, Annotations and Translations

In writing the introduction for a particular volume of the ACT series, the translator or volume editor will discuss, where possible, the opinion of the writer regarding authorship of the text, the importance of the biblical book for other patristic interpreters, the availability or paucity of patristic comment, any salient points of debate between the Fathers, and any special challenges involved in translating and editing the particular volume. The introduction affords the opportunity to frame the entire commentary in a manner that will help the general reader understand the nature and significance of patristic comment on the biblical text under consideration and to help readers find their critical bearings so as to read and use the commentary in an informed way.

The footnotes will assist the reader with obscurities and potential confusions. In the annotations the volume editors have identified Scripture allusions and historical references embedded within the texts. Their purpose is to help the reader move easily from passage to passage without losing a sense of the whole.

The ACT general editors seek to be circumspect and meticulous in commissioning volume editors and translators. We strive for a high level of consistency and literary quality throughout the course of this series. We have sought out as volume editors and translators those patristic and biblical scholars who are thoroughly familiar with their original language sources, who are informed historically, and who are sympathetic to the needs of ordinary nonprofessional readers who may not have professional language skills.

Thomas C. Oden and Gerald L. Bray, Series Editors

ABBREVIATIONS

alt.	altered
ANF	A. Roberts and J. Donaldson, eds. Ante-Nicene Fathers. 10 vols. Buffalo, N.Y.: Christian Literature, 1885-1896; Reprint, Grand Rapids, Mich.: Eerdmans, 1951-1956; Reprint, Peabody, Mass.: Hendrickson, 1994.
CCL	Corpus Christianorum. Series Latina. Turnhout, Belgium: Brepols, 1977-.
Étaix	Raymond Étaix, "Fragments inédits de l'Opus imperfectum," *RB* 84 (1974) : 278-300.
Mali	Franz Mali. *Das "Opus Imperfectum in Matthaeum" und sein Verhältnis zu den Matthäuskommentaren von Origenes und Hieronymus.* Innsbruck: Tyrolia-Verlag, 1991.
Meslin	Michel Meslin. *Les Ariens d'Occident (335-430).* Paris: Éditions de Seuil, 1967.
NPNF	P. Schaff et al., eds. A Select Library of the Nicene and Post-Nicene Fathers of the Christian Church. 2 series (14 vols. each). Buffalo, N.Y.: Christian Literature, 1887-1894; Reprint, Grand Rapids, Mich.: Eerdmans, 1952-1956; Reprint, Peabody, Mass.: Hendrickson, 1994.
PG	J.-P. Migne, ed. Patrologia Graeca. 166 vols. Paris: Migne, 1857-1886.
PW	August Pauly and Georg Wissowa. *Paulys Realencylcopädie der classischen Altertumswissenschaft.* Berlin: 1893-1978.
RB	*Revue bénédictine.* Belgium: Abbaye de Maredsous, 1884-.
RHE	*Revue d'histoire ecclésiastique.* Louvain, 1900-.
trans.	translation
VC	*Vigiliae Christianae.* Amsterdam, 1947-.
ZKT	*Zeitschrift für katholische Theologie.* Vienna, 1877-.

TRANSLATOR'S INTRODUCTION

As Thomas Aquinas was approaching Paris, a fellow traveler pointed out the lovely buildings gracing the city. Aquinas was impressed, to be sure, but he sighed and stated that he would rather have the complete *Incomplete Commentary on Matthew* than be mayor of Paris itself.[1] And yet I doubt that many who stumble across this volume will have heard of the *Incomplete Commentary on Matthew*, or the *Opus imperfectum in Matthaeum*, as it is called in Latin. That is because the work is incomplete or imperfect in several ways.

An Incomplete Work

To state the most obvious, it is an incomplete work because it is missing several important portions of Matthew. The commentary omits Matthew 8:14 to Matthew 10:15 and an even bigger gap of Matthew 14 through Matthew 18. The commentary ends abruptly at Matthew 25, thus leaving out the passion and resurrection narrative, the most crucial parts of the whole Gospel. It was for this reason that earlier generations of Christians gave this work the title *Incomplete Commentary on Matthew*.

Incomplete Information About the Author

The work is also incomplete because the author is unknown. Or, to speak more accurately, it was wrongly ascribed for centuries to John Chrysostom. Under closer analysis, however, Chrysostom cannot have been the author since the style of this commentary hardly matches that of Chrysostom and since he employs apocryphal books (e.g., the *Book of Seth* in his comments on Mt 2:2) that Chrysostom would have been unlikely to use. What is more, the author clearly wrote in Latin, as is perhaps most clearly seen in his comments on Matthew 5:3. After giving a lengthy disquisition on the meaning of "blessed are the poor in spirit," he ends by remarking in passing that the word translated as "poor" meant "beggar" in Greek—a fact that would hardly have merited comment if the work were originally written in Greek and later translated into Latin. Moreover, the Latin text for Sirach differs wildly at times from the Greek and includes much more material than

[1]CCL 87B:179.

the Septuagint does, and it is clear throughout this commentary that it was the Latin version of Sirach that the anonymous author was quoting.[2]

What can we say about this anonymous author besides the fact that he wrote in Latin? First, he clearly lived after the time of Theodosius I, whom he mentions, when Arianism was out of favor and a stricter Nicene orthodoxy was being enforced. Since he mentions Theodosius (A.D. 379-395) as having reigned in the past, he could not have written much before the dawn of the fifth century. Since he mentions Theodosius without any further description (i.e., Theodosius I or II), he might have written his commentary before the reign of Theodosius II (408-450). However, this is not absolutely certain, since one could easily speak of a past reign of a Theodosius while a second Theodosius was on the throne without leading to any confusion. It would be most unlikely, though, that he could have written about Theodosius I simply as Theodosius if he were writing after the death of Theodosius II. Joop van Banning, summarizing the scholarship on this point, suggests that the writer lived in the Roman part of the empire, but somewhere near the Greek sphere of influence. He clearly knew Greek and used Greek loanwords, even if this work is not a translation of an original Greek text. Van Banning also suggests that he could not have lived north of the Danube because he wrote as if he was not living among the barbarians (e.g., the Goths).[3] He suggests Dacia or Moesia or Illyricum (i.e., somewhere in the Balkans north of Greece) as the most likely place for the author to have lived.[4] The author may have visited Constantinople or lived there at some point, since he mentions the schools on the Capitoline.[5] He was a teacher in the church, and hence he would have been a clergyman; the exact rank—whether bishop, priest or deacon—is disputed by scholars. In addition, the author alludes to writing a commentary on Mark and Luke.[6] Thus, even if we know that the author was not John Chrysostom, we still do not know who the author was, and consequently the work remains incomplete.[7]

How did the author's work get confused with a work of John Chrysostom? That is not easily answered. Chrysostom had given a series of sermons on Matthew that is commonly called his *Commentary on Matthew*.[8] Scholars in the West were aware of that work, but it

[2]See, for example, his quotation of Sir 1:27 in his commentary on Mt 13:4 or Sir 11:30 in his commentary on Mt 25:32. There remains, however, a distinct minority of scholars who believe that this is a Latin translation of a Greek original, even if it is not by John Chrysostom. See *ZKT* 34:1-38 and *ZKT* 33:594-97.

[3]See the author's comments on Mt 1:10 and Mt 22:10.

[4]CCL 87B:5. Van Banning argues that the instances where the author uses a Greek derivative rather than a native Latin word indicate that the author might have been in a Latin-speaking area adjacent to the Greek-speaking area.

[5]See the author's comments on Mt 10:18.

[6]He alludes to his commentary on Mark in his comments on Mt 24:32 and to his commentary on Luke in his comments on Mt 1:17.

[7]I have adopted the convention of calling the anonymous author simply "the author" rather than Pseudo-John Chrysostom. I have done so for a few reasons. First, it is easier to write or to say "the author" than "Pseudo-John Chrysostom." Moreover, there is no evidence that the author wrote the work to pass himself off as John Chrysostom, and he would not have agreed completely with Chrysostom's Nicene Christology or Antiochene hermeneutic. More important, it appears that the Latin text to be published in CCL will omit the mention of any author.

[8]For an English translation of Chrysostom's work, see NPNF 1 10:1-534.

existed in an incomplete Latin translation until 1151, when Burgundius of Pisa translated all of Chrysostom's commentary into Latin.[9] Up until then one could easily think that this anonymous commentary on Matthew contained portions of the not yet completed translation of Chrysostom's sermons on Matthew. But even when all of Chrysostom's sermons had been translated into Latin, the *Incomplete Commentary on Matthew* was still ascribed to Chrysostom on the theory that Chrysostom's *[Complete] Commentary on Matthew* was a series of homilies for his parishioners (which it was), but the *Incomplete Commentary on Matthew* was Chrysostom's more scholarly commentary not meant to be preached so much as read.[10] Indeed, the Incomplete Commentary on Matthew was not originally divided into homilies, but these divisions were added later (and kept in this translation) for convenience's sake. Only when Erasmus published his 1530 edition did he argue that the commentary was written not by Chrysostom but by an anonymous Arian.[11]

There are three main candidates for authorship. Those scholars who have argued that this work is a translation of a Greek original have suggested Timothy, an Arian priest in Constantinople well steeped in Origen's exegetical tradition. Since the author is familiar with Constantinople, as his reference in Matthew 10:18 to the philosophers' schools on the Capitoline indicate, and since the exegesis is largely reminiscent of Origen's work, this suggestion makes some sense.[12] The fifth-century church historian Socrates has this to say of Timothy: "I have myself conversed with Timothy, and was exceedingly struck by the readiness with which he would answer the most difficult questions, and clear up the most obscure passages in the Divine oracles; he also invariably quoted Origen as an unquestionable authority in confirmation of his own utterances. . . . Nevertheless although [Timothy and another presbyter, George] remained connected with their own church, still they have unconsciously changed the Arian sect for the better, and displaced many of the blasphemies of Arius by their own teachings."[13]

The other two candidates have been suggested by scholars who are certain that this work is a Latin original, albeit written by someone who knew Greek and was steeped in the earlier Greek exegetical tradition. Most scholars who propose a Latin original and dare to suggest a name hypothesize that it was Maximinus because of the similarity in style, Scripture quotations and motifs in his work. Maximinus was an Arian bishop who accompanied the Goths, although he himself was probably not a Goth, as his name indicates, as they migrated from the Balkans to North Africa, where he debated Augustine, bishop of Hippo.[14]

---

[9]CCL 87B:179.
[10]CCL 87B:206.
[11]For Erasmus's arguments on why it cannot be the work of John Chrysostom but must have been the work of an anonymous Arian rather than a legitimate work with interpolations by an Arian scribe, see PG 56:601-601*.
[12]*ZKT* 34:473-99. See also *RHE* 67:760-63. This Timothy is mentioned in Socrates' *Ecclesiastical History* 7.6; see NPNF 2 2:156.
[13]NPNF 2 2:156.
[14]Meslin 174-80; *RHE* 6:332.

A third possibility is that this is the work of Annianus of Celeda, a Pelagian deacon of the early fifth century and a vocal opponent of Augustine. F. W. Schlatter has argued for this candidate, chiefly because he believes that the work is more Pelagian than Arian and that it was a deacon, not a priest or bishop, who wrote the work.[15] There is one strong piece of evidence that Schlatter could have marshaled to support his case, but for some reason did not: if Annianus is the author, then it is easily understood why the work was falsely ascribed to John Chrysostom. Annianus was responsible for translating several of John Chrysostom's sermons into Latin (those sermons that existed in the West before Burgundius of Pisa completed the translation); Annianus also wrote an introduction to those sermons of John Chrysostom.[16] It is understandable then that a later generation would have been aware of his role as translator of Chrysostom and assumed that Annianus's own commentary on Matthew was Chrysostom's.

Whoever is believed to be the author, it will probably not make much of a difference to the reader. Suffice it to say that the author must have been steeped in the exegetical tradition of Origen,[17] whether he is one of the above three candidates or someone else who lived and died in greater obscurity.

An Incomplete (or Deficient) Theology

Now that we know that the orthodox John Chrysostom did not write this work, we are forced to consider another sense in which this work is incomplete: the author had a deficient theology, namely, one of the milder forms of Arianism that survived in the fifth century. It may surprise the modern reader that this commentary would have been so highly praised by sound theologians in the Middle Ages when its Arianism is at times quite blatant. How could anyone have thought that this was the work of John Chrysostom? The answer is that the explicit Arianism is limited to a handful of passages in the commentary, most notably in the comments on four passages: Matthew 8:9, where he states that the Son is inferior to the Father because he is under the Father's authority and hence not equal to the Father; Matthew 20:8, where he argues that whether the Father or the Son is the householder and the Son or the Holy Spirit the steward, the person represented by the steward must be inferior to the householder; Matthew 20:23, where he notes that the Son derives his authority from the Father and therefore is not equal to him; and Matthew 23:32, where he states that the belief in three equal persons of the same substance and authority is Gentile paganism in Christian disguise. Despite the sharp Arianism of these passages, the author is more concerned about giving a solid exegesis of Matthew than in giving an outline of Arian thought. The medieval scholars recognized the Arian-

[15]*VC* 42:364-75.
[16]*VC* 42:369-70.
[17]On the indebtedness of the author of the *Incomplete Commentary* to Origen's commentary on Matthew, see Mali, especially 324-39.

ism of the text but assumed that an Arian scribe had interspersed his comments into the text. One manuscript, formerly housed by the St. Maartensdal monastery in Louvain and now in the Royal Library in Brussels, handled the problem by excising ten offending passages and putting them together at the end of homily 46 and then leaving a couple of pages afterwards before resuming with homily 47.[18] The sixteenth-century Franciscan J. Manhusius was apparently moved by this manuscript to bracket as inauthentic all the Arian passages plus a couple more that dealt with baptism and the Eucharist.[19] Another practice was to warn the reader that some Arian, perhaps the presumed Latin translator of John Chrysostom, had altered the text and interspersed his comments.[20]

The author's Arianism is of a milder form, although he is no less passionate about it. We do well to remember that the Christian world of the fourth and fifth centuries was not neatly divided between orthodox Nicaeans and radical Arians, with a few Modalists thrown into the mix. Many Christians instinctively recognized the dangers of the extremes (the Anomoean party of the Arians on the one hand and the Modalists on the other) but struggled to express the orthodox truth that lay in the middle. To some degree, language interfered with a speedy resolution of the debate as terms such as *hypostasis* and *personae* were used in ways that sounded like tritheism or modalism to wary hearers. Many people whose basic theological instincts were correct nonetheless misunderstood the Nicene Creed to be espousing a form of modalism, which seemed a more pervasive danger in the Greek-speaking parts of the church. They had no difficulty confessing the deity of Christ by saying that he was like the Father, but to say that he was of the same substance with the Father seemed to be drawing no distinction between the two persons and thus falling into the error of modalism. However, these same people also disliked the direction that radical Arianism would take by the end of the fourth century. Eunomius, bishop of Cyzica, espoused an Anomoean form of Arianism, which argued that the Son was not like the Father in any respect. Eventually, as the three Cappadocian fathers developed a new and clearer terminology, as the dangers of a more radicalized Arianism were perceived and as the mildly Arian party saw that the Nicaeans were not cryptomodalists, the Homoiousian party (the mildly Arian party that taught only a similarity and not an identity between the Father's substance and that of the Son) became reconciled to the Homoousian (or Nicaean) party. The process did not take place overnight and took longer on the fringes of the empire and beyond it. Thus, even if we find the author's doctrine of God quite deficient, he must be credited with believing in the divinity of the Son, albeit in a deficient, subordinationist manner.

[18]CCL 87B:218-19.

[19]CCL 87B:218. Manhusius's brackets are retained for the most part by PG 56:611-946, the primary text that I have used. However, since these bracketed passages are well attested in the manuscripts, they are most certainly authentic. I have removed the brackets and indicated in a footnote that these are the passages that Manhusius deemed inauthentic.

[20]For example, the St. Omer manuscript notes the Arian passages with a theta in the margin (CCL 87B:54-55). Abelard recognized the Arianism in the work and used the Arian passages to form a counterargument in his *Sic et Non* (CCL 87B:186).

Schlatter argues that there is a greater deficiency: *The Incomplete Commentary* is tainted by Pelagianism. While the Arianism is confined to fewer than ten brief passages, most of which consist of two or three sentences each, in Schlatter's view Pelagianism permeates the entire work.[21] Schlatter raises six criteria of Pelagianism and finds that the *Incomplete Commentary* meets them all. (1) Are human beings born without sin, and can they fulfill God's commandments by nature? Yes, answers the author. Even if the flesh does not have control over its will, the soul does. It lies in human power to do the first part of righteousness (avoiding evil), even if the second part (doing good) is not altogether in his power. (2) Are unbaptized babies sinless and therefore not liable to condemnation? The author does not address the question directly, but the implied answer is yes, for the author says that the devil does not lead people to sin until people's sins have led them to the devil. (3) Must the wealthy get rid of all their riches in order to enter into heaven? Yes, says the author, and rails against merchants, who can in no wise enter the kingdom of heaven. (4) Is it wrong to take an oath? Yes, the author explicitly says. All swearing under oaths, not just perjury, is wrong. (5) Must the church be without fault and blemish now? Yes, says the author, the true church is without sin for its members are sinless. (6) Is it wrong for Christians to marry? Yes, says the author, even if it is not a sin per se. In each of these instances, the author has adopted the Pelagian position.[22] Given the author's Pelagian stance on these six major issues, Schlatter argues that the work is more properly called a Pelagian exegesis of Scripture with Arianizing tendencies rather than an Arian work with Pelagianizing tendencies. As Schlatter admits, this blending of Arianism and Pelagianism is a bit puzzling, since by all accounts the Pelagians were orthodox on the doctrine of the Trinity.

Franz Mali has argued in reply (albeit all too briefly) that the author is not a Pelagian, even though there are several points of contact between the author and standard Pelagianism. He notes that the author in one passage, on Matthew 11:12, can speak of people obtaining the kingdom by the efforts of their own free will, while in another, on Matthew 21:8, can say, "Every human being is not only naturally a sinner, but even altogether sin"—hardly a Pelagian statement.[23]

But perhaps a better explanation for the Arianism and possible Pelagianism in this work comes from a remark made by Schlatter in passing: the author is carrying on the exegetical tradition of Origen in Latin.[24] First, the author makes use of both Origen's allegorical method and his exegesis of specific passages.[25] Second, Origen taught an aus-

[21]Since Pelagians tended not to be Arian, Schlatter is not entirely convinced that the Arian passages are part of the original text; instead, they may be interpolations of a later Arian scribe. However, the Pelagianism, he argues, is too integral a part of the work to be a later addition (*VC* 41:283).

[22]*VC* 41:266-83.

[23]Mali 353-54.

[24]*VC* 39:388; *VC* 42:370-71.

[25]For a detailed examination of this, see Mali 91-323.

tere morality that could be called proto-Pelagian. To be sure, there are hints in Origen's works of the need for divine grace, just as can be found in the *Incomplete Commentary*, but as with many of the Fathers before Augustine, especially those in the East, holiness and sanctification receive far more attention than grace and forgiveness, and there is a greater emphasis on the power of the human will to resist evil and to choose good. Finally, Origen's language concerning Christ could be understood in both an orthodox and an Arianizing sense; indeed, his students would end up as leading figures on both sides of the christological debate. Thus, if the author was an admirer of Origen, one of the most learned biblical scholars of the early church, he may well have landed in territory that in the early fifth century would be marked as Pelagian and Arian.

Does the author's deficient theology rule him out as a serious exegete of the Scriptures? The answer since 1530 seems to be yes. Ever since Erasmus published his text of the *Incomplete Commentary* in that year and argued in its preface that this was not the work of John Chrysostom but of an anonymous Arian, the work has suffered neglect. A century ago, Germain Morin called for young scholars to work on this overlooked work, but though there has been some scholarship on the *Incomplete Commentary*, a critical Latin text still awaits publication.[26]

However, I would argue that the reader should not neglect this work for several reasons. First, the Arianism is easily excised from the text. The attentive reader who is well versed in the doctrine of the Trinity should not fear being misled by the author's antitrinitarianism, which is as vociferous and easy to spot as it is rare. And, second, even if the Pelagianism (or an asceticism that may seem Pelagian) is not as easily excised as its Arianism, an attentive reader can separate the Pelagian chaff from the biblical wheat. Without a doubt, few if any readers will adopt the author's moral positions in their entirety, for example, in denouncing the occupation of merchant as unchristian or in saying that marriage is an evil, even if not a sin.[27] Some readers, particularly those from the Arminian and Holiness branches of Christianity, may be more receptive to this work's call to holiness, even if they do not completely adopt his stance on every issue. Others, such as those who espouse a Calvinist or Lutheran confession, will be more wary but will still find much of value. After all, no genuine Christian of any stripe, even one with a strongly anti-Pelagian stance, takes sanctification lightly. But despite his asceticism, the author insists, as in his commentary on Matthew 19:16, that faith comes before works—a truth that will likely endear himself to those of the magisterial Reformation. This leads us to consider a third reason to read this work: the commentaries of Pelagius, who was condemned as a heretic, were widely used by churchmen who rejected Pelagianism, and the works of Origen are still highly esteemed even by orthodox Christians for their scholarship, if not always for every last conclusion of their theology. As the author of the

[26]*RHE* 6:332.

[27]See the author's comments on Mt 21:12 and Mt 1:18.

Incomplete Commentary acknowledges, "Often good doctrine comes forth from a wicked person"[28]—not that the author was necessarily wicked, but certainly a bit misdirected in his theology. Fourth, the author has composed a fine commentary. To be sure, there are the occasional overwrought allegories, and sometimes the exegesis becomes formulaic, but often the author uncovers exegetical gems and then elaborates further by bringing in an abundance of illustrations from the outside world. And, finally, this book was influential in the Middle Ages and in its exegesis. We have already noted the influence it had on Aquinas and Abelard and can add that it also shaped other scholastics such as Bonaventure. But it also helped shape the *devotio moderna* of Geert Groote, as well as the proto-Protestant movements of John Wycliffe and Jan Huss.[29]

An Incomplete Manuscript Tradition

Perhaps no other incompleteness has so troubled me as a translator than the incomplete state of the text. In 1988, van Banning wrote an excellent introduction to the four textual families and their manuscripts; this was done in preparation for the publication of a critical edition of the text. However, nearly twenty years later that edition has not yet been published, although it may well appear in print before this translation does.

In the meantime I have cobbled together a text for translation in this fashion, following suggestions contained in van Banning's introduction. I have used as a basic text that which is found in PG 56:611-946.[30] I have removed the brackets around those passages that were marked as possibly inauthentic by Manhusius. I have also excised those passages that van Banning recognizes as inauthentic, including the twenty-third homily by the numbering of PG, which in reality is a homily by Chromatius of Aquileia. I have added the fragments found by Raymond Étaix and published in 1974;[31] the fourth of those six fragments is a rather large fragment and has now become the twenty-eighth homily so that from the twenty-ninth homily the numbering aligns with that of PG again.[32] Following van Banning, I have kept the division into PG's 54 homilies as a useful convention, although I am fully aware that this division is rather artificial and certainly not original. However, I have omitted the italicized words that occasionally begin a paragraph in PG since they serve less as an introduction to a section as an index of key phrases in the paragraph to follow. While there will be minor variants in readings that will have to be changed once the critical edition is published, for the most part the English reader will be given a more complete text in translation than anyone in the Middle Ages could have had in the original Latin.

[28]See the author's comments on Mt 23:3.

[29]CCL 87B:81, 179-80, 184-88, 190-94, 196, 223-24, 276-78, 302.

[30]Throughout the document, unless page numbers are required, I will refer to this text as PG 56.

[31]Étaix 278-300.

[32]This numbering reflects the numbering system van Banning will use in his critical text (in CCL) with one exception: I have not divided the overly long first homily into 1a and 1b, as he has done.

For if it seems as if I have had to cobble together a text for translation, it is nothing compared with the state of the manuscripts that the medieval scribes and theologians had to work with. None of the manuscripts contain the complete text as it is translated here. The earliest of the four families of manuscripts contains only homilies on Matthew 19 to Matthew 23. A second family of manuscripts added the homilies on Matthew 1 to Matthew 8.[33] The third family of manuscripts, however, broke new ground. This third family came into existence when it was noted that an incomplete manuscript of the commentary of Chromatius of Aquileia, which ended at Matthew 8, was supplemented by materials from the Incomplete *Commentary on Matthew*, at least insofar as it existed: Matthew 10:16–13:13 and Matthew 19:1–25:46. (Clearly, even then the materials from Matthew 13:14 to Matthew 18:35 were missing.) These homilies were removed from Chromatius's commentary and added to the Incomplete *Commentary on Matthew*.[34] Elements from the second and the third family were combined to form the fourth family, which was an attempt to put together the most complete text of the *Incomplete Commentary on Matthew*. Van Banning surmises that this was done by an Englishman (given the penmanship) who visited Italy to search for the missing portions and scoured various homiliaries looking for something that might be in the style of the *Incomplete Commentary*. By and large this Englishman was successful, only once including an extraneous homily, the aforementioned twenty-third homily found in PG 56:754-56.[35]

Further Scholarship to Make the Incomplete Less Incomplete

For those interested in pursuing scholarship on the *Incomplete Commentary on Matthew*, I suggest starting with CCL 87B. This volume, written by van Banning, is essentially a preface to the text of the *Opus Imperfectum in Matthaeum*, which will appear in CCL sometime in the future. Not only does this volume give a good outline of the textual problems of the *Incomplete Commentary on Matthew*, but it also has a good bibliography of foreign language scholarship. His discussion of the family 4 manuscripts is a fine introduction to the *Commentary*'s legacy to medieval theology.

I also suggest reading Schlatter's three articles in *Vigiliae Christianae*, as they are one of the few things available to read in English and build a provocative thesis, namely, that the author of the *Incomplete Commentary* must have been Annianus, a Pelagian deacon of the early fifth century.[36]

Most of the important scholarship has been done in French, Italian and German, which is summarized in the slightly dated bibliography in van Banning's work mentioned

[33]For a general introduction to the four families, see CCL 87B:9-15, especially the useful chart on 15. For an introduction to the first and second families, see CCL 87B:16-17 and 31-35, respectively.

[34]CCL 87B:98-99. Presumably they were written because the author alludes to his commentary on Mt 18:23 in his comments on Mt 25:30.

[35]CCL 87B:148-49.

[36]*VC* 39:384-92; 41:267-84; 42:364-75.

above. For those who read German, I would add Mali's book to van Banning's bibliography. The introductory chapter is a fine summary of the scholarship on this work. Mali also closely examines the *Incomplete Commentary*, Jerome's commentary on Matthew and Origen's commentary on Matthew, both the Latin translation and whatever we possess of the Greek original. He concludes that the *Incomplete Commentary* relies more heavily on Origen's original commentary rather than on Jerome's commentary, a Latin adaptation of Origen's work.

Biblical Quotations

I have quoted throughout from the Revised Standard Version (RSV) unless the Latin text differs so much from the RSV that I have substituted my own translation. In order to make the text more accessible to modern readers, I have updated the archaisms that the RSV had retained in certain contexts; the only exception I have made is to retain the archaic language in the Lord's Prayer because of its familiarity. (At the time of its publication, the editors of the RSV thought that its readers would demand the traditional Jacobean English in all discourse addressed to God, even if they would appreciate more modern English elsewhere. Now, however, such archaisms seem out of place.) Occasionally I have kept the translation of the RSV but substituted a word or two to bring the translation closer to the original text of the commentary. I have noted all significant alterations in the footnotes.

Readers familiar with the King James Version will recognize that the author of the commentary often adopts readings found in the Majority Text.

Clearly, then, this is an *opus imperfectum*, an incomplete work, in several senses. However, given that nothing we do on this side of eternity is truly complete, it will have to do.

James A. Kellerman
The Feast of St. Bartholomew, 2007
Chicago, Illinois

INCOMPLETE COMMENTARY ON MATTHEW
(Opus imperfectum)

Prologue

As commonly reported, Matthew was compelled to write his Gospel for the following reason. When a dire persecution had broken out in Palestine, so that all Christians there ran the risk of being scattered, they asked Matthew to compose a history of all of Christ's words and works for them, so that even if by chance they had to be without any teachers of the faith, they would still not lack their teaching. Consequently, wherever they would end up, they would have an account of the whole faith with themselves. The impious impudence of the Jews, who deny that Jesus Christ was descended from David, forced Matthew to begin with his human birth and to set forth his human origin. Now Matthew ordered the body of his narration in this way: first, his birth; then his baptism; third, his temptation; fourth, his doctrine; fifth, his miracles; sixth, his passion; seventh, his resurrection and ascension. Through these sections he intended not only to set forth the history of Christ's life but also to teach the disposition of an evangelical life. For it makes no difference that we were born of human parents unless we have been born again of God through water and the Holy Spirit, since that which is born of flesh is flesh, but what is born of the Spirit is spirit.[1] After one has been baptized, however, he must stand against the devil, inasmuch as every Christian is anointed for this purpose. And he is reconstituted in baptism so as to undertake war against the Tyrant. Thereafter, when he has overcome every temptation and been made apt to teach, let him teach, if he is indeed a priest. And since it is not always necessary to do miraculous deeds, let him commend his teaching with the deeds of a good life in the place of miracles. But if he is a lay person, let him teach his faith by his works. Let him commend himself to people and God by his works. Then, because we cannot exit the world unless the body, through which we entered into the world, has been detached, we must depart from this racecourse of the world. And because all our life was a period of testing, it remains that the reward and glory of the resurrection should follow our victory over temptation.

Matthew was an evangelist of saints, but nonetheless especially of those who had been sinners, since he proclaimed the gospel to sinners not only by his words but also by the emendation of his life. He had once been a tax collector and had made it his habit to heap up money that would soon perish. He would never have been made an Evangelist, so that he could write discourses that would last for eternity, unless by his own example he invited sinners to the mercy that comes from repentance. He, who once was the circumspect accountant of earthly transactions, now is a most diligent dispenser of spiritual precepts. Formerly he impoverished many by defrauding them of money; now he enriches countless people by preaching righteousness that we may

Prologue [1]See Jn 3:5-6.

glorify the Lord for his sake and say, as does the prophet, "The right hand of the Most High has changed."[2]

The First Homily: On Matthew 1

[1]The book of the genealogy of Jesus Christ, the son of David, the son of Abraham.

This book is a treasury of grace, as it were. For just as in some rich person's treasury each person could find whatever he desired, so also in this book every soul finds what it needs.

What does he mean when he says, "The book of the genealogy of Jesus Christ, the son of David, the son of Abraham"? And how can the prophet Isaiah say, "And who will tell of his genealogy?"[1] Isaiah proclaims that his divine genealogy cannot be told, but Matthew sets forth his genealogy according to the flesh. Therefore, he does not say, "the genealogy of Jesus Christ, the Son of God," but "of the son of David, the son of Abraham." And why does John immediately, at the beginning of his Gospel, show the nature of Christ's divinity? It is because John had been exiled among the Gentiles and wrote his Gospel in Greek style for the Gentiles, who had not learned if God had a Son or how he had begotten him. Therefore, it would have been irrelevant for him to point to the mystery of Christ's incarnation first, when the Gentiles did not know who he was. Therefore, it was necessary first to show to them that he was the true God and the Son of God. Then in what followed he could say that Christ became incarnate: "And the Word became flesh and dwelt among us."[2] But Matthew, as we already have noted above, wrote his Gospel to the Jews in a Hebrew style in order that the Jews might read it and be edified in their faith. The Jews always knew that he is the Son of God and how he is the Son of God. Thus, it was irrelevant to explain to them the nature of his divinity, which they very well knew; however, it was necessary to show them the mystery of his incarnation.

But why does it not suffice for him to say that Christ is the son of Abraham alone or of David alone? It is because a promise had been made to both of them that the Christ would be born as one of their descendants. To Abraham it was said, "And by your descendants shall all the nations of the earth bless themselves."[3] This cannot be understood to refer to anyone but to Christ, since there has never been any stable friendship between the Gentiles and the other Jews (besides Christ). The following promise was spoken to David: "The Lord swore to David a sure oath from which he will not turn back: 'One of the sons of your body I will set on your throne.' "[4] Therefore he calls him the son of both Abraham and David in order to show that the promises to both were fulfilled in Christ. He also does this because Christ would have three titles: king, prophet and priest. Abraham had two sons and two titles: he was a prophet and a priest. He was a priest, as is clear when God says to him in Genesis, "Bring me a heifer three years old."[5] And he was a prophet, as the Lord testified to Abimelech about him: "He is a prophet, and he will pray for you, and you shall live . . . you, and all that are yours."[6] Therefore he was called the son of Abraham and David, so that he might be understood to be a prophet and priest because he is of Abraham and a king because he is of David. Therefore he was not called merely the son of David, since David was a king and a prophet but was not a priest. Thus he was called the son of both, that the threefold office from each ancestor might be recognized in Christ by right of his lineage.

But why did Matthew mention David first, although Abraham preceded him temporally? The first reason—and a straightforward one,

[2]Ps 77:10. **First Homily** [1]Is 53:8 (trans. Kellerman). [2]Jn 1:14. [3]Gen 22:18. [4]Ps 132:11. [5]Gen 15:9. [6]Gen 20:7.

too—is this: since it was the Evangelist's intention to enumerate the genealogy of our Lord from Abraham, if Matthew had first said that Christ was the son of Abraham and then the son of David, he would have had to return again to Abraham and name him twice in the same passage.

The second reason is that the honor of a kingdom is greater than the honor of nature. For although Abraham preceded him temporally, David surpassed him in honor. And how could David be greater than Abraham, since David was once caught in sin? But listen to how David spoke confidently about his very abundant righteousness: "O Lord my God, if I have done this, if there is wrong in my hands,"[7] and "If I had cherished iniquity in my heart, the Lord would not have listened."[8] That is why he was permitted to be ensnared by his flesh—not so that his unrighteousness might be shown but so that his boasting might be restrained. Abraham is the father of the faithful. God wanted him to be an example for the saints and so said to him, "Go from your country and your kindred and your father's house to the land that I will show you."[9] He did this so that all who want to be the children of Abraham and to receive that living land of the promise—concerning which it has been written that "I believe that I shall see the goodness of the Lord in the land of the living!"[10]—might know that they ought to despise their own goods, just as Abraham despised his own land and forsook his own parents according to the flesh and at the same time forsook his kinship with them. But those who do not want to imitate Abraham cannot be his children.

[2]***Abraham was the father of Isaac.***

Isaac means "laughter." Now the laughter of the saints is not the foolish guffaws on their lips, but rather the reasonable joy of the heart, which points to Christ in all circumstances. Just as Isaac was given as laughter to his own parents in their old age, who had long since given up all hope, that it may be known that he was not a son born by nature but by grace, so also our "Isaac"[11] was begotten at the end of time from a Jewish mother to be the joy to all, just as the angel said to the shepherds: "Behold, I bring you good news of a great joy which will come to all the people."[12] For the same reason the apostle says, "But when the time had fully come, God sent forth his Son, born of woman, born under the law."[13] Christ was born of a virgin, while Isaac was born of an old woman—although both were born in a way beyond what nature might hope. Isaac was born after his mother had ceased to be of childbearing age, while Christ was born before his mother should have been able to give birth to him. Now Isaac was born from an old woman already past her prime, whereas Christ was born of a pure virgin, because Isaac would produce sons under a law that would be annihilated, while Christ's offspring would be under a grace that would endure forever. Just as Isaac's mother did not know that he was being led off to be sacrificed but found out that he had been sacrificed only when he returned, so the synagogue did not recognize that Christ was the Son of God when he was being led to death, but the Jews recognized him as such after he rose from the dead. Just as Isaac carried wood to the place where he was to have been lit ablaze, so also Christ carried the wood of the cross to the place he was to be crucified. Just as Isaac did not resist Abraham when the latter wished to kill him, but said, "My father, bind my hands and feet, lest perchance I arise to fight off the sacrifice," so also Christ did not contradict his Father but, ready for all things, answered, "My Father, if it be possible, let this cup pass from me; nevertheless, not as I

[7]Ps 7:3. [8]Ps 66:18. [9]Gen 12:1. [10]Ps 27:13. [11]Christ. [12]Lk 2:10. [13]Gal 4:4.

will, but as you will."[14]

Isaac [was] the father of Jacob and Esau.[15]

Jacob and Esau represent the two ages. Esau, who was altogether hairy from his head down to his toes, represents the first age, which from its beginning to its end was altogether bristling with wickedness as if with very rough hairs. Jacob, in contrast, was altogether handsome and elegant; he represents the age to come, which will glisten with the adornment of piety and in which there will not be found any harshness or black mark of sin. And when Esau left his mother's womb, Jacob grabbed hold of the sole of Esau's foot (hence he was called Jacob in Hebrew, that is, "supplanter"), for as soon as Esau's feet had left the womb, Jacob's head appeared. In the same way, at the end of the first age, the beginning of the second age will appear. And just as Esau persecuted Jacob, so the children of this age persecute the children of the age to come. And Jacob's children overcome their evil opponents by fleeing rather than resisting them, just as Jacob did. For just as Jacob's mother advised him at that time, saying, "Now therefore, my son, obey my voice; arise, flee to [Mesopotamia] . . . until your brother's fury turns away,"[16] so also the church teaches its children daily, whenever they suffer persecution, "When they persecute you in one town, flee to the next,"[17] and "Give way to wrath."[18]

And Jacob [was] the father of Judah and his brothers.

And our "Jacob"[19] produced twelve apostles in spirit, not in the flesh—by word, not by blood. Just as Jacob went down to Egypt with his twelve sons so that they might increase in number, so also Christ went down into the world with his twelve apostles and increased in number throughout the whole world, as the very facts of history bear witness. Moreover, just as Jacob went down to Egypt to eat its marrow, so also Christ with his disciples entered this world in order to eat the marrow of this world, that is, to acquire it for himself. The marrow of this world is the saints. As long as the sap[20] is healthy in a tree, it always flourishes, but when it is consumed, it gradually grows weaker and dries up. In the same way, the world itself endures, as long as the faithful endure. For, just as Egypt was destroyed when the Israelites left Egypt, so also the world will fall when the saints abandon it.

Judah means "praise," since he bore the image of Christ, who would praise his father when he said, "I thank you, Father, Lord of heaven and earth."[21] Now just as Judah was united with a prostitute and gave her his staff and signet ring, so also Christ united himself with the adulterous church drawn from the Gentiles and gave her as payment for that union the staff of the cross and the signet ring of the Holy Spirit through baptism, a token of the preceding faith, as it were, which the kind father ordered to be given elsewhere to the prodigal son on his return. Perhaps for this reason his wife Tamar's name is interpreted "transformed" or "exasperation": from her one is able to have a suitable understanding of the church. Although she appeared chaste, she turned herself into a prostitute and exasperated Judas and angered him, as the book of Genesis states. But the church began as a prostitute and exasperated God, but later she was transformed into a chaste bride through faith in Christ.

[3]And Judah [was] the father of Perez and Zerah by Tamar.

[14]Mt 26:39; the archaic language of the RSV has been updated. [15]The author adds "and Esau." [16]Gen 27:43-44. [17]Mt 10:23. [18]Rom 12:19 (trans. Kellerman). [19]Christ. [20]The word for "sap" in a tree is also used for "marrow" inside a bone. [21]Lk 10:21; the archaic language of the RSV has been updated.

This serves as a figure for the Jewish nation and the Gentiles. Zerah was the first to appear from the womb. The midwife tied a piece of red cord on his hand, which foretold that the Jewish nation would be reddened by the blood of circumcision. But when Zerah withdrew, Perez came forth. For the flesh in which Zerah had been enclosed had been blocked up again, but the flesh in which Perez had been enclosed opened up, and so he came forth first.[22] Thus the Jewish nation was the first to appear in the light of faith, coming forth from the shadowy womb of the world, as it were, and thus it was marked by the redness of circumcision, since everybody thought that that nation would become the first people of God. But what happened? The law was placed as a hedge before Israel's face, so that it might hinder their righteousness. For the law hinders faith and does not help it, as it is written, "Apart from the law, sin lies dead. I was once alive apart from the law, but when the commandment came, sin came alive and I died."[23] Therefore the Jews were hindered by the law so that they did not come to the light of the gospel, but at the time of Christ the hedge of the law, which had previously been between the Jews and the Gentiles, was suddenly torn down, as the apostle says, "[He] has broken down the dividing wall of hostility."[24] In the same way, just as the Gentiles had been closed in and confined in the womb of the shadowy world when the Jewish nation appeared, but after the law had been abolished by the commandments of Christ and the Jewish nation had been thrust out, the Gentiles were the first to come to faith, and thereafter the Jewish people follow, as the apostle says, "I tell you a mystery,"[25] "brethren: a hardening has come upon part of Israel, until the full number of the Gentiles come in, and so all Israel will be saved."[26]

However, it may be that someone will say that Zerah represents the Gentiles, who first appeared in the prophets, and from the very same prophets were designated by the scarlet of the Lord's blood. For while it was foretold that the Gentiles would be begotten anew through the blood of Christ, he was marked by the scarlet of the Lord's blood. Phares, however, represents the Jewish people, who came forth first, while the Gentiles were still excluded by the barrier of the law and would follow afterwards, when the wall of the law was removed, as is aptly said. Therefore he was also called Zerah, which means "one who arises" or "noble." The other was called Perez, that is, "breaking," because the Christian people would always be arising and always would be noble, but the Jewish people would be cut off from them through the intervention of the law.

It also seems that Judah acquired sons from the incestuous marriage to his daughter-in-law Tamar and that she was not really a prostitute. She was not a prostitute because she made herself a prostitute out of her love for the seed of Israel when there was none. Moreover, she was not a daughter-in-law, because none of Judah's sons had her as wife. In the case of Er, Judah's first son, Judah did not want Er to take a wife from among the Canaanites because his own experience had warned him against it. Instead, Judah gave Tamar to Er as his wife, one of the daughters of the Arameans. However, Er's mother, a Canaanite, urged him to take a wife from her own people. Er listened to his mother's advice and did not consummate the marriage, and for that reason God struck him down childless. When Judah's second son heard that Tamar would raise up offspring for his brother and not for himself, he poured forth his seed into the ground and for that reason was struck down by God. And so it was that Tamar remained a virgin. While Judah, ignorant of these facts, lamented and grieved

[22]See Gen 38:27-30. [23]Rom 7:8-9 (RSV alt. by Kellerman). [24]Eph 2:14. [25]1 Cor 15:51, which the author has substituted for the first words of Rom 11:25 ("I want you to understand a mystery"). [26]Rom 11:25-26.

these things that had been done concerning his sons, and as he repented that he had done an unspeakably shameful act in Israel with his daughter-in-law (as he thought) and prayed a long time to God and would not end his sorrow, the angel of the Lord appeared to him and explained all these things to him, just as they had taken place, and comforted him. Nonetheless, Judah was so pious that even after he understood that Tamar had not been his son's wife, he did not feel comfortable to have relations with her because, although she was not a daughter-in-law as God knew, still she seemed to have been so according to human knowledge. He looked for the good, not only in the eyes of God but also in the eyes of people.

Perez [was] the father of Hezron.

We believe that we have been given these names for a good cause and purpose by the providence of God, especially since they are the most eminent of the family of the elect, but only the authors, who recorded these names, and God, by whose providence they were recorded, know for what cause and reason they were recorded. As for us, we will say only what we can understand concerning these names, especially since we have no canonical Scripture to explicate these people. As the interpreters of Hebrew names tell us, Hezron means "one who sees the dart." Darts, however, are enemies, all carnal desires, which the devil hurls inward into the soul, and all temptations that come from adversities, which arise for the faithful at the devil's instigation. Thus, the devil's darts are all unjust people, whom the enemy arouses against the truth (that is, the will of God) or against his servants. The apostle says concerning all of them, "besides all these, taking the shield of faith, with which you can quench all the flaming darts of the evil one."[27] Therefore whoever sees the dart is vigilant against the wiles of the enemy, sees his darts from afar and is careful, or else, having taken up the shield of faith, turns back to the Lord. Thus, the Lord wants all his servants to see the darts that are coming on him. But if he does not see the darts coming on him, how will he turn them aside? One can also understand that the just person is "the seeing dart," so that he is the dart of Christ, as Christ is called the dart of the Father, as Isaiah says, "He made me a polished arrow; in his quiver he hid me away."[28] Such a faithful person is a dart of Christ, inasmuch as he is sent by Christ; he is a dart, not one bereft of reason but one endowed with it, and he sees so that he knows what he should transfix and what he should pass over.

Hezron [was] the father of Ram.[29]

Ram is interpreted "their vision" or "their vexation" or "exalted" or "their light." As the meaning of those names indicates, so I hazard to guess that in the time of that Ram the children of Israel multiplied, were exalted and glorious. Their multiplication had been very enviable in the eyes of the Egyptians, who vexed them, as is written in Exodus: "Behold, the people of Israel are too many and too mighty for us. Come, let us deal shrewdly with them."[30] And perhaps in Ram's day the Lord saw the Israelites groaning beneath the oppression of the Egyptians, as it is written: "I have seen the affliction of my people who are in Egypt and have heard their cry."[31] Therefore, owing to the providence of God Ram was given such a name—either because the Israelites vexed the Egyptians as they grew mightily and were exalted or because God saw the Israelites groaning and toiling. And the whole matter is credible, when one considers that time period. In three ways the Egyptians dealt shrewdly with the children of Israel: first, by forcing them to make bricks; second, through the midwives; and third, by

[27]Eph 6:16. [28]Is 49:2. [29]Latin reads "Aram" for "Ram" throughout this section. [30]Ex 1:9-10. [31]Ex 3:7.

making them expose their infants. Moses was born during the last phase of their oppression. At last Moses[32] took the daughter of Amminadab, son of Aram, the sister of Nahshon, as his wife. Between the first and the last shrewd dealing of the Egyptians some years must have transpired. Consequently, we come to understand that the children of Israel multiplied in an enviable manner in the days of Ram, and that affliction came upon them unexpectedly and that God visited his people. Quite appropriately, however, Ram, who meant "the vexing of the Egyptians" or "their visitation" or "their light," begot his son Amminadab, whose name means "desired nation" or "my willing people." God would not have visited his people unless the nation had been desired and his people had been willing. And even now, those who are desirable and eager for God are envied and make the people of darkness jealous of them. Besides, being a willing people and being a desired nation amount to the same thing. Whoever is eager for God and says, "With a freewill offering I will sacrifice to you,"[33] is desirable before God; and whoever is desirable to God without doubt is eager for him, for God does not love altogether the subjection of people or their servitude, but rather he loves a voluntary subjection and a voluntary servitude. By nature all people are under God, because they have been created by him, but according to their will not all people belong to God, because they yield themselves to the devil as far as their works go.

4*Amminadab*[34] *[was] the father of Nahshon.*

Nahshon means "restoration," that is, "rest." Indeed, whoever is willing for God produces restoration and rest for himself. Most appropriately, then, Nahshon, in whose lifetime the children of Israel left Egypt, and who himself was made prince over the tribe of Judah, was called "restoration and rest," because in his days the Israelites enjoyed rest when they were freed from slavery to the violent Egyptians and from vile, laborious works. In the desert they also pursued refreshment of body and soul: their body was refreshed because they achieved bodily freedom, but their soul was refreshed because they were won over to the knowledge of the living God after laboring under the impure rites of the Egyptians. But Nahshon can also be interpreted to mean "dove-like" or "serpent-like," perhaps because he was prudent in good, just like a serpent, while being innocent as far as evil is concerned, just like a dove. Now as we have already stated, this Nahshon left the land of Egypt and was the prince of the tribe of Judah, as the evidence clearly shows.[35] He would not have been able to become prince if his father had still been alive, unless someone by chance should say that Amminadab was so old that he could not carry out the task of ruling—a possibility that I discount.

What is said in Exodus, namely that in the fifth generation the children of Israel left Egypt, is found to be the case in the generations of the tribe of Levi. Jacob begot Levi, Levi begot Gad, Gad begot Amram, Amram begot Moses and Aaron. Therefore when four generations had died in Egypt—all those up to the generation of Amram—the fifth generation departed, that is, Moses and Aaron. However, according to the generations of the tribe of Judah, it seems that it was the seventh generation that left Egypt after the previous six generations had died in Egypt:[36] that is, Jacob, Judah, Perez, Hezron, Ram and Amminadab; the seventh generation (Nahshon), however, was the one to depart. However, I think that this is due to the fact that the tribe of Judah multiplied more than all the other tribes. The tribe of Levi did not multiply so

[32]The author states that Moses took her as wife, but Ex 6:23 says that Aaron was the one to do so. [33]Ps 54:6; the archaic language of the RSV has been updated. [34]"The willing people" or the "desired nation." [35]See Num 1:7; 2:3. [36]1 Chron 6.

greatly because the Levites were needed only for carrying out the matters for the temple, where only a few men were needed, just as the book of Numbers indicates.

Nonetheless, if there is some significance to the fact that Enoch, who was translated into heaven, was born in the seventh generation, and if there is some significance to the fact that Noah was born in the tenth generation from Adam, who prefigured Christ, and if there is some significance in that Abraham was born in the tenth generation from Noah, and if there is some significance to the fact that from Abraham to the Law, that is, to Moses, seven generations are counted, without doubt also this is significant, that according to the tribe of Levi the Israelites left Egypt in the fifth generation but according to the tribe of Judah they left in the seventh generation. Thus I think that this mystery, namely, that the tribe of Levi left in the fifth generation after four had died in Egypt, is due to the fact that every person is made of four elements, as far as the body is concerned: earth, air, fire and water. Thereafter, however, a person is regenerated through baptism and made a child of God. Thus, the four generations of elements die in him in the world, while he through baptism departs from the world in the fifth generation, namely, that of the spirit. That is to say, whoever mortifies his members on earth,[37] as the apostle says, which are made up of the four generations of the elements, so that he is no longer in the flesh but in the spirit, such a one leaves this world for the perfect one. And no one will truly depart from this world unless those four generations have been mortified and he has begun to live in the fifth, so that the apostle is addressing him: "You are not in the flesh, you are in the Spirit."[38]

Now we consider the generations of the tribe of Judah. It seems as if there is a different significance to the generations, yet nonetheless one that is nearly the same. The number six points to work and labor, because God labored on all the visible things for six days and rested on the seventh day. The number seven alludes to forbearance, leisure and rest, as we have said in many places. Therefore, whoever passes through all visible things and leaves behind whatever things were made within six days, that is, this whole corruptible world, and fulfills what John commands in his canonical epistle, saying, "My little children, do not love the world or the things in the world,"[39] that one is in the seventh day, that is, in Christ and in rest. Christ is our rest, as the prophet David spoke concerning the Jews who would not enter into the rest at all: "I swore in my anger that they should not enter my rest."[40] He truly rests from every work of the world, if he keeps a sabbath holy from evildoing, and he merits forgiveness. If he has done anything humane, he has departed from the world. But whoever is in the world never is in the rest of the seventh day, nor does he ever lie idle from evildoings or ever take a sabbath. Moreover, whoever is in the seventh day's rest is not of the world, while he who is in the world is not worthy of forgiveness.

See how wisely we have explained the reasons that the Levites departed from Egypt in the fifth generation but the royal tribe of Judah in the seventh, because royalty often fail either a little or quite a lot as their power compels them to do wrong, and it is difficult for them to be perfected without ever committing sin. Furthermore, if they sin moderately, they are made worthy of forgiveness. But the Levites, since they are religious and priestly men, perfect and spiritual, ought also to be without fault. Therefore it can be expected of them that after four generations of being mortified in the body they are prepared in the fifth generation of the world. They would have nothing of the flesh in them, except for

[37]Col 3:5. [38]Rom 8:9. [39]1 Jn 2:15; the author adds "my little children" at the beginning of this verse. [40]Ps 95:11.

whatever sustains life, as the apostle expresses it, "if we have food and clothing, with these we shall be content."[41]

Nahshon [was] the father of Salmon.

Salmon means "take the vessel." Salmon was the one who took Rahab as his wife. This Rahab, however, is said to have been the prostitute from Jericho who welcomed the spies and ambassadors of the children of Israel. When the king of Jericho sought them in order to kill them, she hid them in the upper part of her house and kept them unharmed. Once she had heard about the deeds of the children of Israel, she preferred Israel over her own people. And this whole matter seems quite believable to me for two reasons. First, although Salmon was a noble among the Israelites, both because he was of the tribe of Judah and because he was the son of a prince, he saw that that faithful Rahab had been so converted to good, loved by God, drawn away from Jericho by God's command and numbered among the daughters of Israel, as if she had been designated some great woman, she deserved to have Salmon take her as his wife. Second, I believe that this took place because it portended a spiritual truth. The prostitute Rahab was a figure of the church, since she had been a prostitute living among the Gentiles and had been thoroughly defiled by the worship of idols. Yet she welcomed the spies of Jesus Christ, that is, the apostles, into the home of her heart through their words. She hid them again in the memory of her head so that the prince of this world, the devil, might not find them or destroy them. They were lowered down through the window by a red cord, which also served as a sign. Thus she was saved through this foretelling of our Lord's passion, was led from the world, purified and made the bride of Christ.

Salmon was the tenth generation from Abraham. The number ten always refers to the perfect Christ, because it is the number of perfection: the first letter of the name of Jesus is an iota, which is used to represent the number ten.[42] Because Salmon has the mystical number of Christ and Rahab portrays the church, it is not without reason that we believe that the Rahab mentioned in Matthew was the very same Rahab mentioned in Joshua and that Salmon took her as his wife. Perhaps it was for this reason that Salmon's name was interpreted as "receive the vessel," inasmuch as by his very name he was invited by the providence of God to accept the vessel of his choice, Rahab. For just as Paul was deemed worthy of apostleship and made a vessel of election for God, although he had been a persecutor, so also Rahab was thought by the people of Israel to be worthy to be married to Salmon, although she had been a prostitute and a Gentile. Or this might be interpreted spiritually, as referring to the marriage with Christ, because she was made a vessel of election for Christ. Either name of that prostitute fits this mystery.

Previously she had been called Rahab, which means "breadth" or "spread abroad." Either because the church has been called from all the ends of the earth, she is called the breadth of the Gentiles or, because the believing church is established from the whole globe in every part of the world, the church has been spread abroad. After Salmon married Rahab, she was called Rachab,[43] which means "ascension." Just as that Rachab ascended bodily, having been made one of the daughters of Israel and having had the honor of marriage to a noble man bestowed on her, so also spiritually the church ascends. Although the church had previously been an idolater, she was made

[41]1 Tim 6:8. [42]The Greeks used letters of the alphabet to represent their numbers; alpha represented 1, beta 2, and so on. The letter iota stood for 10. [43]The Septuagint renders her name "Raab," both in Josh 2 and Josh 6, but the New Testament prefers the spelling "Rachab," which reflects better the Hebrew guttural consonant that is the second consonant of her name. However, the author of this work has mistakenly assumed that Rahab's name was changed after her marriage.

a friend of the angels, the bride of Christ and the daughter of God.

As for that Salmon, whose name means "receive the vessel," what kind of son did he produce by Rachab? Boaz, whose name means "in virtue" or "virtue in itself" or "prevailing." According to God's design he took Ruth as his wife, who had been cared for by God. In virtue he sired children, who both had virtue in themselves and who prevailed. Indeed, whoever marries owing to the devil's bidding, that is, not with a view toward religion, neither produces children faithful in infirmity or ones who ever prevail and are strong, except in evildoing. Moreover, such parents seem to produce their children as a punishment for their irreligion and not as joy or comfort. And so Boaz took a Moabite woman by the name of Ruth as his wife. I think that it is unnecessary to explain how he came to marry her, since the Scriptures are very clear about all these matters. We will only say that Ruth married Boaz owing to the merit of her faith, since she despised her own people, land and race, and chose Israel and did not despise her widowed mother-in-law, living in exile, but was led more by the desire for her mother-in-law's nation than for her own. She rejected the gods of her ancestors and chose the living God, as she spoke such words to her mother-in-law: "Do not urge me to leave you or to return from following you. For where you go I will go, and where you lodge I will lodge. Your people shall be my people, and your God my God. Where you die I will die, and there will I be buried. May the Lord do so to me and more also if anything but death parts me from you."[44] Therefore Boaz took her as his wife because of her faith, so that royal offspring might be born from such a hallowed marriage. Boaz, who had already become an old man, did not take a wife for himself but for God; it was not for the sake of the lust of his body but for the sake of the righteousness of the law, so that he might raise up a seed for his neighbor. He was made more eager for the marriage not because of his love but rather because of his religion. In age he was an old man, but in faith he had the vigor of youth—and so for this reason he was called "in virtue" or "virtue prevailing in itself." Whoever is in his manly virtue at the age that men get married is not worth mentioning or praising for being in his manly virtue. But whoever is already past the age of marriage and gets his manly virtue for entering into marriage from religion, as Boaz did, is worthy to be praised and named, because he exists in virtue and the virtue of such a great man is in him himself. The manly virtue of a youth is not in himself but in the youthfulness of his body and, consequently, it later is consumed and grows weak. But whoever has the virtue of faith in his soul (just as Boaz did), the virtue of that man resides in himself and thus cannot grow old.

Consequently, Ruth was named "inspiration." Unless the inspiration of God had been in her, she would not have said the things she did, nor would she have done the things she did. What sort of thing is found to be praiseworthy in her? Is it her love of the nation of Israel, or her candor, or her obedience or her faith? Indeed, she did love the nation of Israel, for she greatly desired to conceive sons from the seed of Israel and be united with the people of God. If she had merely desired intercourse with a man like a lascivious girl, she would have rather sought out another young man. But because she did not desire to satisfy her lasciviousness but her piety, she chose instead a holy family rather than the youthful age. She showed her candor because she spontaneously wrapped herself in his cloak and did not think that he would reject her as a righteous man might reject a lascivious woman or think that he might sport with her and—what would be

[44]Ruth 1:16-17 (RSV alt. by Kellerman).

even more serious—despise her once he had had his fun with her, as many do. But she was obedient to her mother-in-law's advice and confidently believed that God would prosper her deed, since she had a clear conscience that it was not lust that had driven her to this deed but rather piety had urged it.

What qualities are mentioned as being in Boaz? Humility, chastity and piety. Humility and chastity because he did not touch her as a lustful man might touch a young woman, nor did he shrink from her as a chaste man might shrink from a lascivious woman, but as soon as he heard her words about the levirate marriage, he did not impute any of these things to lust but rather ascribed them all to piety. Nor did he look down on her as a wealthy man might look down on a poor woman, nor did he fear as an old man might fear taking a youthful bride. Prepared more by his faith than by his body, he went to the gate early in the morning and summoned one of his kinsmen whom he thought would be closer kin according to the law of levirate marriage. He obtained her and prevailed not so much by the law of levirate marriage as by the favor of God who chose him. Perhaps for this reason he was called "prevailing."

What sort of son did Boaz produce with such a wife? Obed, whose name means "submissive." Now those who choose wealth and not character, or who choose beauty and not faith, or who hope to find in their spouses what men are accustomed to seek in prostitutes—such men do not produce children who are submissive either to themselves or to God but rather children who are insolent against their parents and against God, so that their children are not the fruit of their just marriage but rather a punishment fitting their ungodliness. But Obed, who was said to be submissive, what did he beget? Jesse, that is, "consolation." Jesse in the Latin tongue means "consolation." Whoever is truly submissive to God and to his parents produces such children (if God so permits) by whom he may be consoled, for "whoever honors his father is honored by his sons."[45] However, those who are insolent, either against God or against their parents, when they have children, they will not beget consolations for themselves but rather griefs, so that they will receive from their own children what they had done to their parents.

Moreover, I venture a guess because of the names Obed (whose name means "submissive") and Jesse (whose name means "consolation") that perhaps in the days of Obed the children of Israel were handed over to the authority of some other nation because of their sins, as we read in the book of Judges frequently happened. And because they were made submissive to some nation, Obed quite appropriately was named "submissive" at the time of his birth. But, as we can partly surmise from the writing of Kings[46] that David lived for as many years as Saul reigned, so Jesse was almost a contemporary of Samuel. With Samuel as judge and prophet, the children of Israel pleased God in all things and were consoled in the body, freed from foreign domination and did well spiritually. Perhaps for this reason Jesse was called "consolation."

[6]Jesse [was] the father of David the king.

Because God is involved with the generation of the just, the generation of the upright will also be blessed. But can we say concerning David as much as the book of Kings[47] says? We will pass over all other matters and speak only about this one thing, how also David was a type of Jesus Christ. David's name means "sufficient in hand" or "beloved," just as also Christ was. David was brave in war and mighty and beloved by his father. Both in his actions and in his mercy and clemency he was a prefigure-

[45]Sir 3:6 (trans. Kellerman). [46]1 Sam in the RSV. [47]The books of 1 Sam and 2 Sam in the RSV.

ment of Christ. And what else need I say about his just actions or the unjust persecutions he suffered? But even in his most evil sin he was a type of Christ and the church. Just as David saw the beautiful Bathsheba as she was bathing while he was blissfully aloft on his roof, and as he lusted after her and took her while she was still married to another man, a Hittite, so also Christ, while he was still in his most high heaven, still blissful in his own divinity, saw the church of the Gentiles, beautiful in her heart but displeasing to him due to her defiling by her errors, while washing herself with good works. He saw her while she was still the wife of the devil, and he desired her and laid hold of her beforehand. Afterwards he came into the world, just as David did afterwards, once Uriah had been killed, and took her as his wife in marriage. So also once the devil had been destroyed, Christ brought the Gentiles subdued to him into marriage with him. Just as David had intercourse with Bathsheba while she was still married to her own husband and later took her as his legitimate wife, so also Christ did at that time for the church and now does to every righteous soul. Unless God had previously laid hold of either Jew or Gentile, it would have been impossible to lead anyone to faith in him, as, for example, he led Cornelius to faith through the ministry of Peter. But God had previously laid hold of Cornelius's soul and wrought in it diligent prayers and much almsgiving, as the Acts of the Apostles attests.[48] He called the centurion to faith in him, but previously when he was still under the devil's sway, he had laid hold of his soul, working in it a love for God's people and building synagogues.[49] So we see what the devil can do. It is impossible for him to draw any Christian to treachery, unless earlier while he was still under Christ's sway he had laid hold of his soul and worked in it his own kind of work and shown his approval. Look at Judas before the devil had disjoined him from Christ and joined him to himself. The devil had already laid hold of him and worked in him greed and thievery. After Judas had pleased the devil so much in his conscience that conformed to his own will, the devil then compelled him to betray Christ and to pass over to his side.

Bathsheba means "daughter of the mighty one." That name has a suitable significance for the mystery of the church. The church is married to our David and has been made the daughter of God almighty, while previously she had seemed to be the daughter of the devil. Moreover, Bathsheba can mean "seventh well," if we double the letter at the end, which has an appropriate interpretation in both a physical and a spiritual sense. The book of Chronicles makes clear that David had seven wives, from whom he sired children: six of them he married while he was in Hebron, but the seventh, Bathsheba, he married in Jerusalem.[50] In the Proverbs of Solomon, the word "wells" means "wives," at least on the first reading of the passage. (It does have another, deeper meaning, but it still has this meaning of "wives.") When Solomon tells men to stay with their own wives, he says, "Drink water from your own cistern, flowing water from your own well."[51] Therefore if "wells" mean "wives," then quite appropriately Bathsheba is called "the seventh well," because she was the seventh wife. But also Christ is counted as the husband of the seven churches. For although there are countless churches, insofar as the diversity of places allows, nonetheless all the churches are called "seven" because of the seven spirits, by which the whole church is sustained. For this reason both John and Paul the apostle wrote to seven churches,[52] as if they were writing to

[48]See Acts 10. [49]See Lk 7:1-10. [50]See 2 Sam 3; 1 Chron 3. [51]Prov 5:15. [52]John wrote the seven letters to the seven churches in Rev 2–3. Paul wrote epistles to seven churches: Rome, Corinth, Galatia, Ephesus, Philippi, Colossae and Thessalonica. The rest of Paul's epistles are addressed to individuals (Timothy, Titus, Philemon).

all of them. As far as the remaining kings are concerned, it seems unnecessary for me to say something about them, since the book of Kings has enough to say or hear about them for those who desire to do so. But, nonetheless, we have attempted to compare their names with their deeds according to how their names are translated from the Hebrew tongue. We do this to show God's providence also in the very names of people and to obtain spiritual delight for the people who are listening.

David was the father of Solomon.

Solomon means "man of peace." He was called "man of peace" because all the surrounding nations had been pacified and were paying tribute and so he had a peaceful reign, so that he could also build a temple to God, for which he also employed the service of Gentiles. He was a figure of our peace-bearing Christ. All the Gentiles flee to him by faith and offer their spiritual tributes of good works. Thus, he has a peaceful kingdom so that he can build up a living temple for the living God out of living stones—not just the Jews but also the Gentiles.

7 Solomon [was] the father of Rehoboam.

Rehoboam means "in the multitude of the people." I believe that his father named him Rehoboam with good intention, as did the fathers of all the kings, but the providence of God granted him an appropriate name, just as he did for the names of all the kings, naming them according to their deeds, whether good or bad. Thus, when Solomon had expanded his kingdom greatly due to his own merits and those of his father David, because God loved Solomon at first, Solomon named the son born to him at that time Rehoboam, that is, in the multitude of the people, as if it had taken place in the multitude of the people that his son was named according to the state of his kingdom, which had multiplied. But the providence of God gave him the name because Rehoboam was to become a sinner and experience the dissolution of the kingdom so that the kingdom might be said to have been dissolved into a multitude of people. For whatever happens in a multitude of people often easily results in the sedition of the multitude. A multitude is the parent of sedition and arrogance, for most often one cannot overcome what the majority of people do wrong. A paucity of people, therefore, is the teacher of discipline.

I believe that Solomon and Rehoboam were types of Christ. And if they were types of Christ, consequently they also were types of the Christian people. (Since all Christians are the body of Christ, the whole Christian people ought to be understood properly as Christ.) Solomon served as a type of the Christian people who begin well, while Rehoboam serves as a type of the people finishing badly. When Solomon was old and sinning, God stirred up Satan against him and cut off his kingdom to some degree. In the days of Rehoboam, when he rejected the advice of the elders and followed the advice of his youthful contemporaries, the kingdom was split fully apart so that ten tribes withdrew and crowned their own king, while only two tribes remained under Rehoboam's rule. In the same way the Christian people at first did well and prospered, just as Solomon did. But as time went on, when the Christian people began to go astray and to love the things of the flesh and of the world, the daughter of Pharaoh, as it were, whom the devil (the prince of the flesh and of the world) furnished in order to tempt them, God stirred up a spirit of schism among the Christians. At first the Christian people were weakened by some schisms. But now in the most recent history of the Christian people, as iniquity abounds and love grows cold, just as in the days of Rehoboam, the Christian people have been thoroughly split apart so that the majority of Christians are divided into heretical groups and appoint their own bishops for themselves, as if they were their own kings, and scarcely a Christian remains in the church of Christ under Christ. And just as Rehoboam at that time rejected the advice of the elders, followed that of his contemporaries and thereby offered an opportunity for that rebellion, so also at the end the bishops abandoned the counsels of their elders (the apostles and prophets), according to which they should have taken counsel how to keep company with other bishops or to handle their office, and instead they followed the counsels of their contemporaries and young people who were giving counsel that a bishop ought to be rich and inhospitable, that he should not have the fear of God and that he should say all such things as get applause. They gave an opportunity to the devil to make a schism, since they did not pay attention to what the Lord said: "But if that servant says to himself, 'My master is delayed in coming,' and begins to beat the menservants and the maidservants, and to eat and drink and get drunk, the master of that servant will come on a day when he does not expect him and at an hour he does not know, and will punish him."[53] Again Peter commands, "not as domineering over those in your charge but being examples to the flock."[54] Again Paul says, "Have nothing to do with stupid, senseless controversies; you know that they breed quarrels. Their talk will eat its way like gangrene."[55] And "Follow the pattern of the sound words which you have heard from me."[56] It is foretold in the psalm that the people of Christ will first prosper and then experience adversity. It foretells their prosperity at first: "Of old you spoke in a vision to your faithful one, and said,"[57] and the verses that follow. It foretells their later adversity: "But now you have cast off and rejected, you are full of wrath against your anointed"[58] and the verses that follow. See how in the kingdom of Judah some kings were sinners, but some were less so. But in the kingdom of Israel no king was found to be just. So also in the church of Christ good bishops and sinful bishops can be found, but among the heretics no one is found upright at all, but all are perverse, because dross and filth are found in gold, not gold in filth.

Rehoboam [was] the father of Abijah.

Abijah means "the father who is coming" or "this man of my father." Perhaps this Abijah had been born similar to his father in body, so they called him "the father who is coming," as if another father were being born. Or they named him "this man of my father" as if he were the image of his father. The providence of God ordered him to be so named, because just as Rehoboam began correctly but later sinned against God, so also did Abijah.

Abijah [was] the father of Asaph.

Asaph means "ointment." This Asaph was very perfect in heart and pleasing to God, as the book of Kings shows. Perhaps for this reason it was ordained by God that he would be called "ointment," for just as ointment retains its good smell and delights people with its smell and makes them healthy when they have been anointed, even in the winter when flowers have died, so also the just person does not fade in the winter of temptation but remains faithful. So it was in the case of Asaph, who was a man of good reputation, and the history written about him delights the reader, edifies him, makes him healthy and stirs up prudent people to long for his holiness.

8Asaph was the father of Jehoshaphat.

Jehoshaphat means "the Lord is judge." I think

[53]Lk 12:45-46. [54]1 Pet 5:3. [55]2 Tim 2:23, 17. [56]2 Tim 1:13. [57]Ps 89:19; the archaic language of the RSV has been updated. [58]Ps 89:38; the archaic language of the RSV has been updated.

that when the Lord had prospered his father Asaph in all things because of his righteousness and had crushed his enemies before him, as the book of Kings attests, he offered to God, the just judge, by giving that name to his son, calling him "the Lord is judge." Indeed, it is the duty of a just judge to reward those who do good and to punish one who neglects to do good, just as God did to Asaph. For after God defeated the countless forces of Ethiopians and Libyans before him, later he sought the help of the Syrians when the king of Israel, Baasha, turned against him. For this reason God also sent the prophet Hanani to him to say these things: "Because you relied on the king of Syria, and did not rely on the Lord your God, the army of the king of Syria has escaped you. Were not the Ethiopians and the Libyans a huge army with exceedingly many chariots and horsemen? Yet because you relied on the Lord, he gave them into your hand. For the eyes of the Lord run to and fro throughout the whole earth, to show his might in behalf of those whose heart is blameless toward him. You have done foolishly in this; for from now on you will have wars."[59] Because of his lack of trust in God I think that also in his old age his feet hurt him, because the Lord was a just judge for him in all things. The Lord neither leaves unpaid the smallest righteousness of his servants nor refrains from correcting the smallest fault. But he was also a righteous judge toward Asaph's son Jehoshaphat, who was called by this name because Jehoshaphat was consumed by justice, just as his father Asaph had been, but even more so. Therefore the Lord, the righteous judge, exalted him even more fully and glorified Jehoshaphat more than his father Asaph, so that all the surrounding kings brought gifts to him as they had brought to Solomon. But, nonetheless, when he had become friends with Ahab and given him help as he went up to war, chariots surrounded him. And when he was in danger of being killed, he called out to God, and God delivered him. When he returned to Jerusalem after Ahab's death, God sent to him the prophet Jehu, the son of Hanani, who said, "Should you help the wicked and love those who hate the Lord? Because of this, wrath has gone out against you from the Lord. Nevertheless some good is found in you, for you destroyed the Asherahs out of the land, and have set your heart to seek God."[60] Do you see that one ought not to give help to the enemies of God or receive it from them? The aforementioned history of Asaph teaches us that we should not receive help from the enemies of God. The account about Jehoshaphat teaches us that we ought not to give it to them, either. Whoever seeks help from the enemies of God despairs of God's help and thinks that the enemies of God are more useful than God. Meanwhile, whoever helps the enemies of God fights against him. As God is trying to destroy his enemy, such a person attempts to defend him.

Jehoshaphat [was] the father of Joram.

Joram means "the Lord is exaltedness." Just like his father Jehoshaphat, Joram likewise prospered greatly and was exalted in his kingdom. Because Jehoshaphat trusted in the Lord, he called his son "the Lord is exaltedness." It was as if he were saying, "The Lord is my exaltedness, who has lifted me on high not by my own merit but by his mercy." Perhaps it was also the providence of God that granted him to be so named, for Joram would be ungodly and haughty. Joram was raised up to become very rich, and yet he acted very wickedly against God, as the book of Kings and Chronicles attest. He married the daughter of Jezebel, Godoliah by name,[61] and Ahab made use of his counsel, and Joram was wicked against God and rose up against him. He made his own ex-

[59] 2 Chron 16:7-9. [60] 2 Chron 19:2-3. [61] Athaliah is the name given in 2 Chron 22:2.

altation into a god or lord for himself and put his trust in his high estate. Everyone makes the evil he serves his lord. He was so haughty that he killed all his brothers, whom his father had left for him as helpers and counselors. For all these reasons the Lord struck him with a dire and prolonged illness so that two days before he died he expelled his own rotten bowels.

Joram was the father of Ahaziah. Ahaziah was the father of Joash, and Joash was the father of Amaziah. Amaziah was the father of Uzziah.[62] Quite rightly the Holy Spirit teaches us through Matthew to remove up to three generations from the number of kings and not to number them among the ancestors of Christ. They were born from the impure and accursed seed. Joram took his wife from the seed of Ahab and Jezebel. Her name was Godoliah, and he produced Ahaziah with her. Ahaziah begat Joash, and Joash begat Amaziah, in whom the fourth generation of the wicked and accursed seed reached its fruition. Ahab, the king of Israel, took Jezebel as his wife, a daughter of the king of Sidon, a very impious woman opposed to the commandments of God. Ahab committed many acts of godlessness against the Lord at her instigation. Therefore the Holy Spirit warned through a prophet that he would destroy every male from the house of Ahab. Jehu, the son of Nimshi, fulfilled this prophecy after he had been anointed by the lad who had been sent to him by Elisha. Jehu also received the promise that his children would reign over Israel until the fourth generation. Thus, the blessing given to Jehu, who had brought punishment on the house of Ahab, was of equal length as the curse that was placed on the house of Joram because of the daughter of the wicked Ahab and Jezebel, so that up to the fourth generation his sons would be cut off from the number of the kings and so his sin would descend on his sons, as had been written: "I the Lord your God am a jealous God, visiting the iniquity of the fathers upon the children to the third and the fourth generation."[63]

See, therefore, through that passage, how dangerous it is to marry one of the ungodly, as Joram did, and how glorious it is to punish the ungodly, as Jehu did. As far the history of Kings is concerned, Amaziah begat Uzziah. But as far as Matthew is concerned, Joram begat Uzziah. For this reason Uzziah means "noble son." Why his father called him a noble son he was not able to fully judge, unless by chance if someone should think that Uzziah had been a particularly splendid child or had been the firstborn. At that time, the firstborn were held to be noble and honorable. God gave him that name inasmuch as he was noble compared with the kings who had descended from the accursed seed. He was also noble in God's opinion because Uzziah did what pleased God and in all things received help from God. Because this was so, when he had been prospered by God, his heart became haughty, and he thought that he was worthy to carry out the priestly office. When he had arrogated to himself the right to bring the censer into the temple and the sons of Aaron and the Levites resisted him, on the grounds that he was seeking something forbidden by the Law, he threatened them as a king relying on his power. But God immediately struck him down with leprosy, and his leprosy appeared twice on his forehead, and he ran outside and sat at home as a leper until his death. See how it is wrong to usurp that work that has not been entrusted to you by God. A layperson commits this sin when he usurps the work of the clergy to himself. A lector commits the same sin if he usurps the work of a deacon; a deacon sins if he usurps the work of a presbyter; and a presbyter sins if he seeks the power of a bishop.

[62]Matthew omits these names, but the author of the commentary draws them from the accounts of the kings of Judah given in 2 Chron 21–26. [63]Ex 20:5.

As those generations arose from that accursed family and were prolonged, see how iniquity gradually became stronger in them generation by generation. Notice how Ahaziah was worse than all people after his father Joram. Ahaziah means "invisible possession." Although his father had been an ungodly man, we cannot suppose that he would have given such a name ("invisible possession") to his son according to God's will, unless by chance it was according to the devil, by whom he had been seduced and tossed to and fro by various errors. His son Joash was better, but not by much. As long as the priest Jehoiada, who had married into the royal family, lived, he loved the lad Joash mightily and rescued him from the hand of his grandmother Athaliah (who had already killed all her other grandchildren), Joash also did what was pleasing to the Lord. But after Jehoiada died, whom Joash had respected as a holy priest and as the one who gave him his life and his kingdom, Joash changed and did evil before God. When at last the Holy Spirit had come on Zechariah, the son of the very same Jehoiada, and had said to him, "Why do you transgress the commandments of the Lord, so that you cannot prosper? Because you have forsaken the Lord, he has forsaken you,"[64] they rose up against him and stoned him at the command of the king. Therefore, his name appropriately means "prolonging of time," because the prolonging of time changed him for the worse.

Again, Joash's son Amaziah was a little better than Joash. Amaziah pleased God at first, just as Joash did, but afterwards he was corrupted, as was Joash. In this respect he was better than Joash his father: Joash stoned to death the prophet who chided him, and he did this to the son of Jehoiada, the priest who had made him king. But when God sent the prophet Balaam[65] to Amaziah and said, "Why have you resorted to the gods of a people, which did not deliver their own people from your hand?"[66] he did not kill him but threatened him with this reply, "Have we made you a royal counselor? Stop! Why should you be put to death?"[67]

Again, Uzziah (Amaziah's son) was better than all those who had preceded him, even if he was not altogether without reproach because he interfered with the work of the priesthood. Notice how even in this way the judgment of God is just. Just as Uzziah was less evil than others who were born from that accursed dynasty (as the number of generations continued to grow) but was nonetheless not perfect, so also God did not cut him off from the number of the kings, for he did what was pleasing to God. But he did strike him with leprosy because of his arrogance so that he had to stay at home. Consequently, it appears that he was not cut off from the number of Christ's ancestors, but he was partially deprived of the enjoyment of his kingdom.

[9]Uzziah [was] the father of Jotham.

Jotham means "perfect" or "undefiled lord." And truly this Jotham was perfect and undefiled in comparison with the kings who had preceded him, because he did what was pleasing to God and no fault was found in him in the book of Kings.

Jotham [was] the father of Ahaz.

Ahaz means "the support of the Lord" or "virtue." Jotham was upright and faithful to God and believed that the Lord was his support and virtue and that God had prospered him in his reign. Confessing, as it were, that the Lord was his support and virtue, he called his son Ahaz, "the support of the Lord" or

[64]2 Chron 24:20. [65]Neither the Hebrew text, the Septuagint nor the Vulgate of 2 Chron 25 names Balaam as the prophet. [66]2 Chron 25:15. [67]2 Chron 25:16.

"virtue." But Ahaz was not the support of the Lord or virtue. Neither did God strengthen him in good, but rather the devil supported him in evil, for he was Ahaz's lord. He acted very wickedly against God, as the books of Kings and Chronicles attest. That Ahaz was called the support of the Lord or virtue shows the piety of his father but his own hardness of heart,[68] for just as he wandered far from his father's habits, so also he removed himself from properly bearing his name, unless by chance his name refers to that which is written in the book of the prophet Isaiah as follows: "In the days of Ahaz the son of Jotham, son of Uzziah, king of Judah, Rezin the king of Syria and Pekah the son of Remaliah the king of Israel came up to Jerusalem to wage war against it, but they could not yet mount an attack against it. When the house of David was told, 'Syria is in league with Ephraim,' the heart of Ahaz and the heart of his people shook as the trees of the forest shake before the wind. And the Lord said to Isaiah, 'Go out to meet Ahaz, you and Shear-jashub your son, at the end of the conduit of the upper pool on the highway to the Washer's Field. And say to him, "Be careful, be quiet, do not fear, and do not let your heart be faint because of these two smoldering stumps of firebrands, at the fierce anger of Rezin and Syria and the son of Remaliah. Because Syria, with Ephraim and the son of Remaliah, has devised evil against you, saying, 'Let us go up against Judah and terrify it, and let us conquer it for ourselves, and set up the son of Tabeel as king in the midst of it,' thus says the Lord God: 'It shall not stand, and it shall not come to pass.' " ' "[69]

Perhaps Ahaz was comforted when he sired a son and called his name Hezekiah. Hezekiah means "the Lord has comforted." Truly, the comforting of the Lord was accomplished through Hezekiah, whose mind was holier than all the kings who had been before him. Not to mention all the other good deeds that commended him quite deservedly to God, when Sennacherib, the king of the Assyrians, sent him the Rabshakeh (the commander of his army) and a document full of abusive language and blasphemies against God, as Isaiah the prophet describes Hezekiah took that document and entered into the temple to appear before the Lord. He prayed, and immediately Isaiah the prophet was sent to him to announce to him God's protection and to comfort him. At Hezekiah's prayer the angel departed from the face of the Lord and struck 185,000 men in the Assyrian camp. As for the words of the Rabshakeh, the prayer of Hezekiah and the comforting words of Isaiah, read them in Isaiah and discover the reason for the encouragement in the people.[70]

10Hezekiah [was] the father of Manasseh.

Manasseh means "away from the one rising up" or "out of oblivion." The latter meaning is commended by the book of Genesis, where, when Joseph's son was born in Egypt, he named him Manasseh, saying, "God has made me forget all my hardship and all my father's house."[71] If Manasseh is understood as "from the one rising up," we can say that perhaps it was because the Lord freed Hezekiah from Sennacherib who had risen up against him. Thus, he afterwards gave thanks to God as he named his son and called him Manasseh. If, however, his name is understood to mean "out of oblivion," one can think of the reason for his name in another way: because he had not produced a son, therefore when he had begotten a son, he called his name "out of oblivion," as if the son had been born to him when all hope had been given up.

We will think that these things took place

[68]Or read "the difference [from his father]" *(differentiam)* rather than "hardness [of heart]" *(duritiam)*. [69]Is 7:1-7 (RSV alt. by Kellerman). [70]See Is 37. [71]Gen 41:51.

according to the good intentions of the father. Otherwise we must think that Manasseh was named for a different reason, namely, according to his most evil acts, that is, his father called him Manasseh on the basis of his predicted course of life. The providence of God allowed him to be given this name because he would forget all the kindnesses of God conferred on him for the sake of his merit and, goaded on by the rebellious devil, whose habit is to rise up against the human race in order to overthrow it, he would do everything to provoke God's wrath. When at last Hezekiah had become ill at a certain time and the prophet Isaiah had come to visit him, Hezekiah called his son Manasseh and began to command him how he ought to fear God, how he ought to rule the kingdom, and many other things. And Isaiah said to him, "Truly your words are not settling into his heart, but I myself must be killed at his hands." When Hezekiah heard this, he wanted to kill his own son, saying, "It would be better for me to die without a son than to leave such a son behind, who will exasperate God and persecute his saints." But Isaiah the prophet scarcely restrained him, saying, "God has made this plan of yours null and void," for he saw the piety of Hezekiah, since he loved God more than his own son.[72]

Nonetheless, when this Manasseh had done many godless things, God brought the mighty princes of the king of Assyria against him, and they seized him, put him in chains and bound him in fetters and led him to Babylon, and there he was bound and chained in the prison and given a small portion of barley bread and a small portion of wine with vinegar, just enough for him to stay alive. And he was mightily confined in his pain. And behold, when he was afflicted gravely, he sought the face of the Lord his God and prayed to God (who is near to all), and the Lord heard his voice and had compassion on him. And a flame of fire appeared around him and melted all his chains. And the Lord freed Manasseh from all his tribulation, and he returned to Jerusalem and to his throne. And Manasseh recognized the Lord and said, "He alone is God." And he served the Lord God alone with all his heart and with all his soul all the rest of the days of his life, and he was accounted a just man.[73] Perhaps he was called "away from the one rising up" or "out of oblivion" because the Lord freed him from the one who rose up against him, and Manasseh was made mindful of God when previously he had forgotten him.

Manasseh was the father of Amos.[74]

Amos means "strength." If indeed he was born before Manasseh repented, while he was still acting evil, we cannot imagine any pious reason for calling him "strength," but rather only the reason of bodily audacity, as the barbarian nations are accustomed to name their children after beasts, wild animals or rapacious birds, giving them names that point to their destructive power and thinking that such warlike and bloodthirsty children have something glorious in their name. But if Manasseh begat him after he repented, it is quite likely that he called him "strength" for pious reasons. Moreover, Amos can also be understood to mean "of the one burdening" or "of the one tearing apart the people." Now if he begot his son before he repented, I cannot see why he would have named him this. But if it was after he repented, there are good grounds. Mindful of his own past misdeeds, for the sake of humility he called his son "of the one burdening" or "of the one tearing apart the people," to accuse himself, as it were. And it is as if he were to say, "son of a sinner," because the king who sins and burdens himself and tears himself away from God also

[72]The author may have drawn this information from the apocryphal *Ascension of Isaiah*; see *ZKT* 34:16. This event is not recorded in canonical Scripture. [73]See 2 Chron 32. [74]Alternate reading: Amon.

by his own example burdens the people with his sins and tears them away from God, as Manasseh did, who burdened the people and tore them away from God by the example of his godlessness.

Amos himself was not "strength" according to God, but according to the devil. He was extremely unjust, as his own evil deeds appear, with which he had imitated Manasseh, so that he even thought he could deceive God, saying, "My father did many unjust deeds from youth on and in his old age he repented; now I too walk as my soul pleases and later I will be converted to the Lord." And so he was made a wicked "strength" and burdened himself with even more dangerous burdens, and by the example of his wickedness he tore away his people more from God than his father had done. Perhaps for this reason he was so named in accordance with the providence of God. The Lord God quickly wiped him out. Listen carefully, then, o laity, lest some of you think in your heart the way Amos did. Whoever sins while thinking in this way transgresses not by being overcome by the weakness of the flesh but by an evil intention, which is a close friend to evil itself.

Amos [was] the father of Josiah.

Josiah means "where is the offering to the Lord?" or "the Lord's salvation." Perhaps Amos in his heart turned from God and called his son "where is the offering to the Lord?" or "where is the Lord's salvation?" as if to say that that which does not exist cannot be of any advantage. The providence of God, by which Josiah had been foretold, granted him to be called that name "where is the offering to the Lord?" or "the salvation of the Lord," since truly in him was the offering of the Lord. He offered to the Lord God such a sacrifice as no other king either before him or after him offered. And he himself was an offering to the Lord in the manner that the apostle commands: "present your bodies as a living sacrifice, holy and acceptable to God."[75] And during his days he himself was his people's salvation that comes from the Lord. We cannot speak of his praiseworthy deeds as the books of Kings and Chronicles do. Consider that he was such an individual that his name was foretold even many generations before he would be born. Josiah is the third individual whose name had been foretold before he was born. Those three are Sampson, Josiah and John.

[11]Josiah [was] the father of Jechoniah.

But this is not the way it is described in the book of Kings, but rather after the death of Josiah his son Jehoahaz was made king. Pharaoh came and brought him to Egypt because of his sins. In his place Pharaoh put Eliakim his brother as king, another son of Josiah. His name means "adjudged by the Lord." Pharaoh called him by another name, Jehoiakim, which means "preparation of the Lord." But when Jehoiakim also behaved wickedly against God, he was adjudged by God as being ungodly and thus condemned. Later he was prepared for the overthrow of Judah, and the king of the Assyrians led him away to Babylon in accordance with God's wrath. In his place Jechoniah[76] his son was made king, whose name means "preparing for the Lord." When he also behaved wickedly against God, preparing himself for God's wrath, he was led by the king of the Assyrians to Babylon with all of his men. In his place his brother Zedekiah was made king by the king of the Assyrians, under whose reign also all of Judah went into exile. Therefore, this is the genealogy: Josiah begat Eliakim (later called Jehoiakim); Jehoiakim begat Jechoniah.

[75]Rom 12:1. [76]Called Jehoiachin in 2 Kings 24.

[12]*And after the deportation to Babylon: Jechoniah was the father of Shealtiel.*

According to the book of Kings, Jehoiakim is the fourteenth from Solomon, and he himself was the son of Josiah. But Jechoniah was the first in the genealogy down to Christ and was really not the son of Josiah but his grandson and the son of Jehoiakim. According to the Gospel, however, in which Jechoniah is said to be the son of Josiah, if Jechoniah is reckoned as the fourteenth one among the preceding set of generations, the remaining set of generations down to Christ from Shealtiel would turn out to be thirteen. But if Jechoniah is placed first among the last set of generations, the preceding set of generations calculated from David to Josiah would turn out to be thirteen.

What are we to do then? Jehoiakim was removed from the number of the kings, and quite rightly so. The people of God did not seat him on his throne, as had been the custom of seating kings, but Pharaoh had done this through the nobility. Therefore, to that extent Jehoiakim was not king. If it was right to remove the aforementioned three kings from the number of the kings solely because of their mixed lineage derived from Ahab and Jezebel, even though they had been seated on their thrones by the people and by the laws, why then was it not right in like manner to remove also Jehoiakim, whom Pharaoh had made king over a land hostile to him and whom the people of God had not crowned as legal precedent demanded? Consequently, that Jechoniah, who was the son of Jehoiakim (and grandson of Josiah), was put in place of his father Jehoiakim when his father was removed from the number of the kings, as if Jechoniah had been the son of Josiah. And so he is named twice in the Gospel: once before the exile, namely, as the fourteenth in number, and again after the exile as the first in number. It happens in this way: Josiah begat Jechoniah, namely, as the fourteenth descendant. But after the exile Jechoniah begat Shealtiel, as if Jechoniah were the first in the next genealogy. And so Jechoniah here is found to have the number of two people: his father's and his own. Although this Jechoniah was one person, he had two different states. He was a king before the exile, having been crowned by the people of God; he was also made a private citizen after the exile, having been led away as a captive. Therefore before the exile he was reckoned among the kings as a king, but after the exile he was reckoned among the private citizens as a private citizen.

But how do you expect the Evangelist to have written it? If he had said, "Josiah begat Jehoiakim in the fourteenth generation, and Jehoiakim begat Jechoniah, and Jechoniah after the exile begat Shealtiel," aside from the fact that one crowned by Pharaoh (Jehoiakim) would be counted among the kings of Judah, one would moreover find fourteen kings before the exile, but after the exile one king and thirteen private individuals. But if Jechoniah had been placed among the earlier kings, one would find fifteen royal generations before the exile but thirteen generations of private citizens after the exile. In either case the Evangelist seemed to say something contrary to reason and did not show the mystery that he had set forth. You see how wisely the Evangelist wanted Jechoniah to appear twice, first as the fourteenth among the kings and then as a private citizen, the first after the exile among the generations of private citizens. Since it is consistent, I also count Jechoniah so that that there are twenty-eight generations from David to Christ. What harm is there to remove Jehoiakim and to mention his son Jechoniah twice for a sound reason, so that he might explain the mystery that the Evangelist sets forth and still not lie about the number of the generations? Nor is it any objection that he is called the son of Josiah when he was really his grandson, since also grandsons are rightly called sons.

Jechoniah begat Shealtiel, whose name means "petition of God." We read nothing, either good or bad, about Shealtiel. Nonetheless, we think that he was holy and in captivity diligently prayed to God for the calamity that had fallen on Israel, and so he had been called "petition of God."

Shealtiel [was] the father of Zerubbabel.

Zerubbabel means "disregarded flow" or "from a mixture" or "here is a teacher of Babylon." He was lawfully called this, if it is true (I do not know) that the priestly and royal lines were mixed in Zerubbabel, as we will explain below. Therefore, it was perhaps for this reason that he was called "from a mixture."

It was through that Zerubbabel that all the children of Israel were released and returned to their own land with great joy, as the prophet Ezra explains.[77] When Zerubbabel was in the service of King Darius, a dispute arose between him and two other servants of the king as to what was the strongest thing in the world. One said that nothing is stronger than wine, another said that nothing is stronger than a king, and Zerubbabel said that nothing is stronger than a woman and the truth. As they were fighting endlessly over this matter, they appealed to the opinion of King Darius. As he was seated with his princes to pass judgment, the three of them argued, each one for his opinion. Whoever wishes to know the words of their arguments may read the prophet Ezra.[78] Nonetheless, Zerubbabel won, and by the judgment of Darius and all the princes it was pronounced that truth is stronger than everything else. But when King Darius swore an oath to him, "Ask whatever you wish from me, up to half of my kingdom," Zerubbabel answered, "I do not seek your kingdom, but may you enjoy it forever. But this I ask of you, that which your father King Cyrus began before you, namely, that you release the captivity of the children of Israel so that they may return to their own land." Darius granted his wish. Zerubbabel departed and gave thanks to God, saying, "Blessed are you, who has given me wisdom; I give you thanks, O Lord of our fathers."[79] And so he was found to have been rightly named by the providence of God Zerubbabel, that is, "here is a teacher of Babylon." What greater teaching is there than to show that truth is mistress over all things? In him was fulfilled that which had been written: "Your commandment makes me wiser than my enemies, for it is ever with me. I have more understanding than all my teachers, for your testimonies are my meditation. I understand more than the aged, for I keep your precepts."[80] His name could also mean "disregarded flow," that is, because he disregarded the succession to the kingdom that was flowing down to him and chose the redemption of his people.

Now concerning the rest of the generations, I cannot recall having read any part of Scripture or ever heard any tale about them. However, this ought finally to be noted, that whatever kings pleased God reigned for a long time, and God humbled their enemies and put them in their hands, but as many behaved basely quickly had their reign and life cut short by bitter death, and God humbled them under their enemies.

[17]So all the generations from Abraham to David were fourteen generations.

Since the Evangelist could have briefly explained the number of generations by saying, "From Abraham to Christ there were forty-two generations," why did he divide the generations three times, and why did he divide them into three parts of fourteen generations each? It was because three times when fourteen generations had been completed, the state of

[77]See 1 Esdras 4 and Josephus *Antiquities* 11.3. [78]1 Esdras 3:17–4:11. [79]1 Esdras 4:60; the archaic language of the RSV has been updated. [80]Ps 119:98-100; the archaic language of the RSV has been updated.

humankind among the Jews changed. From Abraham until David they were under judges; from David to the exile they were under kings; from the exile to Christ they were under priests. Therefore he wanted to show how, just as when the fourteen generations had been completed the state of humankind always changed, so when the fourteen generations had been completed from the exile to Christ, there must similarly have been a change in the state of humankind—which indeed took place. After Christ, humankind was no longer under many judges or under many kings or under many high priests, but all generations have been subordinated under the one Christ, who is both judge and king and high priest, since he alone has the office of those three estates. Thus, because both the judges and kings and high priests were prefiguring the three offices of Christ, the first to hold those offices always bore the image of Christ. Joshua was the first of the judges; David was the first of the kings; Joshua, son of Jehozadak, was the first high priest. No one can doubt that they bore the image of Christ.

Perhaps for this reason fourteen generations are given, that is, four and ten, that is, four times Christ. The letter iota[81] represents the mystery of Christ. Therefore it was for this reason that there were fourteen generations, because three times Christ was prefigured and shown, but the fourth time the true Christ appeared. We shall explain in its own place why in Luke's Gospel seventy-seven generations are given of Christ as he is being reborn from baptism.[82] But here let us say why forty-two generations of Christ are given as he is being born according to the flesh and appearing in the world. Forty-two is the number of six weeks. Six is the number of work and labor, for in six days the world was made, which has been situated in work, labor and pain. Therefore, quite appropriately forty-two generations of Christ are given at the time of his birth into the world in order to labor and suffer pain. The number forty-two has within itself the portent of work and labor.

18Now the birth of Jesus Christ took place in this way.

As he had stated above, Jacob was the father of Joseph, to whom Mary was betrothed when she gave birth to Jesus. So that no hearer might think that the birth of Christ took place in this way, as the birth of the preceding fathers had taken place, Matthew interrupts the order of his narrative and says in addition, "Now the birth of Jesus Christ took place in this way." It was as if he were saying, "The birth of those fathers concerning whom we have expounded took place just as I stated. But the birth of Christ took place not in that way but in the way that follows." How? "When his mother Mary had been betrothed to Joseph, before they came together she was found to be with child." That is, he was born of a virgin without a father that Matthew, reckoning his birth, might show that Christ was descended from the seed of David according to God's promise, and that Matthew might reveal the mystery of Christ's deity as he unfolds that Christ's birth occurred in a manner beyond human nature. Nor was it seemly that the only-begotten of God should be born in human fashion, since he was not being born for his own benefit but for that of humankind. Humankind is born in the flesh so that it might be subjected to corruption. But Christ was born in order to heal corruption. Therefore, just as it is not reasonable to assume that a corruptible human being is born by being born out of the incorrupt-

[81]The Greek letter iota is the initial letter of Jesus and was used to signify the number 10 among the ancient Greeks. [82]From this remark we can infer that the author of this work also wrote a commentary on Luke. Schlatter suggests that part of the commentary is the *Fragmenta in Lucam* found in the Bobbio palimpsest (*VC* 39:384-92).

ibility of virginity, so it is not reasonable that the only-begotten Son, who was being born in order to heal corruption, would be born out of the corruption of wedlock. Humankind is born out of necessity in order that it may exist, but Christ was not born out of the necessity of nature but rather out of his merciful free will to save us. How then is it fair that necessity and free will have one and the same esteem in the way a person is born? Therefore he was deservedly born contrary to the rules of human nature because he was above nature.

See how the birth of Christ is something new and astonishing, that is, it took place through sinful human beings, through prostitutes and adulterous women and through Gentiles. But such an origin does not soil the dignity of Christ but rather shows his mercy. His mercy was so marvelous that he who made and begot them as his fathers by adoption was born from them as if they were his sons. They were made his fathers, of whom he was not the son. He offered them this distinction, namely, to be their son. They, however, did not offer anything to him so that they might be his fathers. Among humankind, fathers adopt for themselves the sons whom they themselves desire, but this son adopted for himself fathers whom he chose. Among humankind, sons receive the distinction of noble birth from their fathers, but in Christ's case the fathers received this distinction from him, their descendant.

When his mother Mary had been betrothed to Joseph, before they came together she was found to be with child from the Holy Spirit.

Since all the saints would be born of the virgin church, betrothed to Christ, Christ is born of a betrothed virgin so that the servants would not be born in a more glorious manner than their Lord. But in order that his children might imitate in every respect the perfect example of their father's birth, Mary had also been betrothed to a carpenter, because also Christ, the bridegroom of the church, accomplished humankind's salvation and his entire work through the wood of the cross. Now Mary was both betrothed and dwelling in his home, so that her betrothal might be faithful and refute every reproach of fornication from the mother and preserve the glory of virginity[83] for the Lord who was about to be born. If the unbelieving Jews said, "Is not this Jesus, the son of Joseph?"[84] because she gave birth in the home of her husband, how much more would they have said, if she had given birth outside the home of her husband, "Is not this Jesus, the son of the prostitute?" For just as in the case of a woman who conceives a child in the home of her husband she is understood to have conceived within the marriage, so also in the case of the woman who conceives a child outside of the home of her husband she is suspected to have conceived apart from him. Therefore the Lord preferred that his mother be suspected of having conceived within the marriage rather than endure the reproach of being a fornicator.

Before they came together she was found to be with child.

He did not say, "Before she was taken into the home," but "before they came together, she was found to be with child," because she had already been taken into the home. Virginity indeed is imperishability; imperishability is genuine virginity itself.[85] Therefore, before they came together, Christ was conceived, so that the imperishable One might not be born out of what is perishable nor might the Lord make for himself a temple out of the passion of either body. I say this not to trouble married people or lead them to despair but rather to console and praise those who are continent, because marital intercourse is something bad before God. I did not say that

[83]Alternate reading: "in order to preserve the grace of virginity." [84]Jn 6:42. [85]Alternate reading: "but imperishability is truth itself."

it was sin but rather something bad. In its very nature, it is sin, but by the concession of God it was made to be not sinful. How? Mortals had to be born in the world so that they could be tested and, once having passed the test, be crowned with glory. If mortals had been made immortal, they would not have been able to be tested. If they were not tested, they also could not be crowned with glory because they had not felt the testing of their immortality. Therefore it was determined that mortals would be born from the passion of flesh and blood, from burning fire in the loins as the vital fluid ascended, so that something bad might not be born from something good or corruption from impassability, but that bad might come forth from bad and corruption might arise from passion.

Therefore, although marital intercourse was sin, as far as its nature is concerned, permission to marry was given by God's concession. I say permission was given, not that it was made something righteous. Even if for the sake of necessity it ceases to be sin, nonetheless it does not deserve to be called righteousness. Therefore, the marital union does not bring punishment to those who partake of it, but it does not offer a reward either. And if it does not kill, nonetheless it does not save either. Thus, even the prophet was not looking for God's indulgence but at the filth of his deed when he said, "Behold, I was brought forth in iniquity, and in sin did my mother conceive me."[86] That is to say, "Why is it amazing if I sin, since I was born from sin? The nature of sin has followed its own birth." For if marriage itself pleased God, a glorious crown would never have been promised to those who refrain from it, nor would the celibate be loved by God when they hate marriage. It is not the one who flees from the good who is rewarded but rather the one who flees from evil.

But do you wish to know how marriage is permitted, how at some times it was permitted even to have one's own sisters as wives, and how Cain and Abel had them as wives? Rifan and Edoclam are the names of the daughters of Adam whom Cain and Abel had in the beginning.[87] And they did not sin because the paucity of humankind and the need excused that sin. Later, as the number of people grew, this evil returned to its own nature and began to be a sin. However, the custom of permitting one man to have many wives remained in force. Later, as the world was filled, even this evil returned to its own nature, and it began to be a sin. However, the custom remained in force that one man might have one wife. But now after the fullness of time has come and the world has grown old, we know what is God's plan and what he wants and what is pleasing before him. But we have not dared to say this because of the incontinent, in whose body their soul does nothing, but their blood and that most foul heat, which arises from that maddened fire, hold total sway over them. Finally, the angel recommends to Tobit at his marriage, when he will come to that human custom, to first rise and pray and say, "Lord, you know that I did not take a wife for passion's sake but in order to beget children."[88] If he had prayed any other way, his prayer would not have pleased God. You see, therefore, how he excuses that most foul work of the flesh for the sake of begetting children. But now that the world has increased, the necessity for humankind to procreate has been abolished. Now it is not the multitude of people but the love of the saints that delights him.

Notice that it is the same passion that leads to fornication and that governs marital intercourse. But consider that God marked the shores as the boundaries for the sea when he said, "Thus far shall you come, and no farther, and here shall your proud waves be stayed."[89] In the same way he made marriage the boundary for carnal passion so that it might come

[86]Ps 51:5. [87]These names may come from the apocryphal *The Daughters of Eve*. See *ZKT* 34:14. [88]Tob 8:7 (trans. Kellerman). [89]Job 38:11.

that far and restrain itself there. Just as the sea sins if it crosses over its shores, so also a man sins if he goes beyond what is permitted him in marriage. If then there is the same passion among married people as among adulterers, how can the same thing be righteous in half of its cases but sinful in the other half? Either the whole thing is sinful or the whole thing is righteous because it is one thing. But because passion is not righteous, then it is altogether sinful. But no punishment is imputed to that sin until that loathsome and perishable world passes away. Therefore our Lord was conceived before they came together so that he would not be born of the passion of flesh and blood, since he came to unfetter the passion of flesh and blood and change them into spirit.

Who found her to be with child from the Holy Spirit? Without a doubt it was her husband Joseph, who always admonished himself with a zealous love and looked attentively at the life of Mary. Just as a certain history[90] that is not unbelievable or irrational teaches, when those things that Luke describes took place, Joseph was absent. Nor does it even make sense to think that the angel appeared to Mary and said the things he did and Mary answered the things she did, all while Joseph was present. If we grant that the angel was able to appear to her and speak, that Mary at once with haste departed for the mountainous regions and entered the home of Zechariah, greeted Elizabeth and remained with her three months, this would not have been possible had Joseph been present, because it would have been necessary for him to ask the reasons for her absence and lengthy visit. However, after he returned from afar after so many months and found her clearly pregnant, he perhaps threatened her, as if he were her husband, and terrified her with the judgment of God, since he was a pious man. But when she saw that she had fallen innocently into suspicion of guilt nor could she yet defend herself, having been convicted by the testimony of her belly, she swore, crying out with tears and sighs, saying, "As the Lord lives, I do not know how this took place."

When Joseph heard this, he became greatly afraid and partially believed that there was something divine inside of her. (He would not have been afraid unless he had at least to some degree believed her.) Her holy manner of living urged him to believe her words concerning these things. Since he was a just man, perhaps he began to think to himself concerning her, "She never was a reveler or drunkard. Every woman who is a reveler or a drunkard is also a whore." For whether it is in food or in passion, it is the indulgence of the flesh that ruins a person. A woman who does not say no to the pleasures of her throat also all the more does not agree to resist her lust, as even the apostle says, "She who is self-indulgent is dead even while she lives."[91] "She is not fickle, a jokester, a singer, a lover of foul words, as girls for the most part are likely to be, who gladly either speak such things or hear them. (If they are the more shameless type, they gladly speak, but if they still have a sense of shame, they delight to hear such things, even if they are too embarrassed actually to say such things.) She has not looked down on her husband, nor has she stared directly at him. Those things are evidence of a prostitute, as Solomon says, 'A wife's harlotry shows in her lustful eyes.'"[92] As Joseph mulled over these and similar things, he did not find any of them in her, but on every hand he found everything laudable, everything admirable, which cannot be found in human nature without the Holy Spirit. Therefore, since none of the evidence was found by which a woman's adultery is ordinarily found out and proved, the only suspicion yet remaining about her was that it was the grace of God that caused her pregnancy.

[90]Most likely a reference to the apocryphal *Protoevangelium of James* 13; see ANF 8.364; *ZKT* 34:17. [91]1 Tim 5:6. [92]Sir 26:9.

Because of all these things he thought that she was with child with the Holy Spirit. For nothing so commends the chastity of a woman to a man as her disciplined life. Where there is fear of God, there is chastity. Where there is no fear of God, there is no chastity. The flesh urges one on, and the carelessness of a woman aids the flesh. If there is no fear of God present that would resist the flesh, who would restrain the flesh once it had been found? O inestimable praise of Mary! He believed her chastity more than her womb. He believed more the work of grace than of nature. He clearly saw that she was pregnant, and yet he was not able to suspect fornication. He believed that it was more possible for a woman to conceive without a man than for Mary to be able to sin. And what is even greater to see, Joseph dealt with her as a husband would deal with his own wife. Often, if men see their wives cast a flashing glance at another man, they are soon stirred up to jealousy, even though there is nothing to suspect, because their jealousy has arisen out of great love. But in Joseph's case the evidence of her previous manner of life overcame both a husband's jealousy and the accusation of her womb seemingly crying out her guilt.

[19]*And her husband Joseph, being a just man and unwilling to put her to shame, resolved to divorce her quietly.*

Perhaps he thought to himself, "If I cover up her sin, I act contrary to the law of God, and if I make it known to the children of Israel, they will stone her. I am afraid that whatever is in her womb is there by divine influence. Did not Sarah get pregnant and give birth when she was ninety years old? If he made her to flower, who was already like a dried-up tree, what if the Godhead wanted to grant her a birth without man? Did that conception by a woman owe its existence to a man? If the conception by a woman always owed its existence to a man, doubtlessly whenever a man wanted, then also the woman would conceive. But now it is not whenever a man wants that a woman then conceives, but whenever God wants. Therefore, if a woman's ability to conceive is not in the hands of a man but of God, how is it extraordinary if he wanted to give her offspring without a man? What therefore am I to do? I will send her away secretly because in an uncertain matter it is better that an adulteress should escape than an innocent woman die. It is more just that an unjust person justly escape than that a just person unjustly perish, because even if a guilty person escapes once, he can perish another time, but if an innocent person perishes once, he can no longer be called back from the dead. Therefore it is advantageous that she endure reproach by being sent away rather than that she be handed over and killed." But to think this way and to want to do such things is not characteristic of a very just man.

[20]*As he considered these things, behold, an angel of the Lord appeared to him in a dream.*

When Joseph heard the words of Mary and considered her life, such reflection did not allow Joseph to suspect any evil about her. But when he considered her pregnancy, such reflection did not fully allow him to think only good things about her. So his mind wavered back and forth: he both feared to have her as wife and did not dare to hand her back. Because of this, that divine revelation was necessary for him. If Mary herself, who had seen the angel and heard him talking to her about her own pregnancy as well as that of Elizabeth, went into the mountainous regions to see Elizabeth and to have the matter confirmed by her own very eyes, how much more Joseph needed a divine revelation after the words of Mary's pregnancy and his consideration of her life, as he was still wavering.

Therefore the angel appeared to him for

three reasons. First, it was so that a just man would not do an unjust deed out of ignorance, albeit with a just intent. Second, it was for the sake of the honor of the mother herself. For if she had been sent away, she would have never lacked base suspicion from unbelievers, even if not among the faithful. Third, it was so that Joseph could understand the holy manner of conception and guard himself more diligently from intercourse with her in the future than he had previously. Previously he had preserved himself because of his discipline of righteousness, but afterwards out of respect for a birth of this type.

Why did the angel not come to Joseph before the virgin became pregnant? It was so that he might not think those things he was thinking and suffer what Zechariah suffered, who fell into guilt because of his unbelief at the pregnancy of his wife who already was aged. It is, indeed, a more incredible matter to believe that a virgin can conceive than that an old woman can. If the aforementioned priest did not believe that the easier event would take place, how much would that ordinary man not have believed that the more difficult event would take place? If even Mary herself, because of her virginity, almost did not believe when the angel spoke to her about her pregnancy, as she said, "How shall this be, since I have no husband?" how would Joseph have ever believed someone saying that a woman would conceive without a man?

"Joseph, son of David, do not fear to take Mary as your wife, for that which is conceived in her is from the Holy Spirit."

He calls him the son of David because he wants to remind him of God's promise to David that the Christ would be born of his seed. But when he says, "do not fear," he wishes to show that he knows his heart so as to create confidence in the future good tidings that he was about to say about Christ, for "that which is conceived in her is from the Holy Spirit." He calls the only-begotten God the Holy Spirit, as he testifies concerning himself in the Gospel: "It is the spirit that gives life, the flesh is of no avail."[93] And John says, "God is spirit."[94] For the Spirit, the Advocate, did not enter into Mary to take a human body and be born into the world but in order to sanctify the vessel of the virgin. He says, "that which is conceived in her is from the Holy Spirit," as if to say that he would not be born from the seed of some other man, as Joseph in fear was guessing, but from the Holy Spirit. Just as prayer ought to precede whenever a husband and wife are about to lie together, as the angel Raphael commanded Tobit, so that what is about to be conceived might be conceived in holiness, so when the only-begotten God was about to enter the virgin, the Holy Spirit preceded, so that Christ could be born in holiness according to the body, as the Divinity entered in place of the seed.

21"She will bear a son, and you shall call his name Jesus."

He did not say, "She will bear you a son," as he had said to Zechariah, "your wife Elizabeth will bear you a son."[95] A woman who conceives a child with her husband bears a son for her husband because the child comes more from him than from her.[96] But Mary, who had not conceived a child with a man, did not bear a child for him but only for herself. Notice how in every respect this follows the likeness of the very matter that happened in Adam. At that time the woman tasted of the tree, and she alone was seduced and gave birth to death. But Adam did not participate in her seduction, nor did he sin because he was seduced by the

[93]Jn 6:63. [94]Jn 4:24. [95]Lk 1:13. [96]It was commonly thought in antiquity that conception was the male implanting his seed into a woman's womb. The child owed its origin entirely to the father, while the mother merely furnished a place for the child to grow.

devil but because he agreed with the woman. So now, when Mary conceived a child from the Holy Spirit, she alone believed and said, "Behold, henceforth all generations will call me blessed."[97] But Joseph then did not share her trust that led to that conception, but afterwards he was saved by his silent agreement. Thus the angel appeared to him in a dream, not openly, so that just as God created the woman as Adam slept, so also he might vouch for his wife by divine influence, as Joseph was sleeping.

Now the Evangelist interprets what Jesus means in the Hebrew language, saying, "he will save his people from their sins." Therefore if a physician, who does not have any power to save humankind, has no shame to call himself "physician" solely because of his mixing of herbs, how much more worthily is Jesus called Savior, through whom the whole world is saved?[98]

[24]*When Joseph woke from sleep, he did as the angel of the Lord commanded him; he took his wife.*

He did not take her into his home, for he had not yet sent her away from his home, but in his own mind he had put her away, and he took her back again into his mind.

[25]*But [he] knew her not until she had given birth to a son.*

Truly he did not know her beforehand, that is, what honor she had been given, who had been made the mother of the only-begotten God. But after she gave birth, then he knew her because she was made more splendid and noble than the entire world. She alone received in the narrowest chamber of her womb him whom the whole world could not lay hold of and him whom the world did not deserve to receive. Joseph saw that she remained a virgin after her birth. He saw how the mystery[99] of the star stood above the boy's head and showed the lad to the coming magi. It gave witness by standing still because it could not talk. He saw the magi come at last, worshiping him and offering him their divine gifts. He heard their tales, how they had come from the east to Jerusalem, as the star led them, which did not scorn to serve human beings that it might reveal God's glory. Therefore, his incomparable birth, which exceeded the measure of all human birth, showed to Joseph both the divinity of the child who was born and the honor of Mary who gave birth to him. Therefore he said, "But he knew her not until she had given birth to a son." He knew who she was after his birth.

From this statement, some people, following Eunomius,[100] think that until Mary gave birth Joseph did not have carnal relations with her,[101] but afterwards he knew her and she gave birth to children. For this reason he calls Christ the firstborn because we call him firstborn whom other siblings follow. A mad person does not think that anyone is sane; because they dared to say this about her, they also think that Joseph dared to do it. The Evangelist, you see, says that which could have been done was not done, but why would he have thought that it was necessary to say about that which was not able to be done, "It was not done"? Let me give you a couple of examples. A certain individual quarreled with another and, as long as he lived thereafter, he did not speak to him. When I said, "as long as he lived, he did not speak to him," did I imply that after

[97]Lk 1:48. [98]The lines from PG 56:634.60–56:635.14 have been omitted as spurious. [99]Alternate reading: "ministry." [100]Eunomius (d. 395) was a bishop of Cyzicus and leader of the Anomoean or radical wing of the Arians who said that the Son was in no way like (Greek: *anomoios*) the Father. The author of this work is an Arian, to be sure, but of a much milder sort and one as likely to reject the Anomoeans as the orthodox followers of Nicaea would have. [101]The alternate readings "he did not have her in conscience" (*in conscientia*) and "or concupiscence" (*vel concupiscentia*) are not as strong as the emendation "in concupiscence" (*in concupiscentia*).

his death he spoke to him, a deed that cannot be done? So it was also believable that Joseph would have known her before she gave birth, because he did not yet know the full splendor of the mystery. But after he learned that she had been made the temple of the only-begotten God, how could he have taken possession of this temple? Is it that previously, as a religious man, he had not wanted to do this because he expected that he would do it after the marriage, so that he could defile the dwelling place of God with his carnal desires?

Now I have argued these things merely according to common sense. But let us turn to the authority of the Scripture. In accordance with the example of the prophet, the apostle says about Christ: "He must reign until he has put all his enemies under his feet."[102] Now, does Paul mean that Christ will reign only until all things have been put under his feet but that afterwards he will cease to reign? What a foolish idea! He who reigned before all things were subjected to him will reign all the more also after all things have been subjected to him. Again, he says elsewhere, "Till I come, attend to the public reading of scripture."[103] He does not mean "Till I come, attend to the public reading of scripture, but when I come, neglect it," does he?

Now as to the fact that he is "the firstborn," as I have been talking about, it is the usage of the Scriptures to not only call the one who is born first the firstborn, but also him who is an only child. When the Lord says to Pharaoh, "Israel is my firstborn son,"[104] it cannot mean that there is another people, can it? But if you say that he was saying that he was calling the Jewish people the firstborn according to his foreknowledge since he knew that he would make another people out of the Gentiles, I would say to you that he has always had two peoples as far as his foreknowledge is concerned, but he would have one people from the Jews and from the Gentiles alike, just as also he now has.

The Second Homily: On Matthew 2[1]

[1]Now when Jesus was born in Bethlehem of Judea in the days of Herod the king.

When Jacob was fleeing from his brother Esau and had arrived at evening, he saw a dream as follows. A ladder had been placed whose top reached up to the heavens, and angels ascended and descended on it, but the Lord reclined above it. When Jacob awoke, he prophesied at the Spirit's prompting and said, "How awesome is this place! This is none other than the house of God, and this is the gate of heaven."[2] And so the name of that place was called Bethel, which means "house of the Lord." Therefore, when the Lord was born in Bethlehem, the prophecy of that vision was fulfilled. The house of God is the body of Christ, as he said: "Destroy this temple,"[3] and again, "Wisdom has built her house."[4] The gate of heaven is Christ, through whom one enters into the heavenly realms, as the prophet says: "This is the gate of the Lord; the righteous shall enter through it."[5]

Let us furthermore see when Christ is born, namely, "in the days of Herod the king," for this matter is useful, and the Evangelist states the time that he might show that the prophecy of Daniel was fulfilled, which had shown that the Christ would be born after seventy periods of seven years. From that time up until the reign of Herod seventy years of sevens passed by. Because God knew the treachery of the Jews, since they would crucify the true Christ and wait for another Christ, that is, the Antichrist, God removed any pretext for their unbelief and showed them the time when

[102]1 Cor 15:25. [103]1 Tim 4:13. [104]Ex 4:22. **Second Homily** [1]Third homily in some manuscripts. [2]Gen 28:17. [3]Jn 2:19. [4]Prov 9:1. [5]Ps 118:20.

Christ would be born, so that we could believe in that Christ who was born after seventy years of sevens from the time of Daniel, and not in that false Christ who will come in the name of Christ at the end of the age.

In the days of Herod the king.

As long as the Jewish nation was governed by Jewish kings (albeit sinful ones), prophets were sent to cure them. Whatever the need was, such was the help given. But now when the law of God was being governed by the power of a wicked king, that is to say, when the righteousness of God was being pressed by Roman domination, Christ was born, because a great and hopeless disease required a more skilled physician.

Behold, wise men from the East came to Jerusalem, saying, 2"Where is he who has been born king of the Jews?"

"Behold" means that immediately, as soon as he was born, they pointed to the great God in the small human being by their words, deeds and gifts. By their words they showed this because they said, "Where is he who has been born king of the Jews? For we have seen his star in the East, and have come to worship him." By their deeds they showed this because when they had seen him, they worshiped him. They had a faith in them keener than what appeared, for they saw lowly things and understood the lofty. By their gifts they showed this because they offered him gold, frankincense and myrrh, as we will show below. They came as an exoneration of the Gentiles and as an indictment of the Jews, since they foretold the coming faith of the Gentiles and condemned the present unbelief of the Jews. O blessed magi, who were blessed to become the firstfruits of the faithful from all the Gentiles! Those wise men bore the image of the church that would soon be. Just as they believed, sought and confessed the king whom they had not seen, so also we who are of the Gentiles believe and seek the Lord whom we have never seen and confess his power. How well Isaiah prophecies of them, saying, "For before the child knows how to cry 'My father' or 'My mother,' he will carry away the wealth of Damascus before the king of Assyria."[6]

Who are the magi? Men from the East, who came from Persia. Among the Persians the magi are understood to be wise, not evil. For this reason they are called the "wealth of Damascus" because the wealth of that one province is its wise men. The king of the Assyrians is the devil, the prince of demons. Therefore, before Christ in his body knew how to recognize his father or mother, he conquered the power of the devil. He showed as a boy what he would be like later when he became full grown, since he, as he lay in the manger, despoiled the devil of his goods, namely, from those wise men. Consider how he would annul all the devil's power when he came to full warfare: they came from the East, from where the day is born, and from there the beginnings of faith came forth, for faith is the light of souls. When something is born in the West opposite the East, a portent of evil[7] is shown against good people, but when something is born in the East against the West, it is a portent of good[8] against evil people. Thus, because in Christ's time righteousness was about to conquer wickedness and faith was about to conquer unbelief, so the firstfruits of faith came from the East.

"For we have seen his star in the East, and have come to worship him."

Did not they know that Herod reigned in Jerusalem? Did not they understand the justice of

[6]Is 8:4 (trans. Kellerman). [7]Alternate reading: "a reign of evil." [8]Alternate reading: "a reign of good."

the law that whoever proclaims and worships a king while another king is still alive is punished by death as a revolutionary? But while they were contemplating the future king, they did not fear the current king. Did not they have the danger of death before their very eyes, since they were usurping such illegal power? But they showed no worry about death. If they had been worried about death, they never would have dared to come there. Furthermore, they had not seen Christ and yet were already prepared to die for him. O blessed magi, who were made confessors of Christ before the visage of a cruel king, even before they had seen Christ. I have read in someone's writings[9] that those magi learned of this star that would appear from the books of Balaam the diviner, whose prophecy was placed in the Old Testament: "a star shall come forth out of Jacob, and a man shall rise out of Israel, and he will rule all the nations."[10]

I have heard some people referring to a certain writing that, even though it is not fully attested, does not destroy the faith but rather delights one, saying that there was a certain nation placed on the beginning of the East next to the ocean, among whom there was said to be a certain writing named Seth[11] concerning the appearance of this star and the gifts of this kind that were offered to him, which was considered to have been handed down from fathers to their sons through generations of diligent men. And some of them chose twelve even more diligent scholars and lovers of heavenly mysteries, and they commissioned them to wait for that star. And if one of them happened to die, his son or one of his neighbors who was found to be of the same will would be appointed in the place of the deceased. They were called magi in their own tongue, because they glorified God in silence and unspoken voice. Year after year, after the month of harvest, they would ascend on top of a certain mountain situated there, which was called in their language "Mount of Victory." It had in it a cave in the rock, and it was most pleasant because of its springs and choice trees. They would climb up it, wash themselves, pray and praise God silently for three days. So they were doing for generations, always waiting, if perchance in their generation that star of beauty would arise, until at last the star appeared to them, descending on top of that Mount of Victory, appearing as a small boy and having the image of the cross above itself. And the star spoke to them and taught them and commanded them to set out into Judea. The star led them for two years after they set out, and their bags lacked neither food nor drink. All the other deeds that are related by them are found briefly in the Gospel. Nonetheless, when they returned, they continued to worship and glorify God all the more eagerly than before, and they proclaimed to everyone in their nation and made many learned. At last, when the apostle Thomas went to that province after the resurrection of the Lord, they joined themselves to him, were baptized by him and assisted his preaching.

Now inasmuch as the Scripture says, "We have seen his star in the East," it seems to give an opportunity for unbelievers to promulgate astrology, so that they think that everyone is born and lives by the motion of his own star. Therefore it is good to preach briefly about these matters. If indeed the star determines that we are good or evil, then our good should not be praised or our evil reviled, because it was not a voluntary act on our part. What praise would I merit for my good, which I do not by my own will but by the movement of a star? Or shall I receive punishment for my evil, which I did not out of my will but out of necessity? For I can neither flee evil, even if I want to, if the star of my birth drove me to evil. If people commit

[9]Probably the apocryphal *Books of Balaam*; see *ZKT* 34:15. [10]Num 24:17 (trans. Kellerman). [11]The reference is to an apocryphal work, *The Book of Seth*.

adultery and murder through the star, and if the star causes them to die in the commission of a crime, great is the iniquity of those stars—and even more is the iniquity of him who created the stars for this purpose. Therefore we ask: Was the creature made by itself or by another? If they say, "by itself," then let them hear from us that it is impossible for that which exists by itself and is driven by chance to have a certain predictability. But if they say, "by another," then he who made it is unjust. For although God foreknew the future, namely, that so great iniquity would take place through the stars, unless he wanted to correct it, he is not good. But if he wanted to correct it but could not, he is weak. But he is also unjust because he punishes those who sin by the compulsion of the stars as if they had sinned of their own free will. Do not they destroy the very commandments of God not to sin or the exhortations to do good by this folly? Who would exhort someone not to do the evil he cannot avoid or to do the good to which he cannot attain?

Next we ask: if the course of the stars is always the same, why is not the status of people always the same? If they say, "There is a restoration of the stars over a certain period of years, and therefore, those who know the astrological discipline must know that the stars are restored over a period of certain years and must know through how many years this restoration takes place," we say to them in reply: What was that star that caused all people to die in the flood? Did anything exist in it so as to make a flood a second time, or had those people been born under one star? I say this because each and every circular motion had to accomplish its own unfailing purpose. For if the motion of that sort and the circular motion of the stars cause the same evil or the same good, then there should not have been one Abraham or one set of patriarchs or one set of prophets or apostles, but there should have been another set as often as the stars had completed their circular motion.

Finally, the fact that human beings are converted testifies to the truth. Before Christ's coming, what star forced all people to worship idols and to do other wicked deeds? Or after Christ what circular motion made people withdraw from idols and changed ancient customs throughout the whole world? Note that Persians marry their own mothers and daughters, while the Jews are circumcised on the eighth day, and each and every nation has its own habits. If the course of the stars is all the same, how is it that the Persians never retreat from their habits or the Jews from their own? But if it should be said, "The way stars work differs from region to region," how is it that those who have come to faith in Persia have been able to withdraw from the base deeds of that country, even though they stayed in the same region? Or how is it that those who did not come to faith held onto ancestral customs even when they sojourned in a foreign land? The Jews were deported to Babylon and produced children there; how then were they never compelled by the stars of that region to abstain from circumcision and to follow the madness of the Babylonians? Therefore let no one blame the course of the stars, but rather his own manner of life.

[3]When Herod the king heard this, he was troubled, and all Jerusalem with him.

Because he thought that Christ would be an earthly king, Herod was disturbed about the successor to his kingdom, as it were. That is because grand power is always subject to greater fear. Just as even the blowing of the slightest breeze moves the branch of trees situated up high, so also the slightest report of a messenger disturbs lofty people who exist at the height of honor. But humble people live for the most part in tranquility, just as if they were in a valley shut in from all sides. Or he was so disturbed when he heard that the king of the Jews had been born of the nation of the Jews because he himself was an Idumean by nationality and feared that his kingdom would return again to the Jews, that he would be driven out by them and that his offspring would be cut off from the kingdom after him.

I think that Herod was not so much disturbed in and of himself as much the devil who was in Herod. Herod was afraid because he had his suspicions, but the devil was afraid because he truly knew what was happening. Herod thought the king to be a man, but the devil knew him to be God. Already he had heard the angels crying aloud in heaven, "Glory to God in the highest, and on earth peace among men with whom he is pleased!"[12] The more eyewitnesses were added on Christ's behalf, the more the devil feared the destruction of his own power. Therefore, both of them were disturbed in their own fervor and feared the successor to their own kingdom according to their own nature: Herod feared an earthly rival, but the devil feared a heavenly one. Herod would not have been afraid if he had suspected that a heavenly king had been born; nor would the devil have feared if he had suspected that an earthly king had been born. Do you wish to know that Herod was not as disturbed as the devil in him? Look at how the Jewish populace was disturbed. They should have been happy to hear that a Jewish king had been said to arise and one so designated by God. But they were disturbed because these wicked people could not rejoice at the coming of a just man. Or certainly they were disturbed by the fear that Herod in anger at the newborn Jewish king would harass his people. Just as when winds struggle against each other, the sea is shaken violently, so also the people of a realm are harassed when two kings fight against each other.

4And assembling all the chief priests and scribes of the people, he inquired of them where the Christ was to be born.

From this it is most apparent that the devil was disturbed in Herod, inasmuch as he questioned the teachers of the law. Why would Herod have asked them, since he did not believe the Scriptures? But the devil was investigating[13] the matter, and he believed that the Scriptures do not lie. The devil may well lead others into error, but he knows the truth well. Well, what do you want to say? Did Herod believe the Scriptures or not? If he did not believe them, then why was he asking the Scriptures, which he thought to be idle chatter? Or if he did believe that a king would really be born in the place where the Scriptures said he would be, how was he hoping to kill that king, whom the Scriptures said that he would be? Humankind could not change matters so that what God ordained to take place would not take place, could he? But Herod believed in the Scriptures to advance evil but not good; he believed that the king would be born where the Scriptures said that he would, but he did not believe that he would be unable to do anything against the one whom God was sending. This was because he was not governed by his own counsel but was bound and dragged by the chains of the devil.

So are all sinful people in whom the devil works: they believe the Scriptures and yet do not believe them because this very thing that they believe they are not permitted to believe perfectly.[14] What they believe is due to the power of truth because it cannot be hidden to anyone; but what they do not believe is due to the blindness caused by the enemy, for they are made subject to his works and their mind is not free. Think of how all of us who are Christians and read know that the world will come to an end and that we will die—and yet we do

[12]Lk 2:14. [13]Alternate reading: "instigating." [14]Alternate reading: "because this very thing which they believe they are not permitted to accomplish."

not believe this very truth perfectly, nonetheless. For if we believed this perfectly, we would live as if after a brief period of time we would pass over from this world, not as if we would remain in it forever.

5They told him, "In Bethlehem of Judea; for so it is written by the prophet."

They answered the king who asked them but not with good intentions, because they should have concealed the mystery of the king whom God had determined beforehand would save the people of Judah. They should have concealed it especially from the sight of a foreign king, who (if they had wished to consider the matter wisely) was known to be opposed to any king coming after him, not only out of a zeal for his own kingdom but also out of hatred for a foreign people. And yet they not only revealed this mystery but also offered an example from the prophets to give confidence to their words, to the effect that they offered the hidden treasures of their Lord to his enemies and became not preachers of the works of God but rather traitors of his mysteries, and they became not Herod's teachers but instigators of his evil. From these matters we are taught that the secrets of the Scriptures are not to be revealed to the wicked but to the faithful, as Paul commands: "What you have heard from me before many witnesses entrust to faithful people who will be able to teach others also."[15]

And not only did they betray the mystery of the prophecy to the wicked king, but because all of them with one accord excised that one prophesy and did not set forth all of the divinely inspired Scripture, they became the reason that the little children were slaughtered. For how had it been written? "But you, O Bethlehem Ephrathah, who are little to be among the clans of Judah, from you shall come forth for me one who is to be ruler in Israel, whose origin is from of old, from ancient days."[16] If they had set before him the entire prophecy, just as it had been spoken, Herod would have considered that the king who was about to be born was from ancient days and would have understood the antiquity of his honor, because he was not such an earthly king, whose days are from ancient days, and so Herod would not have kindled such great anger against him. But now after this part of the prophecy had been removed, which might have been able to restrain his temper, they brought forth only the first, which could only provoke him. Thus, because they had explained matters to him in this way, Herod thought that a king similar to other kings had been born from Judah, and so he killed the children since he thought that he could kill the Christ along with the rest of the children. O unhappy Jews! They taught Herod that he who would rule the people of Israel would be born in Bethlehem. But they did not teach themselves after he was born, so that they would believe in him. Herod believed them as ones telling the truth so that he consequently persecuted the Christ, and yet they did not believe themselves so that they might welcome him.

7Then Herod summoned the wise men secretly and ascertained from them what time the star appeared; 8and he sent them to Bethlehem, saying, "Go and search diligently for the child, and when you have found him bring me word, that I too may come and worship him."

After Herod heard their answer (which was believable for two reasons: first, because it had been given by the priests, and second, because it had been corroborated with a citation of a prophet), he was not moved to worship the newborn king but to kill him wickedly by trickery. An evil man can indeed understand

[15]2 Tim 2:2. [16]Mic 5:2.

what the things of God are, but he cannot do them, for the intellect of a person was created by God, but his deeds originate from the intention of his will. Herod saw the magis' great devotion toward Christ, and because he could not sway them with flattery or frighten them with threats or corrupt them with gold so that they would agree to murder the future king, he instead planned to deceive them. For it was impossible for them to be seduced by flattery into betraying him on whose account they had undertaken the hard work of a long journey. Nor would they have been frightened of someone so as to hand him over when they had regarded neither Herod nor Caesar but had entered into the middle of their realms and announced a new king. Nor would they have wanted anything more than Christ, since they brought precious gifts for him from such a far-off province. Since he saw that he could not do anything else, he therefore promised his devotion, as he was sharpening his sword and painting over the malice of his heart with the color of humility. Such is the habit of all malicious people when they secretly wish to strike someone direly: they feign humility and friendship with him. He called them secretly so that the Jews might not see the meeting (for he suspected the Jews), lest by chance there might be someone who loved the king of his own nation and understand Herod's shrewd dealing and so betray his plot to the magi. Herod did this, not realizing that the Jews were greater enemies of Christ than Herod himself was. Herod persecuted him because he thought that he was a mere human, but after many miracles and heavenly signs, yes, after the Jews had clearly recognized that he was the Son of God, it was then that they crucified him. Because his divinity was clearer to the Jews than it was to Herod, their iniquity is more vicious than that of Herod.[17]

9And lo, the star which they had seen in the East went before them, till it came to rest over the place where the child was.

From this place is shown how the star had been hidden from the magi after it had led them a little ways away from Jerusalem. When the star had abandoned them, they were consequently forced into Jerusalem to ask about the Christ and to make him known for two reasons. First, it led to the confusion of the Jews, inasmuch as only the Gentiles had been entrusted with the vision of the star and had sought him through foreign lands, while the Jews, who had read the prophecies about the Christ from childhood on, did not welcome him, even though he had been born in their own country. Second, this took place so that the priests might be asked where the Christ would be born and could answer to their own condemnation concerning Bethlehem, since those who explained to Herod about the Christ did not themselves know of his existence. If it had appeared immediately, it would have led them to Bethlehem, and so they would not have been compelled to announce his birth by their asking about him.

And lo, the star which they had seen in the East went before them.

If they were pondering the obedience of the star, they would have understood the majesty of the king and would have said among themselves, "How can this one be an earthly king, when a star serves him?" But how marvelous was it that, when the Sun of righteousness

[17]The modern reader, living after the time of the Holocaust, must take care not to view these words through the lens of modern or even medieval anti-Semitism. The commentator does not have the Jews as an ethnic group in mind, but rather the Jews who rejected Christianity. The commentator is following in the footsteps of the New Testament, especially the Gospel of John (e.g., Jn 6:41; 7:1, 13; 8:48), which refers to the Jews who reject Christ as "the Jews," even if the Evangelists and apostles were themselves Jews and elsewhere acknowledge that there were many Jews who believed in Christ (e.g., Jn 8:31; 12:11; Gal 2:14-15).

would rise, a divine star served him! It went before them to show how all the elements likewise serve those who seek God. So if you think that it is a great feat that a star obeyed Christ, see how there are greater things that serve you, even though you are a mere human being. See the sun runs its course for you and the moon does not cease to shine. If the elements serve you, though you are but a human being, how is it astonishing that a star obeyed Christ? If the elements serve you, sinner though you are, how is it surprising if a star went before those who were seeking Christ? And if angels serve people, even though God made the angels not to obey people but rather to obey him, what great feat is it if the elements serve humankind, when they were created for humankind's sake? When we hear these things we ought both to rejoice and to fear, since the greater favors God has appointed for humankind, the more severe the judgments have been prepared for sinners. And the star stood over the child's head, as if to say, "Here he is," so that it might show by standing still what it could not show by talking.

[10]*When they saw the star, they rejoiced exceedingly with great joy.*

They rejoiced because their hope (namely, that they had not undertaken the hard work of such a long journey for no reason) had not escaped their notice but had been confirmed more fully. For by the discovery of the star that met them a second time they understood that that birth of the king had been divinely shown to them. And through the mystery of the star they understood how the honor of the newborn king surpassed the measure of all earthly kings. Of necessity they thought that he was a more glorious king than the star, since the star so piously obeyed him. How could they have failed to believe that people ought to be made subject to him, when they saw that the adornments of the heavens were subject to him? Or how could the earth rebel against him, to whom even the heavens submitted?

[11]*And going into the house they saw the child with Mary his mother.*

Shall we see what sort of glorious thing they rejoiced to see in the lad, since they had undertaken the hard work of such a long journey in order to see a king? They did not see a palace resplendent with marble, did they? They did not see his mother crowned with a diadem and lying on a golden bed, did they? They did not see a child clad in gold and purple, did they? They did not see a royal courtyard echoing with all sorts of people, did they? But what did they see? They saw a dark and dirty inn, more suitable for animals than for people, a place where no one was content to retire unless compelled by the necessity of a journey. They saw his mother having barely one tunic, useful not so much for adorning her body as covering her nakedness—the type of clothing that a carpenter's wife could have, and that for traveling. They saw the child wrapped in very filthy rags and put in an even filthier manger, because that place was so small that they could not find any other space to put the baby. If, then, they had come to seek an earthly king, they would have been more confused than glad, because they would have undertaken the hard work of such a journey for no reason. But because they were seeking a heavenly king, even though they saw nothing royal in him, nonetheless they rejoiced, being content with the testimony of the star alone. Their eyes could not notice that the boy appeared contemptible because the spirit in their hearts showed him to be one to be revered. Moreover, if they had sought him out as an earthly king, they would have remained with him once they had found him, as often happens in this age, as people leave behind their own king and hasten to another. But they worshiped this king and returned to their own, so that they had a heavenly king over their souls but an earthly king over their bodies.

And they fell down and worshiped him.

Do you think that they would have adored the infant who did not understand the honor of their adoration unless they had believed that there was something divine in him? Therefore they did not honor his youthfulness, which could not understand anything, but rather they honored his divinity, which knew everything. But also the very quality of the gifts they offered testified that they regarded the boy as divine.

Then, opening their treasures, they offered him gifts, gold and frankincense and myrrh.

They fulfilled the confession of the Gentiles in Christ, and they indicated that the prophecy of Isaiah had been fulfilled, who says, "All those from Sheba shall come. They shall bring gold and frankincense, and shall proclaim the praise of the Lord. All the flocks of Kedar shall be gathered to you, the rams of Nebaioth shall minister to you; they shall come up with acceptance on my altar."[18] When at once they recognized him and opened their treasure chests, they showed their offering through the very gifts that were fitting for the Gentiles in Christ. Because they recognize him to be a king and a pure firstfruits and one precious to the saints, they offered the gold that had been stored away for themselves. Because they understood his divine and heavenly origin, they brought him the fragrance of incense, a type of the pure prayer offered in the sweet fragrance of the Holy Spirit. Because they understood his human and temporal death, they gave him myrrh.

Even if the magi did not understand these things at that time, according to which sort of mystery those things were being done or what each of their gifts meant, nonetheless it in no way contradicts what they did. For the grace that urged them to do all these things also ordained that all of these very things would later be understood. Therefore gold represents the faithful who are perfect and wise, as the apostle says: "Now if any one builds on the foundation with gold, silver, precious stones."[19] If someone offers himself then to Christ, filled with the wisdom of faith, he offers him gold. Incense, however, is prayer, as it is written: "Let my prayer be counted as incense before you."[20] If someone offers Christ pure prayer, he offers incense to him. I think that myrrh represents good works, since just as myrrh preserves the body of the deceased from decomposition, so the good works constantly preserve the crucified Christ in the memory of a person and preserve him in Christ. Therefore, first one ought to offer to Christ a reasonable faith, then pure prayer, and thirdly holy deeds. Therefore when you come to the church to pray to God, carry your works with you in your hands. Give to the one who has nothing and ask of him who has that your prayer might be commended by your good works. So also it is written in the Law: "None shall appear before me empty-handed."[21] Weak is the prayer that is not strengthened by the power of alms.

12 And being warned in a dream not to return to Herod, they departed to their own country by another way.

O faith of the magi! They did not contradict the angel who warned them or say, "We came on such a long road and did not fear as we passed before a multitude of countries, neither were we scared of any dread king in any of those places, but we stood and proclaimed the king who had been born and offered him gifts worthy of God. And now you order us to flee furtively like runaway slaves, so that we come

[18]Is 60:6-7. [19]1 Cor 3:12. [20]Ps 141:2; the archaic language of the RSV has been updated. [21]Ex 23:15.

by one way and leave by another?" But they were faithful men. They neither were afraid to be recognized nor too embarrassed to return stealthily, since it was not possible that those who had come from Herod to Christ could return to Herod. Those who leave Christ and go to Herod will frequently return to Christ, but those who leave Herod behind and come to Christ with all their heart will never return to Herod. That is to say, those who pass from Christ to the devil through their sin frequently return to Christ through repentance, but those who leave the devil behind and come to Christ with difficulty return to the devil, because the one who was never amid evils but in innocence is easily deceived, since he does not know what evil is, and so he passes over to the devil. But when he has experienced the evil he found there and remembered the good that he lost, he is driven to return to God from whom he had withdrawn. But he who had been amid evils and was converted to good, since he rejoices concerning the good things that he has found and remembers the evil from which he had escaped, returns with difficulty to evil. But what are we to say? When many leave Christ and sin, they do not repent. Such people were never of Christ, so I said above, "Those who come from the devil to Christ with all their heart." Whoever does not repent after sinning did not sin as one deceived by the flesh, but rather he did evil of his own free will, since he himself was evil. For an evil person does not think that that which is evil to be evil, and so he does not repent when he has done evil.

Or this is the explanation: whoever comes from the devil to God should never walk on that same path through which he came to the devil. If you came on the road of fornication, walk away from him on the road of alms. But if you return by the very same road, you walk again under the kingdom of Herod, and you will betray Christ.

13Now when they had departed, behold, an angel of the Lord appeared to Joseph in a dream and said, "Rise, take the child and his mother, and flee to Egypt."

O angel of God, did you not tell me that that which would be born of Mary is of the Holy Spirit? How then do you order us to flee? How can the Son of God flee before a man? Or what sort of a man is he to free us from our enemies if even he fears his own enemies? Indeed, he fled as soon as possible so that in all things he might preserve the rules of the human nature that he had assumed, in particular the rule that it is appropriate both for human nature and especially for childhood that one flee a power that threatens. Otherwise, if he had done that which was appropriate for God, even though he was in the body, he would not so much have managed the human nature in himself as changed it. Second, he did this so that other Christians, that is, the saints, would not be embarrassed to flee whenever the need of persecution should arise. And why did he go to Egypt? It was not because there was no other land, was it? Egypt, you see, had always been hostile toward his people. But because the Lord, who is not angry beyond all bounds or offended forever, remembered how much evil he had brought on Egypt, he sent his Son there and gave it a sign of great reconciliations and a pledge of perpetual friendship, that one medicine might be able to heal the ten plagues of Egypt. "The right hand of the Most High has changed"[22] so that the nation that previously had persecuted the firstborn people later became the guardian of the only-begotten Son. Those who had violently lorded it over that people now serve Christ with devotion. No longer do they go to the Red Sea to drown there, but they are called to the waters of baptism in order to come alive. So was fulfilled the word which was said: "Behold, the Lord is riding on a swift cloud and comes to Egypt."[23] The cloud

[22]Ps 77:10. [23]Is 19:1.

is his body; it is light since it does not have the burden of sins.

[16]Then Herod, when he saw that he had been tricked by the wise men, was in a furious rage.

After the little Jesus conquered the magi and put them under his command—not by the power of his body but by the grace of the Spirit—Christ did not send an army after them, but rather an unpretentious star in front of them. He conquered them by piety, not by fear. He did not chase after them, but he was sought by them. Quite understandably Herod grew angry because the little Jesus, lying in a manger and wrapped in rags, pleased these men whom he, sitting on a regal throne and clad in purple, could not sway. Herod was tricked, although he wanted to trick the magi; he was promising to worship the lad when he said, "Go and search diligently for the child, and when you have found him bring me word, that I too may come and worship him."[24] He was not perceptive inasmuch as he tried to deceive with human fraud the only-begotten Wisdom of God. Already he raved because he feared the successor to his kingdom. For if kings grow angry for some other reason, they are quickly placated; but their anger cannot be extinguished if jealousy over their reign provoked it. Thereupon the magi added reasons for his grief when they tricked him. Just as if someone were to pour oil on a burning fire and the conflagration were to grow all the more, so the disgrace of his being tricked aroused the burning zeal of Herod.

What did he do?

He sent and killed all the male children in Bethlehem and in that entire region who were two years old or under, according to the time which he had ascertained from the wise men.

Why? He had been tricked by the magi. Just as if someone has wounded a wild beast, which has its own innate ferocity, the anger caused by its pain doubles its innate fierceness and in a blind rage, as it were, now it no longer looks for the one who wounded it but whoever meets it—whether human or another beast—it rips to shreds, as if he were the cause of its wound; so also Herod, tricked by the magi, poured out his anger against the little children. He thought and said in his madness, "Certainly the magi have found that boy whom they were saying would reign, and either they took gold from his parents or were appeased by generous promises; consequently, they did not return to me." For whatever a king thinks to be directed against his own reign he deems to be entirely true. His mind was always suspicious because he was full of jealousy for his kingdom. While he was afraid of everything, he suspected everything. He easily believed whatever he suspected. Just as a man jealous of his wife or a woman jealous of her husband believes every base rumor about her or him, even if the report is not trustworthy, nonetheless the jealousy commends the trustworthiness of the report.

Therefore in this manner he said such things to himself: "Who is that boy who before he was born on earth already appeared in heaven? He does not show himself, and yet all seek him. He does not yet have an earthly nation, and yet already heavenly armies of stars serve him. Who is this one who already has conquered me before he has fought with me, and who already reigns before he has conquered and who already is lord and master before he has reigned? What do you think that that man will do in my kingdom, if he grows up? I both dispense gifts to people and carry a sword so that he who does not fear me will at least love me, and he who does not love me will at least fear me. He does not have a nation, nor has he amassed wealth; and how can he be loved without gold or be feared without

[24]Mt 2:8.

a sword?" So he sent and killed all the small boys so that he could find one among all of them. But he did not find even one among all of them, and yet he gave eternal life to all of them because of the one. Inasmuch as he sought to lay hold of God among human beings, he intended to deceive himself. What did your senseless anger accomplish, Herod? If you did not believe the words that the magi spoke about the future king, why did you rage for no reason against the boys? But if you believe that that which was spoken about the boy and the star to be true, again I ask, why for no reason did you rage against the boys? You do not think that you can change God's mind or destroy the one whom God defends, do you? But how is it anything noteworthy if Herod, a wicked man, thought that he could change the counsel of God? After Solomon had heard from the prophets that Jeroboam would be the king because of Solomon's sins, even this wisest man purposed to persecute him and thought that he could destroy him whom God had raised up, because jealousy does not know how to act wisely and anger has no sound counsel.

[18]*A voice was heard in Ramah.*

Ramah was the city of Saul. Saul, however, was from the tribe of Benjamin, and Benjamin was the son of Rachel, whose monument was near Bethlehem, where these evils were perpetuated. Therefore, because the small boys were killed in Bethlehem, where the tomb of Rachel was, so she is introduced here as weeping. Although Ramah is not near Bethlehem, nonetheless it is said, "A voice was heard in Ramah" because Ramah means "on high" in Hebrew. So he says, "A voice was heard on high," because the voice arose to the heavens at the death of the innocents and so was heard on high. So also Solomon says, "The prayer of the humble pierces the clouds, and he will not be consoled until it reaches the Lord."[25] So also whenever a poor person suffers violence at the hands of a powerful person, even if he does not dare to lift his voice but rather cries secretly, his hidden cry is heard on high, because it is not the loudest plea that is heard swiftly by God, but rather the just one. "Wailing" points to the crying of the children, and "loud lamentation" points to the weeping of their mothers. The children wailed because they were separated from their mothers. Their mothers lamented loudly because they were bereft of their sons and separated from them, as if their own heart had been torn out of them. One could see greater grief in the mothers who survived the incident than in the children who died. The children suffered one moment of pain because they were separated from their mothers and not because they were led off to death. Up to this point they had not even known the fear of death. But their mothers suffered twice the pain: first, because they saw their children killed; second, because they were bereft of their children. In the case of the children, their blessed death ended their sorrow, but in the case of the mothers, whenever they remembered their children, they stirred up grief.

Now after these things Herod was duly punished. For he killed his own three sons—and it was not that he saw them killed by somebody else so that he could show some paternal love for them as he grieved, but he himself killed them so that he both lost his sons and bore the reproach for their death. He tore out his heart in the matter of his sons and did not feel their pain. Consequently, just as the little children of Bethlehem did not feel their death because of their infancy, so also Herod did not feel the pain of his own heart because of his madness. At last he was overcome by many griefs, as history tells us, which would be

[25]Sir 35:17.

long to narrate. He was tortured by as many griefs as he had members of his body. And because he who had killed many infants could not die many times, the punishment for those numerous people killed by him was meted out in the numerous pains afflicted on him. Moreover, when he saw that he was near death and knew that he was hated by all the Jews and that his death would cause joy to many, he gathered all the princes of the Jews and ordered that as soon as he had died, all of them should be killed, so that all the cities might grieve on his death, even if not on account of love for him, at least on account of their own grief. And this took place by the counsel of God, for when the magi proclaimed the star of the future king, all the princes agreed with Herod to seek out the child and kill him. How do we know this? First, because of that Scripture verse that says, "Herod was troubled, and all Jerusalem with him."[26] Second, the very words of the angel proved this when he said, "Rise, take the child and his mother, and go to the land of Israel, for those who sought the child's life are dead."[27] He did not say, "He who sought the child's life is dead," but rather "Those who sought the child's life are dead."

19But when Herod died, behold, an angel of the Lord appeared in a dream to Joseph in Egypt, saying, 20"Rise, take the child and his mother."

Do you notice that Joseph was chosen not to be Mary's spouse but the child's servant? When Mary went down to Egypt and returned, who would have fulfilled the ministry of so great a need for her, unless she had been betrothed to him? At first glance Mary seemed to nourish the child and Joseph kept him safe. In reality, however, the boy nourished his mother, and Joseph was the one kept safe. So the angel did not say, "Take the mother and her child," but rather, "Take the child and his mother," because the son was not born for the sake of that mother but rather because of that son she was readied to become the mother. Nor was it the glory of her child to have her as his mother, but rather it was her blessing to have such a son, as she said: "For behold, from now on all generations will call me blessed."[28]

20"Go to the land of Israel."

He went down to Egypt as a doctor, to visit the country as it languished under its errors, not to remain there. At first glance he went down to Egypt, fleeing from Herod, but in reality he went there to chase out all of Egypt's demons of error out of the land, as Isaiah says: "Behold, the Lord is riding on a swift cloud and comes to Egypt; and the idols of Egypt will tremble at his presence."[29] Do you see then that he went down to Egypt not to flee death but to rout their deadly idols? For one cannot find that the Lord ever went down to Egypt except at this time. Moreover, it must be noted that he fled by night to Egypt but returned by day, because when he was fleeing, he was fleeing Herod's persecution, but when he returned, he was returning after the persecutor had died. Every outbreak of persecution is as night, but every refreshment from it is as day.

22Being warned in a dream he withdrew to the district of Galilee. 23And he went and dwelt in a city called Nazareth, that what was spoken by the prophets might be fulfilled, "He shall be called a Nazarene."

Since he says, "by the prophets" and not "by the prophet," it is clear that he did not cite the certain authority a prophet, but he spoke while uniting the sense of the prophets. For through all the prophets Jesus was called "Nazarene," that is, "holy." Or perhaps they had read also some other prophets who said this, who were

[26]Mt 2:3. [27]Mt 2:20. [28]Lk 1:48. [29]Is 19:1.

not canonized by us. For indeed there were others who prophesied and even wrote, such as Nathan and Ezra. And that indeed it had been prophesied is clear from Philip when he told Nathanael, "We have found him of whom Moses in the Law and also the prophets wrote, Jesus of Nazareth, the son of Joseph."[30] Since Nathanael also knew that this had been prophesied, he answered and confirmed this point: "Can anything good come out of Nazareth?"[31]

The Third Homily: On Matthew 3[1]

[1]In those days John the Baptist came preaching in the wilderness of Judea, [2]"Repent, for the kingdom of heaven is at hand." [3]For this is he who was spoken of by the prophet Isaiah when he said, "The voice of one crying in the wilderness: 'Prepare the way of the Lord; make his paths straight.' " [4]Now John wore a garment of camel's hair and a leather belt around his waist, and his food was locusts and wild honey. [5]Then Jerusalem and all Judea and all the region about the Jordan were going out to him, [6]and they were baptized by him in the river Jordan, confessing their sins. [7]But when he saw many of the Pharisees and Sadducees coming for baptism, he said to them, "You brood of vipers! Who warned you to flee from the wrath to come? [8]Bear fruit in keeping with repentance."[2]

When the sun is getting near its rising point, before it appears, it sends out its rays and makes the east grow light, that the dawn that goes before it may show the coming of the day. So when the Lord was born in the world, before he appeared, he illuminated John by imparting the splendor of his Spirit to him, that he might go before him and announce the coming of the Savior, lest by chance, when he came suddenly and said that he was the Son of God, he would seem unbelievable because of the very great and fearsome proclamation of such a matter. If John proclaimed this, when he was well known as to his person, deemed noble in ancestry (for he was the son of the priest Zechariah) and notable for his manner of life, and still the faithless Jews did not come to believe in Christ through him, how much more would they have not come to faith if no announcement had gone before him? For no matter how praiseworthy his character was, he would not be a suitable witness for his own case.

John came as the faithful preparer of a great king. The messenger of the king was just like the king: he was born by grace, not by nature. Just as an angel had foretold Christ's conception, so also he had foretold John's. Just as Christ's name had been heard before he had been conceived, so also had John's. Just as Christ's power had been shown before he was born, so also John's virtue had been shown before he was born. This was the difference between them: when Christ was conceived, his faithful mother confessed her thanks to God, saying, "Behold, I am the handmaid of the Lord; let it be to me according to your word,"[3] but when John was conceived, the unbelieving father was struck silent. Furthermore, when John was born, the law was silent in other respects, but when Christ was born a little later, grace was about to speak. John indeed had been given to his parents as a reward for their piety, since nature beyond hope gave birth to him in old age.

Because the world too had been made sterile through so many thousands of years, the fruit of righteousness had come about when John was born, whom his parents did not beget so much out of fleshly love but rather merited owing to their devotion to and harmony with discipline, for they were both righteous before God. For it would not have been appropriate for him who was born in order to proclaim the son of the virgin to have been born of flesh

[30]Jn 1:45-46. [31]Jn 1:46. **Third Homily** [1]The fourth homily in Codex Valle Dieu. [2]RSV text alt. by Kellerman here and wherever portions of this passage are used throughout this homily. [3]Lk 1:38.

and blood. Indeed, Judea was a desert—bereft of righteousness, full of sins—that God had planted, the Law watered and all the prophets cultivated. However, it had produced no fruit, except for some sharp thorns, with which it crowned its own Lord.

He said, "Repent." At the beginning he shows that he is the messenger of a kindly king; he does not threaten sinners but promises the forgiveness of sins. Often when a royal son is born, kings grant forbearance in their realms, but beforehand they send very harsh tax collectors to tax everything that they find so that their forbearance seems crueler than the usual tax, so that it has nothing but the name of forbearance and people accept it grieving and robbed. But when God's Son was born and God wanted to show forbearance of sins in this age, he sent John ahead of him as one making demands and saying, "Bear fruit in keeping with repentance." O great demand, which does not impoverish the poor but rather makes them rich! For whenever someone pays the debt of his own righteousness, he does not offer anything to God but rather acquires the gain of salvation.

But what does repentance do? It purifies the heart, it illumines the senses, it hallows the soul, and it prepares human hearts to welcome Christ, just as whenever a great judge or some king comes on a special mission people go before him to make preparations. They wash away whatever is dirty and put together whatever has fallen into disrepair, lest the dainty king by chance see something disgraceful and bristle at the sight. So also when our Lord was about to come to the alien places of this world, John went before him in order to cast out the filth of sin from human hearts with the broom of repentance, and by his establishment of spiritual commands he put together those things that had been scattered by the long insubordination of the devil. Moreover, he adorned everything with the water of baptism so that when the heavenly king came, he would find a worthy entrance into the hearts of the faithful, on account of which he said, "The voice of one crying in the wilderness: 'Prepare the way of the Lord; make his paths straight.'"

A voice is a disorderly sound that reveals no secret of the heart but only means that the one who cries wishes to say something. But the word is rational discourse, which reveals the mystery of the heart. Furthermore, a voice is common to both animals and people, but people alone have words. Therefore John is called a voice, not the Word, because through John God showed neither his mercy nor his righteousness nor his plans prepared before the foundation of the world, but he showed only that God was intending to do something great among humankind. Afterwards, however, through his own Son he revealed the fullest mystery of his will; therefore he was called "the Word."

3 ***"Prepare the way of the Lord."***

To repent of one's sins and to bear fruit worthy of repentance is what it means to prepare the way of the Lord and to make straight his ways. In this way he shows that all the ways of the Lord have naturally been planted in people, but later they were deserted through our arrogance and made tortuous. He would never have entrusted people with the task of repairing them unless he had known that they already existed in people and had been overthrown by the negligence of humankind. Note that the grace of humility existed in people, but since they provoked one another to anger they marred the grace of humility. Now whenever one humbles himself, the other refuses to accept him. Second, if one were to humble himself toward another, he would stir up himself to the grace of humility toward the other. For just as every skill is preserved and augmented by bodily usage, so also every grace is augmented through exercise and diminished through idleness. But now if a lesser individual humbles himself before a greater one—or a poor person before a rich one—the latter does not accept it as a gesture of humility but rather as a duty owed to power. Do you wish to know that previously the grace of humility existed among us? Whence did we learn to be subjected to the mighty? Third, people had wisdom, but since they used their wisdom not to help themselves through their own wisdom but rather to deceive others, their wisdom was discovered to be malice. How would anyone have the understanding of how to deceive another unless he had received the grace of intelligence from God? So people used the good gift of God badly, and they made it to be the evil of the devil. One can understand what happened to all good things according to these three points.

After he showed that he was the voice of one crying in the wilderness, saying, "Prepare the way of the Lord," he wisely at once added also what his lifestyle was, because everyone was deservedly revering him. For he bore witness to Christ, but his lifestyle bore witness to himself. For the testimony of his words would by no means have been appropriate unless the noteworthy conduct of his life had commended him. Nobody can be a good witness for another unless he has already been a good witness for himself.

[4]Now John wore a garment of camel's hair and a leather belt around his waist, and his food was locusts and wild honey.

He did not have clothing made of camel's wool, lest the very softness of his clothing render his limbs dainty and his daintiness then soften the virtue of endurance, but he had clothing made of the coarse hairs of a camel, so that their very roughness might train the soul in the virtue of patience. So he did not say, "of camel's wool" but "of camel's hair." Every piece of clothing serves one of three purposes: either it is a sight to behold (that is, it is for vainglory) or it is a delight for the body or it is a covering for nakedness. It is not appropriate for servants of God to have clothing that is a sight to behold; similarly it is not fitting for those who serve God to delight the body. But what use remains? Only as a covering for nakedness. That John did not have clothing made of camel's wool but rather of camel's hair is clearly shown by our Lord, who said about John, "What did you go out into the wilderness to behold? A reed shaken by the wind? Why then did you go out? To see a man clothed in soft raiment? Behold, those who wear soft raiment are in kings' houses."[4] Do you see then that he wore such clothing so that the very garb of his body might speak about the virtue of his soul?

And a leather belt around his waist.

From the fact that he says "and a leather belt around his waist," as if it meant something new, shows that it was the custom of the Jews to wear woolen belts. Therefore, John put on a leather belt, as if he wanted to do something harder. I think that in his intercourse with the Jewish people, who were living according to the righteousness of the Gentiles, John was showing by his garb a more devout clothing—not a softer one or more delicate, but one made of haircloth, more serious and harsh, one wearing down the body rather than caressing it. For the righteousness of the crooked Gentiles is to hold that these righteous acts are more serious than the other righteous deeds of the Law: "You shall not kill. You shall not commit adultery. You shall not swear falsely. An eye for an eye and a tooth for a tooth. You shall love your neighbor and hate your enemy."[5] Therefore the Evangelist says later, "For if you love those who love you, what reward have you? Do not even the Gentiles do the same?"[6]

[4]Mt 11:7-8. [5]Mt 5:21, 27, 33, 38, 43. [6]Mt 5:46-47.

And a leather belt around his waist.

The waist stands for the pleasures of all sins, because every sin is committed with pleasure. The leather belt represents bodily continence. Therefore he had a leather belt around his waist because even if there were those of the Jewish people who seemed to restrain themselves from sins, they restrained themselves with a self-restraint of the body, not of the soul, inasmuch as they restrained themselves for the Law's sake from the evil deed, but they did not restrain themselves for God's sake from an evil desire, since they did not kill but grew angry without cause. Indeed, they did not commit adultery, but they lusted in their hearts. Perhaps they did not swear falsely, but yet they swore. This is bodily self-restraint, since it satisfies the Law and other people—but not God. The restraint of an evil desire, however, pleases God, because people look at the appearance, but God looks in the heart. They repaid evil for evil and good for good; they loved their friends and hated their enemies. This was bodily righteousness, not spiritual; it pleased people, not God. Do you see how all their self-restraint was bodily, in that it kept the sins of deed in check, but not those of the will?

Moreover, locusts are clean flying creatures, albeit small ones, and ones that do not fly very high; John ate them when he lived in the desert. John was teaching people who were very much like the locusts he was eating. Indeed, they were able to fly, but they were not great flying creatures, nor did they fly very high, because they lived according to the righteousness of the Law in fear of bodily punishment, not according to the spiritual and very lofty commandments of Christ. At last how were the Jews like great winged creatures or birds flying up high, on whom repentance alone was enjoined? Whoever keeps oneself from an evil deed and yet does not in addition do good deeds, he does indeed fly, but not very high. Therefore John ate small flying creatures and such as did not fly very high, but he reserved the larger flying creatures (and those that fly high and can enter the heights of heaven) for Christ who was coming later, as for a great king. When Christ came later, he ate large flying creatures and ones flying high, that is, he taught the twelve blessed apostles and the seventy disciples under the apostles and the rest of the Christians, to whom he also gave very lofty commands: "You have heard that it was said to the men of old, 'You shall not kill; and whoever kills shall be liable to judgment. . . .' You have heard that it was said, 'You shall not commit adultery.' But I say to you that every one who looks at a woman lustfully has already committed adultery with her in his heart. . . . Again you have heard that it was said to the men of old, 'You shall not swear falsely, but shall perform to the Lord what you have sworn.' But I say to you, Do not swear at all. . . . You have heard that it was said, 'An eye for an eye and a tooth for a tooth.' But I say to you, Do not resist one who is evil. . . . You have heard that it was said, 'You shall love your neighbor and hate your enemy.' But I say to you, Love your enemies."[7] Do you see that those to whom John preached repentance of sins were small flying creatures and ones who did not fly high, but those to whom Christ gave spiritual commandments were mighty flying creatures and such as to penetrate the heavens themselves, so that they can say, "But our commonwealth is in heaven."[8] Perhaps for this reason he said, "Fear not; you are of more value than many sparrows."[9]

Honey is the eloquence of God. Therefore, John ate wild honey because as he lived under the Law before Christ and before the Holy Spirit, he used the eloquence of the Law for the unsavory, the boorish and the wild. For

[7]Mt 5:21, 27-28, 33-34, 38, 43-44. [8]Phil 3:20. [9]Lk 12:7.

if the Son of God was placed under the Law, how much more John, who truly was a Jew? But the Son of God was placed under the Law to redeem those who were under the Law and lead them out from under it. But John was born under the Law, not so that he could lead out those who were under the Law but rather so that they could be under the Law, so as to live and teach according to the Law. Therefore he did not do or teach anything outside the Law but only preached repentance, but Christ both taught and did many things outside the Law. He worked on the sabbath, he touched a man with leprosy, and he did many other things, because it was not for the unsavory and wild but for the refined and well-heeled that he employed the precepts of the Law that he had received from his Father. Therefore John ate wild honey, but Christ ate cultivated honey. And John put on a foreign hair shirt, since he was fulfilling every form of the Law and Prophets and with divine virtue he was embodying in himself the appearance of the Gentiles. This hair shirt portrayed that the Law and the prophecies of the prophets have woven together, as it were, its church, which is incapable of decaying or being seized. He wore a belt, that is, he showed his readiness for those who drew near and believed his preaching. He ate locusts and woodland honey, showing that those who lived far away would be near, as the apostle said to the Gentiles: "But now in Christ Jesus you who once were far off have been brought near in the blood of Christ."[10] And he ate woodland honey, teaching that the sweetness of the future faith would be of the barbaric nations, since this faith had gone forth to remove all care.

[5]Then Jerusalem and all Judea and all the region about the Jordan were going out to him.

That is, when the voice was heard in the wilderness, "Prepare the way of the Lord, make his paths straight." And the mode of his life echoed more fully in the desert than the voice of his cry. And he made people fear more by his works than by his words. And perhaps unless his manner of life had commended his preaching, all Judea would never have gone out to him, to his voice. From those words it became apparent that the Lord, being already in the world, had taught his people not only visibly with his sermons but, invisibly working in the hearts of people, he was leading them to faith. For John was not admonishing them to prepare the way of the Lord on the earth but rather to prepare the way of the Lord in the thoughts and hearts of people. Therefore at first glance he seemed to be walking in the body, but in reality he was entering through the hearts and thoughts of people and examining the consciences of each one.

All . . . were going out to him.

Who could think that he was just in comparison with him? His manner of living could not be imitated, and he made everyone's life appear full of fault so that no one any longer trusted in their own works, but all placed their hope in the mercy of God. It is just as if you would look at a beige garment, you would say, "It is sufficiently white," but if you put it next to snow, it begins to look dirty; even if it really is not dirty, nonetheless compared with the snow it is found dirty. So compared with John, every individual seemed impure. And truly the leader of a nation ought to be such a person so that the whole nation always can find something new[11] to imitate in him. Would a nation vie to emulate him and amend their own lives, if it should see that its leaders are more sordid than itself?

[6]And they were baptized by him in the river Jordan, confessing their sins.

[10]Eph 2:13. [11]Alternate reading: "something good."

Confession of sins is the testimony of a conscience that fears God. Whoever fears the judgment of God is not ashamed to confess his sins, but whoever is ashamed to confess them does not fear God's judgment. Perfect fear removes all sense of shame. Confession is regarded as disgraceful where people do not believe in the punishment meted out by the future judgment. Do not we know that the confession of sins has a sense of shame and that to be embarrassed about this very thing is a grave punishment? But God orders us all the more to confess our sins so that we might experience discomfiture rather than punishment.

7But when he saw many of the Pharisees and Sadducees coming for baptism, he said to them, "You brood of vipers! Who warned you to flee from the wrath to come? 8Bear fruit in keeping with repentance."

Just as a skilled physician understands the type of ailment if he has seen the complexion of the patient, so also as soon as John saw the Pharisees coming to him he understood their base thoughts. Perhaps they thought to themselves, "We will go and confess our sins. What does it matter to be embarrassed for an hour? He does not seek any righteous acts from us, nor will he impose any labor on us. We will be baptized, and we will obtain the forgiveness of sins." So they thought, just as even now all who have no intention of doing righteousness but come to baptism, thinking that they can be justified by the water of baptism alone, even if a good disposition did not precede it. You fool, make John to be your doctor and make his word a surgeon's scalpel, by which your conscience full of sins can be excised; think of confession as a surgical removal of impurity and filth that had been closed up inside and think of baptism as a washing of filth that has already exited. As soon as impurity has been surgically removed, you are not already healthy at once, are you? Do you not still have the wound? Do you not need medicine put on it? So also a person needs much diligence after confession and baptism, so that the wound of sins and the incision of confession may be healed.

"You brood of vipers!"

It is the nature of a viper to run immediately to water as soon as it has bitten anyone; if it does not find any water, it dies. So he called them also a brood of vipers who, while committing deadly sins, were running to baptism, in order to avoid the danger of death just as vipers do. Moreover, it is the nature of vipers to burst the belly of their mothers and to be born in this way.[12] Therefore, because the Jews diligently persecuted the prophets and corrupted their mother, the synagogue, "My . . . sons were angry with me,"[13] so they are called a brood of vipers. In addition, vipers are beautiful on the outside, almost as if they have been painted, but they are full of poison on the inside. So he was calling both the hypocrites and Pharisees a brood of vipers because the hypocrites showed a beauty of holiness on their face and yet carried the poison of malice in their heart.

Who gave you this idea? Does not Isaiah the prophet do so, when he says, "Wash yourselves; make yourselves clean"?[14] Perish the thought. For just as he said, "Wash yourselves; make yourselves clean," he also said, "Remove the evil of your doings from before my eyes . . . learn to do good."[15] If Isaiah had really taught you, you would never have put your hope only in water, but also in good works. The prophet David gives you this idea, does he not, when

[12]The author elaborates on this notion (namely, that the offspring of vipers bore their way out of the belly of their mother, thus killing her) in his commentary on Mt 12:34 and Mt 23:33. In antiquity people had many strange notions about vipers; see PW 2 2.1:538-39. [13]Song 1:6. The author omits the word "mother's" before "sons," although it significantly alters the meaning and deviates from the Vulgate. [14]Is 1:16. [15]Is 1:16-17.

he says, "Purge me with hyssop, and I shall be clean; wash me, and I shall be whiter than snow"?[16] But perish the thought, for he says afterwards, "The sacrifice acceptable to God is a broken spirit; a broken and contrite heart, O God, you will not despise."[17] If, therefore, you were disciples of David, you would come to baptism with a broken heart and a sigh from your heart.

9"And do not presume to say to yourselves, 'We have Abraham as our father.'"

What does a noble ancestry benefit him whom his own character defiles? Or how does a base ancestry harm him whom his character adorns? Whoever glories in his ancestors shows that he is empty of all good deeds. What did it benefit Ham that he was the son of Noah? Was not he separated from the midst of his sons? He who had been born a brother according to the flesh was made their slave according to his soul. Nor was his holy family able to defend godless behavior. Or how did it harm Abraham that his father Terah worshiped worthless gods? Was not he separated from his generation and placed at the head of the faithful, so that he could no longer be called a son of sinners but the father of saints? The errors of his father could not besmirch his glory. Gold too is born from the earth, but it is not earth, and gold is chosen while earth is despised. And a silver-lead alloy arises from silver, but it is not silver. Consequently, silver is preserved once it has been extracted, but the silver-lead alloy is driven out. It is better to become noble from a contemptible origin rather than to be born contemptible from a noble origin. Indeed, as for whoever is born noble from a noble lineage, the glory of his nobility is not his alone but seems to be shared with his ancestry. But as for whoever arises as noble from a contemptible lineage, all the glory of his nobility is his alone. Meanwhile, as for whoever is born contemptible from a noble lineage, all the turpitude is his alone. Thus it is better that your parents glory in you for having such a child rather than that you glory in your parents. So also please do not boast, saying, "We have Abraham as our father," but rather be ashamed that you are his children and yet are not heirs of his righteousness. He will convict you with his own testimony that you who did not imitate your father were born of adultery. Let us convert the word spoken to the Jews to apply to Christians because, just as the Jews thought that they had to be saved because of the fact alone that they were children of Abraham, so also many foolish Christians think that they must be saved because of the fact alone that they are Christians. To them John appropriately says, "Do not say, 'We are Christians,' but bear fruit in keeping with repentance."

"God is able from these stones to raise up children for Abraham."

It is difficult to make a stone into a tool, but once a tool has been made from it, it does not know how to fail. So also the Gentiles came to faith with difficulty, but nonetheless once they came to faith they remain forever in the faith.

10"Even now the axe is laid to the root of the trees."

The axe is the keenest anger of the last day, which will cut off the whole world. And if it has been laid, why does it not cut? Or, again, if it was not about to cut, why was it laid? It is because the trees are rational and have the ability to do good or not to do it, so that when they see that the axe has been laid at their roots they may fear themselves being chopped down and so bear fruit. For although an evil

[16]Ps 51:7. [17]Ps 51:17; the archaic language of the RSV has been updated.

person is not corrected even by fear, nonetheless a good person will perish unless he fears. Therefore, although an angry denunciation will do nothing among evil people, nonetheless it separates good people from evil. See how it is not said that the axe was laid to the branches so that they could be repaired when they have been cut off, but rather to the roots, so that they could be eradicated irreparably. Why? It is because, as long as that unjust world, entirely placed under the evil one, was not near the end, sinners were being chastised and not removed—for two reasons. First, because people had to be in the world, even though they were wicked, because also the world itself was wicked. Second, because as long as the world endured there was hope that some just people might arise by chance from the generations of the unjust. But now that the world is soon ending and that holy One has already drawn near, sinners are no longer merely chastised but overturned—for two reasons. First, because there is no longer the hope that perhaps some other righteous people will be born somewhere else from the generations of the unjust. Second, because it is not appropriate that people not be holy in that holy world, as it is written, "The holy shall dwell in the land, but the wicked will be driven out of it."[18] And again Isaiah prays, "Let the wicked be removed so that he does not see the honor of the Lord God."[19]

11"I baptize you with water for repentance, but he who is coming after me is mightier than I, whose sandals I am not worthy to carry. He will baptize you with the Holy Spirit and with fire."

Because John had been sent to baptize—but not because there was a need to give baptism but rather that through this opportunity he might preach the presence of the Son of God to those who were coming to baptism, as he elsewhere attests, saying, "but for this I came baptizing with water, that he might be revealed to Israel"[20]—so now he was both proclaiming to those coming to be baptized that he would appear and he announced the excellence of his power. By "feet" we can understand "Christians," in whom he walks, especially the apostles and other preachers, through whom he runs about, among whom was also John the Baptist. By "shoes," with which his feet are equipped, we can understand the constancy with which all preachers are equipped. Do you wish to know how strong the Lord's shoes are? Hear him speaking to Jeremiah: "And I, behold, I make you this day a fortified city, an iron pillar, and bronze walls."[21] Therefore, all preachers wear the shoes of Christ, and John himself wore them, but he proclaimed that he was not worthy to carry them, so that he could show the greater grace of Christ by his own deeds.

John is a bodily creature, and water is something bodily. Therefore, a body baptizes a body with a body of water. But Christ is Spirit, and the Holy Spirit is a spirit, and the soul is also a spirit. Therefore, a spirit baptizes a spirit with a spirit. And because Christ is a judge who baptizes in fire, that is, in testings, while John is a physical being, John cannot give a spiritual baptism, because every kind person is greater than his act of kindness. No one can give a more worthy benefit than the beneficent person, nor does he do anything else as he himself is not such a person. No human can baptize with fire, because no human being can judge another. Whoever has the power to reward has permission to scrutinize.

Therefore the baptism of Christ did not abolish the baptism of John but included it in itself. Whoever is baptized in the name of

[18]A paraphrase of Ps 37:9-11. [19]Is 26:10 (trans. Kellerman); the author's text differs significantly from the Masoretic text and the Vulgate. [20]Jn 1:31. [21]Jer 1:18.

Christ has each baptism, that of water and that of the Spirit, because Christ was spirit and took on a body, in order to give both a spiritual and a physical baptism. But John's baptism did not include Christ's baptism in itself because whatever is greater includes the lesser in itself, but whatever is less cannot include the greater in itself. Therefore when the apostle found some Ephesians baptized with the baptism of John, he baptized them again in the name of Christ, because they had not been baptized in the Spirit.[22] Therefore, if the apostle could give Christ's baptism over John's baptism, which although it was not yet the complete thing was nonetheless proper, how can you say that you ought not to baptize my better baptism over that baptism that has nothing in itself beyond the name "baptism"? Then when we baptize, we baptize in accordance with the death of him who was crucified. If, therefore, God was not crucified in the flesh according to you, but rather as a pure man, you now baptize according to the death of a mere man.[23] But a mere man cannot give a spiritual baptism, as we said above, and so although your baptism was not proper, nonetheless it was a baptism, that is, it was similar to John's baptism, that is, in water, not in the Spirit. Therefore Paul, following Christ's example, was baptizing those who had been baptized with the baptism of John, because also Christ had baptized again those who had been baptized with John's baptism, as his discourse shows when he says, "I baptize you with water, but he will baptize you with the Holy Spirit." Nor did he seem to baptize a second time, but only once; it appeared a new baptism in that the baptism of Christ was fuller than that of John and was not repeated. Therefore, if after the baptism of John, which although it was not perfect was nonetheless legitimate, Christ was baptizing in order to give something fuller to people, how is it not permitted to give a holy baptism after an impious one?[24]

Let us now see what the usefulness of each baptism was. Although the word *baptism* is not used in this passage, nonetheless because it is the case and the Lord spoke about it[25] ("You are already made clean by the word that I have spoken to you."[26]) and the apostle says, "having cleansed her by the washing of water with the word,"[27] we say also about the first baptism that the word washes away the filth of ignorance and pours on us the light of knowledge, but it does not wash away sin or help the soul or remove evil desires from it or restrain the flesh from evil pleasure. The word of faith does this, which the Law was doing previously: it shows righteousness but does not help the soul because every word is a lamp and not a virtue. Again, the water is of benefit because it washes away the sins that have already shown themselves in action—and it does this, if one repents; but baptism does not hallow the mind, nor does it cut off the evil desires or thoughts of the heart, nor does it drive them away, but it does not even keep carnal longings in check. Therefore whoever was not baptized so as to deserve to receive the Holy Spirit was baptized in the body and his sins were forgiven, but he was instructed in the mind. For thus it is written: "Anyone who does not have the Spirit of Christ does not belong to him."[28] For this reason his flesh spawned worse sins thereafter because he did not have the Holy Spirit preserving himself inside of himself, but the house of his body was empty. For that reason the spirit found his empty home, although made clean by the teachings of the faith, as if by brooms, and he entered and dwelled sevenfold in it because the words of faith, which are called brooms, clean one from ignorance, not

[22]See Acts 19:3-5. [23]The preceding three sentences were excised by Manhusius for doctrinal reasons but are well attested in the manuscripts. See the comments about the text of the *Incomplete Commentary* in the introduction. [24]This sentence was excised by Manhusius but is well attested in the manuscripts. [25]Other manuscripts read, "because the Lord himself also spoke about it." [26]Jn 15:3. [27]Eph 5:26. [28]Rom 8:9.

from sins or evil desires.

But the baptism of the Spirit is of benefit because the Spirit enters and embraces the soul and surrounds it with a certain impregnable wall, as it were, and does not permit carnal desires and thoughts to prevail over it. To be sure, he does not make it so that the flesh has no sinful longings, but rather he lays hold of the soul so that it does not consent to it nor is the soul conquered by it. Therefore whoever has the Holy Spirit indeed has sinful longings in his flesh, but in his soul he is helped by the Spirit so that his sinful longings do not come to completion. The baptism of testing and tribulation is compared here with fire, for it burns the flesh and roasts it so that it does not produce sinful longings quickly and does not even produce such longings. For the soul is a spirit and fears spiritual punishment but does not fear punishment of the flesh. Thus also the saints despise the punishments meted out by this age and fear the coming judgment when the spirits will be tortured. Meanwhile the flesh does not fear spiritual punishments, but fears those of the flesh. Thus evil people do not cease to sin unless fleshly and earthly judgments restrain them. Therefore, because the Lord knows that the flesh fears only fleshly punishments but not spiritual ones, he send fleshly desires, testings and tribulations over his servants so that their flesh, having been burned, might fear[29] discipline and in their fear of their own difficulties might not desire evil. For the flesh, troublesome and full of sinful longings, if left secure, will befoul the holiness of God's servants, even if it does not overcome them, and it will leave them restless and not allow them to rest.

Therefore righteousness flourishes amid testings but is languid in prosperity. Just as if you put a hearth on the ground, it burns the very roots of plants so that in that place no plant sprouts up easily, so also the fire of testing is put on their flesh, and it burns the roots of their sinful desires in their flesh so that it does not easily long for sinful things. Do you see then how water washes away past sins, but the Spirit drives away sinful desires and does not allow them to prevail, while fire burns the very roots of sinful desires? And water removes the past, the Spirit impedes the present, and the fire fortifies against the future?

What it means to baptize in fire is shown in the next clause.

[12]***"His winnowing fork is in his hand."***

The winnowing fork is the judgment through which the Lord will try each person and discern the hearts of all. Therefore it is not as soon as someone has been baptized in water or the Spirit that he has been baptized immediately to completeness, unless when the Lord has invisibly baptized him in the fire of testing, because if someone has not been tested, he cannot have been approved. However, there are many kinds of tests. People are tested either in their weaknesses or in the losses of their goods or in the death of loved ones, as Job and Tobit were. Others are tested in perverse thoughts or in doubts, just as the prophet says: "Prove me, O Lord, and try me; test my heart and my mind. For your steadfast love is before my eyes, and I walk in faithfulness to you."[30] Again Solomon says about Christ, "For at first she will walk with him on tortuous paths, she will bring fear and cowardice upon him, and will torment him by her discipline until she trusts him, and she will test him with her ordinances."[31] Others are tested in persecutions, as the prophet says in the voice of martyrs: "For you, O God, have tested us; you have tried us as silver is tried."[32] Thus, since Solomon knew that the servants of God must be tempted, he

[29]Alternate reading: "lay hold of." [30]Ps 26:2-3; the archaic language of the RSV has been updated. [31]Sir 4:17. [32]Ps 66:10; the archaic language of the RSV has been updated.

admonishes them, saying, "My son, if you come forward to serve the Lord, prepare yourself for temptation."[33] In sum, every adversity that troubles us in this world through no fault of our own is a baptism of fire. If you endure it magnanimously, not murmuring against God, that carnal affliction is imputed to you in the place of the sin that you have committed. But if you have not sinned (which is difficult) and that fire of temptation does not find any filth of sin to devour around your soul, it will make your very soul all the more glorious; and the more dire the temptation, the more it will glorify your soul.

And indeed we are baptized once in water, but in fire almost[34] our whole life long. Just as our life in this world is never pure of sin (for either by living or hearing or speaking or thinking those things that are not proper the mind is soiled), so the fire of tribulation can never withdraw from us. Truly, it is a desirable thing to the wise, for it is written, "Blessed is the man whom you chasten, O Lord."[35]

Although as far as the outcome of the matter is concerned, the fire and winnowing fork have the same meaning, nonetheless as I pursue the properties of these words, I think there is a difference between fire and a winnowing fork, so that every tribulation that befalls Christians according to their flesh is a baptism of fire, but the persecution of the heathen or of the heretics is a winnowing of the heavenly winnowing fork.

"And he will clear his threshing floor and gather his wheat into the barn, but the chaff he will burn with unquenchable fire."

The threshing floor is the church, the barn is the heavenly kingdom and the field is this world. Therefore, just as the head of the family sends out his reapers and reaps the stalks from the field and brings them into his threshing floor so that there he can thresh them and sort out the wheat from the chaff, so also the Lord sent out the apostles and other teachers as reapers and harvested all the nations from the world and gathered them into the barn of the church. Here, then, we must be threshed; here we must be winnowed. Just as a grain of wheat, enclosed in chaff, will not exit it unless it has been threshed, so also a person with difficulty departs from worldly impediments and fleshly things, since he is wrapped up in chaff, as it were, unless he has been troubled by some tribulation. For just as a full grain will leap out of the chaff as soon as it has been lightly struck, but if it were a lighter grain, it will depart more slowly, and if it were empty it will never leave but will be beaten in its own chaff and will be thrown out with the chaff, so all people delight in carnal matters, as grain in the chaff. But whoever is faithful and has the marrow of a good heart runs to God and neglects carnal things as soon as he has been lightly afflicted. However, if he is moderately less faithful, he withdraws with difficulty and returns to God on a great tribulation. But whoever is unbelieving and empty, although he is afflicted, he never departs from fleshly matters and from worldly impediments (just like an empty grain does not leave the chaff), nor does he go to God, but he is beaten there when placed amid troubles so that he ends up being thrown out with the faithless as with chaff.

While wheat is being threshed and after it has been threshed, it lies in one place with the chaff mixed in, but later on is it winnowed so that what has already been disjoined in their bodies might also be separated also in their locations. In the same way also the people in the church are being beaten by the motions of the carnal passions that always press on their soul or by bodily afflictions, as if by some rods or by their mistreatment by the wicked and haughty, as if by the heels of irrational beasts

[33]Sir 2:1. [34]Alternate reading: "often." [35]Ps 94:12; the archaic language of the RSV has been updated.

of burden so that the faithful are disjoined from the unfaithful through various kinds of afflictions. However, although they have been separated by these acts in turn, they are still held, mixed together, in one church. Therefore persecution arises as a wind, so that those who already had been disjoined by their acts might be tossed by the winnowing of Christ and separated also in location, so that just as the pure wheat might be stored in the granaries so also the holy ones who have been approved might be put in the heavenly kingdoms. Do you see that testing does not destroy but reveals the one who did not appear in peace?

But perhaps you say, "Was it not better for God to have called the elect people to Christianity from the beginning, so that the church would not always be winnowed but rather exist in peace?" Listen. You cannot separate the wheat from the chaff while the harvest is in the field, can you? Even if you try, you cannot separate the chaff from the wheat, and you destroy the wheat along with the chaff. So it could not happen that God would separate and call from the Jews or the Gentiles those who were already elect without any testing, since it is not clear that whoever does not know Christ or his truth, if he should happen to err or sin, sins owing to his own evil intention or owing to ignorance. However, if someone knows Christ and his righteousness and errs or sins, it is clear then that he did not err or sin because he did not know who God is or what his will is but rather because he did not love the will of God. How could these things take place without testing? If the palm of victory was not offered in the stadium, you would not be able to find fault with an athlete who did not want to compete and call him weak. It is uncertain whether he does not want to compete because he is weak or because he does not see the palm that is offered. But if he sees the palm and does not want to compete, then it is clear that he does not want to compete owing to his own desire. So also we cannot know whether a Gentile who does not know about the prize or believes that there will be a future judgment does not behave righteously because he does not love righteousness or because he does not hope for any reward for it. But if he has been truly made a Christian and knows that there will be a judgment, then if he sins it is clear that he sins because he does not love what is good.

Perhaps you will say to these things: "You say these things according to human reckoning. But God, who knows the heart and the future, could have known who and what sort of person each one would be." But listen. At the just judgment of Christ the concern will not only be that Christ knows that he is judging a person justly but also that each person himself recognizes that he is being judged justly by Christ, having been confirmed by the testimony of his own thoughts and works, just as it is written: "Their conscience also bears witness and their conflicting thoughts accuse or perhaps excuse them on that day when, according to my gospel, God judges the secrets of men."[36] Again, "Behold a man and his works."[37] Again, "But now I rebuke you and lay the charge before you."[38] Therefore if a person who does not know Christ or his righteousness is condemned by God according to God's knowledge, how will he know that he has been justly condemned? For God, the scrutinizer of the heart, indeed knows that he justly condemns him, but the sinner does not understand that he has been justly condemned and can then say, "If I also had known Christ and his commandments, I would have kept his faith and not strayed from his commandments. Therefore he has led all to recognize the truth so that sinners might be revealed that they sinned not by ignorance of righteousness but by their evil will and that it was not

[36]Rom 2:15-16. [37]This is not a direct quotation of any Scripture passage; cf. Rom 2:6. [38]Ps 50:21.

out of ignorance of Christ that they ran away from him but rather because they loved more the factions of the devil. Therefore if ever they were called out of the Jews and Gentiles, they could not be called elect; how much more can Christians not be made elect since all are born of Christian parents? And yet not only are they made Christians because they believe in Christ or love him but because they are procreated from Christian parents and their calling is determined not by their faith but by their birth. Thus it is necessary that all—good and bad alike—become Christians and all learn to recognize the truth so that later, after trials have been sent, a few may be chosen from the many, in order to fulfill what is said, "So the last will be first, and the first last."[39] You do not criticize why you do not separate the chaff from the wheat and store it away, do you? For it does not make sense to put away also the chaff, because it is not necessary for you to use. And how should we fault God, who separates from the faithful the faithless, who do not redound to his glory? And the chaff is so constituted by nature that it is chaff and cannot be wheat, but the faithless are not so constituted by nature that they are faithless, but they become chaff of their own will as they drive out the kernel of righteousness from themselves. Therefore, if that chaff, which cannot be wheat, is burned with fire, how much more the faithless deserve to be burned, who could have been wheat, unless they had cast out of themselves the kernel of righteousness? And see how he did not say, "he will clean his threshing floor," but "he will clear it." For that reason it is always necessary that the church be held in various ways up until the last day, until it is finally cleared. And so the church of Christ has never been sent away without temptation. Indeed, the Jews were the first to winnow it, then the Gentiles, then the heretics. At last, however, Antichrist will winnow it. Just as when there is a rather small breeze, the whole mass of grain is not cleared but rather the lighter pieces of chaff are blown away by a light breeze, while the heavier pieces remain and likewise the empty grains remain, since it is necessary, then, to await a greater wind so that the heavier pieces of chaff and empty grains might be tossed out, so also when there is a slight testing those who are very unfaithful are tossed out of the church. So a greater testing is needed that all the faithless might be more fully driven out and so the church might be thoroughly purged. And now indeed with only a modest breeze of temptation flowing, the very worst people have withdrawn. But if a greater storm arises, as there will be under Antichrist, even those who seem firm will depart.

The Fourth Homily: On Matthew 3

[13]Then Jesus came from Galilee to the Jordan to John.

When? When John was preaching, saying, "Repent, for the kingdom of heaven is at hand."[1] Then Jesus came that he might accept the witness borne by John, "Behold, the Lamb of God, who takes away the sin of the world!"[2] and so that he might confirm John's preaching, so that all people, seeing Christ being baptized as if he were a sinner even though he was without sin, might say among themselves, "If he concerning whose innocence the Baptist bore witness thought it necessary to be baptized, how can we despise repentance, when we have been covered in sins?" Again John had testified that "I baptize you with water for repentance, but he who is coming after me is mightier than I. . . . He will baptize you with the Holy Spirit and with fire."[3] Then he came for this reason that he might show that this testimony of John was true, so that the heavens might be opened at his baptism, the Spirit descend,

[39]Mt 20:16. **Fourth Homily** [1]Mt 3:2. [2]Jn 1:29. [3]Mt 3:11.

the Father call out from heaven and thereby it become manifest that he who was baptized by John was more worthy than John. For just as when the morning star has arisen, the sun does not wait for the setting of the morning star before it arises, but rather the sun goes forth even as the morning star is still ascending and the sun overshadows its gleam by its own light, so also as John was preaching before Christ came, Christ did not wait for John to complete his course and then come into the midst, but he appeared while John was still teaching, so that when one compared John's teaching and works with Christ's, Christ might make John's preaching not seem to do him full justice. Thus after Jesus began to preach and everybody ran to him, the teaching of John seemed rather base in comparison. Thus when his disciples saw this, they said to him, "Rabbi, he . . . to whom you bore witness, here he is, baptizing, and all are going to him."[4]

Then Jesus came to be baptized, not so that he could receive forgiveness of sins through baptism but so that he could render the waters hallowed for those who would be baptized thereafter. It was also so that he who had taken on our human nature might be found to have undergone the whole mystery of human nature. Although he was not a sinner, nonetheless he had taken on a sinful nature; therefore he himself did not need baptism, but nonetheless his carnal nature needed it.

14John would have prevented him, saying, "I need to be baptized by you, and do you come to me?"

That is to say, "Where I desire to ascend, you descend from there. Therefore it is most logical that you baptize me so that I may be made righteous and worthy of heaven. But what is the reason for me to baptize you? Is it that you may be made righteous? But you yourself are the root of righteousness. Is it so that you can ascend into heaven? But you yourself by nature are in heaven, although by your will you descended from heaven. You are spirit, and I am flesh. Flesh cannot hallow the spirit, can it? Rather, it is the spirit that hallows the flesh. He who has the ability to create also has the power to hallow. What rich person seeks riches from a pauper? Rather, the pauper seeks riches from the rich. Every good thing descends from heaven to earth; it does not ascend from earth to heaven. That old Lucifer,[5] who arose in the morning, thought to himself, 'I will ascend to heaven.'[6] Therefore if that one who had been made an angel was cast down from angelic glory into the shame of the darkness simply for his thought of pride, what would I deserve to suffer, if I, who am a carnal and corruptible man, completed such an arrogant work and deemed myself worthy to baptize the Lord of all creation?"

15But Jesus answered him, "Let it be so now, for thus it is fitting for us to fulfill all righteousness."

He does not deny the eminence of his power but shows the mystery of the economy of grace when he says, "Let it be so now." That is, "I know that it is right for you to be baptized by me, but 'let it be now,' that I might fulfill righteousness for the baptized not just in words but in deeds. First let me receive baptism, and later I will preach." Therefore when he says, "Thus it is fitting for us to fulfill all righteousness," he does not indicate "if he will have been baptized," but "thus," that is, inasmuch as he first fulfilled righteousness by his deeds and then preached. So he did not fulfill

[4]Jn 3:26. [5]Lucifer literally means "light bearer" and is frequently translated "morning star," that is, the planet Venus. Early Christians commonly interpreted Is 14 to speak of an angelic being (Satan) who rebelled against God and was cast down from heaven, and thus the name came to have the negative meaning it does today. [6]Is 14:13.

all righteousness with his words before he did so with his deeds. Therefore Luke also attests concerning him, "In the first book, O Theophilus, I have dealt with all that Jesus began to do and teach."[7]

The phrase "thus it is fitting for us to fulfill all righteousness" also raises the question of how we fulfill the righteousness of baptism. How did Christ fulfill the righteousness of baptism? Without doubt it was according to the incarnation of his human nature. It is characteristic of human beings to have the need for baptism, since all are sinners according to their human nature. Therefore just as he fulfilled the righteousness of baptism, so he fulfilled also the righteousness of being born and growing, of eating and drinking, of sleeping and growing tired. So too he fulfilled the righteousness of experiencing temptation, fear, flight and sadness; so too he fulfilled the righteousness of suffering, death and resurrection. That is to say, according to the direction of his human nature that he had assumed, he fulfilled all those righteous requirements. Therefore he was born not as a mere man but as God and man. As a man he grew, was hungry, was tempted and grew tired—not as mere man but as God and man. As a man he was bound, whipped, crucified and died—not as man but, through the incarnation, God as man. But if as mere man he fulfilled all these things, then he would already have fulfilled all things not according to his incarnation as man but according to his divine nature. But what would the incarnation be or how would it be contrary to his divine nature, if he suffered those things that people, subject to suffering, are likely to suffer? When he said, "let it be so now," to John who had said, "I need to be baptized by you," he showed that afterwards Christ baptized John, although this has been explicitly recorded only in the more arcane books. And John indeed baptized Christ with water, but he baptized John in the Spirit.

[16]*And when Jesus was baptized, immediately he went up from the water.*

I have not discovered why it is written, "Immediately he went up from the water." What difference does it make if he had gone up more slowly? Therefore he could have written this: "And when Jesus was baptized, he went up from the water." But I think that this deed of Christ pertains to the mystery of all the people who would be baptized in the same fashion. Therefore he says, "immediately," and did not say, "he came out," but "he went up." This is because all who are baptized in Christ, since they have been purged and refashioned as worthy people in every facet of righteousness, immediately go up from the water, that is, they make progress toward the virtues and are lifted up to a heavenly rank. They who entered the water as carnal people, children of sinful Adam, at once ascend from the water, having been made spiritual children of God. And so that you should not say to me that many remain after their baptism the same sort of people they were before their baptism, namely, those who are not baptized in repentance or do not repent wholeheartedly that they were the sort of people they had been but are baptized while fully intending to hold on to sin, these people do not progress immediately from the water. Therefore, if some do not progress once they have been baptized due to their own fault, how is baptism to blame? Scripture speaks about the power of baptism. How can baptism be responsible for those who were baptized unworthily?

Or "immediately" may mean that Christ immediately went up from the water, since he was in a hurry to get to the temptations against the devil so that he could free the human race. His compassion urged him on. Just as a general

[7]Acts 1:1.

who has been appointed to fight against a tyrant hastens to depart as soon as he has accepted the signal for the expedition and departure, since he knows that his tardiness means the province's loss (for a tyrant who knows that a commander has been appointed against himself acts cruelly, even if earlier he had acted more leniently), so also as soon as Christ had received the signal of baptism, he hastened to receive the Holy Spirit as spiritual arms, as it were, and to depart, knowing that his lingering would mean the destruction of the world. As soon as the devil heard that the Son of God had descended into the world, he hastened all the more vehemently to close up the hearts of all people in their sins and unbelief, inasmuch as he thought that he could destroy as many people as Christ could not save.

The heavens were opened to him.

It was not the created heavens that were broken open to him, but rather through baptism the sight of his eye was opened so that it might see the things above the heavens. For if the created heavens had been broken open, he would not have said, "They were opened to him," for they would not have been opened only to him. If the heavens had been opened physically, they would have been opened to all. But because they were opened spiritually, they were opened only to those who were illuminated by the Holy Spirit, as Stephen, full of the Holy Spirit, said, "I see the heavens opened, and the Son of man standing at the right hand of God."[8] But someone will say, "What do you mean? Had the heavens been closed to the eyes of the Son of God, who was in the heavens, even as he was on earth?" If you understood well the things said earlier about "thus it is fitting for us to fulfill all righteousness," you will not doubt that the heavens were opened to him according to the mystery of the incarnation. Just as he was baptized according to the incarnation of his human nature, while he did not need baptism according to his divine nature, so according to the incarnation of his human nature the heavens were opened to him, while according to his divine nature he was in the heavens. Therefore the heavens were not opened to God apart from the flesh, nor do I think that they were opened to the human nature apart from God, but to God as man, so that by his example we might understand that all upright people, who were deemed worthy to receive the Holy Spirit by baptism, similarly might have the heavens opened to them and see the things that are in heaven—not by seeing with eyes of flesh but by believing with the spiritual eyes of faith. The heavens are closed to the eyes of the heart of whoever does not believe those things that have been promised by God in the heavens—glorious and fearsome things stored up by God. But whoever firmly believes and strives to that goal that he sees, as it were, to such a person the heavens are opened; even though he is bodily on the earth, in his soul he is in heaven.

But if one must believe that the heavens were truly opened for him, because there had been some invisible barrier previously, by whose resistance the souls of the dead had not been able to enter the heavens—a barrier that no one could see, no matter whether it was closed or open—it still has to be understood that the heavens are perceived to have been opened, whether by this interpretation or by another one, namely, that "the heavens were opened to him," that is, for his sake, by his grace. But the heavens were opened not only for him but also for all people because of him. Even in every single generation there were just people to whom the heavens were opened and again other people (sinners) to whom they were closed. And yet no one could have been so righteous that he was worthy to open the gates

[8] Acts 7:56.

of heaven so that all people could enter. But after Christ was born, baptized and sanctified, by his grace alone the heavens were opened. For example, if a person asked some favor of the emperor but did not have any confidence in making the request or of beseeching his friendship, he would go to the brother of the emperor or to one of his dear friends so that he could intercede for him. So the emperor would say to him, "Behold, I do not grant this favor to him but to you, that is, because of you I grant it to him" (for the favor is not granted to him to whom it is granted but to him because of whom it is granted). So also here he says, "The heavens were opened to him," that is, because of him they have been opened to us. But you wish to know clearly how if the heavens were opened before Christ, they were closed again. For indeed the just were ascending to him, but sinners by no means were. But I have said that perhaps it is the case that it was not pleasing to any of the just that their souls could ascend to heaven before Christ's coming. Otherwise I think that no soul ascended into heaven before Christ ever since Adam sinned and the heavens were closed to him, but all the souls were detained below, for whom Christ also descended to the place of the dead, just as he attests in the book of Wisdom: "I will descend to the nether regions of the earth and I will visit all who sleep and will illume those who hope in God."[9]

The heavens were opened to him.

They were so opened that they have never been closed thereafter. Note that they were opened to Christ when he was baptized, albeit to him alone. But after he conquered the tyrant through the cross and after his resurrection was carried by the angels into heaven, the angels who carried him saw that the heavens were now never to be closed, but all—just and sinners alike—would ascend to heaven and stand before the judgment throne of Christ, since there was no longer any need for the gates of heaven, since the heavens would never be closed thereafter. Therefore, they do not say, "Open up the gates and the king of glory will enter," for now they have already been opened. Instead, they say, "Remove your gates, O princes."[10]

The heavens are the divine Scriptures of the prophets and apostles in which God dwells and concerning which it is written, "When I look at your heavens, the work of your fingers, the moon and the stars which you have established."[11] Therefore when he was baptized and deserved to receive the Holy Spirit, all the Scriptures were thrown open to him so that he could understand what are the mysteries of truth placed therein. But it is for the same reason that the Scriptures are not opened to all because some have a false baptism and so cannot receive the spirit of truth. For others, however, it is not baptism that prevents them from receiving the spirit of truth and the Scriptures being opened to them, but rather a bad intention on their part, even though they received a good baptism. For just as God is concealed in the heavens, so also he is hidden in the Scriptures. And just as everyone sees this physical sky but not everyone sees God dwelling in it, so also all people read the divine Scriptures but not all understand the God of truth placed in the Scriptures, unless someone has been baptized so as to receive the Holy Spirit. Therefore before the apostles were baptized in the Holy Spirit, the Scriptures of the prophets had been closed to them, even though they told

[9]Sir 24:45 (Vulgate numbering; trans. Kellerman). This verse is found only in the Latin versions, not in the Septuagint. This is one reason against this commentary's authorship by John Chrysostom or any other Greek, as well as compelling evidence that this was written by a Latin-speaking commentator. Sir 24 has forty-seven verses in Latin but only thirty-four in Greek. [10]Ps 24:7 (trans. Kellerman). The word translated "remove" (*tollite*) can also have the meaning "lift up," but the author does not see this word quite as a synonym of *aperite* ("open"). [11]Ps 8:3; the archaic language of the RSV has been updated.

of Christ, as it is written, "O foolish ones, and slow of heart to believe all that the prophets have spoken!"[12] After he opened their meaning to them, as the Holy Spirit breathed on them, then all the Scriptures were unlocked in front of the eyes of their hearts so that they could understand what things had been written about Christ. And so perhaps it is said here, "the heavens were opened." In Mark, however, he saw that the heavens were sundered; according to Matthew, the Scriptures were made clear, not sundered, for examples are daily taken from them to strengthen faith. But according to Mark, the Scriptures were sundered and made useless because after Christ we no longer use the Law and the Prophets, but the gospel of Christ, a loftier and nobler heaven, as it were.

And he saw the Spirit of God descending like a dove and coming to rest on him.

By this mystery by which Christ was born he also received the Holy Spirit. And, as a matter of fact, when the Son of God accepted baptism and the Spirit came down, one was standing in human form, while another came down in the form of a dove, and the third did not stand in human form or come down in the form of a dove but was heard only in the voice that came down from above.

Like a dove.

The Holy Spirit took on the form of a dove because more than any other animal it is a cultivator of love. The servants of the devil can have by imitation all the likenesses of righteousness that the servants of God can have in truth. For the devil has mild and humble people; he has chaste people, givers of alms, and people devoted to fasting. Every kind of goodness that God created to save people the devil has also introduced its very likeness in order to seduce them so that there might be a confusion between genuine goodness and feigned goodness and so that simple folk, who cannot carefully understand the difference between genuine goodness and feigned goodness, might run into the devil's henchmen when they had been seeking good people of God. The love given by the Holy Spirit is the only thing that the unclean spirit cannot imitate. Therefore every type of righteousness can be found among imposters, but the grace of true love is alone not found except among the servants of God alone. Therefore the Holy Spirit has preserved for himself alone this particular kind of love so that the Holy Spirit's presence cannot be discerned through anyone's righteousness or testimony as much as through the grace of charity.

17"This is my beloved Son, with whom I am well pleased."

Also see how he said on the mountain, "This is my beloved Son, with whom I am well pleased; listen to him."[13] Here, however, he said only, "with whom I am well pleased," because on the mountain they already partly knew him to be the Son of God. But because they erroneously thought that Christ was similar to Moses and Elijah, he added, "listen to him." It is not that they were not to listen to the Law and the Prophets, but rather that they were to listen to the gospel more fully than the Law and the Prophets so that they might know that Christ is the Lord of the Law and Prophets. But here, since they did not yet know the person of Christ, it was not appropriate to say, "listen to him," since a person's teaching can be faithfully accepted once the authority of his person is recognized, since the honor of a person commends the doctrine of a person.

[12]Lk 24:25. [13]Mt 17:5.

The Fifth[1] Homily: On Matthew 4

[1]Then Jesus was led up by the Spirit into the wilderness to be tempted by the devil.

By adding "to be tempted by the devil," he shows that he was led by the Holy Spirit but not as an inferior ordered by the command of a superior or even as a superior ordered by the exhortation of an inferior. For it is not only those who are led by someone else's authority who are said to be led or influenced, but also those who are moved by the reasonable exhortation of someone else. Take as an example what is written about Andrew: "He first found his brother Simon, and said to him, 'We have found the Messiah' (which means Christ). He brought him to Jesus."[2] Note that he did not bring him by his authority but rather moved him by reason. It is just as if a military advisor should happen to see a domineering tyrant and should happen to advise a king, saying, "Go out to meet him because the whole province is perishing; your reputation is stronger than my virtue." Such a king will be led by his military advisor, and nonetheless the king is not inferior to the one who influenced him. Jesus was led to the devil to be tempted. The devil comes to people to tempt them, but people do not go out to the devil to be tempted by him. But since the devil could not go out against Christ, so Christ went out against the devil.

Without doubt there are five baptisms among us. One takes place in the word, as Christ also says, "You are already made clean by the word which I have spoken to you."[3] Second, there is the baptism in water, as is clear to all. The third baptism is in the Spirit, as it is written, "for John baptized with water, but before many days you shall be baptized with the Holy Spirit."[4] The fourth baptism is the baptism of fire, which is the present testing. That people are baptized also in fire, the Lord testifies in the words of Isaiah: "The Lord shall have washed away the filth of the daughters of Zion and cleansed the bloodstains of Jerusalem from its midst by a spirit of judgment and by a spirit of burning."[5] In a corresponding manner the prophet says, "For you, O God, have tested us; you have tried us as silver is tried."[6] A little later he says, "We went through fire and through water; yet you have brought us out to a place of abundance."[7] Just as gold or silver is worked as the dross is burned off in the furnace, so a person is sent into the furnace of temptation and is sanctified once the sins have been put aside. The fifth baptism takes place in death, as he said, "I have a baptism to be baptized with; and how I am constrained until it is accomplished!"[8] The apostle teaches that sin is forgiven in death when he says, "For he who has died is freed from sin."[9] What sort of sin it is that is forgiven in death is known by him who understands through what sort of sin death was introduced. For if a person dies because of sin, indubitably that sin is absolved on account of which he dies. So after the Lord was baptized in the word, he was made subject to the Law. He was baptized by John in the water, and he was baptized by the Father in the Spirit. Now is he led by the Spirit into the desert to be baptized in the fire of temptation, and later he would be baptized with the baptism of death.

Come now, let us see who are those who are baptized in fire and when they are so baptized. To find the answer, we must see what this phrase means: "Then Jesus was led." When? When the Father cried out from heaven, "This is my beloved Son, with whom I am well pleased." You see, then, that no one is baptized in the fire of temptation unless he has been made a child of God. As long as a person is a mere catechumen, he has not yet more fully renounced the devil and all his works. But when

Fifth Homily [1]Sixth in some manuscripts. [2]Jn 1:41-42. [3]Jn 15:3. [4]Acts 1:5. [5]Is 4:4. [6]Ps 66:10; the archaic language of the RSV has been updated. [7]Ps 66:12 (trans. Kellerman). [8]Lk 12:50. [9]Rom 6:7.

he is baptized, he offers himself to Christ, saying, "I renounce Satan and all his works." And so the devil spares him as long as he is a catechumen, as if he were one of his own, but after baptism he persecutes him with all his power, as if he has been made to belong to another. Baptism is a mark of faith. A soldier is not marked after his enlistment so that he could still sit and take it easy, is he? But rather he is marked before his enlistment so that thereafter he can wage war and work. An athlete is anointed before the contest so that he can wrestle. So also a person is anointed spiritually with the oil of chrism, so that he can wrestle as a spiritual athlete against the devil.

But what are we to make of the fact that when many are tempted they are overcome and perish? Such people are not led by the Spirit to undergo temptation, nor are they children of God: "For all who are led by the Spirit of God are children of God."[10] Instead, such people are driven out by their own sins. But whoever is led out to temptation by the Spirit of God is not overcome. But the servants of the devil are not baptized in fire. Why? He cannot be purified by having his filth removed if he is altogether filth. Go ahead and try to wash mud—will it ever become clean? No, the more the dirt is removed, the filthier it becomes. That which has something good in itself (by which it can be purified) can be purified. Think how, if a good person will become defiled with carnal vices, he is tempted in order that the good that resides in him may be purified. But what can be purified in that person in whom there is no good? According to this, when you see some faithless Christian never grow sad or put in harm's way, or when you see that a heretic never suffers the trial of temptations, do not be offended or say, "How is it that the heretics never suffer persecutions but only the faithful do? How is it that evil people never are in any danger, but only good people are?"

Know that those alone who are children of God are baptized in the fire of temptation. Recall what the apostle Paul taught you, saying, "Indeed all who desire to live a godly life in Christ Jesus will be persecuted."[11] But evil and seductive people will grow worse, as they err and send others into error. Now let us see how they are baptized in fire. After a person has been baptized in the word, that is, instructed in the faith, and after he has been baptized in water, and after he has been baptized in the spirit, in the fourth place he is baptized in fire. But even though many people are baptized in water, they are not baptized in the spirit. Unless someone before his baptism has so cast off from himself every intention of sinning so that he might be worthy to receive the Holy Spirit in the temple of his heart, he is not baptized in the spirit because the Holy Spirit flees a false person and does not dwell in a body handed over to sins—and thus such a person does not become a child of God. These are the sort of people who are overcome and perish whenever they are tempted; they appear to have become the children of God because of the water of baptism, but in reality they are not the children of God because they are not in the spirit of the baptized. Indeed, they have been baptized in the body and catechized in the mind, since the water baptizes the body and the spirit baptizes the soul. Therefore, not only Christ was led into the wilderness by the Spirit, but also all the children of God who have the Holy Spirit are led by the Spirit into the desert in order to be tempted by the devil. Those who have the Spirit of God are not content to sit idly, but the spirit that is in them compels them to undertake some great work against the devil, who is in the wilderness.

In order that you can understand that every good thing (that is, every thing that is good in God's estimation) is in the desert, let us see what the desert is. There is God's desert, and

[10]Rom 8:14. [11]2 Tim 3:12.

there is the devil's desert. The carnal nature is the abode of the devil, and every act of wickedness is his feast. But it is a place deserted by God because there is no righteousness of God in it. In contrast, the spirit is the abode of God, and every act of righteousness is his feast. But such a place is deserted by the devil because there is no wickedness in it, in which the devil delights. And why is the nature of the flesh the abode of the devil? It is because every evil is contained in the flesh because it acts according to the will of the flesh. And every evil belongs to the world because it follows the will of the world. But every good thing belongs outside the flesh, because it does not follow the will of the flesh, and it is outside the world, because it does not follow the will of the world. Do you see then how every spiritual matter is outside beyond the bounds of the flesh and is in the desert, as it were, and outside beyond the world? Thus those who live according to the commandment of God are said to have departed from this world. They are said to have departed from the flesh not in body but in their mode of living and are said to be in the spirit. God's abode is the spirit because every good resides within the spirit because every good follows the will of the spirit. Meanwhile, every evil resides outside the spirit because it does not follow the will of the spirit. Do you see then how every carnal matter lies outside—beyond the boundaries of the spirit—and in the desert? Therefore, as far as God is concerned, the fleshly nature is a desert where there is no path of righteousness and in which no water of the Holy Spirit can be found, and so it is a despicable desert. The prophet spoke about it: "My soul thirsts for you; my flesh faints for you, as in a dry and weary land where no water is."[12] But as far as the devil is concerned, the desert is every spiritual matter—and such is a praiseworthy desert. God spoke about such a desert to Pharaoh: "Let my people go, that they may hold a feast to me in the wilderness."[13] In such a desert God wants all of his faithful to serve him. All the children of God, who have the Holy Spirit, go to such a desert to be tempted.

Inasmuch as you pledged not to marry, the Holy Spirit has led you into the desert, that is, he has taken you beyond the bounds of the flesh and the world that you may be tempted by the concupiscence of the flesh because chastity has nothing in itself so that you would delight in it according to the flesh. If, however, you were in the flesh and in the world, that is, if according to the nature of the flesh and the world you took a wife, you were not being tempted. How could someone be tempted by lust when he is with his wife daily? Or you pledge to fast, and you went out beyond the limits of the flesh and the world so that you could be tempted with hunger by the spirit of the belly. If, however, you ate and drank well situated within the confines of the flesh and the world, you would not have been tempted with hunger by the spirit of the belly. How could someone be tempted with hunger by the spirit of the belly when he has never known hunger? So also our Lord would have never been tempted with hunger unless he had fasted for forty days and known hunger at that time. Again, you intend to give alms, and you went outside because the nature of the flesh and the world does not take delight in giving but rather always in getting something. But if you did not give, you would not have been tempted by the spirit of avarice. Again you intend to preserve a spirit of humility. You went out into the desert to be tempted by the spirit of arrogance because the flesh and the world do not delight in humility. Some angel of the devil will arise who will treat you with contempt and enrage you that you have preserved a spirit of humility, while you see that in this age humility is despised and arrogance honored. And when

[12]Ps 63:1; the archaic language of the RSV has been updated. [13]Ex 5:1.

you will have conquered all these spirits, you will be promptly tempted by the spirit of vainglory. You will begin to boast that you have conquered because a spirit of vainglory is nourished chiefly from holiness.

But we ought to know that the children of God are not able to be tempted by the devil unless they go out into the desert, according to those things that we have said, that is, unless they have intended to vie for some virtues. The children of the devil, meanwhile, since they exist in the flesh and the world, are broken and perish. How? For example, if a good man has a wife—for that is to be in the flesh—he is not tempted by lust, that is, he does not commit fornication, but his wife suffices for him; but an evil man who exists in the flesh and has a wife commits fornication and is not content with one woman. So a child of God, that is, a good person, if he eats and drinks while in the flesh, he is not tempted by the food. That is to say, he does not get drunk, nor is he a glutton, but he eats and drinks moderately. Meanwhile, a child of the devil, though he eats and drinks inwardly, is not content with modest amounts of food and drink, but he gets drunk and exerts himself for richer fare. Again, a servant of God, even if he exists in the flesh, is not tempted if he does not give anything to anyone, because he does not take away anything from anyone either, but an evil person gives to no one and still takes away what belongs to others, and so you will find if you examine what takes place in every circumstance.

Do you see then that there is a distinction between the children of God and the children of the devil? The children of the devil do not go out to the devil to be tempted, but the devil comes to them to tempt them. That is to say, they do not go outside of the flesh to him, but they are ruled by him inwardly in their flesh. What need does one who does not desire victory to go out to the battle? But the devil comes to them as to his own family. But the children of God go out to be tempted by him, that is, they go out beyond the boundaries of the flesh because if they were still within the boundaries of the flesh, the devil would not be able to come to them, because they are children of God and he cannot tempt them, as we said above. Therefore, because the devil cannot come to them, those who are more glorious children of God go out beyond the limits of the flesh against him because they espy the glory of victory. Therefore in this passage the devil does not come to Christ in order to tempt him, but Christ goes out to the devil to be tempted by him, giving an example to his beloved ones. We have said all of these things in comment on the words "Then Jesus was led up by the Spirit into the wilderness to be tempted by the devil."

[2]***And he fasted forty days and forty nights, and afterward he was hungry.***

He was not only tempted because he fasted, but also he fasted so that he could be tempted.[14] Fasting is not only a means by which the passion of the flesh is provoked but a way that it is fought against. Therefore if you have fasted so that you will not enter into temptation, but it pleased God to lead you into it, do not say, "I have lost the fruit of my fasting." For although your fasting did not benefit you so as to keep you from temptation, nonetheless it without doubt will benefit you so that you will not be overcome by temptations, just as Christ's fasting benefited him. In many ways the devil had heard that Christ was born in the world—either from the angels who proclaimed the news to the shepherds, or from the shepherds who brought the news to Mary, or from the magi who sought to worship him in Jerusalem, whose star they had seen, or from John who had pointed to him: "Behold, the Lamb of God, who takes away the sin of

[14]Alternate reading: "he fasted because he was being tempted."

the world!" But his fleshly nature made the devil uncertain. He thought to himself, "This cannot be the son of God who was born of a woman and a man." For he was born from a woman who had been betrothed and had been living in her husband's home so that the virgin birth might be concealed from the devil. If he had been born of an unbetrothed virgin, the devil could easily have recognized that he was the Son of God, for he would have thought to himself, "Mary did not commit fornication, for if she had, I doubtlessly would have known, since every act of fornication is committed through my agency. Without a doubt her offspring is the Son of God, for it cannot be that a man can be born from a woman without a man." Thus, now the devil was compelled to ask, "Did Mary, when betrothed, enter Joseph's house so that Christ's conception might be thought to have arisen from their marriage and the birth of the only-begotten God not recognized? This is the king of glory—the one who lies wrapped in rags and who could not find any room in the inn, but was placed in a manger? This is the creator of the world, who grew up and step by step rose through the stages of life? This is the holy One, who is baptized with sinners as a sinner? What will I do then? I myself will tempt him, and if I find him to be a man (as I think he is), I will master him, just as I have mastered all people. But if I find him to be the Son of God (as I hear he is), I will withdraw a little from him, and I will not fight against him because anyone who goes against a stronger person provides the opportunity for the latter's victory, but if he withdraws himself, he will empty his power."

The Lord knew the thoughts of the devil, namely, that he wanted to tempt him. He set out against him, not as God but rather as man—and yet not entirely as God nor entirely as man. For just as it was not characteristic of human nature to not hunger for forty days, so it was not characteristic of God ever to hunger. He fasted, therefore, for forty days for two reasons: first, to give us an example of fasting against temptations; second, to limit our fasting to forty days. He hungered, however, so that he might not be clearly understood to be God by fasting far beyond human limits and thus extinguish any hope of the devil to tempt him and thereby impede his own victory over the devil. Consequently, when the devil had grown despondent watching Jesus fast for forty days, he began to have hope again when he perceived that Jesus was truly hungry, and so he approached him who was outwardly hungry and found one who was never inwardly hungry. And while the devil tempted the one who was hungry, he was defeated by the one who was not hungry.

3And the tempter came and said to him, "If you are the Son of God, command these stones to become loaves of bread."

O manifest blindness of the devil! How did he suspect that he was not the Son of God, when he perceived that after forty days he was hungry and did not understand that he had not been hungry during the forty days? Just as it is characteristic of human nature to grow hungry, so it is not characteristic of human nature to not grow hungry for forty days. He did not recognize that one who truly does not hunger can voluntarily suffer hunger, but he who truly hungers cannot fail to grow hungry during so many days. A strong person cannot descend to those things that are weak, while a weak person cannot ascend to those things that are stronger. The fact that Jesus had not grown hungry for so many days is an even more compelling argument that the devil should have understood that he was God than the fact that he became hungry after so many days proved that he was man. For God can do human things, but a human cannot do divine things. But perhaps you will say that Moses and Elijah fasted for forty days—and they were men. But they hungered as they fasted and yet were sustained; Christ, however, did not hunger during those forty days. That is what it means when it says, "And he fasted forty days and forty nights, and afterward he was hungry." It belongs to human experience to become hungry and not to eat, but it belongs to the divine nature not to become hungry. Therefore when he did not hunger for forty days but later became hungry, he showed that his hunger was voluntary and not necessary.

What does this verse mean then? Just as the devil always blinds all people so that they do not understand what is good, so he was in an imperceptible manner blinded by Christ so that he could not recognize the truth. The devil thought to himself, "If he will be able to make bread out of stones, he truly is God's Son; but if he cannot, he is a mere man." But what was it that he was thinking? By this logic he would never have recognized whether or not he was the Son of God. First, if he had been the Son of God, he would not have hungered. How could he have failed to conquer the needs of the fleshly nature, since he himself had planted those needs in nature? And why would he need to make loaves of bread out of stones when (had he so desired) he could have made the bread out of nothing, as he had made everything else? Furthermore, even if he was hungry because of the body and wished to do something, he would do it when he wanted to, not when the devil challenged him. If then Christ should happen not to do this feat (as he indeed declined to do), how would the devil know whether Christ did not do this because he was unable to do so as a mere mortal or (as was the case) because he as God did not want to do so? Not only did he not turn the stones into bread, he also did not say, "I could do it, but I do not want to" (if he had, he would have shown himself to be God's Son) and did not say, "I cannot" (if he had, he would shown himself a liar, since he would confess that he was a mere man when he was also God).

But what did he say?

4"Man shall not live by bread alone, but by every word that proceeds from the mouth of God."

He did not say, "I do not live by bread alone, but by every word that proceeds from the mouth of God," so that it might not appear that he was talking about himself, but he says more modestly, "Man shall not live by bread alone." What else could he have answered, thereby both hiding himself as Son of God so as not to show what he can do and excusing himself as an astute man, so that he would not show what he could not do? So, then, when from this one response he was not able to learn anything certain about whether he was God or man, he took him to another temptation, saying to himself, "Even if this one who is not overcome by hunger is not the Son of God, he nonetheless is holy. For holy and spiritual people are so strong as not to be overcome by hunger. But after they have conquered every need of the flesh, they fall through vainglory." So he began to tempt him with vainglory.

5Then the devil took him to the holy city.

When you hear him say, "he was led by the devil," do not think anything of the devil's might, that he could lead Christ, but rather be astonished at Christ's patience, since he endured being led by the devil. Therefore there is no weakness in the Lord's following the devil, but rather patience; there was, however, no virtue but only arrogance in the devil's leading him, because he led Christ who was willing, while the devil did not understand and acted as if he were leading an unwilling individual. He was led so that we might not follow the will of the devil.

And set him on the pinnacle of the temple.

But perhaps we will think how he could put him who existed in a body atop the temple, when all could see? If we consider the power of Christ, all sorts of intelligible reasons can be found. Perhaps while the devil was assuming (as much as he could) that Christ could be seen by all, Christ was acting invisibly while the devil did not realize this, so that he could not be seen by anyone, as was written about him, "But passing through their midst, he went away."[15] If Habakkuk, who was an ordinary man, was not seen by anyone when he was carried by the hair of his head by an angel from Judah to Babylon, how much more credible it is that Christ was not seen when he was willingly led up by the devil?[16]

And set him on the pinnacle of the temple.

He thought to himself, "If he throws himself through the air, I will know that he is the Son of God; without a doubt he will throw himself, so that what he is can be known; but if he will not be able to throw himself, I will know that he is mere man. Thus, just as by the desire for vainglory he will rush headlong from the sky; for although he were an angel, wishing to show himself to be God, even that which he was will perish, since he wished to appear that which he was not." So he thought that Christ too was borne by the desire for vainglory. For just as one who is himself good with difficulty suspects that someone is evil, so one who is evil suspects with difficulty that someone is good.

6And he said to him, "If you are the Son of God, throw yourself down."

Through this statement, how was it possible to recognize if he was the Son of God or not? First, it is not the essential work of God to fly through the air because this is not useful to anyone, either in body or soul. Therefore, if it was not necessary for anyone, neither would it redound to anyone's salvation. Someone would only fly on provocation; he would do this only to show off, and this pertains more to the devil than to God. Therefore, if it is sufficient for a dignified and wise person that that which is exists and it is not necessary that what does not exist to appear to him, since what is seen by others does not benefit anyone, but rather what is in oneself, how much more would the Son of God not deem it necessary for him to show without any useful grounds that to whom nothing was necessary to show, but what he possessed entirely in his nature, concerning which no one is able to recognize to what extent it is in himself. Therefore, if he did not fly, how would he know through this act whether he was not able to do so because of his weakness as a human or because he did not wish to do so out of vanity because he was God? For he had not been believed but tempted by the words, "If you are the Son of God, throw yourself down." See the arrogance of the enemy, how his very invitation is insulting. He could have said, "Descend, walking on air," couldn't he? But what does he say? "Throw yourself down." Nor did he have any fear, thinking, "If by chance he will be proved to be the Son of God, I will be found to have injured him." But whoever does not leave anything for himself to hope for does not hesitate to say or do. And see that he does not push him or touch him or draw near him but only says, "Throw yourself down, if you are the Son of God," so that we may know that everyone who obeys the devil throws himself down. For the devil can exhort to evil but cannot compel anyone.

"It is written, 'He will give his angels charge of you,' and 'On their hands they will bear you up.' "

O devil, you read how the Son of God is being borne on the hands of the angels, and did you

[15]Lk 4:30. [16]Bel 1:33-37.

not read that he would tread on the adder and the thorn? But he brings forth that first passage, since he is arrogant, but he keeps quiet about the other, since he is astute. For in truth the Son of God is not borne on the hands of the angels, but rather he bears the angels. No creature bears the creator, but the creator bears the creature. But if the creature carries around the creator, then before the creator had made the creature, by whom was he carried? Indeed, although he is carried on the hands of angels, he is not carried so as not to strike his foot against the stone, as if he were weak, but rather he is carried because of the dignity of his power, since he is Lord. It is written, "You who are enthroned upon the cherubim, shine forth."[17] To be sure, the passage that the devil cited is true, because it is spoken in the person of Christ, as it is written: "Because you are my hope, O Lord, you have made the Most High your refuge."[18] But this is said not only concerning Christ but concerning every just one whose person Christ has welcomed.

[7]Jesus said to him, "Again it is written, 'You shall not tempt the Lord your God.'"

He did not say, "You shall not tempt me, the Lord your God," lest he reveal that he was God, but he said, "You shall not tempt the Lord your God," which every child of God was also able to say when tempted by the devil, because also he who tempts a child of God is a member of the devil.

So then from this answer he passes on uncertain to the third. He says to himself, "I have these three nets stretched out over the whole world, so that whoever escapes from the net of the belly runs into the net of vainglory; whoever escapes from the net of vainglory falls into the net of avarice. However, no human escapes perfectly these three nets, and if he does escape, he does so not safe and sound, but worn out. This man, however, has ripped apart the net of the belly and passed through the net of vainglory. I will put the net of avarice before him, and I will show him all the kingdoms of the world. If he will desire those things, I will know that he is a mere man. For all people serve me because of their belly or because of their greed for money or because of vain ambitions; if he will despise those things, I will know that he is the Son of God. For he cannot desire what things he made, nor can he who enjoys heavenly things be delighted by earthly things." For although the devil lies to others that all things belong to him, he inwardly knows that they are not his but God's.

[8]Again, the devil took him to a very high mountain [which the devil, since he goes around the whole world, knew was higher than all the rest] and showed him all the kingdoms of the world and the glory of them.

Perhaps you wonder what sort of mountain it was from which all the world could be seen or, if it was above the entire earth, how could he show him the whole world, at least to his flesh? For although he saw it as far as his divinity is concerned, nonetheless, as far as the devil is concerned, he could not show the world to him whom he counted a mere man. But the phrase "took him to a very high mountain" must be understood to mean that to the degree that the mountain was higher, the earth seemed broader to the one looking down from it. Thus, he shows him not so that he can see the kingdoms themselves or their states or their people or silver or gold, but rather the parts of the earth, in which each kingdom or the cities of each kingdom has been situated, inasmuch as if you climb on top of a lofty place I can point my finger and say to you, "Look, there is Rome," or "There is Alexandria." In this way I am not showing you so that you see those

[17]Ps 80:1; the archaic language of the RSV has been updated. [18]Ps 91:9 (trans. Kellerman).

very cities but the parts of the earth in which they are located. If sailors look at one star and direct their course without wandering or deviation to not one province or island but to one city or to individual locations, how much more the devil, who as the prince of the air not only knew the whole earth but also saw it, could point out to Christ individual places with his finger with absolute certainty and explain the glories of each kingdom and their status? For it is not said that he pointed out only that which can be pointed out and seen but also that which can be explained and understood, as it is written, "Come, let us go up to the mountain of the LORD, to the house of the God of Jacob; that he may teach us his ways and that we may walk in his paths."[19]

9*And he said to him, "All these I will give you, if you will fall down and worship me."*

Consider how every promise of his is irrational and deceitful. Certainly he could not give all things to one unless he had taken everything from everyone; but if he took everything from everyone, he would not be worshiped by anyone, because the devil is not worshiped by anyone out of love or fear but because he promises wealth or gives it. How would it help the devil to take everything from everyone and give it to one person so that he would be despised by all and worshiped by one? But we cannot even say that each one possesses his own goods, but rather that he is over them. There never is one person over the whole world or ever was or can be without someone else not being subordinate to him. This is the case, first, because of God, who does not allow the devil also to do this. Second, it is because of the devil himself. What gives the devil joy, glory and power other than arrogance, envy, anger, vainglory and the like? Where these things are pursued, one kingdom cannot stand but must be divided into many. But where these things are not pursued, the devil is not worshiped, nor does he reign there. How then could the devil take the kingdom away from himself and give it to another? Then, what if there were saints who held sway over some kingdom in the world? For if he can give and take away wealth to a sinner, he can neither give to nor take from the saints. Do you think that he always wanted to take away Job's riches? But he could not, unless it had been permitted to him. Did not he want to take away the kingdom from the hand of David, if he could? For truly the world is not the devil's, nor are the kingdoms his. It is written, "By me kings reign, and rulers decree what is just."[20] But those things that are accomplished through iniquity in the world, as when you acquired riches through theft or force or you received glory at the expense of your soul, the devil gave those riches to you, but they are not the riches of the devil himself but rather their promise.[21] But wealth itself belongs to him who made it in order to test saints and sinners. And in two circumstances he puts wealth in the middle so that both the devil and God can give it. For when he gives power to the devil, he does not release it from himself so that if it were acquired through sin, it was given through the devil. But if it was acquired through sin, it was nonetheless acquired through God. Look at how he created our eyes, ears, mouth and other limbs to be between two conditions, so that both the devil and God could open the eyes of people. If a person opens his eyes to a base object, the devil opened his eyes, but if he opened them to righteousness, God opened them. You would not say from this that because our limbs are guided sometimes by the devil, as we ourselves will, that now our limbs belong to the devil, would you? So also wealth is sometimes given by the devil, but nonetheless it does not belong to him. If you truly consider the question, wealth

[19]Is 2:3. [20]Prov 8:15. [21]Alternate reading: "their providence."

itself is more in humankind's power than in the devil's. For the devil cannot give wealth to those whom he wishes to, but rather to those who will receive it from him. But a human being has it in his power to choose from whom he wishes to accept it, whether from the devil or from God.

[10]*Then Jesus said to him, "Begone, Satan! for it is written, 'You shall worship the Lord your God and him only shall you serve.' "*

He put an end to the devil's tempting of him by saying, "Begone, Satan!" so that he might not continue to tempt him further. Just as it pertains to the reason to understand, that is, just as it can be understood rationally, the devil withdrew not as if he was obeying the precept, but rather either the divinity of Christ or the Holy Spirit, who was in him, struck the devil. This is greatly useful for our comfort because the devil does not tempt people of God as long as he wants but as long as Christ (or the Holy Spirit who dwells in them) permits him. The devil would never cease from tempting, insofar as it depended on him, nor does he have anything else to do. He does not eat or drink or sleep or do any other kind of work except tempt, deceive and subvert. This is his food, glory and joy. For this reason he is tireless in evil, but the power[22] of God drives him away, although he permits him to tempt for a little while in order to test their faith but nonetheless drives him away because of their weak nature.

Notice further, when in his first temptation Christ suffered an insult, as the devil said to him, "If you are the Son of God, command these stones to become loaves of bread," he was not exasperated, nor was he stirred up to scold or refute him, but he endured the abuse and remained meek, but against the words of the temptation he gave apt examples. Similarly also in the second temptation, although he was injured when the devil said to him, "If you are the Son of God, throw yourself down," he was not disturbed, nor did he abusively say to him, "Begone, Satan!" Now, however, when the devil arrogated for himself the glory of God, saying, "All these I will give you, if you will fall down and worship me" (and the fact that he allowed all these things to be done to him by Christ that ought to be done to God alone), he was exasperated and grew angry and railed against him and drove him away, saying, "Begone, Satan! for it is written, 'You shall worship the Lord your God and him only shall you serve,' " so that we may learn from his example to endure magnanimously the insults against us brought by the impious whether in word or deed but not to allow any insults or contempt against God even to be heard, because it is praiseworthy for someone to be patient when he is being insulted, but it is very godless to ignore the insults against God.

We have spoken up to this point about the temptations with which our Lord was tempted. Now let us draw together what the temptations of Christ mean for our edification.

Often we say that it is the fast of the body to abstain from food but the fast of the soul to abstain from every evil matter, because just as the body is delighted by food, so the spirit delights to abstain from the sin of the flesh. According to this fast of Christ, we understand that there is an abstinence from sins in us. If Adam's eating from the tree of knowledge of good and evil was wisely understood by all, the appetite is for prohibited sin, and consequently the fast of Christ must be understood as abstinence from sin. But if fasting is abstinence from an evil thing, without doubt hunger is also the desire for that very thing, and the enjoyment of that very evil is understood as food. Therefore Christ, proposing a fast for himself and not overcome by a desire for the

[22]Alternate reading: "mercy."

bread set before him by the devil, teaches us not to interrupt anyone if he chooses a great deed and goes out into the desert, as the Son of God did (as we said earlier), and proposes that he abstain from any bodily or pleasant enjoyment, that is, to fast on account of the life-giving commandment of God. But if the devil should speak in his thoughts and urge him to use that object and thus interrupt his fast, the point is not so much that he made use of that object but that he sins by using it, that is, he turns a stone into bread. And although he decided to abstain from that object that he could have enjoyed without sin, if he had not so decided, nonetheless because he decided to abstain from it, he judged his enjoyment of that item to be sin, that is, a stone. For that reason, if he has made use of it, he has brought for himself sin into the use, that is, he has changed a stone into bread for himself, which breaks into pieces rather than nourishes. Just as the apostle said to those who were pledging widowhood, "When [the younger widows] grow wanton against Christ they desire to marry, and so they incur condemnation for having violated their first pledge."[23] But let such a one repress his desire as if it were hunger and answer the devil who is persuading him in his thoughts that a person does not live perfectly in the use of that very item, and if he lives, he lives according to the body and not according to the soul. He lives most fully in the observance of God's commandments, and so he does not simply happen to say, "Say to a stone that it turn into bread," lest it be understood that he had spoken about any and every kind of stone, but rather, "say to this stone," that is, "to the one that I show you."

Moreover, the ascent to the top of the temple is understood morally to refer to the exaltation of the heart of the saints in their holiness. Standing on top of the pinnacle of the temple is the moment of that very exaltation. For whenever someone, puffed up by the mind of his flesh, has been exalted as a holy person and has boasted as if he were perfect, he has been led up by the devil above the temple, as it were, and whenever he has thought that he stood at the height of holiness and tarried in the very estimation of his boasting, he has been placed at the pinnacle of the temple and stands there. Therefore quite appropriately and in due order the Evangelists have expounded the matter. After they expounded that Christ had overcome the devil in the temptation of fasting, they explain in a following passage that he was led by the devil above the temple because victory over temptation and the completion of another's great work effects boasting and becomes an occasion for vainglory. But see how Christ undertook the fast, but the devil led him above the temple, so that you, who are a child of God, might freely and swiftly hasten to some moral fasting, that is, to a praiseworthy abstinence from some object, but do not acquiesce to be lifted up to the height of holiness because no one lifts himself up to the heights of holiness unless led by the devil. For Christ did not agree to be led and placed on top of the temple so that you might imitate him morally in this regard, ascending through the boasting of your heart to the height of holiness. For he did not willingly ascend, as far as the body is concerned, but he consented to be led there and placed on the pinnacle of the temple to hear the words of the precipice: "If you are the Son of God, throw yourself down," so that he could show you to fear the demise that comes from exaltation, that is, to show you the danger of ruin that all who boast are wont to pursue, as Wisdom attests, saying, "Before destruction a man's heart is haughty, but humility goes before honor."[24] Consequently the Lord too says, "For everyone who exalts himself will be humbled, and he who humbles himself will be

[23]1 Tim 5:11-12. [24]Prov 18:12.

exalted."[25] Therefore, if you fear a fall from the height of holiness, flee the height of your heart to holiness and you will not suffer a fall from the height of holiness. The reason why ruin pursues everyone who boasts is clear. Everyone who is confident in his own works and boasts is secure; but whoever is secure does not fear and whoever does not fear takes no caution; and whoever takes no caution, when he does not expect it, is supplanted by the devil and cast down. But whoever thinks that he is nothing and stands in the lower part of the temple, as far as he is concerned, he is concerned about himself for the sake of humility. But whoever is concerned also fears; and he who fears looks about himself and does not allow himself to be led by the devil above the temple. Such too was the one who said, "Not that I have already obtained this or am already perfect."[26] If Paul feared to call himself perfect, who will dare to think himself to be perfect? If you are a perfect child of God and have undertaken some laudable abstinence, going out into the desert, as it were, the Lord was testing by these two temptations for your sake, that you might not interrupt your work but be led to perfection, and when you are led to perfection, that you will not boast.

But if you are a mediocre child and do not dare to enter any struggle for virtue, you are tempted with the third temptation. For you he was led atop a high mountain and heard the dangerous words, "All these I will give you, if you will fall down and worship me," so that you might not desire to become great and lofty in this world. The ascent of that mountain is the advance to greatness and grandeur of the riches and glory of this world, because the very advancement of those things descends from the haughtiness of the heart. And see the order of what he says: first he is led on top of the mountain, next the glorious things of the world are shown to him, and then the condition is given to him that all will become his if he worships the devil. So also it happens to you, who hasten to become grand and great in the world, and you ascend to the mountain, which the devil has chosen for himself to seduce you. As soon as you wish to become grand and great, that is, to ascend to the mountain, at the devil's leading you begin to think day and night about acquiring wealth and receiving honors and always to place before your mind's eyes all those things. Know that the prince of this world shows you the glorious aspects of his kingdom. But when he senses that you have been stirred by thoughts of this type in longings for such goods for a long time, he provides for you arguments that it is necessary for you to worship the devil and abandon your trust in God, if you wish to obtain those things, and for you to serve him and neglect the righteousness of God, but if you choose to worship God in faith in him and to serve him according to his commands, you will not obtain all those things. So Paul the apostle teaches, "But we urge you, brothers . . . to aspire to live quietly, to mind your own affairs, and to work with your hands."[27] And again, "But if we have food and clothing, with these we will be content. But those who desire to be rich fall into temptation, into a snare, into many senseless and harmful desires that plunge people into ruin and destruction. For the love of money is a root of all kinds of evils. It is through this craving that some have wandered away from the faith and pierced themselves with many pangs."[28] Therefore all things were promised to Christ, and yet Christ despised all things so that he would not give the glory of God to the devil, so that also, even if the whole world were given to you, if only you rejected God, you would not count wealth greater than the glory of God. For it is not right to despise the creator for creation's sake, but rather to despise creation for the cre-

[25]Lk 14:11. [26]Phil 3:12; cf. 1 Cor 4:4. [27]1 Thess 4:10-11. [28]1 Tim 6:8-10.

ator's sake, because God can give you wealth, but wealth cannot give you God. He was not tempted for his own sake but for ours; and he prevailed not for his own benefit but for ours.

11Then the devil left him, and behold, angels came and ministered to him.

He did not say, "And the angels of God came *down* and ministered to him" to show that the angels were always on earth to minister to him but then, at God's command, they withdrew from him to give the devil room against Christ, lest by chance he see the angels around him and not draw near to him. So it happens to every Christian invisibly. There are two angels who remain with people, namely, a good angel and an evil one. As long as the good angel is around us, the evil angel can never drive us into temptation. At God's direction, however, the good angel withdraws for a brief time. However, it is not so much that he withdraws as hides himself, making himself invisible to the devil because, unless the good angel so wills, he cannot be seen by the devil. He removes himself, then, to give the devil permission to tempt, and yet he stands nearby and awaits the outcome of the temptation. Therefore, when some longing for an evil thing climbs up into your heart and agitates some kind of sin, the good angel is not near you, but the devil is speaking into your ear and tempting you and at the same time urging you. If you endure, shattering your heart, or rather shattering the devil in your heart, he will depart from you because he has not been able to conquer you. When, as the sinful longing recedes, your heart begins to exult because you have escaped that evil attack and a certain spirit rejoices in you quietly, as it were, and gives thanks to God, know that the devil has withdrawn from you and an angel has drawn near after the victory over temptation and ministers to you and speaks in you and creates joy.

We know that the angels ministered to him, but we do not know in what matters they ministered to him. Whether it was to heal his infirmities, as God healed Tobias through the angel Raphael[29] or to restore his soul or to put the demons to flight—because God does many of his own works through angels, it is true. As angels do these things, he himself seems to do them, because he gives them the command and the power to do them. Nonetheless, it is most clear that although they ministered to him in his work, they did not minister to him because of a necessity arising from his weakness but rather because of the honor of his power. For they ministered to him and did not materially help him.

The Sixth Homily: On Matthew 4

12Now when he heard that John had been arrested, he withdrew into Galilee.

From whom? Without a doubt from God because no one can do anything against a holy person unless God has handed him over. For perhaps a sinner can do something against another sinner, because a sinner too is not by and large under the care of God, but without a doubt he can do nothing against a person of God because "he is a shield for all those who take refuge in him."[1] So he also says elsewhere, "Are not two sparrows sold for a penny? And not one of them will fall to the ground without your Father's will. But even the hairs of your head are all numbered."[2] Before anyone has done some iniquity, however evil he may have been, he is rather slow to do the work of iniquity; but if he has begun to do iniquity once, he becomes more prepared for every unrighteous deed. Just as a wild beast does not easily hurl itself against a human being, even if it has been stirred up, however savage it

[29]Tob 3:17. **Sixth Homily** [1]Ps 18:30. [2]Mt 10:29-30.

might be by nature, but if it has killed a person or some other wild beast and gotten a taste of blood, now if it sees a human, without any delay it rushes on him, so also Herod, even if his intention was iniquitous, nonetheless after he had been made savage because of the reproof for his adultery, he dared to do the very worst deed and shut up John in a prison, since he had become more iniquitous than he had been. And indeed he had been emboldened when all the Jews agreed to the death of John with him.

When the Lord knew about this, he withdrew from there, not because he feared death but because of two reasons. First, to preserve his passion for an opportune time; second, to give us an example of fleeing the danger of temptation. It was not because he feared the danger of temptation but because we otherwise would not be able to endure every temptation. Therefore, if he went before us as our teacher through every path of righteousness, so that we might follow him as his disciples, it is clear that he did not think about what he could do but what we were able to fulfill. If, however, Christ had done those things that he had been able to do and we could not, we would not be able to be his disciples, since we would not be strong enough to follow him.

13*And leaving Nazareth he went and dwelt in Capernaum by the sea, in the territory of Zebulun and Naphtali,* 14*that what was spoken by the prophet Isaiah might be fulfilled:* 15*"The land of Zebulun and the land of Naphtali, toward the sea, across the Jordan, Galilee of the Gentiles."*

As history teaches, these tribes migrated to Babylon before all the rest. Most aptly, then, the mercy of the Lord visited first those whom the wrath of God had struck before all the rest, and those who were first to be led into bodily captivity were themselves led back earlier from their spiritual captivity.

16*"The people who sat in darkness have seen a great light, and for those who sat in the region and shadow of death light has dawned."*

The Jews were sitting in darkness, since they were under the Law, in which the righteousness of God had not been manifested; even though there was righteousness there, nonetheless it had been covered in certain figures and types of carnal matters. What sort of light of righteousness was there in the circumcision of the foreskin? They were largely shadows according to the Law, which had not been given to reveal the righteousness of God but to punish the hardness of their hearts, as the Lord says, "For your hardness of heart he wrote you this commandment."[3] It was given not to save them but to blind them so that, inebriated by the Law, they might not recognize the light, which they did not deserve to see in the shadows, that is, in their sins.

The great light is Christ. There were many lights among the Jews. Moses and Aaron and Joshua and the other judges and prophets were lights. Every teacher was a light of theirs, whom he illuminated by teaching, as it is written, "You are the light of the world."[4] But the great light is Christ. The Gentiles sat in the region and shadow of death either because they were doing deadly iniquities or because they worshiped idols and demons, whose worship led them to eternal death. But the Jews, who were doing works according to the Law, were thus in the shadows and not in the region and shadow of death, because even if it was not truly righteousness that they were doing, nonetheless eternal death (if not glory) does not befall those who do it, because they were keeping God's commandments. I deem that the shadow of death is the sin of idolatry. Just as those who live in recognition of God and Christ, however

[3]Mk 10:5. [4]Mt 5:14.

much life itself is recognition of him, nonetheless as long as they are in this age, they are not in true life but in the shadow of life, because they walk by faith and not by sight, and they see in a mirror in an enigmatic fashion, not face to face, so those who live in the errors of idols, even if error itself is death, nonetheless they are not in true death but in the shadow of death as long as they are in this age.

That the ignorance of God is the shadow of death is proven by the prophet, who says, "You have turned our steps from your way . . . and covered us with the shadow of death."[5] Without doubt he covers with the ignorance of God one whose life has turned away from the path of God. The region of death is this world. Just as that land is the land of the living concerning which it is said, "I believe that I shall look upon the goodness of the Lord in the land of the living!"[6] so this earth is the region of death. Therefore we cannot fully please God as we live in it, because although we ourselves live on account of the living works and faith in Christ, nonetheless inasmuch as we live in the world, which the devil governs, we are co-sinners with him. Thus even Paul said, "Who will deliver me from this body of death?"[7] This body is a body of death because it has been subjected not to life-giving but rather to deadly pleasures.

And see how accurately the prophet said that the Jews had seen a great light, but that the light had arisen for the Gentiles. Among the Jews there was some recognition of the Son of God, but they did not see him because they sat in the shadows of the Law or of sins, but among the Gentiles there never was any awareness of the Son of God. Therefore he is said to have been seen by the Jews but arisen for the Gentiles. Capernaum is said to have been located at the boundary between the Jews and the Gentiles.

[17]*From that time Jesus began to preach, saying, "Repent, for the kingdom of heaven is at hand."*

"From that time," that is, since John bore witness about him. For he would not have been able to preach in a credible fashion, nor would the witness of the Father have existed, unless it had been attested by John, because no one is able to be a suitable witness of another unless he himself has been attested by another. But Christ was attested by John in this way: "Behold, the Lamb of God, who takes away the sin of the world!"[8] This is so that everyone who is ordained to preach might have the good testimony from the people and from those who are outside, as the apostle says. Whoever lives well saves himself alone, but whoever has a good reputation edifies many. What advantage is there, if by living a good life you save yourself alone, and you scandalize very many people by having a bad reputation?

"From that time Jesus began to preach," that is, from the time he was baptized by John in the water. Now I am speaking according to his humanity that he was baptized in the Spirit by the Father so that he could baptize others from himself because if he had not been baptized, he would not have been able to baptize others.[9] How can a naked person clothe another naked person, or how can a beggar make another rich? So also how could he who was not baptized be able to give baptism to another? We speak in this manner also about the heretics because wherever there is faith, there is the church; where the church is, there is the priest; where the priest is, there is baptism; where baptism is, there is a Christian. But where there is no faith, there is no church present either; where the church is not, neither is there a priest; where the priest is not, neither is there baptism; where there is no baptism, no one is made a Christian.

[5]Ps 44:18-19 (trans. Kellerman). [6]Ps 27:13. [6]Rom 7:24. [8]Jn 1:29. [9]The last half of the sentence beginning with "because" was excised by Manhusius for doctrinal reasons, although attested by the manuscripts.

Why then does he find fault with baptism as a secondary matter when he does not understand that it is a primary matter?

"From that time Jesus began to preach," that is, from the time when he was tempted. He overcame hunger in the desert, he scorned greed on the mountain, and he drove back vainglory on top of the temple—to show us that he who can argue against his own stomach, who can despise the goods of this world and who does not desire vainglory ought as Christ's vicar to preach Christ's righteousness, because from those three forges every flame of diabolical fraud is set on fire.

Again, it was when John was arrested that Christ began to preach. For if he had begun to preach while John was alive, without doubt he would have made John of little value, and his preaching would have been found superfluous compared with Christ's teaching, just as if a light were to arise with the morning star, it would only conceal the beauty of the morning star. How wisely, then, he took as the beginning of his preaching that which John was accustomed to preach ("Repent, for the kingdom of heaven is at hand"[10]) not so that he could despise John's doctrine but rather confirm it. For if Christ had preached these same things while John was still teaching, he would perhaps seem to despise him, but now because he repeated it while John was in prison, it was found to be a confirmation rather a rejection of his teaching. But he confirmed John's doctrine to show that John had been a true witness. Because if John was a true witness, also his testimony about Christ is true, but if he is a false witness, all of those glorious things that he had spoken about Christ were also false. Therefore, while the Lord confirms John's teaching, he commends himself.

"Repent."

The creator of human nature knows what human nature needs. Since the Lord knows that no human sins through ignorance of righteousness but rather while he follows carnal delight and despises spiritual glory, so he did not at once preach the righteousness that all recognize, but rather repentance, which all needed. Who then has dared to say when he comes before the judgment of God, "I want to be good, and I cannot"? The Lord, who preached first not righteousness but repentance, showed that the fault not of an ignorant nature but of a will lies in sinners. Repentance is a correction of the will, not an emendation of an evil nature. For if repentance were the emendation of nature, our creator Lord would have come into the world to correct the fault of his own work rather than our errors.

"The kingdom of heaven is at hand."

That is, the blessing of the heavenly kingdom, which God has prepared for the faithful, is at hand. It is furthermore as if he should say, "Prepare yourselves through repentance and through patience to lay hold of the blessing of the heavenly kingdom, which will draw near the time of meting out reward. You who fear calamities or desire good things, pay heed, because the kingdom of heaven will draw near. If calamities do not terrify you, then let good things delight you; or if you do not long for the kingdom, at least fear the torments. Let the just rejoice because soon their troubles are ended and good things begin. Let sinners grieve because already their goods are passing away and their troubles are beginning. How does it harm just people to have suffered troubles when they have begun to be amid good things? For even a memory of past troubles not only does not harm but also furthermore greatly delights. As long as troubles are present, they seem grave, but when they have

[10]Mt 3:2.

passed, their recollection is grounds for boasting. Or how does it help sinners that they have pursued good things when they have begun to be amid troubles? For the recollection of past goods not only does not help but further burdens one. As long as they are present, they seem delightful, but when they have passed, their memory rather afflicts.

And what sort of fruit did Christ's preaching of repentance bear him? He sowed a word of repentance and harvested undefiled preachers of repentance.

The Seventh Homily: On Matthew 4

18As he walked by the Sea of Galilee, he saw two brothers, Simon who is called Peter and Andrew his brother.

Before he says anything or does anything, he calls the apostles so that nothing either of his words or deeds may be hidden from them, so that afterwards they may faithfully say, "We cannot but speak of what we have seen and heard."[1] He saw them, not physically but spiritually, looking not at their faces but at their hearts. And he did not choose them as apostles, but he chose them because they could be made apostles. Just as a jeweler, if he sees precious, uncut gems, chooses them not on what they are but what they can become, and since he has knowledge of the skill, he does not despise something good that is still rough, so also our Lord saw them and chose not their works but their hearts.

Casting a net into the sea.

And so he prophesied through the work of their trade the grace of their future office. It was so that we might understand that not only that second, spiritual fishing had been given to them by God but also that first, physical fishing had been ordained for them by the providence of God. For just as he who tosses nets into the sea does not know what fish he will capture, but the fish whom God has sent him enter into the nets, so also when a teacher tosses the net of divine speech over the people, he does not know who will draw near to God, but whomever God stirs up, they stick to the teaching. Therefore, just as only the labor of fishing is sought in a fisherman, while God sends the catch, so also in a teacher nothing is sought except perseverance in teaching; it is not a person who corrects the people, but rather God does. So also the Lord says through the prophet, "Say these things to Joshua, the son of Jehozadak, the high priest, 'If you will guard my courtyard, I will give to you those who may dwell in it.'"[2]

19And he said to them, "Follow me, and I will make you fishers of men."

That is to say, "I will make you a teacher so that with the net of God's word you may lay hold of people from this false world—one tossed about by waves, stormy, unstable, treacherous, ever dangerous and safe for no one, where people do not walk but are carried unwillingly. The violence of the devil works in many sinful longings and lies to them that he will do their will, because with delights he compels them into evil deeds so that people devour one another, just as the stronger fish always devour the weaker ones, lest they be brought to dry ground and live in the fruitful earth of the body of Christ, having been made members of his body—in the fruitful earth, the sweet and ever tranquil earth, where there is no storm to destroy everything, unless by chance it is for the testing of their faith and the fruitful bearing of patience. They walk about as people and are not carried about so that its inhabitants may not devour one

Seventh Homily [1]Acts 4:20. [2]Cf. Zech 3:7.

another but cherish one another. Behold, from you there will be a new gospel in your hands and another net of various sayings and of parables bound together, with frequent narrations of admirable virtues and manifold doctrines—a net woven together for those running about here and there as on waves, a net bound together by threats of judgment and promises of blessings in indissoluble nets, as it were, a net confirmed by foreknowledge and awareness of hidden thoughts, by the confessions of demons and the resurrections of the dead. This is so that in your most safe bosom it may lay hold of a catch of reasonable human beings so that it may not give them any opportunity to leave, as it were, through some hole overlooked by the Holy Spirit, who wove the net."

And someone will say to himself, "It was not without cause that they followed Jesus who promised such things." But what about you? Did he promise you rather small things in return? He promised you a heavenly kingdom if you behaved well, didn't he? And eternal life? And an angelic nature? And an inheritance with him? And why do you not follow him? But they followed him because they were lovers of heavenly goods, not earthly ones. But you do not follow him because you are a lover of earthly goods, not heavenly ones. The carnal person, you see, does not believe that anything is good unless it is carnal, and he never believes that there is anything pleasant except that which is on earth. Therefore they do not desire the honor of being a teacher but the pay for a teacher's work, as the outcome has borne witness. For if they were made apostles, they enjoyed the honors of their apostolate and doubtlessly desired the honor of an apostle. But if they not only did not enjoy the honors of their apostolate for humility's sake but also suffered various afflictions for humankind's salvation and Christ's glory, it is clear that they did not desire the honor of an apostle but merely the task of the toil and labor of being an apostle. They knew that a person's soul is precious, how pleasing its salvation is to God and what reward there is in building a person up according to God. They desired these things and followed, but you do not desire these things. How do you desire that another can be saved when you do not take care to save yourself?

[20]Immediately they left their nets and followed him.

Lest any Christian should say, "We cannot love wealth and please Christ, can we?" the apostles taught us by leaving their nets behind that no one can own anything earthly and come perfectly to heaven. Consider how the air placed in the middle between heaven and earth separates each creation in order to show that there can be no mixture between the heavenly and the earthly. Heavenly things are spiritual and light and naturally always seek what is above. Earthly things are weighty and always pull downward. Therefore, if you are held by spiritual things, they lead you upward; if you are held by earthly things, they draw you downward. Therefore they left their nets lest their nets create an impediment for their labors rather than an addition of usefulness.

[21]And going on from there he saw two other brothers, James the son of Zebedee and John his brother, in the boat with Zebedee their father, mending their nets, and he called them.

They were fellow citizens in their habitation, harmonious in their love, equals in their skill of duty, conjoined in the ties of brotherhood. So he called also those men, so that these men, men conjoined in so many good things, would not be separated by different callings. Someone graciously spoke of this double usefulness of brothers because the entire church was to

[3]Jn 15:12.

be built chiefly on love, as he says, "This is my commandment, that you love one another as I have loved you,"[3] and again, "By this all men will know that you are my disciples, if you have love for one another."[4] Just as in a physical building stone is bound together to stone through the mortar between them, so in the building of the church Christian is joined to Christian through the love between them. He so constructed the foundations of the church on the brotherhood of love that, abounding in the roots of love, it might ascend as sap into the branches. And this is in addition to a natural love so that that love might be held all the more firmly not only through grace but even by nature. God acted in this way in the Old Testament: when he was about to build that people through the Law, he put the brothers Moses and Aaron above the rest as the beginning of the building. Since the grace of the New Testament was going to be more abundant than that of the Old Testament, he consequently built the people of the Old Testament on one brotherhood but the people of the New Testament on two.

Mending their nets.

This greatly indicates their poverty. They were mending old nets because they did not have any resources to buy new ones. And a point that refers to their great sense of duty: amid such great poverty they helped their father so that they carried him in their boat, not so that he could help them in their work but so that they could comfort him with their presence. I do not believe that it is without reason that Peter and Andrew are mentioned by all the Evangelists as casting their nets, but James and John are mending their nets, especially since they could have said so without any loss of meaning, "And he saw James and John" and not said, "mending their nets." Moreover, we do not dare to think that Peter and Andrew were quicker to preach, as it were, because they were casting their nets, but James and John were lazier because they were mending their nets at this point—I say this because it belongs only to God to know the difference between them. Perhaps it was for Peter's sake that the former were said to have been casting their nets and it was for John's sake that the latter were said to be mending their nets, because Peter only preached the gospel and did not write it down,[5] but Mark wrote down the things that had been preached by him; meanwhile, John both preached the gospel and wrote it down himself. And he did not only write it down, but he also mended the nets of all the Evangelists. For while all the Evangelists wrote down almost only the human deeds of Christ, John mixed in with them his divine deeds so that the Holy Spirit might not leave any opening in them from which the fish might depart. And so that we may now say what earlier we omitted in the weaving of the nets: he puts around it also leaden weights, that is, the ponderous punishments of inextinguishable flames and undying worms, so that it can easily penetrate the depth of human hearts.

22Immediately they left the boat and their father, and followed him.

See how Peter and Andrew are said to have left behind the nets, but James and John are said to have left behind their father and the boat. The three things are generally everything that everyone who comes to Christ ought to leave behind: carnal deeds, worldly wealth and fleshly parents. Through the fishing nets it is meant that carnal deeds must be left behind;

[4]Jn 13:35. [5]The author has a play on words here that eludes translation. The same word (*componere*) that means "to mend" when used with the object "nets" also means "compose" or "write down" when used with the object "gospel." That play on words continues through the rest of the paragraph; wherever either "mend" or "write down" appears in this paragraph, the reader can be assured that it is translating the Latin *componere*. This play on words is one more indication that this commentary is a Latin original rather than a translation of a Greek work.

through the ship, wealth; through the father, all parents. And see that the fact that the nets were left behind first, then the ship, and in the third place the father means that it is first appropriate to leave the deeds of the world, for they are what are chiefly harmful to the spiritual. Second, wealth, because it is not as harmful to have something in the world as it is to do some action; nonetheless it is also harmful to have it. Lastly, parents, who themselves indeed are harmful but nonetheless are less harmful than the riches and deeds of this age. Therefore they left behind the ship in order to become helmsmen of the ecclesiastical ship; they left behind their nets so that they might no longer carry fish to an earthly city but people to a heavenly city; they left behind one father to become fathers of all spiritual people.

The Eighth Homily: On Matthew 4

23*And [Jesus] went about all Galilee.*

Every king who is about to fight against a hostile force first gathers his army and then goes out to battle. So also the Lord, who was about to fight against the devil, first gathered the apostles, and so he began to preach the gospel through all Galilee. The preaching of the truth is the taking of the devil by storm; the preaching of righteousness is the deadly arrow in his innards. The work of signs is his ejection; the conversion of the faithful is the plundering of his power. And an earthly king gathers an army that he might obtain glory by their labors, but Christ gathered the apostles not so that he could obtain glory by their labors but rather by his labor he might offer them victory.

He went about all Galilee, as a diligent doctor walks around those who are direly ill and applies the medicines appropriate for each individual affliction—because those who are weak could not come to the doctor. And the Lord was walking around each individual region. However, we who are shepherds of each single region, although we do not have the need to go around the regions, we ought nonetheless to go around and consider the individual types of afflictions of the people; that is, we ought to attend diligently those among the people who labor under the disease of avarice so that we can make some sermon about the evil of avarice to serve as a medicine for the healing of him who is troubled by the goads of avarice, in accordance with the opinion of Paul, who says, "If we have food and clothing, with these we shall be content. But those who desire to be rich fall into temptation."[1] Again we ought to provide for those among the people who labor mightily under the burning fevers of passion so that, to remedy their affliction, we can also offer some medicine in the church from the medicinal apothecary of the apostle, who says, "Every other sin which a man commits is outside the body; but the immoral man sins against his own body."[2]

And as the diligent head of a household knows what each one needs in his house, so also a priest ought to acquaint himself with the habits and actions and lifestyle of each one in order to minister such medicine as will be necessary for each: to whom consolation is needed, consolation; to whom rebuke is needed, rebuke. He ought not be angry to whom the more bitter medicine of rebuke has been prescribed according to the nature of his affliction because not even a sick person grows angry against the doctor, if he has applied some more biting medicine. For he does not consider the bitterness of the medicine and grows angry, but rather he considers the benevolence of the doctor and endures it because he desires that it help him rather than harm him. However, just as a patient who comes to the doctor now is partially already healed, so also a sinner who comes to a priest and seeks the medicine of doctrine or of repentance is

Eighth Homily [1]1 Tim 6:8-9. [2]1 Cor 6:18.

already partially righteous. But a grave illness holds one whom the priest pursues with words; and such a person does not sense the medicine of spiritual words or get better but, like those whose stomach ails, he throws up again whatever he has eaten or drunk. So is also the soul that endures whatever it has heard but immediately casts it out from its senses, and so are those unbelieving Jews to whom it was said, "They loathed any kind of food,"[3] that is, every food of doctrine that nourishes the soul.

Teaching in their synagogues and preaching the gospel of the kingdom.

It is one thing to teach and another to preach the gospel. He was teaching them, saying to them natural acts of righteousness that, even if he had not spoken, natural reason itself would teach them: namely, chastity, humility, patience, and other things similar to these. Even if people do not listen to these things, nonetheless they understand all by themselves that they are good, as the apostle says to the Romans, "When Gentiles who have not the law do by nature what the law requires, they are a law to themselves, even though they do not have the law."[4]

But perhaps you say, "If he was teaching them those things that all understand, what need did he have to teach them?" Listen. Teaching was invented not so much for the sake of revealing obscure matters as much as for the sake of stirring up the heart and spirit. Such is human nature: inasmuch as carnal delights prevail in humankind, the knowledge of natural righteousness that is in humankind is shut out and, having been led into forgetfulness, as it were, is driven out of memory and has fallen asleep. Therefore, when a teacher begins to admonish and drive back fleshly evils and to strike terror concerning the coming judgments, as the carnal delights are being removed, as it were, he again returns knowledge into their memory and renews it in their senses. Thus divine discourse is also called a sword because, just as a sword cuts through flesh, so also divine discourse cuts through carnal desires. And just as if you remove weeds from a field, the wheat prevails in it, so also if sinful desire is excised from humankind, righteousness prevails, because just as the weeds choke out the wheat, so also fleshly desires choke discipline. Do you see then that teaching does not introduce new knowledge but makes plain what had been forgotten? Thus if mere human speech has such virtue when it offers a sound to the ears, what do you think the Lord's discourse was doing, since it was a living spirit, not only sounding in ears but also working in hearts?

When he was preaching the gospel, however, he was promising the mystery of righteousness. The gospel is good news. Now good tidings are announced to people whenever heavenly blessing, forgiveness of sins, adoption as children, the resurrection of the dead and everlasting life, the inheritance of a heavenly kingdom and possession of eternal glory, fellowship with the angels, communion of the Spirit, fraternity with Christ and the fatherhood of God are promised to them. The people of old clearly had neither heard nor hoped for all these things. Consequently, since they did not hope for a reward for their good work, they despised the labor of righteousness and dedicated themselves to carnal delights. Because every righteous act is troublesome to all who live in the flesh, for that reason the labor of righteousness is not sustained unless their reward is awaited. So then he proclaimed the good news of a heavenly blessing to stir up their hearts to the patience of good works and a desire of heavenly rewards, either by teaching or interpreting to them the prophecies of his own coming so that it might be a very teaching

[3]Ps 107:18. [4]Rom 2:14.

of the interpretation for the sake of rebuking and an act of spreading good news for the sake of announcing the future honors he would have.

And healing every disease and every infirmity among the people.

He wanted to apply the word *disease* to the bodily afflictions, but when he says "every infirmity" he wanted to apply the word to the spiritual afflictions of the soul. For no fewer diseases afflict the soul than the body. And if he had said, "healing diseases and infirmities," we could have understood each as applying to bodily passions so that diseases would be understood as the more dire afflictions and the infirmities the lighter forms of exhaustion. But now since he says "every disease" and includes every type of affliction, whether dire or trivial, the addition of another phrase seems superfluous, unless we understand the one to refer to bodily afflictions and the other to spiritual ones. Nonetheless, we can understand each phrase to refer to both types of afflictions, that is, "every disease" (whether bodily or spiritual) and "every infirmity" (whether bodily or spiritual), so that we understand disease to be a more averse sickness of the soul, while infirmity means unfaithfulness, since one who has been handed over to the sickness of greed or lust or vainglory suffers a disease of the soul, but whoever ignores the mystery of the calling of God is deemed weak in the faith. Many are those who can do good works and please God but do not do it because they do not know the mystery of God's calling and are themselves weak. Some have been sold to fleshly passions to such a degree that even if they know the mystery of God's calling, they nonetheless are not allowed to do good and are themselves having a disease.

Now he healed the bodily afflictions by the virtue of his divinity, but he healed their spiritual afflictions by the word of piety. Just as medicine helps a sick body, so the word helps a sick soul. See, furthermore, that he did not write first "healing every disease and every infirmity," but he wrote first "preaching and teaching the gospel of the kingdom" and afterwards "healing"—for two reasons. First, it was because the miracles of gallant deeds build up souls in accordance with the words of piety. Thus, what is thought to be more necessary is stated first. Second, it was because the words of piety did not commend the great deeds of the miracles, but the great deeds of the miracles commended the discourses of truth. Nor was Christ believed to be able to do great deeds because he preached the truth, but he was believed to be preaching the truth because he was able to do great deeds.

24And they brought him all the sick . . . and he healed them.

In some places he writes, "He cured many,"[5] just as he also said there, "And as many as touched it were made well."[6] Here, however, he simply says, "And he healed them," meaning that he healed all. Just as a novice doctor who enters into a city and wishes to give proof of his skill cures all who come to him and does not think of taking pay as much as building up his reputation, but when his reputation has become well-known, then he begins also to exact pay for his labors, so also when the Lord began to preach, he did not heal select ones according to his judgment but rather healed all indifferently, but after all Judea came to know him, he proffered the benefits of healing at the worthy price of faith, saying to each one, "According to your faith be it done to you."[7] But he did not do it to all but to those whom he had prepared according to his foreknowledge before they came.

[5]Lk 7:21. [6]Mt 14:36. [7]Mt 9:29.

The Ninth Homily: On Matthew 5

[1]Seeing the crowds, he went up on the mountain.

Whenever a craftsman sees an opportunity to ply his profession, he rejoices. If a carpenter sees a good tree, he desires to cut it down to make it a work of his craft; if a farmer sees fertile soil, he desires to plow it. And what am I to say about rational people? If an irrational horse, leaping from the stable, sees a wide-open field, it grabs hold of the bridle and is roused to run; so also the Lord, seeing a great gathering of people, was roused to teach. So also when a priest sees a full church, his soul rejoices and he delights to teach; but if he sees an empty church, he is confounded and cannot say anything.

He went up on the mountain.

He was not unable to teach where the people already were, was he? But he went up on the mountain for two reasons. First, it was to fulfill the prophecy of Isaiah, who says, "Get you up to a high mountain, O Zion, herald of good tidings."[1] Second, it was to reveal the mystery of godliness. His ascent is the height of virtues. Therefore he went up on the mountain to show us that he who teaches the righteousness of God ought to dwell in the height of spiritual virtues, and likewise he who hears. Let him who teaches be an example of his own words so that he might teach more by his action than by his speech, as the apostle said to Timothy, "Set the believers an example."[2] But whoever walks in the deep valleys of earthly life treads shadowy paths and speaks lofty discourses—such a one does not instruct another but rebukes himself. Nobody can stand in a valley and speak about a mountain, but either speak where you stand or stand where you speak. If your mind is on the earth, why do you speak about heaven? Therefore, if you stand on the earth, speak about the earth, but if you speak about heaven, then take your place in heaven, so that you can say with the apostle, "Our commonwealth is in heaven."[3]

Moreover, the people who hear the righteousness of God ought to take their stand on the heights of good works, because a disciple ought to be an imitator of his teacher. But if you should happen to live in sins and hear someone teaching words of righteousness, you acquire for yourself judgment, not salvation. Indeed, you hear, so that you do not have the excuse of ignorance before God. Behold, if a person wants to learn any art wholeheartedly, such as to paint or to build, when he has often heard or seen his teacher, he secretly goes and takes a tool and tries himself—if he already can do it—to do what he has often heard or seen. So also, if you do not wish to do righteousness, why do you listen to the preacher of righteousness? Why do you call him "teacher" when you do not wish to be his student? Therefore, understand: I am speaking to you a natural fact according to the Scripture of that passage. If you are on top of the mountain and yet there is a preacher in the valley, you listen from on high to that person's voice because the voice has risen better; but if you stand in the valley and your teacher speaks on top of the mountain, his discourse does not benefit you very much.

Therefore the people first ought to consider what sort of people they are and then what sort of priest they have, because a bad teacher does not harm good people very much, but a good teacher cannot help bad people very much. Nowadays, however, the people do not look at themselves, which they ought to do first, but they always sit down and judge the character of the priests. Therefore the present passage teaches us that the people who want to hear

Ninth Homily [1]Is 40:9 [2]1 Tim 4:12. [3]Phil 3:20.

the teaching of godliness should go up on the mountain of holiness as much as the teacher.

Or this may be the interpretation: the church is called the mountain, concerning which the prophet says, "O mountain of God, O fertile mountain."[4] Therefore Christ went up on the mountain in order to give his disciples the mysteries of the truth, showing that everyone who wishes to learn the mysteries of the truth ought to ascend to the mountain of the church, but not on every mountain, but on the fertile one. Indeed, there are also the mountains of the heretics, but they are not fertile but fatty soil, in which the mysteries of the truth are not given, but rather lies that fight against the truth. And so those who go up on such mountains the Holy Spirit rebukes through the prophet, saying, "Why look you with envy, O mountain full of fat?"[5] The churches of the heretics are called full of fat because "their heart is gross like fat."[6]

[3]*"Blessed are the poor in spirit."*

Although the Evangelist Luke also partially sets forth the Beatitudes themselves, nonetheless these beatitudes must be understood to be more perfect than Luke's because the latter were spoken on a plain but Matthew's to perfect people on a mountain. Luke's were spoken to ordinary people but Matthew's to the perfect and the rulers of the people, as they were the apostles to whom these things were said. The reason for this difference we have explained more amply there. So in Luke he simply says "the poor," but here "the poor in spirit." The poor in spirit are humble of heart, that is, one who does not think great things about himself has a poor spirit. In contrast, one wealthy in spirit is understood to be one thinking great things about himself and an arrogant person who does not fulfill the commandment of Christ, who says, "Truly, I say to you, unless you turn and become like children, you will never enter the kingdom of heaven."[7] Whoever has been converted and becomes like a child, he is also poor in spirit. And whoever is poor in spirit, that one has been converted and made as a child. And according to the testimony of Christ and the apostle, "Love is the fulfilling of the law,"[8] but humility is the nurse of love and arrogance is the mother of every evil hatred. Therefore humility is the beginning of every good thing and arrogance of every evil. Finally, the beginning of damnation began with arrogance through the devil, and the beginning of salvation by humility through Christ. For that reason he aptly made humility the beginning of all the Beatitudes.

And why did he not openly say, "Blessed are the humble in spirit"? I have been able to find only this hint of an explanation: it was to point out not only the humble but also the indigent humble people who are so humble so as to be beggars of God's help. Therefore in Greek[9] he does not say, "Blessed are the poor," but "Blessed are the needy" or even "Blessed are the beggars." For a poor person is someone who has difficulty but not so much difficulty so as to be forced to beg. The prophet too speaks about this difference: "Blessed is he who considers the beggar and the poor."[10] Therefore he says, "Blessed are the beggars in spirit" so that he might show the humble in their ultimate need. If he had said, "Blessed are the humble in spirit," he would have meant nothing more than "humble people," but now he means both the humble and those who are humble in faith and understand from whence comes humankind's help. There are many who are naturally humble in spirit and yet not out of faith. Such

[4]Ps 68:15 (trans. Kellerman). [5]Ps 68:16 (trans. Kellerman). [6]Ps 119:70. [7]Mt 18:3. [8]Rom 13:10. [9]This is one indication that John Chrysostom or another Greek writer could not have written this work. The author is clearly explicating the Latin text, although obviously he is able to understand Greek. [10]Ps 41:1 (trans. Kellerman).

people do not implore the help of God. But whoever are humble in faith and understand, even while they are very afraid concerning themselves, they do not cease to implore God's help.

"For theirs is the kingdom of heaven."

What? Does not the kingdom of heaven belong to those who pursue other virtues too? Yes. Just as other vices lead to hell, but arrogance especially does this, because arrogance is the root of all evils, so also all virtues lead to the kingdom of heaven, but humility especially does this, because arrogance is the root of all evils, and without a doubt humility is the root of all good things; and because it is appropriate that he who would exalt himself be made humble, so also he who humbles himself will be exalted.

4***"Blessed are those who mourn."***

Those who grieve over their own sins are blessed, that is, they are moderately blessed; but more blessed are those who grieve over other people's sins because those who grieve over other people's sins certainly do not have sins of their own over which to grieve. It is appropriate for all such people to be teachers and those who stand on the mountain. For because all teachers are parents of the Christian people, how can they be without grief when they daily see the souls of Christians falling all the way into hell? For Ezekiel writes concerning the angels who will go out at the end of the age to mark the servants of God and who grieve for the sins of others: "Go through the city, through Jerusalem, and put a mark upon the foreheads of the men who sigh and groan over all the abominations that are committed in it."[11] Jerusalem, to be sure, is the church of Christ, whose foundations are on the holy mountains.

"For they shall be comforted."

If the consolation of those who grieve is the cessation from their grief over their punishment, because those who grieve over their own sins will be comforted by obtaining forgiveness in the coming age, how will those who grieve for other people's sins be comforted in that age? They will not cease to grieve for sinners, will they? Indeed, they will. As long as they are in the world and do not know the providence of God or understand fully those who transgress at the devil's compulsion and those who love evil but not out of bad intention, they grieve for all who sin, since they think that all are surrounded and compelled by the devil. But when they recognize God's providence in that age and understand clearly that those who were of God could not perish, but those who perished were not of God, because no one could take them from God's hand, they will put aside their grief and be comforted, and without any mixture of any grief they will rejoice in their blessed state alone. For as long as the saints show love to sinners, there is also grief. But in that place there will be no love of saints toward sinners or grief, even if they were kin, as the parable teaches in which the rich man says to Abraham, "Father Abraham, have mercy upon me, and send Lazarus to dip the end of his finger in water and cool my tongue; for I am in anguish in this flame."[12] Abraham did not show any compassion for his own son who was burning, did he? For he who had been a lavish diner was being tortured in that part of his body that had sinned more, that is, in his throat.

5***"Blessed are the meek."***

The meek neither provoke trouble nor are

[11]Ezek 9:4. [12]Lk 16:24.

provoked by trouble; neither does any cause for sin prevail against them, nor does any cause for sinning arise for somebody else because of them, but instead they are content to suffer an injury rather than to cause one. For unless a person is content to be harmed, he would never be without sin, because just as weeds are always found in a field, so also instigators of trouble are everywhere in the world. One is truly meek who does not think to do evil or do it when he has been harmed.

"For they shall inherit the earth."

Without a doubt, the land of the living, concerning which it is written, "I believe that I shall see the goodness of the Lord in the land of the living!"[13] This earth, as some say, as long as it is in this state, is the land of the dead because it has been subjected to futility; but when it will have been freed from servitude to corruption and turned into the freedom of the glory of God's children, it will be the land of the living, as immortals inherit immortality. I read someone else who explained that heaven, in which the saints will dwell, is called the land of the living, which is called the heaven in comparison with our lower region, but which in comparison with that heaven that is above it is called a land. Others say that our body is on earth, and as long as it lies underneath death, it is the land of the dead; but when it will be transformed and made like the glorious body of Christ, it will be the land of the living and eternal people will inherit that eternal earth, and spiritual saints will inherit that spiritual and saintly earth.

6"Blessed are those who hunger and thirst for righteousness."

To hunger and thirst for righteousness is to desire the righteousness of God. When people either do the righteousness of God or hear it, they do it not as if they hear or do the righteousness of God unwillingly but out of their heart's desire, because every good deed that people do but not out of a love for that very good, is displeasing to God. Thus in John's Gospel our Lord called only the thirsty and not everyone indiscriminately when he said, "If anyone thirst, let him come to me and drink."[14] I think that it is not without reason that he speaks about hungering and thirsting for righteousness. One who desires to walk according to the righteousness of God (which comes from a right heart) now hungers for righteousness, while one who desires to obtain knowledge of God thirsts for righteousness, which can be pursued from a study of the Scriptures, which belongs to a teachable person.

"For they shall be satisfied."

Namely, with the generosity of God's reward, for greater are the rewards of God than the wildest desires of the saints.

7"Blessed are the merciful, for they shall receive mercy."

Not only one is merciful who shows mercy either to a pauper or an orphan or a widow, for this mercy is also commonly found among those who do not know God, but he is truly merciful who shows mercy to his own enemy and acts kindly toward him, as it is written, "Love your enemies, do good to those who hate you."[15] For God too does not give rain only to the grateful or orders his sun to shine on the grateful, but also on the ungrateful. Thus he also says, "Be merciful, even as your Father is merciful."[16] And truly such a person is blessed because his mercy benefits him in addition to his righteousness, if indeed he does not have

[13]Ps 27:13. [14]Jn 7:37. [15]Lk 6:27. [16]Lk 6:36.

sin (which is a difficult thing among humankind); but if he does have sin, it benefits him as forgiveness of sins because he is able to say faithfully, "Forgive me my debts as I also forgive my debtors."[17]

[8]"*Blessed are the pure in heart, for they shall see God.*"

There is a twofold way of seeing God: in this age and in the age to come. In this world it occurs as it has been written, "He who has seen me has seen the Father."[18] They are pure in heart who not only do no evil or think it but also those who do every good deed and think about it. It is possible sometimes to do a good deed and yet not think about it, such as those who do a good deed but not for God's sake. Such a good deed God does not reward because what is rewarded by God is not the good that is brought about but that which is well done. But whoever does a good deed for God's sake, without a doubt he also thinks about the good. Then God sees whoever does every act of righteousness and thinks in his own mind, because righteousness is an image of God. For God is righteousness. Then to the degree that someone has removed himself from evil and done good, to that degree he has also seen God—whether confusedly or purely, moderately or fully, partially or perfectly, occasionally or always, or as much as humanly possible. In this very same way also he who thinks about and does evil sees the devil because every evil is an image of the devil. However, in the age to come the pure in heart will see God face to face and no longer enigmatically in a mirror.

[9]"*Blessed are the peacemakers, for they shall be called sons of God.*"

Peace is the only-begotten God, concerning whom the apostle says, "He is our peace."[19] Those who love peace are thus children of peace.

Not only are those who reconcile enemies with peace called peacemakers, but those who love peace are also those who are forgetful of injuries. There are many who gladly reconcile other people's enemies in peace and yet they themselves never are reconciled with their enemies from the bottom of their heart. Such people are mockers of peace, not lovers of it. That peace is blessed that is situated in the heart, not in words. Do you wish to know who is truly a peacemaker? Listen to the prophet who says, "Keep your tongue from evil, and your lips from speaking deceit."[20] That is, let not your tongue say any evil talk. For just as fire drawn from a small spark kindles a great blaze, so also wicked talk about a trivial slight inflames great enmity. One's lips speak treachery if he speaks peace on his lips but keeps malice in his heart. If you are a Christian, either think what you are saying or say what you are thinking. "Depart from evil, and do good."[21] He did not say, "Do not approach evil," but "withdraw from evil." However, it is the one who is drawing near who is ordered to withdraw. Because our merciful God knows our intemperance—because if he had said, "Do not approach evil," either a few people or possibly no one would have been able to fulfill this, for nearly all people have been prepared for evil—so he says, "It is good if you did not even approach evil, but if as a natural human being you have been stirred up by the fleshly emotions and drawn near to evil, at least withdraw from evil out of consideration of divine anger." Perhaps it is characteristic of human weakness to draw near to evil in accordance with the flesh, but to remain in evil or to pursue it is characteristic of malignity and not mere weakness.

"Seek peace, and pursue it."[22] He did not say, "If peace follows you, lay hold of it," but

[17]Cf. Mt 6:12. [18]Jn 14:9. [19]Eph 2:14. [20]Ps 34:13. [21]Ps 33:14. [22]Ps 33:14.

"And if it flees from you, pursue it." If you go to court with someone (as commonly happens to people) and if that person first invites you to peace, inasmuch as peace follows you, welcome it with joy. But if that troublemaker remains in his evil, peace is hidden from your eyes; as a child of peace pound on the door of peace, that is, seek after peace. Do not say, "He hurt me first and ought to ask me first." You are more honored if you seek peace when injured than if you want revenge. Therefore seek peace, that you may find the reward of peace: "Blessed are the peacemakers, for they shall be called the children of God."

10"*Blessed are those who are persecuted for righteousness' sake.*"

He did not say, "Blessed are those who suffer persecution by the Gentiles," lest you think that only one is blessed who suffers persecution for not worshiping idols. So also blessed are those who are persecuted by the heretics because they do not abandon the truth, for they suffer for righteousness' sake. The heathen deny Christ, but the heretics deny the truth of Christ. But whoever denies the truth of Christ denies Christ himself. Christ is the truth. And so the heretics who do not persecute because of Christ but because of Christ's truth at first appearance seem Christian, but in reality they are heathen. Not only if a heretic but also if some other powerful person who appears to be a Christian will become your enemy (perhaps after he has been corrupted on account of his own sins) and persecute you, you are blessed with John. For also John the Baptist was not killed because of heathenism or because of heresy but because he rebuked Herod for his adultery. So also all the prophets were killed not by heathen kings but by their own kings, not because of heathenism but because they rebuked their sins. But if he who suffers something at the hands of his own kings for the sake of God does not have a reward, then neither did the prophets have a reward. But if it is true that the prophets are martyrs, without doubt also one who suffers something for God's sake, even if he suffers at the hands of his own kings, has a reward. So the Scriptures do not note the station in life of those who persecute but only the reason for the persecution, so that you might not look at who is persecuting you but why he is persecuting you.

What, then, if someone will persecute you not for the sake of God but over some private matter? Say, for example, that he took away something belonging to you; he indeed who persecuted you without cause is guilty, but you are not blessed because you did not suffer persecution for righteousness' sake but over a private reason. Clearly you will be blessed if you wish to fulfill what is said, "If anyone strikes you on the right cheek, turn to him the other also; and if anyone would sue you and take your coat, let him have your cloak as well,"[23] because even if in the beginning you did not suffer persecution for God's sake, you later suffered either loss or injury for God. But if you resist with sin and cannot suffer, you lose the reward of blessing.

11"*Blessed are you when others revile you.*"

After he spoke about enduring persecutions, it is almost as if someone answered God, "Lord, what if we do not suffer persecution for your sake or for righteousness but come into disrepute and the blasphemy of wicked people?" and he said, "Blessed are you, not only when you are persecuted but also when people revile you. Behold, many people are your enemies for the sake of God's cause, but they do not openly persecute us, perhaps because they cannot; nonetheless, they go around everywhere and

[23]Mt 5:39-40.

blaspheme us and say about us whatever things are shameful."

"Blessed are you when others revile you and persecute you and utter all kinds of evil against you falsely on my account."

Just as it is true that whoever offers a cup of water to us does not lose his reward, so also when someone injures us with the slightest word, our soul is not bereft of reward. Therefore, in order that the one who is blasphemed may be blessed, these two things are necessary: that he is blasphemed falsely and for the sake of God. Otherwise, if one of these two requirements is missing, there is no longer a reward or blessing. For example, if someone says about you what is a base lie but does not do so for the sake of God's cause, but rather because he is grieving over some private cause for enmity, he indeed sins, but you do not have the reward of righteousness, unless by chance when you are able to revile him in turn, you do not do so for the sake of the righteousness of God, or you do not take revenge even though you could—and then you are blessed and the private matter has become God's cause. But if you are blasphemed for the sake of God's cause, but the evil that is said about you is true, again you are not blessed because the truth has been spoken about you—and that blasphemy applies not toward a reward of righteousness but as a punishment for sin. For that reason he added both phrases "falsely" and "on my account."

12"Rejoice and be glad."

Why?

"For your reward is great in heaven."

Weigh the earthly disturbance with the heavenly glory, and see if what you suffer on earth is not much lighter than what awaits you in heaven. But perhaps you say, "Who when being reviled falsely can endure it magnanimously—I dare not even say 'rejoice'?" It is whoever does not delight in vainglory. Whoever desires whatever things are in heaven does not fear reproach on earth, nor does he think about what people are saying about him, but rather what God judges about him. Whoever rejoices in the praise of people also rejoices as much as he is sad. He is sad at the vituperation of people and is sad to the same extent that he is happy. But whoever is not excited by the praise of people also is not humiliated by their vituperation. Where each person seeks his glory, there he fears disturbance. Whoever seeks glory on earth fears disturbances on earth. One who does not seek glory except only with God does not fear any disturbance except that caused by God. If a soldier can endure the danger of war, provided he hopes for the spoils of victory,[24] how much more ought you not to fear the reproaches of the world, since you await the prize of a heavenly kingdom?

The Tenth Homily: On Matthew 5

13"You are the salt of the earth, but if salt has lost its taste, how shall its saltiness be restored?"

It is as if the apostles were asking to whom he was speaking all these things, whether generally to the people or to them, and Christ, wishing to show them that he was chiefly speaking these things to them, added, "You are the salt of the earth." That phrase "you are the salt of the earth" points to that which he said before, namely, that a teacher ought to be adorned with all virtues. He ought to be poor in order to rebuke greed with a free voice. He ought to be sighing and grieving, whether for his own sins or those of others, in order to confound those

[24]Alternate reading: "hopes to take from thence the spoils."

who do not hesitate to sin before they sin or are sad because they have sin after they have sinned. He should so sigh and weep in order to show thereby that the world is a grave and dangerous place for the faithful. He ought to hunger and thirst for righteousness in order by the word of God or the scourge of rebuke to be strong to stir up the idle toward good works or at least reading faithfully—more by example than by his voice. He ought to be accustomed to rule the church more by forgiving than by punishing so that he may be loved more than feared. He ought to be merciful to others but strict with himself, so as to put the heavy burden of righteousness on himself but a light burden on others. He ought to be pure in heart so that he does not get himself involved with worldly business but not even think about the world. Just as the eye becomes purer the longer it sees, so also the further a soul is from worldly trouble the more fully it is closer to God. But if the eye of a person's heart gazes at the world, his mind cannot see God. Let him be a peacemaker so that his whole church may be of one mind. But where there is no harmony, neither is prayer heard nor is the sacrifice accepted because neither is God there where disharmony reigns. He ought to also be ready to suffer, not having the vain hopes of martyrdom but the constancy of faith worthy of the martyrs. For as far as the wise are concerned, that soldier is not said to be prepared for war who desires to go out to fight, but rather he who is able to go out. Thus, if he has been adorned with all these virtues, then he is very good salt, and all the people are edified from him more by seeing him than hearing him. For the first teaching is to see a good person, and the second is to hear him.

14*"You are the light of the world."*

While we consider what is the function of salt and that of light, he admonishes to seek the reason the apostles were compared with salt and the reason they were compared with light. It is the function of salt to preserve an object in the state in which it is found it so as not to allow it to be changed for the worse, but salt cannot make it better. For example, it preserves meat from spoiling, but it cannot make spoiled meat fresh. It is the function of light to break up the darkness and to light up those things that were in darkness. So also the apostles and other teachers are the salt of the Christian people who already know God, since they preserve them in their very knowledge of God and holiness, that is, they are the salt of the cultivated land, which has been subjected to the word of the cross as to the tiller and the plow. But they are the light of the heathen, bringing them to the light of knowledge, or the light of others who by chance have fallen in the church in the darkness of their sins. Again, the priest's good manner of life without a word keeps them holy in holiness through his own example, but it cannot lead the ignorant to knowledge of the truth. Again, the word can lead the ignorant to knowledge of the truth even without a good manner of life, but to keep them in faith or holiness cannot be done without a good manner of life, but rather he also scandalizes them, as we will show below. Therefore for the sake of their good lifestyle the priests are salt because the priests' good manner of life is the preservation of the people. Because of the word of doctrine they are light because the word is light to the ignorant.

First he called them salt, afterwards light, either because it is the first priority to preserve what you have and it is the second priority to call those whom you do not have, or because living well comes first, and then teaching well. For through a good manner of living one can ascend without doubt to knowledge, but from knowledge I do not know if one can altogether come to a good manner of living. For that reason we see many knowledgeable people without the fear of God, but we do not see those who do not fear God without having any knowledge. Or because of the Jews they are first said to be salt, since they did not lead them to the knowledge of God but preserved them in that knowledge. They are light, however, because of the Gentiles who were called in the second place.

Consequently, introducing the matter through an apt comparison, he adds, "A city set on a hill cannot be hidden." Although it might wish to be hidden, the mountain itself that carries it makes it clear to all. So also the apostles and priests who have been founded on Christ, the lofty mountain, are not able to be hidden; and if they wished to hide themselves, Christ reveals them, since he carries them. What is this city? It is the church of the saints, concerning which the prophet says, "Glorious things are spoken of you, O city of God."[1] Its citizens are all the faithful, concerning whom the apostle says, "You are fellow citizens with the saints and members of the household of God."[2] Its towers are the prophets, about whom it is written, "Peace be within your walls, and security within your towers!"[3] Just as arrows are fired from the towers against all the enemies, so from the prophetic books salutary examples of the truth are set forth against the idle tales of the heathen and the mad disputations of the heretics. Its gates are the apostles, concerning whom it is written: "The Lord loves the gates of Zion more than all the dwelling places of Jacob,"[4] because through them all the people enter into faith. Its walls are the priests and other teachers, concerning whom the prophet says to this spiritual Jerusalem, "Foreigners shall build up your walls,"[5] because once they were called from the Gentiles, they were made priests and rulers of the church. Just like walls, they take every blow of the heathen and of the heretics, who strike the clergy, that is, the wall of the church, with frequent persecutions as with battering rams. And just as walls receive deadly arrows, so the teachers like living stones receive the mad words of their perverse thought, which proceed from the impious quiver of the heart; and like walls the teachers bind the church together by the virtue of faith. Therefore this city has been placed on top of a mountain; that is, the apostles, prophets and other teachers have been built in Christ. The mountain is Christ, concerning whom Daniel says, "As you looked, a stone was cut out by no human hand, and it . . . became a great mountain and filled the whole earth."[6]

Now through another comparison he wishes to show why Christ reveals his saints and does not allow them to be hidden.

[15]"Nor do people light a lamp and put it under a basket, but on a stand, and it gives light to all in the house."

Who are the ones who set the lamp on fire? The Father and the Son. What is that lamp? The divine word, concerning which it is written, "Your word is a lamp to my feet."[7] "It gives light"—that is, it appears and illumines those who are in the house of the church or in the house of all the pure. What is the lampstand? The church, which bears the word of life. Consequently Paul also says, "Among whom you shine as lights in the world, holding fast the word of life."[8] Consequently, every ecclesiastical person who has the word of God is called a lampstand. The baskets are worldly people, devoid of God and of all things that are God's. They are called baskets because just as baskets are empty on top but full below, so all lovers of the world and of the flesh are devoid of spiritual and divine things, which are rightly called things above, but in the lower things, that is, in worldly and terrestrial things, they seem to some extent to be full and wise. For that reason, just as if you wish to put some-

Tenth Homily [1]Ps 87:3. [2]Eph 2:19. [3]Ps 122:7. [4]Ps 87:2. [5]Is 60:10. [6]Dan 2:34-35. [7]Ps 119:105; the archaic language of the RSV has been updated. [8]Phil 2:15-16.

thing in a basket, it must fall into its lower and darkened area, so if you say something that is of God to a carnal, worldly, empty person, he does not hold it in the upper part of his mind or heart or carry it in his mouth, but immediately it falls from his mind and heart down into the terrestrial and dark regions, so that it never benefits him or others. But if some testing occurs because of the word of truth, it is immediately turned over onto the earth, and, looking at the earth, just like a basket, he holds the word of God hidden underneath him. He is turned over and looks at the earth and hides the word underneath himself whenever he does not dare because of some earthly reason to speak the truth of faith. Or they fear fleshly injuries[9] or death or loss or the other things that hinder carnal people, so that they do not dare to freely profess the word that they believe.

But now knowing that he is a praiseworthy teacher who does what he teaches, he adds and says,

16"In the same way, let your light shine before others, so that they may see your good works and give glory to your Father who is in heaven."

So shine, teach, not so that people can only hear your words but so they can see your good deeds, so that those whom you illuminate through the word as a light you can establish through the example of your works as salt, because he who teaches and does what he teaches truly teaches, but whoever does not do what he teaches does not teach another but condemns himself. And it is better to do and not teach rather than to teach and not do. Because he who does, even if he keeps quiet, corrects others by his example; but whoever teaches and does not do not only corrects nobody but moreover scandalizes many. Who would not be moved to sin when he sees the teachers of piety sinning?

Therefore God is glorified through those teachers who teach and do, but he is blasphemed through those who teach and do not do. For example, if the teachers teach well and live even better, the heathen say when they see this, "Blessed is the God who has such servants. Truly their God is God. For unless he himself were just, he never would preserve his people in righteousness as he does. For the discipline of a lord is shown by the behavior of the family. They are not like our philosophers, who speak great things and do not even do ordinary things." However, if they see them teaching well and behaving badly, they see it and say, "What sort of God is their God, who does such things? He would not sustain them when they do such things, unless he agreed with their works, would he? Our ancestors, worshiping idols, as they thought best, preserved all righteousness, but they speak glorious sermons and do shameful works." Do you see how God is blasphemed through evil Christians? Nor can a lord who has an evil family have a good reputation. Thus it was spoken to the people of God, "The name of God is blasphemed among the Gentiles because of you."[10]

17"Do not think that I have come to abolish the Law or the Prophets."

For two reasons he says that he did not come to abolish the Law but to fulfill it. First, to challenge his disciples with these words to follow his example, whom he had taught earlier that they ought to be adorned with good works, so that just as he fulfilled every law, so also they might hasten to fulfill completely even the smallest details of the Law. Second, because it would happen that the Jews would accuse him of working on the sabbath and

---

[9]Alternate reading: "or fleshly ill will." [10]Rom 2:24.

touching leprosy, as if he were breaking the Law, so before he runs into their calumny, he satisfies his accusers by saying, "Do not think that I have come to abolish the Law or the Prophets; I have not come to abolish them but to fulfill them." The Law and the Prophets do these two things: they both prophesy about Christ, and they establish a law of how to live, both of which Christ fulfilled. He fulfilled the Law concerning himself when he was born and called Emmanuel, when he was circumcised, when he was presented in the temple and a sacrifice was offered for him, namely, two turtledoves or two doves, and when he was in Egypt. When he returned to Nazareth, when he rode a donkey to the temple, when he was praised by children, when he was crucified between wicked men, when he drank vinegar and gall, when he commended his spirit into the hands of his Father, when he left behind his clothing to be divvied up, when he descended to hell and visited all who slept there, when he ascended in a crashing sound, when he sat at the right hand of God, when moreover he will come, calling the earth from east to west, when he will sit in the valley of Jehoshaphat and judge all the nations, he fulfills the prophecies, because unless these things had happened, all the prophets would be liars. But now they have been fulfilled and will yet be fulfilled, when the stars fall and the sun is darkened and the moon is turned the color of blood and when the sky will be folded like a book.

But inasmuch as it is a law of how to live he fulfilled the Law in two ways. First, he set free the outward forms of the Law but fulfilled completely its inner truths. For example, in the Law it commands that one ought not to do any servile work on the sabbath except what is necessary for the soul, namely, that which is necessary for human life. This is symbolic because God ceases from his work on the sabbath. But spiritually, according to the truth of the gospel, the servile work is sin because "everyone who commits sin is a slave to sin."[11] But every good work is not a servile one but a free one and is done for the freedom of the soul, although it seems that the very work is a physical work at first glance. Do you see then that Christ fulfilled the Law when he worked on the sabbath and did not break it? That he revealed it, not hid it? Again, it had been written that one ought not to touch leprosy. This has a figurative meaning, for leprosy is understood to be sin. Thus, when Christ touched leprosy, he did not break the Law but fulfilled it. By cleansing the leper, he worked righteousness, not sin. And thereby he touched righteousness, not sin, which is truly leprosy. For he who did not sin, nor was any deceit found in his mouth, certainly did not touch leprosy, that is, sin.

Quite rightly he says then,

18"For truly, I say to you, until heaven and earth pass away, not an iota, not a dot, will pass from the Law until all is accomplished."

Because the mysteries of those things that would be from the beginning of the world to the end have been prophesied in the Law so that it might not seem that God had not thought previously about any of those things that came to be, he says, "The heavens and earth cannot pass away until everything that has been prophesied in the law will be fulfilled in very substance." If a frank person is caught in a base lie, he blushes; and how would God not do that which he promised in the Law or do it differently? Whatever a wise person says he does not leave his word empty; and how could the divine words remain empty without fulfillment? God punishes a person if he does not do what he teaches; how could Christ not fulfill in deed what had been spoken in the prophets? Thereupon he fulfilled the Law in even its least matters.

[11]Jn 8:34.

[19]"Therefore whoever relaxes one of the least of these commandments and teaches others to do the same will be called least in the kingdom of heaven."

But first let us see what are the least of the commandments. Some people hold to one interpretation and others to another. But I think that the Lord clearly shows what they are when he pointedly says, "If someone relaxes one of the least of these commandments," that is, "the ones that I am about to say." For such is the manner of speaking in the Scriptures; those things that are about to be spoken are pointed out as if they had already been spoken, as in the passage, "Hear this, all peoples!"[12] What does the word *this* mean except the things that he was about to speak in the following verses?

Therefore, the commandments of Moses are easy to do: "Do not murder, do not commit adultery." Consequently, they are little in consideration of their reward, but they are great in consideration of the sin against them. But the commandments of Christ, that is, "Do not become angry or lust," are difficult things by the very act, and so they are great when one considers the reward but are little if one considers the sin. It is obvious that it is easy to abstain from murder or adultery. For the very magnitude of the offense drives back the will to do them, and so one who abstains from these things does not have praise, because it is no great labor to abstain from those things. For in every case, the more dire the offense is, the easier it seems to be to not do it, and it makes the sin all the more dire if it is done. But in practice it is difficult not to grow angry because it is not easily kept by many since the fault is thought to be rather minimal. And it is much harder work to be able not to get angry because irascibility has been naturally planted in humankind.

And so they are great commandments because it is difficult and hard work to abstain from them. For that reason, if a person becomes angry or lusts, he is indeed a sinner because it is an evil, but nonetheless it is not a grave sin because it is difficult to abstain from them. Therefore these commands of Christ are called "the least of these commandments," namely, "You will not be angry, you will not lust." In observing them there are great rewards, but in sinning against them they seem very small, at least to people who neglect them. Therefore those who commit rather trivial sins are least in the kingdom of God. That is to say, one who gets angry and, though angry, does not put a great sin into action is free from punishment, to be sure, but nonetheless he is not in glory, because even if he does not commit any such sin, nonetheless he sinned because he followed his anger and did not restrain it in his heart. Thus the prophet orders us to repent and restrain irascibility in our hearts, knowing that if we sinned through anger, trivial as it might be, we are sinners. Again, he who lusts has sinned, even if he has not done anything. Why? Because he at any rate wanted to. The teacher, then, who abstains from all these things is great, but if he has committed any of these light sins, the honor of his priesthood does not benefit him at all, but rather he is cast out for the first ecclesiastical choir and placed among those who are not in punishment because they have not committed a grave sin but nonetheless are not in glory because they took the wrinkle or blemish of sin.

The Eleventh Homily: On Matthew 5

[20]"For I tell you, unless your righteousness exceeds that of the scribes and Pharisees, you will never enter the kingdom of heaven."

The righteousness of the scribes and Pharisees is the commandments of Moses, but the

[12]Ps 49:1.

fulfillments of those commandments are the commandments of Christ. Thus the meaning is, "Unless someone fulfilled, in addition to the commandments of the Law, also these precepts of mine, which among them is thought to be the least, he will not enter into the kingdom of heaven, because Moses' commandments (as we said) free one indeed from the punishment that is owed to transgressors of the Law, but they do not lead one into the kingdom. But these commandments both free one from punishment and lead into the kingdom."

But since it is the same thing to break the least of these commandments and to not keep them, why does he say previously concerning the one who breaks them, "Whoever then relaxes one of the least of these commandments . . . shall be called least in the kingdom of heaven," thereby showing him to be still in the kingdom, even if the least, but here he speaks about those who do not keep them, "Unless your righteousness exceeds that of the scribes and Pharisees, you will not enter the kingdom of heaven"? For whoever will not enter into the kingdom of heaven will be outside the kingdom. But see how to be least in the kingdom is the same thing as not entering the kingdom. For someone to be in the kingdom is not the same as reigning with Christ but only to be in the people of Christ. It is as if he were to say, "Whoever breaks these commandments and teaches the same will indeed be among the Christians but will be the least Christian or among the least Christians." But whoever enters into the kingdom is made partaker of the kingdom with Christ, just as elsewhere he says to the good servant, "Enter into the joy of your master,"[1] that is, "You will rejoice with your Lord." Consequently also he who does not enter into the kingdom of heaven will not have the glory of the kingdom of heaven with Christ but will be in the kingdom of heaven nonetheless, that is, in the number of those over whom Christ rules as king of heaven. Now he begins to show and to teach what are those least commandments, whose breaking he had proclaimed to be dangerous. He says:

21"You have heard that it was said to the men of old, 'You shall not kill; and whoever kills shall be liable to judgment.' 22But I say to you that every one who is angry with his brother shall be liable to judgment."

This second fulfillment of the Law was done according to the law of how to live. When Christ did these things and taught them, he fulfilled the Law and did not break it. For the commandment of Christ is not contrary to the Law but is broader than the law. The commandment of Christ includes the Law in itself, but the Law does not include Christ's commandment. Therefore whoever fulfills the commandments of Christ tacitly fulfills in them also the commandments of the Law, for whoever does not grow angry all the more does not kill. But whoever fulfills the commandment of the Law does not altogether fulfill the commandment of Christ. Often an individual does not kill because he fears punishment, but nonetheless he is angry. Do you see then, that the Law is fulfilled by grace but not abolished? Then without these commandments of Christ the commandments of the Law are not able to stand. For if license is granted to become angry, a reason for committing homicide is also given, for it is from anger that murder originates. Remove anger, and there will be no murder. Everyone who is angry without cause, as far as his will is concerned, commits murder, even if he does not do so out of fear. Consequently, there is not as much grief as if it had happened, but the sin of the angry person is just as great. So John in his canonical

Eleventh Homily [1]Mt 25:21.

epistle says, "Anyone who hates his brother is a murderer."[2]

See the wisdom of Christ. Wishing to show that he is the God who elsewhere spoke in the Law and who now commands in grace, he now places at the beginning of his commandments that very commandment that he had placed before all others in the Law. First of all it was written in the Law, "You shall not kill."[3] So here at once he begins with murder so that he might be discovered to have been the magistrate of law and gospel through the harmony of the commandments.

"Every one who is angry with his brother without cause shall be liable to judgment."[4]

Therefore everyone who is angry with cause will not be guilty. For if there is no anger, neither does doctrine profit, nor do judgments stand, nor are offenses restrained. A just anger is the mother of discipline. Consequently, not only do they who get angry with cause not sin, but contrariwise, unless they become angry they sin; they sin because an unreasonable patience sows vices, nourishes negligence and invites not only evil people, but even good people, to evil, because an evil person is not corrected, to be sure, even if he is not reproved,[5] but a good person perishes unless he is reproved because evil prevails more in the body[6] than good does. The anger that is with cause is not anger but judgment. Anger is properly understood as a movement of passion. But whoever is angry with cause, his anger does not come from passion but from a cause. So he is said to judge and not to be angry. However, I think that Christ is not speaking of the irascibility of the flesh but of the spirit. Nor is he speaking to the flesh but to the soul, as we will show in what follows. For our Lord knows that even if he commands the flesh, the flesh will not obey him. Nor is it possible that flesh not be disquieted: "For the mind that is set on the flesh is hostile to God; it does not submit to God's law, indeed it cannot."[7] Nor can, as Job says, "man that is born of a woman," full of irritability, not grow angry. Therefore whenever a person grows angry and yet does not wish to do what anger compels him, his flesh is angry, but his mind is not angry. Therefore, there are many whose flesh grows angry, but their soul does not. Again, there are many whose flesh is not angry, but their soul is angry, that is, those who seem patient and quiet and yet secretly think evil and always seek an opportunity to harm.

"Whoever insults[8] his brother shall be liable to the council,"

that is, that it might be one from the council of those who had opposed Christ, just as the apostles are interpreted by their own canonical councils. "And whoever says, 'You fool!' shall be liable to the hell of fire." *Racha* seems to be "empty" in Hebrew, although it is the same to say "fool" and *Racha* as far as the meaning of the word is concerned. For whoever is empty is a fool, and whoever is a fool without doubt is empty, and there seems to be one injury from each word. For just as it is an unworthy thing to say "fool" to him who has spiritual wisdom in himself by his knowledge of God the Father and Christ, so it is an unworthy thing to say that a person is empty who has the Holy Spirit in himself. For nobody is called empty who has the Holy Spirit inside of himself, and nobody is a fool who knows Christ.

And why does the one word, that is, *Racha*, have the punishment of the council, but the other word, "fool," the punishment of hell? For if it is one sin, there ought to be one punishment for both. For inasmuch as it depends on

[2]1 Jn 3:15. [3]Ex 20:13. [4]The author adds "without cause." [5]Alternate reading: "even if he is reproved." [6]PG 56:690 suggests "heart" for "body." [7]Rom 8:7. [8]Literally, "says *Racha* to." See the exegesis below.

the intention of the speaker, these words already have a difference, even if they are similar in meaning. *Racha* was a vulgar word among the Jews, which they were saying not out of anger or hatred or some other vain passion but more out of self-confidence than irritability. For every region has in its usage some word of rebuke, which they are fond of saying to them whose confidence they have, not for the sake of a quarrel but familiarity. For example, when a patron receives his freeman or a wealthy person a pauper or a city dweller a person of the countryside, he despises his character rather than hates him. But perhaps you say, "If *Racha* is not said for the sake of anger, why is it sin?" Because it is said for the sake of contemptuousness rather than edification. For even if the character of that individual seemed contemptible to you, nonetheless the dignity of his Christianity was not contemptible. And if you did not want to look at him, nonetheless you ought to have looked at Christ who is in him.

Then for another reason it is a sin to say *Racha*, because even if a person deserved to hear some empty comment, nonetheless it was not right for you to say some empty comment, as it was written, "I tell you, on the day of judgment men will render account for every careless word they utter."[9] Whatever is not light is darkness; so also whatever is not good is evil. The apostle says, "Let no evil talk come out of your mouths."[10] And he does not add, "but only such as is good," but "only such as is good for edifying." If thus we ought to say not even a good word without cause, unless it is for the opportunity of edification, lest the good word itself be found to be idle and thus made evil, since it is said without cause, how much more ought we not to say that word that by itself is naturally evil and pertains to the injury of the hearer?

Next, shall we use our mouth in the service of vanity, that body part that was created for the edification of others, whether for the use of the body or the glory of God? Every idle speech that is spoken is brought forth as an impure spirit speaks. Therefore, when we say an idle word, not only do we sin because we injure someone through that word, but also we give place to impure spirits in us to do what they want. Because Solomon knew this, he said to the Lord, "Two things I ask of you; deny them not to me before I die: Remove far from me falsehood and lying."[11] If it is a sin and danger to take holy vessels and employ them for private use, as Belshazzar did, who drank in the hallowed chalices and was deprived of his kingdom and his life,[12] if it was dangerous to take these hallowed vessels and employ them for private use in which the true body of Christ was not placed but the mystery of his body is contained therein,[13] how much more ought we not to give the vessels of our body, which God has prepared for himself as a habitation, as a place for the devil to do in them whatever he wants?

"And whoever says, 'Fool.'"

It is commonly understood everywhere, "without cause." That is, one who was angry without cause, who said *Racha* without cause and who said "fool" without cause. If, however, it is not sin to kill with cause, how much more is it not sin to say "fool" with cause? For even an evil word is a certain type of chastisement and is harsher than a whip for a wise person. But what if there were such a reason proffered to be punished not with words but with beatings? Behold also the apostle says "fool" when he says, "O foolish Galatians! Who has bewitched you?"[14] But he did not sin because there was a just reason for him to speak this way. So our Lord spoke to the disciples on the road: "O

[9]Mt 12:36. [10]Eph 4:29. [11]Prov 30:7-8; the archaic language of the RSV has been updated. [12]Dan 5. [13]The words "in which the true body . . . contained therein" were excised by Manhusius for doctrinal reasons. [14]Gal 3:1.

foolish men, and slow of heart!"[15]

[23]***"So if you are offering your gift at the altar."***

Because earlier he had said, "Everyone who is angry with his brother," and "whoever insults his brother," and "whoever says, 'You fool!'" he consequently appends, "So if you are offering your gift at the altar, and there remember that your brother has something against you." He has something, namely, if you were angry at him without cause, if you said *Racha* or "fool" without cause. Therefore, if for these small reasons your brother has been offended and is not pleased with you and it is impossible for an offering to be offered to God or received by him, how will they who mistreat and plunder their brothers and do many other unspeakable things to widows and orphans enter before the face of God?

We ought to know first that as long as faithful people have some dissension among themselves, God cannot be friendly to them, nor is their sacrifice accepted, nor is their prayer heard, or if they have done some other good thing, because nobody situated between two enemies can be a faithful friend to both. For example, if you speak well of the one in the other's hearing, you displease the latter and you are suspected of loving him more; and if you speak well of the latter to the former, you displease him and are suspected of loving him more. So God does not wish to be the friend of the faithful as long as they are hostile to each other, because if he shows mercy to the one, the other is saddened. Even if he is not saddened because he cannot do anything against God, nonetheless he does not rejoice with the other in God's act of kindness toward him. But if he had been able to do something against God, he would have gotten angry at God because he had pitied his enemy. Similarly, if God had shown mercy to the second individual, the first one would be saddened. Consider what sort of conscience God had toward us and how he maintains his faithfulness toward humankind because he loves us perfectly and so does not wish to be a friend to our enemies. For example, you are two faithful people who are enemies; to the degree he does not wish to be friendly to you because he is friendly to him, to the same degree he also does not wish to be friendly to him because he is friendly to you. Therefore, loving you, he is an enemy to him, and, loving him, he is an enemy to you. God accepts our gifts not for his sake but for ours, does he not? God opposes the one while he preserves the conscience of the other; and while he loves both, he does not want to be friend to either because of the hostilities of both. Therefore, since God preserves his faithfulness to us, he does not wish to be a friend of our enemies, and yet we do not keep our faithfulness to him if we love his enemies and hate his friends. Whoever is a friend of the unfaithful and an enemy of the faithful hates the friends of God and loves the enemies of God. But if we were to maintain our faithfulness to the Lord, as he does to us, we would never nurture friendships with unbelievers, and we would never join ourselves in marriage to unbelievers.

[24]***"Leave your gift there before the altar and go; first be reconciled to your brother."***

See the mercy of God, how he looks more at the advantages to people than at his own honors. For if he were regarding his own honors, he would have said, "Meanwhile, offer your sacrifice and later go and be reconciled." Now, however, he says, "Go, first be reconciled to your brother, and then come and offer your gift." It is as if he would say to him, "Go. I am gladly despised and freely suffer the loss of my honor, and I, your Lord, willingly await you my servants, only so that you can come in friend-

[15]Lk 24:25.

ship. Go, then, so that you can know that I love the harmony of my faithful more than sacrifices”—because the sacrifices of humankind do not profit God, but indeed their love effects God’s glory. Do not say, “He harmed me; I did not harm him. He ought to make amends with me, not I with him.” If for the glory of your salvation the Lord orders you to make him your friend, you ought to ask him, even though you have been harmed, so that you might obtain a double glory: first, because you were harmed; second, because you asked first. For if you had harmed that person and so entreated him, God spares what harm you have done because you asked first; nonetheless, you have no reward because you asked when you were guilty. But if he injured you and you asked first, you will have great reward. Hasten then to establish friendship with your enemy before he does, lest by chance, as you are tarrying, he ask you first and seize the reward of piety from your hands. For if he harms you and entreats you, your friendliness is pointless. What sort of righteousness have you done before God, if you were reconciled when he asked you? It is not because God wants you to throw yourself beneath his feet that he orders you to ask first, but it is because he wishes to offer you the glory of humility.

But perhaps you say, “Behold, I wish to be reconciled, but tell me, how will I be reconciled?” The same sort of reconciliation ought to follow as the nature of the offense that preceded it. If you offended by thought, be reconciled in thought. If you offended in words, be reconciled in words. In the same way every sin is committed, in the same way let it be repented of. For example, you thought badly of some Christian; you cannot offer your sacrifice before God because you have the intention of harming him in your heart. Think over again—this time for good—that which you have thought in an evil way and have repented. For the sin of thought is dissolved by its contrary thought. Who says so? The prophet does: “Commune with your own hearts on your beds, and be silent.”[16] Do you see that it belongs to nature to grow angry, but it belongs to one’s nature to pursue anger? If you harmed your brother with words, go and reconcile him wholeheartedly with your words, and you have repented. Aaron attests that the sin of words is dissolved by an apology of words. For when he had made disparaging remarks about Moses, he came and asked him in words, saying, “Oh, my lord, do not punish us because we have done foolishly and have sinned.”[17] But if you have offended someone by your deeds, for example, if you have taken away someone’s money by fraud or some other object by violence, give back to him what you took and you have repented. Zacchaeus attests that the sin of taking an item is atoned for by paying back those things: “Lord, if I have defrauded anyone of anything, I restore it fourfold.”[18] But if you did not take someone’s property but by chance you unjustly punished a weak person, give to him something appropriate for his injury, as it is written in the Law, “If he knocks out the tooth of his slave, male or female, he shall let the slave go free for the tooth’s sake.”[19] According to this it is understood, even if you have punished someone, the sin of injuring him must be atoned by an act of kindness. In general, unless you have placated with deeds him whom you hurt by your deeds, in vain you pray to the Lord, in vain you give alms from your property, which you have robbed from others. How does it help you if someone prays on your behalf to God and another troubles God with remarks against you? Even if God wishes to show mercy to you for the prayer of the former, the latter’s objection does not allow it. It is better that you harm no one, even if you benefit nobody, than to rob some people and clothe others.

[16]Ps 4:4. [17]Num 12:11. [18]Lk 19:8. [19]Ex 21:27.

[25]"Make friends quickly with your accuser, while you are going with him to court, lest your accuser hand you over to the judge, and the judge to the guard, and you be put in prison."

The Lord hastens that we may hasten into friendship with our enemies as long as we live in this life (for the life that is common to all humans is that life in the flesh, through which all people pass, both good and bad), since he knows how dangerous it is if one of our enemies dies before we can make peace; for even if later they wanted to make peace, they cannot, once they have been separated. For if as long as you are on the road of this life you do not make peace with your adversary whom you harmed, but the two of you, still enemies through death, go before Christ the judge, your adversary will hand you over to Christ, arguing at his tribunal that you are guilty, and the judge will hand you over to his servant, that is, the cruel angel of punishments, and he will send you to the prison of hell. But if you had made peace in this age, you would have been able to receive forgiveness for even the gravest misdeed, as it is written, "Love covers a multitude of sins."[20] Once you are condemned and sent to prison, now no longer for grave sins but even for an idle word that you have spoken, that is, if you had said *Racha* to anyone, you must pay the penalty for it. Your adversary will hand you over to the judge, even if he asks you first, for Solomon says, "If your enemy is hungry, give him bread to eat . . . for you will heap coals of fire on his head."[21] What else does "heap coals of fire" mean other than to make someone guilty before God? Accordingly, if someone who shows kindness to an enemy makes him guilty before God, then also he who asks his enemy first makes him guilty before God. Often people in this age are sent to prison for sin, that is, they are sent into various difficulties and tribulations. Often those who sin against people are sent into various tribulations, but we do not perceive it. The troubles of this world are called "prisons."

The Twelfth Homily: On Matthew 5

[27]"You have heard that it was said, 'You shall not commit adultery' [28]But I say to you that every one who looks at a woman lustfully has already committed adultery with her in his heart."

Note another commandment, indeed a very small one among the Jews then and now among all who do not care much about the soul or judge their heart, who think that getting angry with one's neighbors for no reason is not a sin, also do not think that merely lusting after another man's wife is a sin, as long as the work does not follow the lust. But it is a great commandment among those who fear God and judge their heart. It is also a great commandment in God's estimation, who does not look at a person's work as much as his heart. By this commandment the Law is not abolished but fulfilled because without this commandment the commandment of the Law cannot stand. Every adultery arises out of lust. How then will adultery (as per the commandment of the Law) be removed unless lust be cut off (as per Christ's commandment)? Because just as anger is the mother of murder, so lust is the mother of adultery, consequently just as he who is angry at his brother without cause murders him in his heart, even if he does not kill him out of fear of being punished[1] or because of his weakness, and it is homicide in God's eyes (who does not consider the deed more than the desire), so also he who lusts after another man's wife has already committed adultery with her in his heart, even if he has not had her because some reason intervened, and he is also an adulterer in God's eyes (who

[20]1 Pet 4:8. [21]Prov 25:21-22. **Twelfth Homily** [1]Alternate reading: "out of fear of those who see."

looks more at the will than the deed), because he lacked the deed of committing adultery but not the will.

Some people, ignorant of human nature, consider that in general all fleshly nature has been subjected to those passions and there is nobody among mortals, not even among the saints, who is strong enough to separate himself entirely from anger or lust. Lest by chance they think that since Christ is commanding these impossible things, he is seeking an opportunity by which to make people guilty, because everyone who orders impossible things sows occasions for offense and seeks reasons to mete out punishments, so let us discuss a few points about the division of the wills of the soul and body. Just as we have two natures in us, namely, the soul and the flesh, so we have two wills: one of the soul, the other of the flesh. We have two angers: one of the soul, one of the flesh; two lusts: one of the soul and one of the flesh. And the nature of the flesh cannot separate itself from all these. For it holds it necessary to get angry and to lust, even if it does not wish, because it was not brought forth in the power of its own free will. That is to say, it is not now under its free will, as it had been created, but rather under the law of sin. It was sold under sin, for which reason the apostle says of it, "For the mind that is set on the flesh is hostile to God; it does not submit to God's law, indeed it cannot."[2] But the soul was brought forth in the power of its own free will according to the law of the righteousness of God. For that reason it is able both not to become angry, if it wishes, and not to lust, if it wishes.

Therefore, whenever we get angry and lust, if we displease ourselves and hasten to check either our anger or our lust, it is clear that our flesh alone is angry or lusting, not our soul. But whenever we delight ourselves in these things and consider if we are able to fulfill our anger or our lust, then also the soul is getting angry and lusting along with the flesh. For that reason God, who knows that the nature of the flesh was not subjected to him and that it cannot not grow angry, does not command of the flesh the things that he commands. For what wise person would place a precept on him who could not obey, even if he wishes to? But he addresses the soul and commands the soul, which can obey God in all things and which has the ability not to grow angry and not to lust, even if the flesh is growing angry and lusting. Therefore, if he addresses the soul and speaks about the lust of the soul when he says, "Everyone who looks at a woman lustfully has already committed adultery with her in his heart," that is, not "if someone has lusted according to the inevitable desire of the flesh," but rather "if someone desires according to the will and consent of the flesh, pondering and deciding what it can fulfill," such a person (even if he has done nothing) already is an adulterer nonetheless before God, because perhaps he was prevented from the deed, but he was not contrite in his will.

[29]*"If your right eye causes you to sin, pluck it out and throw it away."*

I think that every reward for our righteousness has been made to hinge on our struggling against the flesh all the time, "for the desires of the flesh are against the Spirit, and the desires of the Spirit are against the flesh."[3] The prophet says thus, "I am utterly bowed down and prostrate; all the day I go about mourning. For my loins are filled with burning, and there is no soundness in my flesh."[4] Thus, if according to the prophet there is no soundness in our flesh, how many eyes or how many right hands in his body must he have, so that the penalty of those limbs would suffice for the evil caused by the flesh?

[2]Rom 8:7. [3]Gal 5:17. [4]Ps 38:6-7.

But let us see lest by chance it is possible to understand it in this way about the bodily eye or hand. As long as an entire human being sins, he lives in sin and is dead to righteousness, as it is written, "When you were dead through the trespasses and sins,"[5] but when an individual is converted to righteousness, he lives for righteousness but has died to sin. In the same way, as long as each and every member of the body (for example, the eye) looks bad, it is whole and healthy for sin and is thrown away from righteousness, but when it has ceased to look badly, it has been cast out from sin and made whole and healthy for righteousness. But not even in this way does the interpretation fit. It does not fully explain why he says, "If your right eye causes you to sin." What does that mean? When the right eye causes you to sin, what is the left eye doing? Does it contradict the right eye so that the right eye is thrown away as guilty, while the left eye is preserved on the score that it is innocent? But I think that all these matters apply to the soul, as we said earlier. He calls the mind through which the soul sees the eye of the soul. Elsewhere he speaks about it: "So, if your eye is sound," and so forth.[6] But that fleshly eye is not the eye, but it is the mirror of that inner eye, that is, the mind. The body also has its mind, just as it also has its own soul, as the apostle attests when he speaks about the mind of the soul in this way: "So then, I of myself serve the law of God with my mind, but with my flesh I serve the law of sin."[7] But concerning the mind of the body he speaks thus: "Puffed up without reason by his sensuous mind, and not holding fast to the Head."[8]

The same thing applies to the hand and the foot. A person's right hand is the will of the soul; the left hand is the will of the body. But this bodily hand is not the hand but an organ of that hand. For unless a will (whether good or bad) moves it, it does not move toward anything. And so a person's right hand is the will of the soul, but his left hand is the will of the body. For the parts of the soul are called "right," but those of the body "left," because the soul was created in the power of its own free will, to whatever it wanted to incline, whether to good or evil, and it was created under the law of righteousness so that it might see and hear the correct things and do and walk in them. The parts of the body are called "left," because the flesh was created not in the power of its own free will so as to be able to do whatever it inclines to, whether good or evil, but it was created in evil under the law of sin, and it cannot either see or hear or do anything correctly. So also all the saints are called "right" but sinners "left."

Therefore each of us has a right eye and a left eye: the right is the mind of the soul, but the left is the mind of the flesh. Each of us has a right hand (the will of the soul) and a left hand (the will of the flesh). Therefore, whenever we lust out of the passion of the flesh as people do, but with our mind we resist our lust, the left eye causes us to sin, that is, the mind of the flesh, not the mind of the soul. The left hand causes to sin and not the right hand; that is, the will of the flesh, not the will of the soul. See now that he does not order us to throw away the mind of the flesh or to cut off the will of the flesh. Nor can it be done in such a way that the flesh will ever cease from its evil desire. But we can restrain the desires of the flesh so that we do not do what the flesh desires, while we are still not able to cut it off so that it does not desire. But whenever we wish some evil out of the intention of our soul, then our right hand, that is, our right eye causes us to sin and so does our right-handed will. He orders us to cut off this eye and that hand as much as we can, because the soul is in the power of its own free will, so that it is robust enough to incline to whatever it wants.

[5]Eph 2:1. [6]Mt 6:22. [7]Rom 7:25. [8]Col 2:18-19.

But the flesh is not in the power of its own free will but in the power of evil; it was sold under sin and cannot wish for the good. So the flesh is called "left" and the soul "right" because the flesh was created for us as a temptation but the soul for our salvation.

This is the true interpretation of this passage, as I think. Nonetheless, we can find yet another hue of interpretation. The pondering or consideration of the mind is the eye of the soul, namely, the will to effect some work, and it is the eye that moves the hand to some task. (In this interpretation, the hand of the soul is as we have described it above.) For example, there was a certain religious woman (either a virgin or a widow). I saw her and pondered and said, "I ought to visit that woman diligently so that, if she as a woman should be ignorant of something, I can instruct her and strengthen her in that very good intention." That intention is good, and it is the right eye, but while I diligently visit her, I fall into the trap of desiring her, and that good intention of mine (a right-handed one) became a cause of sin for me. What then ought to be done? Throw out that good intention that had begotten a bad one for me.

Or it may happen in this way. I saw a certain orphan and said, "I ought to take her into my home and raise her until it comes time for her to marry." And I went and began to supply her with whatever was necessary. This is a good work and right-handed. But while I see her in order to take care of her, I have fallen into the trap of longing for her. And that good work of mine, right-handed, has become an occasion for sin for me. Or it might happen this way. Some people who have seen me acting confidently with her have been offended, saying, "What does he want for himself that he speaks so familiarly with the girl?" Therefore I ought to cut off such a good work, which creates evil either for me or for another. For whatever evil it creates for another, it also creates for me because it was brought about through me that another was caused to stumble on my account. And we say these things to make a general principle: in general, we ought to cut off every good thing from us that causes either us or others to sin. For what sort of good is it from which evil arises? It is better that we are saved without one intention or one good work than that we perish with all good works while we are wishing to do good works.

But others interpret this passage differently. They say: Christ wants that we not only are cautious of the danger of our sin as we keep ourselves from every evil desire, but also that our neighbors or someone akin to us may not do something base. For example, you have someone (a son or brother or friend) who looks kindly on your affairs as if he were your own eye and you deem as dear as your right eye. Or you have someone who so cares for your property as your right hand does and so to you he is like your own right hand. And yet if you recognize that he has done something base, cut him off from your soul and throw him away from you because he is causing you to sin because we will give an account not only for our own sin but also for the sin of those closest to us that we are able to restrain, unless we either restrained it or drove them from us. And because all of us Christians are one body and members one of another, it is better that we are saved without one or another member than that we perish with them because we wanted to cling to such people.

31"It was also said, 'Whoever divorces his wife, let him give her a certificate of divorce.' 32But I say to you that every one who divorces his wife, except on the ground of unchastity, makes her an adulteress; and whoever marries a divorced woman commits adultery."

Now he gives a third commandment, a very little one among the undisciplined and lascivious who do not think it to be a sin to divorce a woman with a certificate of divorce, without which the commandment of the Law cannot stand. How? As soon as Moses led the children of Israel out of Egypt, they were Israelites by lineage but Egyptians in their customs. Because of that custom of the Gentiles it happened that a man would hate his wife. And because he was not permitted to divorce her, he was ready to kill her. Or if he did not kill her owing to the fear of the Law, he nonetheless afflicted her with constant tortures. Therefore he ordered them to issue a certificate of divorce, not because it was good but because it was the remedy of a greater evil so that, since they were forbidden to do one evil, they would not do something even worse. Homicide does not take place only in the deed, does it? Does not it also take place in the will? As far as people are concerned homicide takes place by a deed, but as far as God is concerned it takes place in the will. Just as the one who is angry at his brother without any cause, even if he could not kill him, nonetheless kills him in his heart, so also the one who lusts after a woman, even if he had not taken her, has committed adultery with her in his heart because his will was impeded, not corrected. But whoever hates his wife (except because of her fornication) and hates her to such a degree that he divorces her also hates her so that he kills her, unless he had permission to divorce her. He kills her in his heart, as far as God is concerned, because the deed of homicide was lacking but not the will to kill her.

Do you see then that the law that commanded the giving of a certificate of divorce diminished the deed of homicide but not the sin? And not only did it not remove the offense of homicide (as far as God was concerned), but it also introduced another sin, that of divorce. Because the certificate of divorce is a testimony to the dissolved marriage, it is not a just explanation for the dissolved marriage, is it? Therefore when the certificate is given, the dissolved marriage is indeed made public, but the sin of the dissolution is heightened all the more.

Nonetheless, when he spoke about getting angry without reason and about not lusting, he aptly brought in the commandment about not divorcing women. For if the one who is angry at his brother without cause is guilty at the judgment, how will he not be guilty who so hated his wife (who was not guilty of any fornication) that he sent her away?

But you say, "My wife has many faults." What? You yourself are without fault? If we ought to bear with the imperfections of those outside our family, as the apostle says, "Bear one another's burdens, and so fulfill the law of Christ,"[9] how much more ought we to bear the imperfections of our wives? If someone sees a woman so as to lust after her, he commits adultery with her in his heart; how will he not be condemned for adultery who divorces his wife and gives her the opportunity to commit adultery, so that she commits adultery with another man and the other man with her? For a Christian man ought not only not make himself guilty, but also not give an opportunity for others to make themselves guilty. Otherwise, their offense would overflow into the sin of him who had become the reason for the others to commit their offense.

See also that those who give a certificate of divorce in accordance with the Law commit four iniquities: first, there is homicide as far as God is concerned; second, he did not divorce a woman who was committing fornication; third, he made her commit adultery; fourth, also the one who married her commits adultery. None of these things is done wherever Christ's commandment is kept.

33"Again you have heard that it was said to the men of old, 'You shall not swear falsely, but shall perform to the Lord what you have sworn.' 34But I say to you, Do not swear at all."

[9]Gal 6:2.

Behold a fourth commandment, which the greedy think to be a very little one, who do not think that to swear honestly is a sin, without which the commandment of the Law cannot stand. For unless an oath is forbidden, perjury cannot be curtailed. For it is from an oath that perjury is born. For there is nobody who swears frequently and yet does not sometimes commit perjury. For this reason Solomon admonishes, "Do not accustom your mouth to oaths, for there are many ways to stumble by it."[10] For just as those who make it their custom to speak many things must also speak importune things sometimes, and whoever makes it his custom to strike with his hand must also sometimes strike unjustly, so those who make it their custom to swear in private matters often also must commit perjury, even against their will, in trivial matters, since their custom induces them to do so. For we do our habit in all matters whenever we wish, but we do not reject it whenever we wish. And Solomon teaches what the sentiment of God is against those who take oaths: "a man who swears many oaths will be filled with iniquity, and the scourge will not leave his house."[11] Thus, if the scourge does not depart from those who swear, how will it ever depart form those who commit perjury?

Tell me, friend, how does it help you to swear? If your opponent believed that you would swear honestly, he would never have forced you to take an oath, but because he thinks you would commit perjury he forces you to swear. And when you swear, he does not keep silent because he is pleased with the truthfulness of your oath, but he leaves as if he had been vindicated by the condemnation of your perjury. For an oath never has a good outcome. Some will think that you have sworn because of greed, and others will think that you have committed perjury. Those who want to think well of you, even if they do not believe that you have committed perjury, nonetheless cannot affirm that you have sworn in truth. Nobody can defend you on the score that you have also acted piously. Consequently, when you swear, you come into opprobrium with your enemies but under suspicion among your friends.

But perhaps you say, "What will I do? He does not believe me or wish to believe me unless I take an oath." Rather lose your money than your salvation. Let your soul seem more valuable to you than your property. If you lose a portion of your property, you can still live, but if you lose God, how will you live? Or do you not know that for whatever you lose unwillingly because you fear God you will have a greater reward than if you had given alms? We are more worthily crowned for whatever we do with a greater struggle.

Behold, friend, I admonish you not to ever compel someone to take an oath. If you think that he is sworn honestly, withdraw from him, or if you think that he has sworn dishonestly, withdraw all the more from him, because even if he has sworn honestly, you have become a reason for his perjury as far as your conscience is concerned because you forced him to take an oath with the intention of having him not swear, but commit perjury. But if you thought that he would swear honestly, you would not have compelled him even to take an oath.

You fool, who forces another to swear, you do not know what you are doing! Even if he commits perjury, he may well commit perjury to his profit, but you are found to be a participant in his perjury without any profit. Whoever does not hesitate to lie also does not hesitate to commit perjury, for whoever lies transgresses the truth in his heart; but whoever commits perjury violates God in his words. What difference is there between violating God and transgressing the truth, since God is truth itself? This alone is the differ-

[10]Sir 23:9 (trans. Kellerman). [11]Sir 23:11.

ence: we violate the truth when we lie in our heart, but we violate God with words when we commit perjury, for we satisfy people with a word but God with our conscience. God, who forbade us to commit perjury, also commanded us later not even to swear. Therefore whoever does not fear to neglect the commandment of God in taking an oath will also not fear it in committing perjury. But what do you want? He fears God or he does not fear God. If he fears him, he does not lie, even without an oath. But if he does not fear him, neither can he say the truth with an oath.

Listen, you clergy, who offer the holy Gospels to those taking oaths, how are you able to give no heed to that oath, when you are planting the seed of perjury?[12] He who carries the fire from which a conflagration is set ablaze is not exempt from responsibility for that conflagration, is he? Or is not he who offers a sword by which a homicide is committed an ally of that murder? So also those who offer an opportunity of perjury are a colleague of that perjury. If it were right to swear honestly, you would rightly say, "We give them the gospel so that they can swear, not so that they can commit perjury," but now because you know that it is a sin even to swear honestly, how can you be free when you give an opportunity when sin is committed against God?[13] Let the fire cease, and the conflagration does not come into existence. Take away the sword, and no homicide is committed. So take away the oath, and there is no perjury.

These things are spoken about those who swear by God. The iniquity of those who swear by the elements is all the more damnable. God created heaven and earth and everything else for himself, not for something for people to swear by. Note that in the law it is commanded not to swear by anyone except by God. Therefore whoever swears by heaven or earth, or whatever it is by which he swears, turns it into a god. For that reason everyone who swears by God through some other object turns himself into an idolater, even if it were right to have taken an oath, because he did not give his oaths to the Lord his God but to the elements, and so he doubly sinned: first, because he swore; second, because he deified that through which he swore.

And see how he explains element by element, why someone ought not to swear by the elements.

"Do not swear either by heaven, for it is the throne of God,

that is, it is not God,

35or by the earth, for it is his footstool,"

that is, not a goddess,

"or by Jerusalem, for it is the city of the great King,"

that is, not the great King himself.

36"And do not swear by your head, for you cannot make one hair white or black."

And of what importance are you that you swear by yourself? You do not have the power even to make one black hair white or a white one black, do you? Therefore, whether someone swears by his own children or by himself or by anyone else, he makes that individual greater than God, at least in his own eyes.

38"You have heard that it was said, 'An eye for an eye and a tooth for a tooth.' 39But I say to you, Do not resist one who is evil."

This fifth commandment is very trivial, as far as those cruel people are concerned, who think that they do not sin if they return evil for evil,

[12]Alternate reading: "when you give a holy object to perjurers?" [13]This sentence was excised by Manhusius for doctrinal reasons.

since they do not consider what is said in the psalm: "If I have requited my friend with evil or plundered my enemy without cause."[14] Let Christians know that if they requite those who pay them with evil, they will suffer all those things the psalmist reckons that he deserved to have suffered, if he had paid back evil to those who were requiting evil to them. For such vain people are about to be killed by their enemies; their enemy will persecute them and lay hold of them and trample their life on their earth and turn their glory into the dust.

Nonetheless, without this very small commandment the commandment of the Law cannot stand. How? The law that commands an eye for an eye and a tooth for a tooth has this intention that each one would spare his neighbor's limbs since he fears for his own and so no evil person will be found. But woe to the world because of its offenses! As long as we live in this world, which the devil rules, cursers, strikers and persecutors must abound. Therefore if we begin to repay evil for evil to everyone in accordance with the command of the Law, both the purpose of the Law has been removed and it makes even good people evil, although it wished to make evil people good. But if in accordance with Christ's commandment resistance is not given to the evil person, even if evil people are not harmed, nonetheless the good remain good, and thus through the commandment of Christ also the commandment of the Law is fulfilled. For whoever fulfills the commandment of the Law does not at the same time also fulfill that of Christ, but whoever fulfills the command of Christ also at the same time fulfills that of the Law. For example, whoever strikes someone acts contrary to the Law. But whoever strikes back acts according to the Law but not according to the commandment of Christ. But whoever according to the commandment of Christ does not strike back even when struck has tacitly also fulfilled the will of the Law. For whoever has not struck back when struck all the more did not strike at the beginning—because Christ did not come to abolish the Law but to fulfill it.

But you say that the one who struck you contrary to the Law deserves to be struck back. True. But you do not deserve to be the one to strike back because you are the disciple of that one who, when reviled, did not revile in reply and who, when struck, did not strike in return and who, when crucified, prayed for those crucifying him. If you strike back, then first you deny that you are a disciple of Christ, not by your words but by your deeds. Then when you have gouged out his eye for your eye and broken his tooth for your tooth, your body part will not thereby be restored in its own place, will it? Thus, if you do not repay evil for evil, even if you have lost a part of your body, you will obtain the reward of patience. But if you pay him back, you suffer the loss of your body and of your salvation.

"But if any one strikes you on the right cheek, turn to him the other also."

You see, the devil does not rejoice so much in the wounding of a human body, but more in the wounding of a soul. Therefore he stirs up someone to strike you so that when you are stirred up and strike him you may sin, and in one blow he can wound you both. For he knows that a wound in the body is quickly healed, but the wound of the soul can scarcely be healed in some people even with great labor, and in other people it can be healed. Therefore, if you strike him, at first glance you seem to have overcome him, but in reality you have been overcome by the devil. And you think that you have taken your fill of him, but in reality the devil has taken his fill of you. But if you do not strike him back, you seem indeed to have been overcome by a human,

[14]Ps 7:4.

but you have overcome the devil.

These things accord well with the righteousness of God. But let us see how they also accord well with fleshly usefulness. Now if you strike him back, you have not restrained him so that he will not strike you, have you? But instead you have provoked him so that he will keep on striking you. For anger is not restrained by anger but is provoked all the more. It is just as if you join one fire with another, a greater flame is kindled, but if you do not strike him back, he will soon stand still. If he is indeed wise, he will be confounded; but if he is not wise, he will have had his fill, and not only will he not strike you again, but perhaps he will be stung in his heart and repent that he struck you even once. Nonetheless, even if he is so angry that he does not understand your patience so that he is confounded in his deed, you would not be able to punish him more than God will avenge you, would you? And so if you strike him back, you have lost the claim to being avenged because you have avenged yourself, and you have freed him from the hands of God because you paid him back what he had done. Therefore, if you get very angry, endure it more patiently that you might be avenged better, namely, through God.

40"*And if any one would sue you and take your coat, let him have your cloak as well.*"

First, it is not an appropriate matter for a faithful individual to stand at court before the sight of an unbelieving judge. For even if he is not an unbeliever, certainly he is secular. And he who ought to have respected you because of the nobility of your faith now judges you because of the exigencies of the lawsuit, and you lose the nobility of Christ for the sake of the world's business. Is it not better that you lose earthly property rather than eternal glory? For if you lose your property for Christ's sake, Christ can restore it to you, but if you lose Christ for the sake of property, it cannot restore Christ to you. Next, it is necessary that you humble yourself before the judge and that you become submissive to him for the sake of the exigencies of the lawsuit. And perhaps you who would not humble yourself for God's sake will humble yourself for the sake of profit and make property dearer than God. Third, every judgment is an incitement of the heart and of evil thoughts. As soon as you have entered into court, you no longer desire that the truth of the case may appear but that somehow or another you may come out the winner. But if you see that your suit, as often takes place in trials, is being assaulted by words or trickery or money, it is necessary that you hasten to help your case either by words or trickery or money. And if you did not have advice to do so from the beginning, the necessity of the very controversy will force you to do so later. For at first you were only hastening for gain, but afterwards you vie even for shamelessness. And you are even more content to sin, provided only that you win, than to be overcome, provided only that you do not sin.

God commanded these things to those who love God more than the world. For whoever thinks that the profit of the soul is great thinks that the loss of property is trivial, for whoever thinks that the loss of property is great thinks that the profit of the soul is very little. Therefore whoever thinks that it is more difficult to let go of something than to enter the court also thinks that it is more difficult to leave the court without sin. For it is easier to let go of something before the court than it is for the court to avoid sin. For before the court, as we said, one condition (greed) compels you, but after it has begun another condition (shamelessness) compels you. And how could you, who could not overcome one condition out of the fear of God, overcome two conditions? Therefore just as Joseph let go of his cloak in the hand of the adulterous woman and fled with the better cloak of chastity, so also you cast off your cloak into the hands of the false accuser and flee with the better garment of righteousness, lest by chance you lose the most precious clothing of the soul while you wish to win back the clothing of your body.

Thus, if the unbelievers see that you, a Christian, repay more oppressive injuries for injuries received in behalf of earthly property and that you go so far as to agitate secular courts against an unjust thief, even to the peril of your soul, how can they believe that the hope of a heavenly kingdom is true, which Christians proclaim? Those who hope for heavenly things easily spurn earthly things. But as for whoever greatly embraces earthly things, I do not know if they firmly believe the heavenly things that have been promised. Therefore we ought to endure and not oppose him who takes from us what belongs to us—not only because of the wound that strikes our souls but also as a demonstration of the indubitable promises of Christ, so that he who sees that you are neglecting your own injuries and despising earthly property as if it were nothing may understand that the hope of Christians is most certain in heaven, more precious than all earthly things and a more pleasant life than all enjoyment of that carnal life.

41 ***"And if anyone forces you to go one mile, go with him two miles."***

This is so that your patience might overcome his cruelty and you may show that the kindness of God is greater in his saints than the malice of the devil is in unjust people. But if you go only as far as he compels you, how can you be recognized as a servant of God? For goodness does not appear in necessity. Therefore whatever he compels you, go because of the force employed by a violent person; but whatever he does not compel you, go because of the glory of a kindly God. If you go one mile, he thinks that you have done as any such person would, and he does not repent that he has impressed you into service; but if you go beyond, he understands that you are a servant of God, and so he begins to regret that he has impressed you into the service for one mile, and this addition of yours does not turn out to be a greater help for him but rather a punishment of his earlier audacity.

Therefore whoever gives much money fulfills both the law and grace. For whoever gives freely of his own goods also does not all the more steal another person's goods. Thus a rich person cannot be tested or tried by suffering because nobody will quickly do any violence to him; but he is tested and tried in his generosity. Again, a poor person cannot be tested and tried by generosity because he does not have the means to be generous, and so he is tested and tried by suffering, if his kindness is not changed by an injury.

Finally, if we wish to consider the truth and understand the reason: our riches are not ours but God's. God wanted us to be distributors, not lords, of his wealth. And so he gives it to whomever he wishes and removes it from whomever he wishes. That is appropriately called ours that is in our power to have, if we wish. But how can that be called ours that we cannot have, even if we want it, unless it has been given to us? Then consider why he entrusted wealth to you rather than to your friend. He did not make you out of one lump of clay and him out of another lump of clay, did he? And he did not hand over Christ for your sake but one of the angels for your friend's sake, did he? If he loved your friend as much as you in all things, then he did not give you riches for you to hold onto them but so that you could be tested by them. So the apostle admonished, "As for the rich in this world, charge them not to be haughty, nor to set their hopes on uncertain riches but . . . to be rich in good deeds, liberal and generous."[15]

[15] 1 Tim 6:17-18.

For the poor person is better in his holiness than you are in worldly matters. Your property is advantageous for keeping him alive in this age, so that his holiness might be advantageous to keep you in the age to come, just as a fruitless elm gives its sap to the vine and the vine bears fruit for itself and for the elm.

Therefore Christ orders us to lend money, but not with interest, because he who makes a loan with interest at first glance appears to give, but in reality he is not giving his own goods but is taking away somebody else's. For he seems to help someone's need, but in reality he is casting him into greater need. He releases him from one chain and binds him with many. And he does not give for the sake of God's righteousness but because of his own gain. Money lent at interest is similar to the bite of an adder. Just as one who is struck by an adder goes to sleep in delight, as it were, and so he tarries in the sweetness of drowsiness, so also he who receives money lent at interest is delighted for a while, as if he were receiving an act of kindness, and so he does not perceive how he has been made a captive by the sweetness of this "act of kindness." Just as the poison of the adder secretly runs through all his limbs and destroys them, so usury runs through all of his possessions and converts them into a debt. Just as the little yeast that is mixed into much flour leavens the whole lump and draws it toward itself and makes it all leavened, so whenever usury enters into someone's home, it draws his whole property toward itself and converts it into debt.

The Thirteenth Homily: On Matthew 5 and 6

43 "You have heard that it was said, 'You shall love your neighbor and hate your enemy.' 44 But I say to you, Love your enemies."

Notice this sixth commandment that fulfills the Law, which is thought to be a very small commandment among hateful people and those who hate in return, who are not ashamed to pronounce with a wicked voice that one ought to hate one's enemy. But if it were right to hate our enemies, God never would have taken you, an enemy from the Gentiles, into his love. For you he led even his own Son through all the shame of human suffering, even to the point of death,[1] he adopted you his enemy, he made you an heir with his only-begotten Son—and you do not wish to give pure love to your enemy? But what is astonishing, if he seems to them to love seriously his enemies who do not even keep a pure conscience with their own friends? For as long as this world exists full of scandals, if they wish to love only their friends, they will not be able to find anyone to love. Today one person offends the other in some such matter; tomorrow the latter will offend the former in another matter; and so it happens that if someone has decided to hate his enemies, he must hate all people and be hated by all. You see that just as murder arises from anger and adultery from lust, so even the love of friends is cut off by the hatred of enemies. But if you sustain him who is an enemy for a while, you will love him as a friend shortly thereafter, once he has been overcome by your kindness.

I think that Christ commanded those things not so much for our enemies as for us—not because they are worthy to be loved by another but because we are not worthy to hate another. Hate is a spirit of darkness, and wherever it settles in, it besmirches the beauty of holiness.[2] Therefore he orders us to love our enemies not so much in order that we love them as in order that we drive away from us whatever is evil. And so I will not say, "If you wound your enemy," but "if you merely hate him," you have harmed yourself in your soul

Thirteenth Homily [1]Alternate reading: "For you he handed over even his own Son to shame through all the events of human suffering, even to the point of death." [2]Alternate reading: "beauty of health."

more than you have harmed him in his body. And perhaps you do not harm him at all by hating him, but you wound yourself without a doubt. Therefore, if you spare your enemy, you have spared yourself more fully than you have spared him. And if you have acted kindly toward him, you have benefited yourself more than him.

I will mention again what I said earlier: to those who do not know the mystery of human nature, it seems impossible to love one's enemy. And it is truly impossible as far as the nature of the flesh is concerned because it lies under the control of the passions. But as far as the soul is concerned, it is possible because it is under the sway of its own judgment and can rule and restrain the flesh from its passions. For the soul would never rule the flesh with its passions if the soul itself were subjected to the passions. I think this commandment is just like the command "But I say to you, do not look at a woman lustfully"; it was not spoken by God to the nature of the flesh, which cannot achieve the state of not desiring what is his own, but to the soul, which is able not to desire. For whenever someone is stirred up by the impulses of his body, his will nonetheless does not incline to do the work that he is being urged to do, but with steady intention, self-restraint and the working of righteousness, he breaks the irrational impulses of his body. And if he desires with his body, his mind does not desire, but if he agrees to fulfill what he is thinking, then he truly is said to desire with his mind. So also in this place: the flesh indeed cannot love its enemy, just as it is not even possible to not feel an injury inflicted on oneself, but the soul can love one's enemy, because the soul's love and hatred lie in its feelings, but the soul's love and hatred lies in its understanding. For this reason the soul changes according to reason, but the flesh is held unchangeable in its experience. The soul is free and under God's reign, but the flesh is captive and under the lordship of the devil, just as also the world is, which has been placed in wickedness, because also the flesh itself is of this world.

Therefore whenever we are injured by someone, even if we hate him, we do not nonetheless follow up on our hatred, because we consider the righteousness of God and instead break up the impulses of our grief and bless him and act kindly toward him. I recognize that indeed our flesh, which cannot love once it has been hurt, hates our enemy, but our soul loves our enemy. Otherwise, if each and every person were to consider the impulses of his own flesh, he would be found to do no good, because we fulfill every good, while the nature of our flesh opposes it and we ourselves contradict our flesh. Next, if you begin to consider that whoever injures you innocently is possessed and led by the devil and that the devil fulfills his own will through the agency of the one who harmed you, not only will you not get angry at him but you will further have pity on him—and pity will stir up feeling for him.

Therefore, do you wish to love your enemy? If you suffer an injury, do not look at the present injury, but consider the glory that you will obtain as a reward on Judgment Day. If you want to bear it calmly, if you suffer a loss, do not look at this loss but at that gain that comes from your suffering. All this seems difficult to those who do not hope for the reward of the coming judgment.

"And do good to those who hate you."[3]

Since our Lord knew that the flesh's love (where it had not existed earlier) arises from acts of kindness done in the flesh and is also nourished by them (where it had existed earlier), so he orders us to do good to our enemies in order that their hatreds might be

[3]The author (like the Vulgate) adds this phrase in the middle of verse 44 before "and pray for those who persecute you."

restrained by our acts of kindness. For if a friendship which had not previously existed arises out of giving and receiving, consequently also every enmity is restrained by the diligence of kind acts. Therefore do good to those who hate you that they might judge themselves by your kindness that they unjustly hate you.

"And pray for those who persecute you."

Praying for your enemies, we commend not so much them as ourselves to God, and we are heard all the more when we pray for our enemies than when we pray for ourselves. For whoever prays for himself does not pursue a work of grace but of nature. For who does not pray for himself? But whoever prays for his enemy is worthily heard because he is pursuing a work of grace.

45"So that you may be sons of your Father who is in heaven; for he makes his sun rise on the evil and on the good, and sends rain on the just and on the unjust."

He carefully put the sentence in order when he said, "on the just and on the unjust," not "on the unjust and on the just," because God gives all good things on earth not for the sake of all people but for the sake of the few holy ones. For he is more content for sinners to enjoy the good gifts of God contrary to what they deserve than for the righteous to be robbed of his good gifts contrary to what they deserve. Likewise, whenever the Lord is provoked by sinners, he sends his punishment not for the sake of good people but rather because of sinners alone; nonetheless, it equally touches the righteous as much as sinners. For just as he does not separate sinners from the righteous in good matters, so he does not separate the righteous from sinners in evil matters.

"So that you may be sons of your Father."

By what other measure will it be known that we are children of God except that we were like God? Often children in the flesh imitate their parents in the flesh, either in appearance or manner of speaking or way of laughing or in some token of the body. But spiritual children imitate their Father in holiness. And even if children in the flesh are like their parents, they do not deserve any praise, and if they are unlike them, they deserve no censure because it is not in the power of humankind to determine what bodily trait they will inherit. But the children of God must be praised if they are like him, but they are to be censured harshly if they are unlike him, because the capacity of doing righteousness is in the power of each and every person.

46"For if you love those who love you, what reward have you? Do not even the tax collectors do the same?"

Whoever loves his friends loves them because of himself, not because of God, and so he has no reward, for that very love of his delights him. But whoever loves his enemy does not do so because of himself but because of God; therefore he has a great reward because he opposes his own impulses. For wherever a work is sown, there the fruit is harvested.

48"You, therefore, must be perfect, as your heavenly Father is perfect."

Whoever loves his friend does not commit a sin, to be sure, but he does not work righteousness. It is half a good deed for a person to depart from evil and yet not follow good; but it is a perfect good deed not only to flee evil but also to do the good. So he says, "You must be perfect," so that you will both love your friends in order to avoid sin and love your enemies in order to hold to righteousness, because the former frees one from punishment, but the latter leads to glory, nor is it a complete image of

God that does not imitate God in his works.

6:1 *"Beware of practicing your piety before men in order to be seen by them."*

In the earlier verses Christ commanded us to love our enemies and do good to them. Since he saw that a trap of the devil lay hidden in the very act of kindness, which is accustomed to destroy the fruit of good works (for in the same way that the vain nature of the flesh is difficult at first to do any good, so even if it does something good it easily turns to boasting about the good deed), Christ for this reason instructs in this part by saying, "Beware of practicing your piety before people" so that your good might not benefit you by serving your vanity but by being useful for your salvation. Because he understood that among humans this is more dangerous than all fleshly vices, he commanded us to be aware of this more carefully when he said, "Beware of practicing your piety before people," because almost all evils harass the servants of the devil. But a desire of vainglory assails not only the servants of the devil but even the servants of God and faithful people; in fact, it assails the servants of God more than the servants of the devil. For wherever a glorious matter is being carried out, there an opportunity for boasting more readily finds room.

"Beware."

But what shall we attend to? Shall we seek a secret place where there are no people? But how does it help if people were not in a place but a vain thought was in your heart? Therefore it is better that a vain thought not be present in your heart than that there be no people in a place. Thus, if we ought to attend to our heart, we must not look with carnal eyes but keep watch over the heart with our perception, for the serpent for whom we are ordered to keep watch is invisible and slippery and secretly enters into our senses and seduces them. So the filthy flesh cannot see him, but a pure soul can. Just as if there is a modest amount of dirt in a clean and splendid place, it appears from afar, but if the place itself is dirty, no matter how much dung lies there, it is not apparent, nor can it be asked if there is any dung there when the whole place is dung, so also if the creeping of the enemy draws near to a pure heart, a just person soon discerns that his own heart is being attacked by a foreign spirit. But if the heart is full of wickedness, it does not readily understand the prompting of the devil inside of himself. How then is he to understand the entrance of him who always resides in him? And so earlier he said first, "Do not become angry, do not lust, do not swear, do not pay back evil for evil, do not hate your neighbor," because one who is subject to all those evils cannot attend to his heart or understand the devil's seduction in it, because a blemish quickly is spotted in a piece of white clothing but is not quickly spotted in a black piece of clothing, even if the whole garment is dirty. And how can it happen that we do not practice our piety before people or notice that we are doing it? If a poor person runs up to you while someone else is present, how can alms be given to him secretly? For even if what is given is not seen, nonetheless it is obvious that he is being given something, as you take him to the side.

But notice that he did not say only "before people," but added, "in order to be seen by them." Therefore whoever does not do it to be seen by people, even if he did it before people, nonetheless appears not to have done it before people. Therefore, if it is not possible to give alms in such a way that nobody sees or perceives it, it is possible to do it with the intention that we are not seen by people. The Lord says, "Let your light so shine before people, that they may see your good works."[4] There-

[4] Mt 5:16.

fore, just as a lamp cannot be hidden once it has been lit, so neither can a work of righteousness be hidden.

Therefore the alms that are seen by people are not displeasing to God, but only those that have been given in order to be seen by people. For example, everyone who does some task considers in his heart also the person for whose sake he does that which he is doing. You make a letter so that you can greet your friend; as long as you are writing you always see in your heart the personage of that friend for whom you are writing the letter. Another example: an artisan holds his project in his hand and always has before his eyes the one who commissioned the project to be done by him, while he thinks how he ordered him to make it. So also he who gives alms for God's sake sees nobody in his heart except the person of God alone for whose sake he gives it. So even if it happens that he does it while some people are present, nonetheless his mind does not see those people, even if he himself is seen by them.

Have not you ever gone down a road while thinking about something and been seen by many people, but you yourself saw nobody, because you were intent on that which you were thinking about? This is because the mind can see apart from the body all by itself what it is thinking, but the body cannot see anything without the mind. Therefore likewise the reverse can happen: someone gives alms with nobody present, and yet he seems to have acted as if people were present. For example, he who gives alms because of people, that is, he who desires to be seen by people, always sees the visages of people in his heart. Thus even if it happens that nobody is present when he does it, he still seems to have done it before people because his heart saw the visages of people.

"For then you will have no reward from your Father who is in heaven."

He both gives the commandment and establishes the punishment so that even if the love of righteousness does not hold onto human vanity, at least fear of loss of reward might hold it back. The Lord knows that the nature of the flesh was subdued by vanities because everyone delights to appear to others, as far as the flesh is concerned. Nor can it happen that the flesh, which was born of vanity, would not itself be a lover of vanity; nor would the Lord admonish us not to do anything before people unless he knew that all people want to do things before people. Who commands someone, "Do not commit fornication," unless he understands him to be lascivious? Who orders someone, "Do not be drunk," unless he recognizes him to be drunk? So also the admonition of Christ to flee vanity is proof of human vanity. Even if the vain flesh desires vanity and an earthly creature seeks its glory on earth because the earthly nature cannot long for heavenly glory, Christ commands nonetheless that the soul, which arose from truth, can flee earthly vanity. The flesh was made subject to the soul, not the soul to the flesh. For the flesh can strive against the soul but cannot overcome it unless the soul itself has agreed to be overcome. The soul also strives against the flesh and overcomes it. Therefore he who does something wholeheartedly because of other people appears to have done it because of other people, but a vain thought has ascended above his heart, desiring to appear to people, but he whose soul understood it and opposed the vain thoughts and drove away the counsel of his flesh does not seem to have done it because of other people, since he indeed wanted to do it as far as his flesh was concerned but not according to his soul. And what he thought was the passion of the flesh, but what he chose was the judgment of the soul. For if we say that alms given because of the vain desire of the flesh is displeasing, no good deed of people can be acceptable before God, since a person can do no good deed freely, but we always do good against the evil desires of the flesh.

Who is the chaste person? It is not he who has never lusted, is it? Far from it: it is he who overcomes his lust. Who is the tame person? It is not he who does not grow angry, is it? Far from it: it is he who restrains his anger. So the one who seems to give alms for God's sake is not one who does not desire human glory but rather one who shatters human glory by the opposition of his soul. Otherwise in every good work we would not have any reward, unless we are urged on by contrary evils through the flesh. In every good work a snare of the devil has been placed, as it has been written about the demons: "By the wayside they have set snares for me."[5] Thus a good work itself is not secure, if it is alone, but it is placed next to an evil work and always tested and tried. For just as wherever there is wheat, weeds must also be found there, so wherever there is a good work of God, there also is a trap of the enemy.

What shall we do then? You intended to give alms, but the desire to appear before others entered into your heart. Should you withdraw your hand so that you do not give way to a vain thought and say to yourself, "It is better not even to do good lest I be found to have done it for the sake of other people"? Far from it! Instead, complete your work lest you lose the good work while you wish vainly to resist the thought. Let what our Lord said about the wheat and the weeds come into your mind: "Lest in gathering the weeds you root up the wheat along with them, let both grow together until the harvest."[6] The wheat is the good will that God planted in humankind. The weed is an evil thought that the devil sowed through the flesh. Therefore because an evil desire also clings to every good will, if you wish fully to remove your evil thought, you would also remove the good work. For the devil planted his own weeds in the wheat of God with the intention that his shameless weeds might choke out the wheat of God—or if someone wishes to remove the weeds of the devil he will at the same time uproot also the wheat of God. Has a celibate man or a virgin already fallen as soon as he or she has lusted? As long as they have not lusted with their full will so as to wish to fulfill their lust, but if instead they have lusted out of the exigency of the flesh and have opposed their own lust, then they have not sinned, but the outcome is all the more glorious because they overcame the temptation as though they had not been smitten by temptation.

Therefore, what does the Scripture say? "Allow both to ripen," that is, "Complete your work and lead it to perfection." In this way that vain thought is dried out like a weed, that is, it is emptied and perishes, but the good work like wheat remains. For thus you will understand if that vain desire came about from your own will or from the exigencies of the flesh. If it was from your own will, you are grieved if nobody sees you giving alms, but if you rejoice later that your alms were given silently, know that your desire came not from your mind but from the exigencies of the flesh—and so it dried up like a weed. Likewise a celibate person can test his lust. If what he lusted after came from his mind, and if he still has the will to sin even after the lust has passed, then his lust came from his will. But if he rejoices because the enemy did not prevail against him with lust but instead his lust was defeated and withdrew, let him understand that the weed arose from the exigencies of the flesh and it was not the will of his mind.

"For then you will have no reward from your Father who is in heaven."

What will you who have given nothing to God receive from God? For whatever is given for God's sake is given to God and received

[5]Ps 140:5. [6]Mt 13:29-30.

from him. But whatever is done for people's sake is scattered to the winds and hoped for by nobody. What else is the praise of people than the sound of winds passing by? People have ceased to speak, and a person has lost its fruit because he did it for the sake of people, in order to be praised by them. But what is wisdom: to give wealth and to run after idle words, or to despise the reward from God that would remain forever in heaven and to choose the fleeing orations of people?

It is better not to do something than to do it for people's sake. Whoever does not do something, even if he does not find anything in heaven, at least he does not lose something on earth. But whoever does something for people's sake both loses something on earth and finds nothing in heaven. Or look at the person from whom you await praise. What does he think about you? He praises you because he thinks that you are doing this for God's sake. But if he were to understand that you are doing it to please him, he would not praise you but scorn you all the more. Why, then, do you hasten to please him who would mock you if ever he understood you? So is the individual who does good to please people: he is like an evil hireling who devours all his pay within the time of his contract; when the time is up and he leaves, he departs destitute. So he who desired to receive the reward of all his good deeds in this age[7] goes empty to God.

2"*Thus, when you give alms, sound no trumpet before you, as the hypocrites do.*"

Truly he is a hypocrite who acts to please people. He has one thing in his heart and shows something else in his deed. He does something because of people's need, or so it appears, and he appears merciful, but in his heart he behaves because of his vainglory and is a merchant of vainglory. The trumpet is every act or deed through which boasting about the deed is made known. Think of one who gives alms whenever he sees someone present but does not do so otherwise. This is a trumpet because his boast is proclaimed through this. Again, he who gives alms when someone intercedes but does not do so when there is no intercessor—this behavior is a wicked trumpet. Moreover, whoever gives alms if he sees a more trustworthy individual who can report the matter (even if he gives alms secretly) and gives nothing to a pauper who is bound in his passions—this too is a trumpet. Even if it took place in secret, it nonetheless was with the intention that he might seem praiseworthy: first, because he did it; second, because he hid it; the very act of hiding it is the trumpet of his alms. A trumpet is that which a person does through which it appears (or he wants it to appear) that he has done it because through that very thing the alms cry out about themselves while it takes place. So it is not only the place or the deed that must be safeguarded, but rather the hidden will. For in every fleshly act the devil can accomplish some deceit, but the conscience is the only place where deceit cannot be brought about, because we persuade other people, but we are an open book to God.

Does not everyone know that it is vain to wish to be seen by others? But such a person is compelled to love that which he understands to be vain. What can be more wretched than human nature? Every animal can love that which it understands to be good for itself and to hate that which it understands to be bad. Humankind alone is forced to love that which it understands to be evil and to hate that which it understands to be good, for it has two natures at war inside of itself. Whatever pleases the flesh displeases the soul, and whatever pleases the soul displeases the flesh, so that, as Job says, our whole life is one of struggle. But if all our

[7]Literally, "in the age." Alternate reading: "of this world."

life is a struggle, all our life is also profitable.

[3]*"But when you give alms, do not let your left hand know what your right hand is doing."*

We have already noted that these things were spoken to the soul, not the flesh, a fact that this sermon clearly states. Otherwise, as far as the body is concerned, how could the left hand not know what the right hand is doing, since both hands were created to help each other, so that one hand serves the other and one would not readily find something that can be done by one hand without the other? But as we said above, the right hand is the will of the soul, always striving for the good. The left hand is the will of the flesh, always opposed to God. Therefore let the left hand (the will of the flesh) not know what the will of the soul is. Therefore, whenever we have the will to give alms to please God, it is the will of our soul and our right hand. If we suppressed the vain will that arises in us that wants to be seen by people, that is, the will of the flesh (or left hand), the left-handed will does not know what the right-handed does. But if we consented to a vain will of this type that arose in us, we joined the left-handed will to the right-handed and the right-handed will to the left-handed and we made known to our left hand what the right hand was doing.

Certainly it can be understood in a different manner, as the apostles interpret it in the book of canons that concern bishops.[8] The right hand is the Christian people, who are at the right hand of Christ, but the left hand is all the people who are at his left. Therefore he says this so that an unbeliever (who is the left hand) might not look on a Christian giving alms (who is the right hand). If a Christian sees a Christian giving alms, it is not against Christ's commandment because both are the right hand.

[4]*"So that your alms may be in secret."*

Not so much in a secret place as in the secret place of the conscience. For if the soul has been enclosed around the bulwark of a good will, we can hide our bodily works. But if our soul has wandered through vain thoughts, it is of no advantage to hide the deeds of the body because the more we hide them, the more broadly we publicize them.

"And your Father who sees in secret will reward you openly."[9]

See that it refers to the hidden place of the heart, not of a location. God is in the hidden place of the heart but not in a hidden place. Consider that God does not want us to do this in secret to the degree that our work does not appear. Otherwise how does he say, "Let your light so shine before men, that they may see your good works and give glory to your Father who is in heaven"?[10] But it is so that he himself might reveal them. For every good work that is hidden by us and revealed by God is more pleasing. For if you show yourself off, there are few who will praise you, namely, those who do not understand that you could have done this secretly. But those who realize that you could have done so will censure you more and not praise you. But if God shows you off, nobody will find fault with you, except perhaps a troublemaker, to whom a good person is displeasing.

It is impossible that God would dismiss the good work of an individual done secretly, but he will reveal him in this age and glorify him in the age to come, because it is the glory of God. Just as the evil work of an individual redounds to the devil's glory, for in it the power of his wickedness is shown, so also a good work is God's glory, for in it his glory is shown. Therefore just as the devil, who suggests that evil

[8]See the *Constitutions of the Holy Apostles* 3.14.1; ANF 7:430; *ZKT* 34:20. [9]The author (and the Vulgate) adds "openly." [10]Mt 5:16.

be done, himself makes known that evil (for example, he suggests that one commit adultery, and he makes the affair known; he suggests murder, and he then publicizes the affair), so God, who grants that good is done, himself openly publicizes every good thing, that is, in that age to come, because here there cannot be a clear reward for righteousness. Think if he has made you rich for your good work because here there are not only good wealthy people but evil wealthy people too; in fact, there are more evil wealthy people than good ones, and so the reward of righteousness does not appear in wealth. If he grants you to have children and grandchildren (who are found to be both good and evil among good and evil parents alike), then also the reward for righteousness cannot be made known since every good thing that is desirable in this age is held in common by good and evil people alike. Thus, if it were given to the good, it would not appear. But the goods of the age to come are not held in common among the good and the wicked, but they belong to the good alone. Thus it is clear that whomever God blesses there it is because he earned that good gift as a reward for his righteousness—unless by chance he had made it manifest in this world, making him known to all and glorifying him so that all might know that he is a person of God and respect him.

Or if one should happen to appraise the situation according to the works, one could also evaluate the conditions of the goods of this world. For example, many, both good and evil, run into troubles in this age. Thus we understand who is being tested by these troubles as a good person and who is being punished as an evil person by looking at their works. If we should happen to see the good works of one person, we know that he is being tested as a righteous person. But if we happen to see evil works, we say that he is being punished by the troubles as a sinner. So we also see that even sinners have the goods of the world, and sometimes so do the just. It is for that reason that it is made manifest according to their works. If an evil person has attained good things in this world, we say that his wickedness is being nourished here so that it might perish all the more severely there. But if a good person has obtained them, we say that God has rewarded him for his righteousness.

5 ***"And when you pray, you must not be like the hypocrites; for they love to stand and pray in the synagogues."***

Concerning prayer we have a discourse that alone the soul offers to God as a spiritual treasure from our inmost being. Every act of righteousness that an individual does, he does according to his power and offers it from his power, but prayer alone he does according to his faith and offers it from his faith. Do you wish to know how precious prayer is? No act of righteousness is compared with incense, except prayer alone, as is shown in the Revelation of John, how a great angel went before the sight of the altar, having in his hand the censer of fragrant incense, and it was said, "[These] are the prayers of the saints."[11] Just as well-selected incense delights anyone who smells it, so the prayer of the righteous is sweet before God.

Do you wish to know its great honor? As soon as the prayer leaves the mouth, angels take it on their hands and offer it before God, as the archangel says to Tobit: "I brought a reminder of your prayer before the holy One."[12] Do you wish to know its power? The prayer of the three boys made it so that the burning fire did not consume them but rather delighted them, so that it seemed to be a flame in appearance but was a parasol in its function. The more glorious prayer is, the more carefully it ought to be preserved, lest it

[11]Rev 5:8. [12]Tob 12:12.

be made of no account because it was used to please people.

"They love to stand and pray in the synagogues."

Do you think that he is forbidding people to pray in the synagogue, that is, in a gathering of people? But he is forbidding people to pray with the intention of being seen in the gathering; otherwise it is praiseworthy to pray in the gathering of the faithful, as it has been said, "Bless God in the great congregation,"[13] and "Worship the Lord in his royal sanctuary."[14] But I think that the Lord is not applying this to the place but to the intention of the one who prays, because the mind of him who prays in order to be seen by people does not look at God but at the people who are there and thus seems to pray to himself in the middle of many. Such a person prays in the synagogue, as far as his intention is concerned. But the mind of one who is praying looks to God alone, if in that hour his mind is such that he does not have anyone around himself because his mind sees no one, if he is not praying to please anyone. And so even if he prays in a synagogue, nonetheless he seems to pray secretly all by himself. Moreover, he prays in such a way that he does nothing new that others might look at, nor does he raise his voice to be heard by others, nor does he stretch out his hands, as did the Pharisee in the temple, so that he could be seen by many. Nor does he openly strike his breast but does so privately, as the publican did in the temple, nor does he shamelessly raise his eyes to the temple to become conspicuous. And so him whom nobody hears making an outcry nobody regards as doing some such thing, and even if he is standing among many people, he is in private.

"And at the street corners."

He did not say, "in the streets" but "at the street corners." He did this not so that if they pray in the streets, they might be rebuked as people who feign piety, but so that they might not appear to pray in secret if they pray in the corners. O astute vanity! They know that it is more praiseworthy to pray in secret; therefore they craft a way to hide themselves in order to be doubly praised: first, because they pray; second, because they pray in a hidden manner; and they show more clearly that they have hidden themselves for this very purpose. Tell us, hypocrite, why do you wish to be seen praying? It is not because prayer is a praiseworthy matter, is it? Why then do you not wish to be praiseworthy, when you desire to be praised? O mad vanity! They do not wish to be the sort of person that they desire to appear to be.

"Truly, I say to you, they have received their reward."

Wherever each person sows, there he harvests, and whatever he sows, that he also harvests. They pray to please people, not to please God. So they are praised by people, not by God. They pray mendaciously, since they are really not praying—and they are praised mendaciously, because they are not really praiseworthy people. They sell an empty form of piety and buy an empty word of praise. Just as their prayer does not delight God, so the praise of people does not really adorn them. Whatever is put in a word lasts as long as the word does, but whenever the word has come to an end, so too has that good thing that was put in the word.

[6]***"But when you pray."***

That is, you who wish to be heard and not to be seen, you who wish to be truly praiseworthy and not merely appear to be so, you who speak

[13]Ps 68:26. [14]Ps 28:2 (trans. Kellerman).

in the ears of God, not in the eyes of people.

"Go into your room and shut the door."

This is so that there will be nobody there except you who pray and he to whom you pray, and so there will not be another person with you except for him whom you need. A witness burdens one who prays and does not help him because God is not compelled by prayers as much as he is pleased by them. I am speaking of another person who has a different heart. But wherever they are of the same heart, even if there were many people who were praying, they are one because one spirit prays in all of them, as it is written, "Now the company of those who believed were of one heart and soul."[15] These things are understood spiritually as having been spoken to the soul. The room is the heart or inner understanding, that is, the spiritual understanding, as it is written, "Commune with your own hearts on your beds, and be silent."[16] The door is the outer, carnal senses, through which all good and evil things enter into the soul. It is as Wisdom says in the person of the church: "Hark! My beloved is knocking. 'Open to me, my sister, my love.' "[17] Christ knocks at the door of a Christian either by speaking through the divine Scriptures or by leading good thoughts into his heart. He who welcomes them opens the door to Christ, but whoever drives them away closes the door to him. Therefore he orders the soul to enter the inner mind when it prays so that it does not think about anything except what it is praying for and to whom it is praying. He orders the soul to close the door of its fleshly senses so that it might shut out all carnal thoughts and worries. But if when praying you think about carnal matters, you have not entered into the inner mind, nor have you closed the door of the senses, and so your soul, speaking silently with extraneous thoughts, destroys the time of prayer.

What was said earlier can be understood in this way too. Whoever prays in the middle of a multitude of evil thoughts prays in the middle of a synagogue, since he is surrounded by worldly worries on every hand. Whenever he prays, he thinks about his wife, his children, his purchases, his home, his possessions, his cattle, military service, profit, treasure chest, and all the other things that cannot be counted that ascend into the heart of a person praying heedlessly. Does this not appear to be a synagogue of evils? All those various types of thoughts are various impure spirits. How then is your soul not praying in the middle of a synagogue when it has so many impure spirits with it as spectators and interlocutors?

We can also understand the door of the house to be the mouth of the body so that we do not pray to God with a loud voice but with a quiet desire. For many evils arise out of a loud prayer, especially these three. First, whoever prays loudly does not believe that God is everywhere and can hear in the hidden places. Consequently, whoever prays secretly honors God twice: first because he prays and second because he believes that God can hear in the hidden places, as indeed he does. For God must not be beaten down by a loud voice but rather pleased by a clean conscience, since he does not listen to the voice but to the heart. The second evil is that you entrust the secrets of your petition, which perhaps nobody ought to know except for you and God, to the ears of good and evil people alike. You are not heard only by God because you have prayed in an undisciplined manner, but you are moreover laughed at by those people to whom you have revealed your secrets. Now the third evil is that you do not allow anyone else to pray next to you when you pray loudly. By your voice you draw his attention to your words, and so not only are you not heard because you are praying

[15]Acts 4:32. [16]Ps 4:4. [17]Song 5:2.

badly, but furthermore you heap up more sin as you do not allow others to pray. Therefore pray as you heard Hannah, who prefigured the church, prayed in the book of Kings, about whom it was said, "Hannah was speaking in her heart; only her lips moved, and her voice was not heard."[18]

"And your Father who sees in secret will reward you openly."[19]

This is so that people can recognize what[20] you prayed for when they see that you have received what you prayed for.

[7]***"And in praying do not heap up empty phrases as the Gentiles do."***

Let us see to whom the Gentiles pray so that we may know why they pray in this way. They pray to demons, who cannot heed them, even if they do hear them. For they cannot cause any trouble unless God permits it. They pray to dead kings (Jupiter, Mercury, and the rest), whose scandalous acts are better known than their names and who could not help others even when they were alive. They pray to unfeeling idols, which cannot hear or give a response. Rightly then they cry out for a long time where there is no one who could hear them. For that reason, when the priests of Baal called on their gods in order to set the sacrifices on fire, Elijah mocked them and said, "Cry aloud . . . perhaps he is asleep and must be awakened."[21] So also one who attends his prayer with long discourse accuses God of sleeping, as it were.

[8]***"Your Father knows what you need before you ask him."***

If he then knows beforehand what we wish, we do not pray to explain to God what we wish but to please him by offering to him what we desire. And if God must be pleased, not taught, then a long explanation is not necessary, but rather a good will.

[9]***"Pray then like this."***

The Fourteenth Homily: On Matthew 6

[9]***Our Father who art in heaven, hallowed be thy name."***

He wanted to be called "Father" more than "Lord," so that he could give us great confidence to ask him and an abundant hope of obtaining it, because servants do not always obtain what they seek, nor do they always seek with a good conscience those things that are proper. For often servants do not consider what pertains to the advantage of their lord but only to their own advantage; as a result they do not always deserve to be heard. Children, however, always obtain it, because they seek with a good conscience whatever things are proper, nor do they think more about what pertains to their own advantage than to their parents'; as a result they always deserve to be heard. And if you believe that you are a child of God, ask those things that are expedient for you to receive and are proper for him to give. But if you always ask for carnal and earthly things from him, you will obtain them with difficulty or perhaps you will never obtain them. When you do not have these things, how will he willingly give them to you, since he admonishes you everywhere to despise them even if you were to have them?

"Our Father."

He says "our," not "my." God gladly hears when

[18]1Sam 1:13. [19]The author (and the Vulgate) adds "openly." [20]Alternate reading: "whom." [21]1 Kings 18:27.

a Christian prays not only for himself but for another. It is part of our nature to pray for ourselves, but it pertains to grace to pray for another. A need for something compels us to pray for ourselves, but brotherly love urges us to pray for another. But the sweeter prayer before God is not that which the need for something compels but that which brotherly love commends.

"Who art in heaven."

He wants us to know that we have a heavenly Father so that we may be ashamed to yield ourselves to earthly things when we know that we have a heavenly Father. Just as a degenerate child leads to the shame of a noble parent, so also a wicked Christian leads to the blasphemy of the just God. For just as God is glorified through good Christians, he is blasphemed through evil ones.

"Hallowed be thy name."

How can he who sanctifies people be sanctified by a person? Or can something be hallowed that already is holy? But his name is holy in and of itself; this is what is sought: that it may be kept holy among us, that is, that we may keep it holy in our midst so that he may sanctify himself in us while we sanctify his name among us. For whoever does not sanctify God is not sanctified by God. Now we sanctify God among us when we know him to be holy and fear him and diligently keep watch that we do not perchance violate[1] the holiness of his name among us through our evil deeds. Just as someone who is wearing splendid clothing avoids every filthy object so that it by chance does not get dirty and lose the charm of its luster, so everyone who receives God in his heart and spirit ought to be careful so that he does not contaminate God, knowing that if God has been contaminated among us, he will remain uncontaminated in his own nature, but he will punish us with our death for the offense of his being contaminated.

10"Thy kingdom come."

The kingdom of God is said to be the reward or suffering that the just receive as a reward for their righteousness or sinners for the fault of their sins. The kingdom of God is also called "the saints," as it is written, "And the weeds will be gathered from his kingdom,"[2] that is, from the Christian people. The kingdom of God is also called "righteousness," as it is written, "Therefore I tell you, the kingdom of God will be taken away from you and given to a nation producing the fruits of it."[3] From all these things there is one meaning: it is one thing to be a king and another to reign. See, God is by nature king, but he does not reign among all people, nor are all people his kingdom because not everybody does his will. For God does not reign over the wicked, but the devil does, for they do the latter's will. Thus the apostle wisely says, "against the world rulers of this present darkness."[4] He did not say "against the rulers of this world" but added "world of this present darkness," because the demons are not lords of the whole world but only over the darkness that is in the world. Wicked people are called the darkness of the world, just as the saints too are called the light of the world. It is as the apostle says: "Once you were darkness, but now you are light in the Lord."[5]

Just as God is shown in this world through the saints, so he is obscured by unrighteous people. And God indeed has the power among human beings[6] to destroy all of them, if he so wishes, just as he can destroy the very prince of sinners, the devil. Although the devil is under

Fourteenth Homily [1]Alternate reading: "destroy." [2]A conflation of Mt 13:40-41. [3]Mt 21:43. [4]Eph 6:12. [5]Eph 5:8. [6]Alternate reading: "among his honors."

the power of God, nonetheless, because he does not want to belong to God, as far as his own intentions are concerned, he is not of the kingdom of God. In the same way, although all sinners are under God's power, they nonetheless are not the kingdom of God, because they do not want to be under God. For it is truly a righteous kingdom whenever both the king wants to have people under him and people desire to be under him. But whenever a king compels others to be under him by violence, that is not truly a kingdom but a tyranny. Thus, although God also has people under his power, he nonetheless welcomes only those who wish to be under him so that he may not be a tyrant but a king. The devil clearly is a tyrant because he compels people to do his will, even when they do not wish to.

What then is he saying? In the meantime there are two kingdoms in the world, that of God and that of the devil, that is, the kingdom of the righteous one and of the unrighteous one. And we seek that the kingdom of the devil (that is, of the unrighteous one) may be abolished and that the kingdom of God (that is, of the righteous one) would only come. Consequently, he says, "Thy one kingdom come," because in the meantime not everyone is of God. This will take place when all wicked people are sent into the fiery lake of the damned along with their prince, the devil. All the saints, however, will rise and come into the air in order to meet the Lord, and they will always be with him in this world so that everything that is in this world might altogether belong to God. So one must understand about righteousness, how now both righteousness and iniquity reign. But when iniquity will be extinguished and the devil has been removed, then righteousness alone will reign.

"Thy will be done, on earth as it is in heaven."

Does not God do everywhere whatever he wishes? It is said because "Whatever the Lord pleases he does, in heaven and on earth, in the seas and all deeps."[7] But we seek that God's will may be done among us, that is, that we may do it. As long as the kingdom is mixed on this earth, the will of God is done on earth but not as in heaven. In heaven all the angels want to do the will of nobody other than God. But on earth not everybody does the will of God, for the wicked do the will of the devil. Thus, when the kingdom of the devil departs, that is, when the wicked have been removed from this world, then all who remain on the earth will do the will of God alone, just as all the angels in heaven. What he says here ("on earth as it is in heaven") ought to be taken to apply to all the petitions. That is, "Hallowed be thy name, on earth as it is in heaven," and "Thy kingdom come, on earth as it is in heaven."

"Thy will be done, on earth as it is in heaven."

See how cautiously he spoke. He did not say, "Father, sanctify your name among us, bring your kingdom to us, do your will among us," so that God might seem to sanctify himself among people or to bring his kingdom to those who wish it or to do his will among those who wish to do it—and thereby God be found to show favoritism. Nor does he again say, "Let us sanctify your name, let us welcome your kingdom, let us do your will on earth as it is in heaven," so that it might not seem that it belongs to humankind to sanctify God or welcome his kingdom of do his will. Rather he adopts the middle ground and speaks impersonally, that is, "May it be hallowed, may it come, may it be done," so that he might show the necessary work of each person because humankind needs God and God needs humankind in order to do righteousness. For just as a person cannot do good unless he has the help

[7]Ps 135:6.

of God, so neither can God work a good deed in a person unless the individual wants it. Just as neither land without seed nor a seed without the land bears fruits, so neither a human being without God nor God without a human being can work righteousness in a person. And if he should say, "If you do these things, you pray for these things," you are worthy children of this kind of father.

[11]***"Give us this day our daily bread."***

At first glance it appears as if the words implied that those who pray "Give us this day our daily bread" do not have bread prepared for tomorrow or the day after tomorrow so that they might be able to say, "Give us this day our daily bread." How can anyone who has bread prepared for tomorrow or for five days or ten days say, "Give me this day my daily bread"? One seeks that which one does not have, but why would one further seek that which one already possesses? But if that is the case, then that petition can apply to few people or perhaps to nobody. Who is so faithful an individual that he does not reserve more for himself than daily food, even though he could have more? Perhaps it was appropriate for the apostles alone, who wandered about through individual cities all the time for the sake of teaching, and their very wandering did not allow them to possess more than daily food. But we ought to apply Christ's teaching so that all might benefit from it, lest the medicine of righteousness, common to all and prepared for the salvation of all, might be found to be superfluous since it is of advantage to very few or to nobody. Therefore it must be understood that we not only pray, "Give us our bread," so that we may have something to eat, but also that we may receive from the hand of God that which we eat. It is common to all, righteous and sinners alike, to have food to eat. In fact, sinners often have more abundant provisions than the righteous. But it is not common to all to receive bread from the hand of God, but that belongs only to the saints. Therefore these words do not forbid us to prepare matters beforehand, but only to do so with sin. For God gives the bread that he eats to whoever prepares things beforehand with righteousness, but the devil, not God, gives to him who prepares it with sin. To be sure, all things are created by God, but all things are not furnished by God.

Or it has to be understood that inasmuch as it is given by God, it is hallowed and received. And so he does not say, "Give us this day daily bread," but adds, "our," that is, "the bread that has already been prepared beforehand in our midst; give it to us so that it may be hallowed as it is being given by you." For example, if a lay person offers bread to a priest so that the priest may take it and hallow it and offer it back to him, the fact that it is bread makes it belong to the one offering it, but the fact that it is has been hallowed makes it the service of the priest.

Did it not suffice for us to say, "Give us this day our bread"? Why then did he add, "daily"? To restrain delicacies. It is so that each person may eat as natural reason compels, not as much as lasciviousness of the flesh urges. If you were to weigh out at one banquet as much food as was able to suffice for many banquets, for example, for a hundred people living moderately or for you yourself living for a hundred days in a disciplined manner, you are no longer eating daily bread but the bread of many days. Or certainly, just as he said earlier about alms or prayer that we should not do it before people, not because this was altogether possible but in order to teach us to flee the sight of people so as not to be seen, if at all possible (which in fact is not possible), so also here he wishes to teach us not to be worried about anything in this world, except about simple food alone, and so he commands us to pray, "Give us this day our daily bread." It is not because he deemed it wrong for a Christian to have more than daily bread but because he desired to teach this so that, if it is possible, not to have more than daily bread—which is not possible as far as human ability is concerned.

Again, why did he not only say, "Give us daily bread," but added "our bread"? He did so for two reasons. First, because God who gives everything to us (whether we pray or serve him) does not give to us alone but also to others through us, so that we give a portion to the weak from that which we have received. Therefore whoever does not give to the poor from his labors cannot say, "Give my bread to me," for he does not eat only his own bread but also that which belongs to another. Second, whoever eats bread justly obtained eats his own bread, but whoever eats bread sinfully obtained eats someone else's.

[12]***"And forgive us our debts, as we also have forgiven our debtors."***

With what hope does someone pray who harbors enmity against another person by whom perhaps he was harmed? For just as he is lying when he prays (for he says, "I forgive" and does not forgive), so he seeks forgiveness from God and yet it is not granted to him. Thus, if he who has been injured prays to God without hope unless he forgives him who has wronged him, how do you think that a person prays who has not been hurt by another but hurts and burdens others by his wickedness? But many people who do not wish to grant forgiveness to those who sin against themselves flee to pray this prayer. What fools! First, because he does not pray as Christ taught, nor is he Christ's disciple. Second, because the Father does not gladly hear a prayer that the Son has not composed. For the Father acknowledges the intentions and words of his own Son but does not accept whatever human arrogance has thought up but only those things that the wisdom of Christ has taught. Therefore you can indeed say a prayer, but you cannot circumvent and deceive God, nor do you receive forgiveness unless you yourself have first forgiven.

[13]***"And lead us not into temptation, but deliver us from evil."***

Because he has commanded people many magnificent things in the foregoing (to call God their Father, to recognize their own heavenly origin, to seek that the kingdom of God would come, not to be worried how they will be fed—all of which are tokens of great hope and righteousness), so now the teaching about humility is added so that they may recognize that they are weak when they say, "Lead us not into temptation," and the consideration of their weakness may quench any grounds for boasting.

Therefore we seek two things: first, that he not lead us into temptation; second, that he free us from the danger of temptation if he has led us there. For truly, if God were to examine people according to the truth of his righteousness, nobody could be saved. But he tests us with that limited degree of difficulty because he knows our weakness. Or if he tests us, he does not test us as long as we can overcome the temptation, but only as long as we show that we wish to overcome it. That is to say, he does not test our virtue but our will, as the apostle confirms and says, "No temptation has overtaken you that is not common to man. God is faithful, and he will not let you be tempted beyond your strength, but with the temptation will also provide the way of escape, that you may be able to endure it."[8] Because he wishes to glorify a person, he tests him—not so that he may boast with great approval but so that he may not boast without reason.

"For thine is the kingdom and the power and the glory."[9]

[8]1 Cor 10:13. [9]These words are found in a footnote in the RSV. These words are not to be found in the better manuscripts of Matthew and are omitted from the text of the RSV.

He introduced these three items that pertain to the three items that he has previously mentioned. Earlier he had said, "Hallowed be thy name; thy kingdom come." If someone should say, "Therefore does God not have a kingdom on earth because you pray for it to come?" this clause ("For thine is the kingdom") addresses that concern. Again, he had said, "Thy will be done on earth as it is in heaven." If someone should say, "Therefore, does that mean God cannot do what he wants on earth because you are praying that his will would be done?" this clause ("Thine is the power") would answer as if to say, "We do not hope for your kingdom in our midst or your will being done on earth as if your kingdom were not on earth (as if your kingdom were not in the world and you could not do whatever you want to on earth) but because your kingdom is everlasting life and your will is righteousness. For that reason you do not compel anyone under your kingdom unless he wants it; nor do you work your will in anyone unless he agrees to it. For that reason we pray that, illuminated by you, we may desire to welcome your kingdom in our midst and hope to do your will." Again, because he had said, "Give us this day our daily bread; and forgive us our debts, as we also have forgiven our debtors; and lead us not into temptation but deliver us from evil," he answers to those petitions, "For thine is the glory." For it truly is God's glory if those who fear him lack nothing; it is God's glory if he forgives the sins of those who forgive their debtors; but it is not God's glory if he forgives those who do not forgive because it is not his righteous judgment. It is God's glory if he does not lead us into temptation or if he frees those led there for some righteous reason. And in general it is God's glory when he accomplishes whatever he commanded us to pray for above.

[15]***"But if you do not forgive men their trespasses, neither will your Father forgive your trespasses."***

For also when he said earlier, "Forgive us our debts, as we also have forgiven our debtors," he did not say, "as we will forgive," so that God would forgive us first and afterwards we would forgive our debtors. God knows that all people are liars because, even if they receive the forgiveness of their sin, they do not forgive their debtors. Thus he says, "Forgive us as we forgive," so that first we may forgive and afterward seek forgiveness and receive the forgiveness of sins from God.

The Fifteenth Homily: On Matthew 6

[16]***"And when you fast, do not look dismal, like the hypocrites, for they disfigure their faces that their fasting may be seen by men."***

Of all the vices the chief and most powerful vices are three: gluttony, avarice and vainglory. The Lord over temptation has undertaken war against these things and fought on our behalf: against gluttony in the desert, against avarice on the mountain and against vainglory on the temple. Again, of all the good virtues the chief and most powerful good virtues are three: almsgiving, prayer and fasting. And notice how the three good virtues have been discovered against the three vices: almsgiving fights against avarice, fasting against gluttony, and prayer against vainglory.

Say to us, "Look, fasting opposes gluttony because fasting is the opposite of gluttony, and almsgiving opposes avarice because avarice piles up but almsgiving disperses. But how does prayer oppose vainglory?" Listen. All the vices that are in the world have opposing virtues through which those vices can be overcome. For example, fornication has the opposing virtue of chastity; arrogance, humility; and anger, gentleness. And there is no vice that does not have an opposing virtue through which it can be overcome, except for vainglory. Consequently, the more good you do, while wishing to restrain vainglory, the more you stir it up. And the reason is that every vice arises from evil, but only vainglory proceeds out of a good deed. Consequently, it is not squelched through good but is sustained all the more. Finally, the temptation to vainglory does not take place among sinners. For how would an adulterer or a thief be tempted by vainglory, when they do not have anything of which to boast? But those who have something of which they could boast experience the temptation to vainglory. Therefore there is no remedy against vainglory except prayer alone, and even prayer itself can produce vanity, unless you look carefully to see if you are praying well.

The threefold distinction of alms, fasting and prayer can be found written in the Law: "None shall appear before me empty-handed."[1] Whoever comes to pray but gives no alms enters before God empty-handed. Not only in the Old Testament but also in the New it is commanded that every Christian put something into the alms box every week when he comes to pray, just as the apostle says: "On the first day of every week, each of you is to put something aside and store it up, as he may prosper, so that contributions need not be made when I come."[2] Again, Solomon says, "Before making a vow, prepare yourself."[3] Whoever comes to prayer while giving alms prepares his soul before prayer. Just as oil sets ablaze the light of a lamp, so also good works rouse the faith of the heart and give confidence to the soul praying in God's presence. Therefore alms are a preparation for prayer. Again, fasting is the aid of prayer because prayer without fasting is slender and weak. For that prayer is strong that takes place in a humble spirit and a troubled heart, as also the prophet says: "The sacrifice acceptable to God is a broken spirit; a broken and contrite heart, O God, you will not despise."[4] But a spirit that eats and drinks and enjoys delicacies cannot have a humble and contrite heart because bread strengthens the heart and wine gladdens it.[5] The strength that comes from bread does not allow the spirit of the flesh to be humble, and the pleasure that comes from wine does not allow the heart to be contrite. So whenever the saints wished to pray to God for some necessity, they joined a fast with their prayer, as Daniel and others did. Therefore, because the power of prayer is fasting, they should never be separated from one another but always be put together. Prayer and fasting free one from death. Again, "But this kind never comes out except by prayer and fasting."[6] Just as neither a soldier is anything without his arms nor arms without a soldier, so neither is prayer without fasting nor fasting without prayer.

But of these three virtues the first is prayer because alms comes from one's property and fasting from the body, but prayer proceeds from neither one's property nor one's body but from one's soul and heart. Consequently, the treatment of prayer has been placed between the other two virtues on the score that it is more worthy than the other two. First come alms, then prayer, then fasting. And why does almsgiving precede prayer? It is because it is a mediator and preparer of the way before the face of prayer so that the prayer that follows almsgiving may find a place of mercy prepared in God's sight. Consequently, fasting follows prayer because prayer is not the aid to fasting, but fasting is an aid to prayer. And prayer is not done for fasting's sake, but fasting for prayer's sake. Thus, fasting does not precede prayer, but prayer precedes fasting.

A third distinction. To give alms or to pray or to fast does not pertain to all people but only to the just. But whoever sins and gives

Fifteenth Homily [1]Ex 23:15. [2]1 Cor 16:2. [3]Sir 18:23. [4]Ps 51:17; the archaic language of the RSV has been updated. [5]An allusion to Ps 104:15. [6]Mt 17:21, footnote in the RSV. These words are not found in the best manuscripts of the New Testament and are omitted in the text of the RSV.

alms loses what he does. The alms of a sinner are given in place of the sin that has ceased, not in place of the sin that is occurring, that is to say, whenever we repent of what we have done, not so that we may by our sin obtain permission to sin. Again, whoever does not sin prays, but whoever sins and prays does not pray to God but mocks him. Again, whoever does not sin fasts, but whoever sins and fasts does not fast for God's glory, nor does he humble himself but spares his wealth. Finally, consider in the previous passages where Christ began to give salvific commands to his apostles, he did not at once command them about alms, fasting or prayer, but first he expelled vices and later introduced good things. "You have heard that it was said to the men of old, 'You shall not kill,' . . . but I say to you that every one who is angry with his brother shall be liable to judgment. . . . You have heard that it was said to the men of old, 'You shall not swear falsely . . .' but I say to you, Do not swear at all. . . . You have heard that it was said, 'You shall not commit adultery.' But I say to you that every one who looks at a woman lustfully has already committed adultery with her in his heart. . . . You have heard that it was said, 'An eye for an eye. . . .' But I say to you, Do not resist one who is evil. . . . You have heard that it was said, 'You shall love your neighbor and hate your enemy.' But I say to you, Love your enemies."[7] Then, after he has deprived humankind of all these evils, he says, "Beware of practicing your piety before men,"[8] showing that a person does these virtues for no reason unless he has first withdrawn from all those vices. First one must get rid of vices and thus undertakes virtues because one cannot become a new person unless he has ceased to be the old person. But whoever does not get rid of vices but undertakes virtues loses the grace of his own virtues, just as if someone put something sweet mixed with bitterness into his mouth, that sweetness does not give its flavor.

"And when you fast, do not look dismal, like the hypocrites."

Whether he was speaking about alms, he says, "Let it not be done before others," or prayer, "Do not be like the hypocrites who pray on the corners"; so he says this about fasting. Do you see how the Lord knew that vainglory proceeded from every virtue? So he orders us to cut off the thistle of vainglory that grows diligently in good soil, lest the thistle of vainglory choke out the fruit of fasting.

Can it happen that the person who fasts does not feel it? But it is better that your fast shows you rather than you show your fast. Because the Lord knows that the one who fasts cannot happen to be joyful, so he does not say, "Do not be dismal," but "Do not look dismal." It is one thing to be dismal and quite another to become dismal. Whoever is naturally sad because of his diligent fasting is sad, but he does not look so, but whoever appears to be pale through some deceptions is not dismal but looks so. Therefore, if someone who fasts and makes himself look dismal is a hypocrite, how much more guilty is he who does not fast but by certain facial expressions paints rented pallor on his face as a sign that he is fasting, as it were! His own nature displeases him because it cannot lie about that which it is not doing, and the wretched face of flesh, innocent of any wrongdoing, is chastised by certain facial expressions because it does not agree to the deception.

I think that every sensible person understands that these words are not to be understood in a carnal manner. For it cannot happen that a person who is fasting does not look dismal, nor does the Lord command what we cannot fulfill. Therefore, if he orders us not to look dismal so that we may not appear

[7]Mt 5:21-22, 33-34, 27-28, 38-39, 43-44. [8]Mt 6:1.

by that very sadness to others to be fasting, why does he order us to anoint the head and wash the face? So also the very anointing of the head and the washing of the face, if they are always observed by those who fast, will no less become signs of a fast. But these things are applied spiritually to the soul so that the spiritual sadness may not banish one's spiritual face. The spiritual face of a soul is its conscience or heart, as the prophet shows when he says, "My heart says to you, 'Your face, Lord, do I seek.' "[9] The face made of flesh does not seek God, but the conscience does. Moreover, Jacob shows that the face is another name for the conscience, as when he wrestled with a man: "For I have seen God face to face, and yet my life is preserved."[10] Indeed, he did not see God face to face at that time because God wrestled against him in the form of a man. For the bodily form was a veil of God, not the true nature of God. But with his mind he saw God. Therefore he was also called Israel, that is, "a mind seeing God." But if his face had seen God, he would have been called "the face seeing God." What can we conclude then? The face of the soul is called the conscience. For just as a beautiful face became pleasing in the sight of people, so also a pure conscience is a sight to behold in the eyes of God.

Moreover, there is a bodily joy and a spiritual joy. Laughter is bodily joy, as is joking and other carnal delights. But spiritual joy is hope, as the apostle says: "Rejoice in your hope, be patient in tribulation."[11] Do you see how it can happen that while we are sad in the flesh we rejoice spiritually in hope? The prophet says this about the Holy Spirit: "There is a river whose streams make glad the city of God."[12] Moreover, there is a bodily sadness and a spiritual sadness. A bodily sadness is the affliction of the flesh, but spiritual sadness is despair and unbelief of the soul. Therefore when he says, "Do not look dismal," he says, "Do not fast for other people's sake." For whoever fasts for other people's sake makes his own conscience sad, that is, makes it to despair. How can his conscience be joyful and hopeful in God by his fasting when he does not fast for God's sake but for other people's sake? So also all the hypocrites, who fast for other people's sake, disfigure their own faces, that is, their own consciences. How do they not have disfigured consciences before God when they pretend to fast for God's sake but are not fasting for God's sake but for the sake of other people, and wish to deceive both God and others?

Or one can understand the words "Do not look dismal, like the hypocrites" to mean, "Do not fast without hope and faith." But whoever does not refrain from sin and does not behave righteously fasts without hope. For just as good works beget hope, that is, spiritual joy, so evil works beget despair, that is, spiritual sadness. Whoever fasts while sinning fasts without hope. That is, he does not have anything on which he may hope and rejoice, but his soul is in despair and sad.

Now nobody is ignorant of how sin and despair disfigure the face of the conscience. For the conscience of one who sins is always wounded. Therefore all hypocrites fast in this way, not cheering up their conscience in hope by their good deeds but rather saddening it into despair by their evil works. Therefore everyone who fasts while sinning is a hypocrite.

Therefore, what does it matter to fast with joy unless you first fast spiritually, then in the flesh? For just as every virtue is spiritual, so it is also something done in the flesh; and every vice is something spiritual and something that can be done in the flesh. For example, fornication in the flesh is whoring, but spiritual fornication is lying. Chastity of the flesh is not to know a woman; spiritual chastity is to be faithful to God. Humility of the body is to stand up for somebody and to speak a gentle

[9]Ps 27:3; the archaic language of the RSV has been updated. [10]Gen 32:30. [11]Rom 12:12. [12]Ps 46:4.

word; spiritual humility is to think in one's heart that the other is better than himself. So also there is a fasting that takes place in the body and a fasting that takes place in the spirit. Bodily fasting is to abstain from food; spiritual fasting is to abstain from sins. For just as the flesh delights in eating, so the spirit of the flesh delights in sinning. Therefore wise people call every sin "desire" because we commit every sin with delight. Consequently, the organ of desire was circumcised so that in this prefigurative act delight in all evils might in general be removed, since these evils make the soul sad, that is, to despair. Whoever fasts from food but not from evil works appears to fast, but not really because to the degree that he fasts as far as people are concerned he most wickedly feasts on vices as far as God is concerned.

"Truly, I say to you, they have received their reward."

The pleasure of praise is enjoyed as long as it is heard, but as soon as it has passed through one's ears, so the pleasure of praise passes away.

17***"But when you fast, anoint your head and wash your face."***

You who are merciful, who fast more with the heart than with the body, who refrain from sin more than from food—you consequently fast for God, not for others. For those who fast while sinning fast for others and not for God, and so they are hypocrites, but those who fast truly for God do not refrain from food as much as from every wicked deed because just as food delights the flesh, so every evil delights the spirit of the flesh. What shall we say then? It is truly vain if we pour oil on our head whenever we fast, even if we wash our face with water. And who goes out with an unwashed face? If we do this, we publicize all the more that we are fasting through these signs of washing and anointing. What can we say then? The simple interpretation of this passage is this, that those things must be understood through hyperbole, as were the rest of the things previously said. It is as if he were to say, "You ought to keep yourself from showing off your fast so that if it can be you do not do even that which is not natural, namely, those things that seem to be indications of a variety of luxury and feasting." Spiritually this takes place, as is clear from the previous passages, that the face of the soul is understood to be the conscience. Therefore, cast off from you the filth of greed, the dung of perjury and the rot of malice, and you have washed your face, that is, your conscience with the water spoken of by the prophets, concerning which Isaiah says, "Wash yourselves; make yourselves clean; remove the evil of your doings from before my eyes."[13] For if you remove iniquity from your soul, you have washed your conscience and are fasting well.

Moreover, your head is Christ. Give the thirsty something to drink, feed the hungry, clothe him who is cold, and so you have anointed your head, that is, Christ, with the most precious myrrh, that is, the oil of mercy, as Christ proclaims in the Gospel, saying, "As you did it to one of the least of these my brethren, you did it to me."[14] Because every act of righteousness consists of two things, first that you do not do evil and second that you do good, he said, "Wash your face" to that which pertains to fleeing from sin and "Anoint your head" to that which pertains to doing good works. And you will be beloved just as Mary,[15] who after she had washed her conscience with

[13]Is 1:16. [14]Mt 25:40. [15]See Jn 12:1-4 (and its parallels in Mt 26:7 and Mk 14:3), as well as the account of the anointing of Jesus by a sinful woman (Lk 7:37-41). Earlier exegetes were quick to identify Mary, the sister of Martha and Lazarus, with the sinful woman of Lk 7, and even to identify this Mary with Mary Magdalene. Modern scholarship is more skeptical about these identifications.

tears of repentance later poured out oil on top of Christ's head and the house was filled with the fragrance; so also the report of your works, if you are like her, will fill the whole church.

And how rightly he said to wash the face and not to wash the head but to anoint it. As long as we are in the body, our conscience is always filthy with sins. But our head, Christ, does not need any washing, but only anointing because "he had done no violence, and there was no deceit in his mouth."[16]

[19]"Do not lay up for yourselves treasures on earth."

This present passage does not seem to follow logically from the preceding passage because that passage spoke about fasting, but this passage speaks about alms. What does this mean then? If we remember, the Lord taught nothing about alms or prayer or fasting above but only restrained their counterfeits so that they may neither do those things before others in order to be seen by them, not because it is possible to do them in such a way that others do not see them (as we said above), but he makes a person consider how much he is striving to do those things so as not to be seen so that that very good work, as far as a Christian is concerned, might take place in the disposition as in the deed. And because the commandments of the law mentioned earlier ("You shall not kill," "You shall not commit adultery," etc.) looked more to the deed than to the disposition, Christ appropriately introduced more spiritual commands to supplement them, more directed toward the disposition than to the deed: "But I say to you, 'do not be angry,' 'do not lust,'" and so on. So also here they are given so that their good works might remove pretense of virtue[17] and look more to the heart than to the appearance. Therefore, just as we stated, because Christ had not taught anything about those things, now he introduced three consequences of his teaching in accordance with the three aforementioned forms of righteousness (almsgiving, prayer and fasting): one pertains to almsgiving, the second to prayer and the third to fasting. We will show this about each one in its own place.

And to almsgiving this is the doctrine that follows: "Do not lay up for yourselves treasures on earth," so that the order of discourse is as follows: "Thus, when you give alms, sound no trumpet before you, as the hypocrites do in the synagogues and in the streets, that they may be praised by people. Truly, I say to you, they have received their reward. But when you give alms, do not let your left hand know what your right hand is doing, so that your alms may be in secret; and your Father who sees in secret will reward you in secret.[18] Do not lay up for yourselves treasures on earth."[19] And here he gives the advice to give alms; second, he shows what use there is to giving alms; third, that not even fear of the poverty that might befall should hinder the will from giving alms. "Do not lay up for yourselves treasures on earth," because you are not of the earth, nor did you come from the earth, but for a while you received earth from the earth so that you might conquer the earth through the earth. But you are of heaven, and you came from heaven and again will return to heaven, unless you wish of your own accord to remain on earth. Therefore store up your wealth where you have your homeland. Do you wish to know that you are a pilgrim in this world? Hear the prophet who says, "I am a sojourner on earth; hide not your commandments from me!"[20] Then what is that folly that makes you content on earth? That is, do you wish to serve the devil on foreign soil when you could reign with Christ in heaven, that is, in your own land?

[16]Is 53:9. [17]Alternate reading: "every pretense." [18]The author (and the Vulgate) adds "in secret." [19]Mt 6:2-4, 19. [20]Ps 119:19; the archaic language of the RSV has been updated.

"Where moth and rust consume and where thieves break in and steal."

A threefold destruction destroys all the goods of the world. Either they grow old by themselves and become moth-ridden, like clothes, or they are devoured by their owners who are living luxuriously, like other provisions, or they are snatched away by others either by trickery or force or calumny or some other unjust method. That is because all people who hasten to make someone else's property their own are called thieves.

But you say, "Do all who have these things lose them? I show off my garment, and it does not grow moth-ridden. I am thrifty, and my provisions do not rust; I guard my property, and it is not taken by thieves." Meanwhile let me say that many people lose their property, even if everybody does not. What can we conclude? Is it better to store up treasures on earth where the outcome of attempts to preserve them is uncertain, or is it better to do so in heaven, where their preservation is certain? If you do not keep watch here, you will lose it, but if you keep watch you will be tortured by fear and worry. But in heaven such things are preserved by God even if you sleep, and when you remember them you rejoice because of your hope. But what folly is it to leave everything behind at that place you are about to leave and not to send it on ahead of you to the place where you are going! Indeed, even if you did not lose your wealth physically, you lost it spiritually because it was kept safe very poorly because it does not benefit you for your salvation. Whatever you do for your soul, that is yours, but whatever you leave behind, you have lost. For whatever is badly gathered together physically is seen to be scattered spiritually and lost, but whatever is well scattered physically is seen to have been gathered spiritually and stored up in heaven.

Now he puts forth what advantage there is to giving alms, saying:

21 ***"For where your treasure is, there will your heart be also."***

Whoever stores his treasures on earth does not have something to hope for in heaven. For what will there be for him to look at in heaven, where he has nothing stored up? For that reason, if he rejoices, he rejoices in carnal and earthly matters, or if he is sad, he is sad about carnal and earthly matters. But whoever stores his wealth in heaven does not have his hope on earth. What could delight him on earth when he has nothing on earth? So if he rejoices, he rejoices in spiritual things, or if he is sad, he is sad over spiritual matters. Therefore even the joy of sinners is bad and their sorrow worse because either they rejoice about some earthly gain or they are saddened about some earthly loss. But the joy of the righteous is good and their sadness is better because either they rejoice in righteousness or they sorrow over sin. For if some cause of death draws near, if indeed his hope is on earth, he is saddened, as if going from his own home abroad, not to mention going off to torment; but if his hope is in heaven, he rejoices as if he were returning from abroad to his own home, not to mention the heavenly kingdom.

Second, whoever stores up treasures on earth sins doubly: first, because he heaps them up evilly; second, because he has his heart on earth and never remembers what things belong to God but always remembers those things that belong to the earth. And whoever stores up treasure in heaven is doubly righteous: first, because he is investing well; second, because he has his hope in God and always thinks and meditates on the things that belong to God and not what belongs to the earth. And just as for him who has begun to gather goods on earth, his earthly desire makes him all the more worried—not only so that his wealth will not diminish but also so that it will increase all the more—so also for him who stores up his treasures in heaven, his spiritual desire makes him worried not only so that he does not lose what he has but furthermore that he may increase it beyond what he has.

[22]*"The eye is the lamp of the body."*

We ought to keep in mind first that the discourse is not speaking about the eye of the body or about this body, which appears outwardly. Otherwise he would have said, "If your eye is healthy or weak," but now he said, "sound" and "not sound." For not everyone with good vision has a body that is altogether full of light, nor does everyone with poor vision have a body in darkness. If someone has a good eye and yet a diseased one, will his body be in the light? Or if it is poor and yet healthy, will his body be in darkness? Therefore "of the body" refers not to the outside but to the inside, that is, to the corporeal nature. Its lamp is the mind, through which the soul sees God. For this reason Jacob was called Israel. Israel in Hebrew means "the mind seeing God." Therefore, after he said, "Lay up for yourselves treasures in heaven . . . for where your treasure is, there will your heart be also,"[21] he fittingly added, "The eye is the lamp of the body. So, if your eye is sound, your whole body will be full of light," to show that whoever gives alms ought to have a heart toward God, but whoever has a heart toward God has an eye full of light. That is, his mind is spiritual and pure. It is not befouled by earthly desires, as it is written: "Blessed are the pure in heart, for they shall see God."[22] Just as he who has difficult vision sees better if you put him in a dim or dark place, but if you put him in the sunlight, he sees nothing because his eye does not endure the gleam of the sun, so the worldly person, who has his eye (that is, his mind) soiled by earthly desires and turbulent, if you put him in worldly matters is wise and astute; but if you draw him to spiritual matters, it grows dark and he knows nothing, because his mind has been corrupted by earthly desires and does not perceive the good of righteousness. I say, "He does not perceive," not "He does not know." Instead, he knows but does not perceive the good of righteousness because he does not also delight in it, for his heart is preoccupied with earthly delights.

[23]*"But if your eye is not sound, your whole body will be full of darkness."*

What is the darkness in us? Fleshly, malevolent and wicked attitudes, which always desire what belongs to darkness and not to the light. In what else does the nature of the flesh delight except in greed, lust, arrogance, pleasures, and other evils, which lead one downward to dark death? And whoever understands what it means that "the desires of the flesh are against the Spirit"[23] understands that the nature of the flesh is darkness. Therefore, whoever has a pure eye, that is, a spiritual mind, always looking at heavenly things, keeps his body full of light, that is, without sin. For if the flesh desires those vices that we spoke of, a person who in accordance with his nature has a clear mind and hope in God distinguishes the flesh out of consideration of righteousness and drives it back with the fear of divine fear. And so he keeps it full of light, that is, without sin, even though it does not wish to be so.

Therefore, do you understand how he who has a sound eye has a body full of light, but whoever has a dark eye, that is, whoever has a mind darkened by some evil or disturbed with the lust of riches, possesses a body full of darkness? For whatever things make a person's spiritual mind to be clean, those very things in the opposite direction make it carnal and dirty. Just as the mind of one who gives alms and has his hope in heaven

[21]Mt 6:20-21. [22]Mt 5:8. [23]Gal 5:17.

becomes pure, and his hope in God makes his mind spiritual and pure, so he who heaps up wealth with sin puts his hope on earth; but as for whoever has his hope on earth, his mind is carnal and impure. Therefore all his flesh is in darkness, that is, in sins. How? When the perverse flesh lusts according to its own nature (as we have already said) and a person has his hope on earth and a mind disturbed by desires, he does not oppose it, nor does he make any distinction out of consideration of righteousness, nor does he drive it back by the power of the coming judgment because he neither sees (because he is blind) nor understands that what is evil is evil, and even if he wishes to do so, he cannot, because he does not have any hope except in this age. But we know that hope offers us strength to resist fleshly desires; and yet one who does not have his hope in heaven does not have the power to resist his desires, and so his whole flesh becomes full of darkness.

And so as to explain this more briefly and clearly: before the soul sins, it was comforted by divine aid and was the queen and mistress of its body, and as a freeborn queen it sat on the throne of its heart and it governed its body as its palace, as it were, nor was the flesh able to overcome it. But if it has entangled itself with dire sins, then it, bereft of divine aid and driven under the power of unclean spirits, becomes weak and sickly, so that it is no longer the mistress of its own body but rather its maidservant; and now the flesh is no longer subordinate to the soul but the soul to the flesh, nor does the flesh do what the soul wishes, but the soul does whatever the flesh forces it to.

Do you understand then how the whole body is full of darkness when someone has a filthy eye of the mind? "If then the light in you is darkness, how great is the darkness!" As we said above, the nature of the flesh is always dark because it is always a sinner. Even if it does not sin because the soul opposes it, nonetheless it is rightly called a sinner and full of darkness because the flesh always has the intention to sin so that it often creeps up on the righteous soul in order to get it to do what is sinful. For who is so faithful that he never has been at least in part conquered by his flesh? And if there is such a person, he is rare. But the light in the heart, as you often hear, is the soul that sees God, that is, the spiritual soul. If then the soul, although it is divine and given to lighting that flesh, becomes carnal, as it were, and grows dark with earthly desires, always looking to earthly things, see how the flesh of such a person has been wrapped in the darkness of sins. But if, as we have already said, in the case of a good person the flesh creeps up on the soul even when the rational soul opposes it and gets it to do what is fleshly, how much more do you think that the flesh wraps itself in wicked deeds in the case of an evil person, since the soul, which ought to have opposed it, agrees with it and desires similar things? Luke explains the same interpretation, albeit in a different form, when he first commands, "Fear not, little flock, for it is your Father's good pleasure to give you the kingdom. Sell your possessions, and give alms; provide yourselves with purses that do not grow old, with a treasure in the heavens that does not fail," and so forth.[24] Then he says, "Let your loins be girded and your lamps burning, and be like men who are waiting for their master to come home from the marriage feast."[25] He shows that nobody can have his loins girded to go out from this world or have lamps burning or await his master except for those who sell what they have and give alms and provide themselves with purses that do not grow old and a treasure in the heavens that does not fail.

[24]Lk 12:32-33. [25]Lk 12:35-36.

The Sixteenth Homily: On Matthew 6

[24]*"No one can serve two masters; for either he will hate the one and love the other, or he will be devoted to the one and despise the other."*

Let us see, first, how the present words follow the preceding things that have been spoken. Earlier he commanded to give alms, saying, "Lay up for yourselves treasures in heaven," because whoever stores up treasures for himself in heaven has his heart in heaven and his hope in God; he has a sound eye of the soul, that is, a pure and spiritual mind, one that also always meditates not on earthly things but on heavenly matters. But whoever has a pure and spiritual mind can keep his body clear, that is, without sin. But whoever does not give alms does not have his heart in heaven or his hope in God, nor does he have a pure and spiritual mind, nor can he keep his body clear, that is, without sin, because nobody is able to serve two masters, God and mammon—that is, wealth. Wealth, you see, is called *mammon* in the Aramaic language. Therefore, just as one who has two masters must love the one and hate the other or despise the one and obey the other, so also whoever wishes to love God must hate wealth, but whoever wishes to love wealth must hate God, and whoever wishes to do the commandments of God must hate riches, and whoever wishes to obey the commandments of God must despise the thought of doing the commandments of greed, and whoever wishes to do the commandments of greed must despise the commandments of God.

Consider, moreover, that he did not say, "Nobody can have God and wealth," but "no one can be a servant of God and wealth." It is one thing to have wealth and quite another to serve wealth. If you have wealth and your wealth does not make you haughty or violent, but you give to the poor as much as you can, you are master of your wealth, not its slave, because your wealth does not possess you, but you possess your wealth. But if your wealth makes you arrogant or violent and you do not give anything to anyone because you have been restrained by your greed, then you are a slave of your wealth and not its master, because your wealth possesses you, not you your wealth.

Now he teaches that the fear of poverty should not hinder the will from giving alms, as he says:

[25]*"Therefore I tell you, do not be anxious about your life, what you shall eat."*

Worry is the daughter of despair because despair begets worry. What does "Therefore I tell you" mean? And what is he saying? To give alms so as to store up in heaven and have a pure heart, as you hope in God. But whoever hopes in God is not worried about what he or she will eat or wear, because there is nothing that causes people to despair in some need except for one thing, namely, that they do not have hope in God. Therefore do not say to me, "I want to worry, do I not? But the very need compels me. I want to trust in God, do I? But I cannot. My heart does not listen to me." You do not know what you are experiencing. You languish, and you do not know the cause of your languishing. Do you wish me to show you the reason so that you will never despair in any time of need? Do good and act righteously so that you may have hope in God, and you will not despair on earth. You see, good works are those things that make one to hope, and evil works force one to despair. Furthermore, the prophet did not say, "Trust in the Lord and dwell in the land and be fed by its riches," but "Trust in the Lord, and do good; so you will dwell in the land."[1]

"Do not be anxious about . . . what you shall eat."

Sixteenth Homily [1]Ps 37:3.

He did not say, "Do not work," but "Do not be anxious." Therefore we are forbidden to be anxious but are ordered to work. So also the Lord, speaking to Adam, did not say, "With worry you will win bread for yourself," but "with labor and the sweat of your brow."[2] Therefore bread must be acquired not by spiritual worries but by physical labors. Just as, with God's assistance, bread abounds as a reward of their diligence for those who labor for it, so it is taken away as a punishment for their negligence from those who sleep and neglect their duties.

"Is not life more than food, and the body more than clothing?"

He confirms our hope, first by descending from the greater to the lesser, then by ascending from the lesser to the greater. If he has given the soul, how will he not give food? If he formed the body, will he not provide clothing? If he had not wanted that which exists to be, he would not have created it. But because he has created it in such a way that it is preserved through food, he must give food to it for as long as he wishes that which he has made to exist.

What is the argument from the lesser to the greater?

26"Look at the birds of the air: they neither sow nor reap."

If he offers nourishment to the birds, will he not offer to humankind food to nourish them? If those who do not labor find food, will not people find food, to whom God has given both the wisdom to work and the hope to enjoy it? God made all animals for humankind's sake, but he made humankind for his own sake. Therefore, if he serves animals for humankind's sake, will he not serve humankind for his own sake? God made all things in wisdom, but he made humankind not only in wisdom but also according to his own wisdom. Therefore, to the degree that the creation of humankind is more precious than that of animals, to the same degree God's solicitude over humankind is greater than that over animals. God made all animals so that they would exist as long as they do, but when they die, they would become as if they had never been, but he made humankind so that he would live not only before death but even after death. Indeed, he would live more after death than before death because he lives before death in temptation but after death in glory. Therefore, if he helps those whom he has created so as to live for only a little while, will he not help humankind whom he has made so that they may live forever?

27"And which of you by being anxious can add one cubit to his span of life? 28And why are you anxious about clothing?"

Therefore, if you cannot add a little part to your body, how will you be saved in your whole body by thinking? God, who formed you out of nothing in the womb, also rescued you from one danger after another, as you were being born from your mother's womb, while you were not only not pondering such things but were not even conscious. God, who day by day grants increase to your body, also does this by his wisdom, even though you do not understand. Therefore, if he daily works his providence in your very self, how will he cease in the midst of your needs?

"Consider the lilies of the field, how," that is, at an opportune time, "they grow."

At the appointed time they are fashioned. On their leaves they are clad in splendor and filled with fragrances. God bestows on them what the earth had not given to the root or the root to them. Nor does he give more to some

[2]Cf. Gen 3:19.

and less to others, but the same abundance of providence is preserved in all of them, so that they may not be thought to have been born of themselves or made by chance, but so that they may be discerned to have been arranged by the providence of God.

"They neither toil nor spin."

By saying "they do not toil," he wishes men to be understood, and by saying, "they do not spin," he wishes women to be understood, because the life of men is supported by farming but that of women by weaving.

29***"Even Solomon in all his glory was not arrayed like one of these."***

This is because although Solomon was not toiling, nor was he worried about what he would wear, he nonetheless either gave orders or made arrangements or knew about such things. But wherever there is an order or arrangement, displeasure is often found there in the servants and the anger of the one giving the orders is stirred up. But these lilies do not know how they will be adorned.[3] People served Solomon, but God serves the lilies.

30***"But if God so clothes the grass of the field, which today is alive and tomorrow is thrown into the oven, will he not much more clothe you, O men of little faith?"***

Therefore, if he helps the flowers, who were born so as to only be seen and then perish, will he neglect human beings, whom he created not so as to be seen for a time but to exist forever? Whoever understands what a human being is does not despair of God, but whoever despairs of God does not know what he is, because a human being is in God and God in a human being.

31***"Therefore do not be anxious, saying, 'What shall we eat?' or 'What shall we drink?' "***

God created these things in nature, entrusting a rule to the earth, as it were, "Let the earth put forth vegetation."[4] Therefore whether or not it wants to, it produces vegetation for good and evil people because the earth has been ordered to serve, not to judge. But he did not create good and evil in nature, but he put them in our will so that we may be whatever we wish to be. Therefore he offers a prize to the good but punishment to the wicked. Therefore what wisdom is it to worry about that which you will have even if you are not worried about it—and not to worry about that which you will lose if you do not worry about it? For you will find food, even if you do not worry about it, but you will not obtain righteousness unless you worry about it.

32***"For the Gentiles seek all these things."***

It is because they believe that luck, not providence, inheres in human affairs, and they do not think that their lives are governed by the decision of God but by are influenced by an uncertain outcome. Thus they rightly are afraid and rightly worry and despair as though they have no one who is in control. But those who believe that they are governed by the decision of God and are not influenced by an uncertain outcome entrust their food to the hand of God and know that neither hunger nor nakedness kills anyone without the will and decision of God. But such a person thinks about good and evil, knowing that unless he is worried about them, he will neither flee evil nor obtain the good. Consequently, he says:

33***"But seek first his kingdom and his righteousness."***

[3]I follow the suggestion of PG 56:724 to read *ornantur* instead of the text's *coronantur* ("crowned"). [4]Gen 1:11.

The kingdom of God is the reward of good and evil works, but righteousness is the way of godliness through which one arrives at the kingdom. Therefore, if you think day and night about what the glory of the saints will be or what the destruction of the impious and sinners will be, you by necessity will withdraw from evil, since you have been terrified at the threat of punishment, or you will hasten to the good, since you have been stirred up out of a desire for glory. And if daily you think about what the righteousness of God is and what it hates or what it loves, that righteousness itself will show you its paths. For just as righteousness flees from those who hate it, so it pursues those who love it. Nor will we give a thought as to whether we have been poor or rich, because this was also not in our power, but rather we will think if we have behaved well or badly, which lies in the power of our will. Man was told, "Cursed is the ground because of you."[5] Do you see that the earth was cursed because of the sins of humankind so as to not bear seed but is blessed when we do good works? Therefore seek righteousness and bread will not be lacking, because just as the fruits of the earth are removed because of evil works, so because of good works they are abundant. For this reason he says, "Seek first his kingdom and his righteousness, and all these things shall be yours as well."

34*"Therefore do not be anxious about tomorrow."*

We have already said that "today" means only that which we need in our present life. When he says "tomorrow," he is pointing to whatever is superfluous to our need. Therefore do not strive to have what is superfluous other than what is necessary for you in the present life for your daily life. Whatever is superfluous, whatever is "tomorrow," will take care of itself. And it is as if he should say, "Whatever superfluous things you have gathered will take care of themselves." Indeed, if you do not enjoy them, they will find many masters who can care for them, just as it will please their very selves. Therefore why are you concerned about those whose power you will hand off to others? "Let the day's own trouble be sufficient for the day," as if to say, "Sufficient is your labor and misery that you suffer in life because of your daily needs. Do not work superfluously for superfluous things, lest the labor be yours but another enjoy it." He calls "trouble" the very affliction of the day of present worries and labors—not as the Manicheans, who say that evil itself is a creature of God.

The Seventeenth Homily: On Matthew 7

1*"Judge not, that you be not judged. Do not condemn and you will not be condemned."*[1]

Some interpret this passage according to the sense of something like this, saying that the Lord by this commandment does not forbid Christians to kindly chastise other Christians who are worthy of chastisement, but he forbids them to chastise by speaking evil of many people and especially hating others and condemning them based solely on suspicions for the most part and pursuing their own hatred under a veil of piety. He orders this so that sinners might not look down on Christians because of their boasting about their righteousness. And so that not even Christians may chastise other Christians in this way, the command applies that says "judge not." But I do not know whether the saying "that you be not judged" applies if they have not chastised.[2] This cannot mean that if they

[5]Gen 3:17. **Seventeenth Homily** [1]The first sentence of Mt 7:1 is in the RSV; the author has added the second sentence (cf. Lk 6:37). [2]Some manuscripts omit "not."

have not chastised sinners that they will obtain forgiveness for their sins, in accordance with the words "and you will not be judged," can it?[3] For if those who judge do evil, as it is not right to judge, then without doubt those who do not judge do not obtain forgiveness for their earlier sins because they have not judged in an evil manner. For who obtains forgiveness for his earlier evil because he did not compound it? Certainly, if those who did not judge those sinning against them, they themselves will not be judged by God for their own sin. We say these things to show that this command was not established concerning not judging one's neighbors who sin against God but concerning not judging those who sin against us.

What does this passage mean? Up to now he has explained the pursuit of righteousness pertaining to alms, but now he begins to explain the pursuit of righteousness pertaining to prayer. And this teaching is in some way a part of prayer itself, as the order of saying a prayer is as follows: "And forgive us our debts, as we also have forgiven our debtors; and lead us not into temptation, but deliver us from evil."[4] Whoever does not judge his neighbor for the sin that he does against him God will also not judge for the sin that he does against him, but God will forgive his debt, just as the individual also forgives his own debtors.

Just as he commanded all the other commandments in a general manner to all people—priests as well as lay people, but nonetheless especially to teachers, who ought to be more perfect in discipline to the degree that they are higher in rank—so also this commandment about not judging one's neighbors pertains indeed to all, but especially nonetheless to teachers. Therefore, if you diligently examine the matter, there are some commandments that do not apply to the laity at all or at most just a little, but by all means apply to teachers. An example of this kind of commandment is that which follows.

[3]"Why do you see the speck that is in your brother's eye, but do not notice the log that is in your own eye? [5]You hypocrite, first take the log out of your own eye, and then you will see clearly to take the speck out of your brother's eye."

Everybody can see the speck that is in the eye of a brother, and yet not everybody can remove it, but only teachers can, who can cast out sin (be it large or small) from the mind of his brother through teaching or godly rebuke. Just as that saying goes,

[6]"Do not give dogs what is holy; and do not throw your pearls before swine."

Not everybody, but holy people have the ability to have holy things or pearls and to know how to dispense either good or bad things and to discern which people are dogs and which are swine. Therefore God wants all the teachers of Christians first to do this and then to teach it, just as in every other form of righteousness, so that they may commend their good doctrine with an even better life and implant knowledge by teaching well but implant fear by living well, because such people are salt of the earth, flavoring all with the example of their lives, and they shine brightly as they illuminate others with their teachings. But who would listen to any teacher who does not listen to himself?

So he says to all, but especially to teachers, "Judge not, that you be not judged." If a teacher is mindful of an injury or grief and keeps the memory of the evil deed alive in his soul, the whole state of the church collapses—whether you look at the time of the apostles or our own. At that time, as we read, they found it difficult to convert others to faith in Christ, unless previously they had suffered many torments. For

[3]Lk 6:37. [4]Mt 6:12-13.

once the devil had been wearied, so to speak, and overcome by their suffering to the point of death, and as the apostles were leaving behind the hearts of the unbelieving and now no longer have any strength to further arm their hearers, the grace of God drew near and their hearers were converted to Christ. But if the apostles had been mindful of injuries that they had suffered from the unbelievers, the apostles would never have taught them afterwards in love and would never afterwards have willingly received them into faith in Christ. But since also now teachers are wronged by lay people, whether justly or unjustly, as the devil sows surprise attacks, if the teachers are mindful of injury and pain, they destroy the whole church. For wherever there is a recollection of injury or pain, the teacher does not gently teach the laity, and the laity do not gladly hear him. Perhaps the teacher opens his mouth unwillingly to teach, but because the laity altogether lack the fear of God, they are not content to hear him looking at him face to face but turn their back on him and exit, despising both themselves and the preacher—and themselves more than the preacher—and do not perceive the loss of their soul, since they have been enraged just as a beast that has been exasperated by a wound that has pierced itself does not perceive anything. The Evangelist Luke broadly pursues this subject when he says, "Judge not, and you will not be judged; condemn not, and you will not be condemned; forgive, and you will be forgiven; give, and it will be given to you; good measure, pressed down, shaken together, running over, will be put into your lap. For the measure you give will be the measure you get back."[5]

And who is that sort of person who does not even judge? And who is that sort of person who judges and yet does not condemn? And who is that sort of person who indeed condemns and nonetheless forgives? And who is that sort of person who gives? We have already explained to you. And because an abundant measure is given to one who does not even judge, a large measure is given to him who judges but does not condemn, but a good measure is given to him who condemns but forgives. Just as an abundant measure is greater than a large measure and a large measure is greater than a good and just measure, so he who does not judge is more perfect than he who judges and does not condemn, and he who judges and does not condemn is better than he who condemns and forgives. Therefore Matthew summarizes all these things in a brief discourse, saying, "Judge not, that you be not judged. For with the judgment you pronounce you will be judged."[6] He understands that the discourse about judging pertains to all those things. For whoever judges only one who sins against himself and does not condemn him nonetheless judges, and whoever not only judges but also condemns also judges, for this very act of condemning is judging. Therefore, where Luke says, "judge not," or if you judge, "condemn not," Matthew says, "with the judgment you pronounce you will be judged." That is to say, if you judge and do not condemn, you will be judged by a like judgment by God, but you will not be condemned. But if you judge and condemn, you will be judged and condemned by a like judgment. And while Luke says, "Forgive, and you will be forgiven; give, and it will be given to you," Matthew says, "The measure you give will be the measure you get." If you forgave your neighbors their sin even when not asked, but only out of respect for God, God also will forgive you before you can ask him. But if you offered forgiveness when asked, God too will give you forgiveness when you ask him with worthy prayers and fitting lamentation.

Therefore, because he had spoken the words "judge not that you be not judged" chiefly to teachers, as we have noted, he fitting adds and says, "Why do you see the speck that is in your

[5]Lk 6:37-38. [6]Mt 7:1-2.

brother's eye but do not notice the log that is in your own eye?" That is to say, if you do not see the log in your own eye, why do you see the speck in your brother's eye? It is as if he were to say, "It is better not to teach or upbraid the laity than to teach and upbraid them and subject yourself to the reproach that such teaching of a teacher is not to be heard but laughed at. For this reason, let every priest first teach himself, if he wishes to teach the people. But if he does not wish to teach himself about whatever he teaches or to scold himself about everything that he is scolding, then let him not teach others or scold anyone, so that even if he does not escape the judgment of God at least he may not experience the reproach of other people.

4"Or how can you say to your brother, 'Let me take the speck out of your eye,' when there is the log in your own eye?"

That is to say, with what pretext do you scold the sin of your lay brother, while you yourself stand in the same sin or in a greater one? Do you not fear that you will hear in return, "Physician, heal yourself"?[7] If it is scandalous for a doctor who does not have the ability to heal another or himself to wish to heal others, though he himself is weak and bears his own malady in his body a witness of his own lack of skill, how is it not scandalous for a teacher to want to rescue others from their sin while he himself is in greater sins, given the assumption that one can rescue oneself from a sin more fully than others?

"How can you say?" means "With what intention are you thinking?" Are you speaking out of the love of your heart so that you can save your neighbor? No, but you are speaking so that you can pretend to be righteous. But if you scold your neighbor out of the love in your heart, so that you could save him, you would first save yourself. It is not possible to be kinder to another than to yourself, is it? Why then do you wish to save another when you do not wish to save yourself? Therefore every teacher who upbraids another person in some kind of fault while he, having the same fault, does not rid himself first of it, certainly does not wish to save others as he speaks in the church, but he wishes to hide his own evil deeds through good teaching, and he seeks praise from people, not the reward of edification from God, and so he is a hypocrite. Therefore, he fittingly adds,

5"You hypocrite, first take the log out of your own eye, and then you will see clearly to take the speck out of your brother's eye."

Every teacher who does not first do good works and then teach them is a hypocrite. While he teaches good things, he professes that he is righteous before humankind, but while he behaves in an evil fashion, he establishes himself as a sinner on the inside. Therefore he says, "Do you wish to freely and faithfully upbraid the laity and take out the sin from the eye of his mind? First cleanse your mind of every evil so that when you scold the laity for their sins, they will not have anything to turn against you for your sin in reply. For he will begin to respect you inwardly when he cannot find anything to condemn in you. But every sin is judged not according to its deed (i.e., whether it is modest or great), but according to the person who sins. Even if a lay person has done a great sin, it is a modest one and a mere speck—I am talking in comparison with the sin of a priest—because he is a lay person. But even if a teacher has done a small sin, it is a great sin and a log—I am talking in comparison with the sin of a lay person—because he is a teacher.

6"Do not give dogs what is holy; and do not throw your pearls before swine, lest they tram-

[7]Lk 4:23.

ple them under foot and turn to attack you."

Our Lord had given the command above to all people, but especially to teachers—namely, the commands to love our enemies to do good to them, and again (as just stated) to not judge those who sin against us—since he reckoned that those who persecute the priests of God or injure or harm them are for the most part unbelievers such as the Gentiles or heretics, or even if they are Christians, they are filthy and insensate because they do not reckon or understand that the priests of Christ are Christ's vicars and Christ himself and that whoever honors a priest of Christ honors Christ and whoever insults Christ's priest insults Christ. However, lest by chance the priests should say to themselves, thinking along these lines, "If we are ordered to love our enemies and do good to them, and if we are commanded not to judge those sinners who sin against us, then just as we ought to love them and do good to them so doubtlessly we ought not to judge those sinners who sin against us so that we share not only our goods but also those that belong to God so that our mercy might be full, just as God's is," he restrains their thoughts by the prudent admonition, "Do not give dogs what is holy, and do not throw your pearls before swine."

And it is as if he were to say, "I commanded you to love your enemies and not to judge them so that I may show you as merciful to them that you may benefit them with your bodily goods, not out of my spiritual goods, because they share a common nature with you, not a common faith. I commanded you to not judge those who sin against you. But I did not order you to exhibit the secrets of my mysteries to those who blaspheme and despise them because they do not want to know me. Look at God, your Father, whose example I want you to follow in being merciful: he offers bodily blessings indiscriminately to those who are worthy and those who are not, but he does not offer them spiritual graces in the same way, does he? Nor did I say to you about him who orders the Holy Spirit to descend on the grateful and ungrateful and gives his blessings on the just and the unjust. For this reason be honest and kind in dispensing your goods, but be prudent and cautious in dispensing mine."

But if you demand that your tailor be diligent and the keeper of your cellar be faithful, how much more God demands that a dispenser of his graces be so, since by managing his graces well he makes people more pleasing, but by not handling them well or by dispensing them badly he renders them unprofitable. Just as if you give a holy thing to dogs or pearls to swine, that which is holy does not sanctify the dogs, nor do pearls feed the swine, but on the contrary the dogs defile the holy item and the swine befoul the pearls or crush them, so if you give something holy to people who have a dog-like or swine-like character, or you entrust them with secret mysteries, that which is holy does not sanctify them, nor do the mysteries of the truth illuminate them, but on the contrary they defile that which is holy and blaspheme the mysteries of the truth.

A dog and a pig are both unclean animals, but a dog is altogether unclean, for it neither chews its cud nor has a cloven hoof. But a pig is partly unclean because it is clean to the degree that it has cloven hoof, but it is deemed unclean because it does not chew its cud. Therefore I think that the dogs should be understood to be the Gentiles or the heretics that are altogether defiled, for even if they are unclean because of their evil deeds, they are also all the more unclean because of their unbelief or idolatry. But I think that the swine are those Christians given over to fleshly and impure pleasures because they are clean on account of their faith, to be sure, but are deemed unclean because of their filthy acts. Or the dogs are Gentiles but the swine are the heretics because of their limited purity inasmuch as they seem to call on the name of the Lord, but from their character you understand who are dogs and who are swine. It is naturally shameful that a dog never uses its voice for any other reason than to drive off those who come near it (as all the other animals do); instead, it howls into the air now and then for no good reason. The Gentiles (as well as the heretics one cannot approve of) are like them, barking much against the servants of God, barking now and then against God with blasphemies, howling openly, and never opening their mouth to good but always to evil. Again, it is the pig's nature to roll in the mud and never to look toward heaven or to seek its master except when it is hungry. They are like Christians who delight in the filth of the flesh and do not ever look to heaven or seek God except when they are in need. And the Gentiles, who vomit evil, whenever they are well judged of their evil return to their vomit like dogs whenever they do evil nonetheless. And wicked Christians cast off the dung of their sins whenever they repent, but they return like pigs to their dung whenever they seek the life they had let go of.

Now let us see what the holy things and what the pearls are. He did not distinguish which holy thing to give and which not to give, although there is a difference of holiness between one holy thing and another. Instead, he forbade us in general to give everything that is holy. Therefore baptism is a holy thing; for that reason one ought not to give it except to those who already have faith. The grace of the body of Christ is holy; therefore it ought to be given only to those who already have been made children of God through baptism and the imposition of hands. The blessed bread is a holy thing; therefore it should be offered to those who have been made capable of blessings through faith. Again, the mysteries of the truth are pearls, because just as pearls are placed inside of oysters in the depths of the sea, so also the divine mysteries have been enclosed inside of words and placed inwardly in the depths of the meaning of the holy Scriptures. And just as not everyone can dive and draw pearls out of the deep unless he is a master of the craft who knows how to use that skill, so not everyone can descend into the depths of meanings and find there the hidden pearls of the mysteries, unless he is a spiritual person who has training in the spiritual narratives of God. Therefore pearls ought not to be given except to those who desire the truth and to those living in accord with human reason. If you give the pearls of the secret mysteries to wretched people such as are like swine, they are weighed down by a mind of a life mired in delight and so do not understand the value of the pearls but think that they are similar to other worldly fables and so trample on them with their fleshly deeds. After they have for a short while reversed through their disobedience, they rush against those who offer the pearls. Often they take offense at them and speak lies against their teachers as if they were teachers of new doctrines. And if you give holy things to people such as are dogs, as we have called them, they take them like dogs without any discernment and trample them with their filthy deeds and think that the things they have received are worth nothing. When they return to their own arguments, as to mindless barking, they rush against the preacher of the truth.

And I think that it is not without a reasonable difference that the Lord forbade us to give that which is holy to the dogs and pearls to swine. Can we say of the pearls that if they are forbidden to be given to the swine, how much more they should not be given to the dogs? But about giving that which is holy we cannot come to the same conclusion. If it is not appropriate to give to those who are more unclean, is it proper to give to those less unclean? Therefore we understand that it is neither forbidden nor commanded because we often lay hands on and bless those Christians living as pigs, not because they deserve to receive the blessing but because we venture to give it contrary to justice, lest they be offended and despair. So it is not ordered because it is unjust, but it is not forbidden either because the weakness had to be forgiven.

But because we have begun to speak about holy people, one cannot overlook that sanctification is one thing and the state of sanctity is another. Sanctification is whatever makes another holy, but a state of sanctity cannot sanctify another person, although it itself is holy. For example, you point to your bread that you eat and say, as Paul says, "it is consecrated by the word of God and prayer."[8] You sanctified it, but you did not make it a means of sanctification. But whatever a priest gives out of his hand is not only sanctified but also a means of sanctification because not only is sanctification (which is seen) given, but also that which is sanctified (which is understood). Therefore one may boast about the blessed bread to animals and give it to unbelievers because it does not hallow the recipient. But if that which is eaten at the table is of the same sort as that received at the hand of the priest, all have eaten from the table, and nobody has received it from the hand of a priest. Therefore, also the Lord not only blessed bread on the road but from his own hand gave it to Cleopas and his fellow traveler. And as Paul was sailing, he not only blessed bread but offered it with his own hand to Luke and the other disciples. But whatever has been offered by the hand of a priest should not be given to animals or offered to the unbelieving, because it is not only sanctified but also a means of sanctification, and it sanctifies the one who receives it.

The Eighteenth Homily: On Matthew 7

7 *"Ask, and it will be given you; seek, and you will find; knock, and it will be opened to you."*

It is difficult to find the transition that leads from one passage to another. So we set forth various transitions according to the various reckonings of the interpreters. It is because the Lord knew that the things he had commanded above were impossible for people to do and were beyond nature's power as far as human nature is concerned. For how can those who cannot restrain themselves from murder restrain themselves from anger? How can those who cannot restrain themselves from fornication restrain themselves from lust? How can those who cannot restrain themselves from perjury restrain themselves from taking an oath? How can those who do not cease to strike others offer themselves to be struck? How can those who do not love their own friends sincerely love their enemies? But what is so impossible as to give alms or pray or fast and not show off to others? And what is more difficult than to not judge the one sinning against oneself or to not say or give anything holy or secret to the unworthy? It is necessary then to make many people one's enemies. Therefore, because the commandments were greater than human power, he sends them to God since nothing is impossible for his grace: "Ask, and it will be given you." This is so that whatever cannot be accomplished by you human beings may be fulfilled through the grace of God.

It is because God created the material creation to be armed and fortified. He fortified some with the swift running of the feet, others with claws, still others with swift wings, others with teeth, and still others with horns. With regards to humankind alone, however, he so arranged it that he himself would be its strength. And insofar as he made humankind weaker than all creatures he wanted them to be stronger in himself. For God knew that it is eternal life to know and worship God, but to ignore or despise him is eternal damnation. So he did not he create humankind so

[8] 1 Tim 4:5.

weak that they could not do any good at all, lest he whom he made to be over all creatures and for whom he had made all creatures be found to be weaker than all, nor did he create them to be so mighty that even without God's help they could do all by themselves whatever they wanted, so that compelled by the necessity of their own weakness they might always need their Lord. And truly it is a most fitting thing that a creature needs its maker. For if all the power of humankind is in God and they nonetheless despise the author of all their good things, how much more would they neglect God if their power lay in themselves?

Or this is the explanation: because he had given them some commandments to observe virtue so as to hallow their prayer when he said, "Judge not that you be not judged," he fittingly added, "Ask, and it will be given you," as if to say, "If you show mercy to your enemies as I have commanded you, ask for whatever you want, and it will be given to you; seek whatever you want to find, and you will find it; and whatever seems closed to you, knock, and it will be opened to you." As grace accompanies you, ask in your prayers, praying day and night. But if God has withdrawn his mercy for a while as he wishes to test the constancy of your faith, do not withdraw from your prayers. Just as a truly hungry person seeks food until he fills the need of his body, nor can he cease seeking, for his need urges him since he cannot live without food, so also whoever truly desires the grace of God cannot cease from seeking, because he knows that he cannot be saved without the grace of God. Moreover, seek by asking the priests and others who have knowledge of the spiritual Scriptures, as the Law commands: "Ask your father, and he will show you; your elders, and they will tell you."[1]

Seek with zeal and diligence, reading the Scriptures of the Law and the Prophets. For God did not so arrange it that we can acquire the bliss of knowledge without the grace of God and without studying and laboring in the Scriptures, lest we chalk up our knowledge to our own efforts. Nor do we obtain grace unless we have been zealous and labored in the Scriptures, lest the gift of God be given to those who shirk their duty. Grace is the help for human weakness, but help is not given to the sleeping but to those who hasten and prevail.[2] Just as in a war not everybody who fights wins, but nobody can win unless he fights, so not all who study and read acquire spiritual knowledge, but nonetheless nobody can acquire it unless he has been diligent at reading or assiduous at hearing. And even unbelievers and those who do not fear God find knowledge by reading and studying, but they do not find that knowledge that is from God and given by the Holy Spirit but that which is from the fleshly nature and is acquired through the exercise of the flesh, which also the diligent of the Gentiles have.

There is a great difference between those two forms of knowledge. Whoever does not strive with prayers and good works but becomes knowledgeable only through the study of the readings does not know what he preaches whenever he preaches to others. If he speaks about the wrath of God, he perhaps terrifies others, but he himself does not fear. If he speaks about mercy, perhaps he comforts others, but he himself does not rejoice. He admonishes others to believe, and he himself does not believe those things that he says. But whenever he teaches others, his conscience inwardly laughs to himself about his words because his knowledge, which comes from reading only, comes out of his mouth, but the knowledge that comes from the Holy Spirit is brought forth from the heart, and so a real spiritual knowledge is not only spoken but also felt. It is not only read in the Scriptures but also prompted from the heart. Consequently,

Eighteenth Homily [1]Deut 32:7. [2]Alternate reading: "and do not prevail."

if such a preacher terrifies others, he himself fears all the more. If he consoles others, he himself rejoices even better. And everything that is spoken he has not only read but also tested by experience. Therefore let us ask God and do good works that we may merit not fleshly but spiritual knowledge.

And this is what "knock, and it will be opened to you" means. Whoever does good works before God in prayer, fasting and alms knocks on God's door. Just as whoever knocks on a door does not only call out with his voice but also his hand, so whoever does good works knocks on God's door with good works as his hand, as it were. It is written, "If you desire wisdom, keep the commandments, and the Lord will supply it for you."[3] But what are you saying? I am seeking this very thing in order to know it and do it—and how can I do it before I receive it? Do whatever you can so that you can do more, and preserve whatever you know so that you can know more. Righteousness produces itself and reveals itself. How? While you bring about righteousness in yourself, righteousness brings you about in itself. For every skill accomplishes itself. For example, you work on a vineyard and collect its fruit, and you work even better once you enjoy it. Do you see that the vineyard itself cultivates itself for you to enjoy while it is being cultivated? So, in the opposite way, whoever pursues the work of sin works a delight of sin in himself, since sin itself is an unclean spirit, with the consequence that he sins all the more because he delights in sin. So also whoever effects righteousness creates a delight of doing righteousness in himself, since righteousness itself is the Holy Spirit, with the consequence that he does more righteousness, taking his delight in it. This is what Wisdom says: "Reflect on the statutes of the Lord, and meditate at all times on his commandments . . . and your desire for wisdom will be granted."[4]

Do you see how righteousness produces itself as you are only beginning and laboring? But it opens itself fully whenever it is cultivated. Just as the mind of whoever sins grows darker and darker while he sins and withdraws from the light of truth, so much so that no knowledge of salvation remains in him but only evil (as Solomon says, "the knowledge of wickedness is not wisdom"[5]), so also the mind of whoever produces righteousness grows clearer and clearer as long as he is doing it, and he ascends to the knowledge of greater wisdom, and righteousness itself offers itself as a mirror before the eyes of his heart.

Then, if you do not do the works of righteousness, that is, if you do not knock, you cannot pray out of faith either. For the power of prayer is the work of righteousness. But the prayer of a good work is like the fragrance of pleasantness. Therefore just as some object can be without an aroma but an aroma cannot exist without some object, so a good work can exist without a prayer, but a prayer is nothing without a good work—and even if you pray, you do not pray out of faith. For just as a lamp is not lit by oil but is fed by it, so faith does not originate from works but is fed by them.

Or this may be the explanation: after he had ordered all, but especially teachers, to love their enemies and not to judge as sinners those who offend them, he continued, as we already have said, so that they would not share the holy things of God and his secrets with them on the pretext of love and kindness, as he said, "Do not give dogs what is holy." Now, however, he gives the good counsel if they, as imitators of a benevolent God, love their enemies and wish to save them in accordance with God's will: they should seek God for them, and it will be given them; they should seek those who have perished in their sins, and they will find them, as the grace of God shows; they should knock those who have been locked in by their

[3]Sir 1:26. [4]Sir 6:37. [5]Sir 19:22.

errors, and God will open them so that their witness will have an entrance into their souls. And if he should say this about those Christians who by themselves have lost the image of God because they live in the manner of swine and who have fallen and been transformed from human beings into swine and perished, then it means, "Seek them by kindly admonishing them and promising them the mercy of God and leading them to hope." For so Paul sought and found by God's grace him who, living more like a pig than a human, had defiled his father's marriage bed.[6] But with constant teaching pound the Gentiles or heretics who have been fenced in by the persuasive power of lies that seem true and have been locked up under the bolts of unbelief, and God will open them, unbarring the bolts of unbelief, and you will find an entrance to them, as Christ says in the Revelation of John: "Behold, I stand at the door and knock; if any one hears my voice and opens the door, I will come in to him and eat with him, and he with me."[7] Therefore we ought to be able to desire to save sinners, Gentiles and heretics not by defiling the holy things of God under the pretext of mercy—for that is a pretext of rashness, not kindness—but by asking God for them or seeking them out ourselves, if they are perishing, or by knocking, if they are locked inside. And then, if we ask in a worthy manner and they also have been made receptive to healing, they will be reformed and made holy people instead of unclean dogs and swine, and so they will participate in the holy things righteously and worthily and will hear the secret mysteries.

[8]*"For every one who asks receives, and he who seeks finds, and to him who knocks it will be opened."*

Because he had said, "Ask, seek, knock," he did not want any sinners to hear this and say, "Yes, he urges worthy people to do those things, but we are unworthy, and if we ask, we will not receive, and if we seek, we will not find, and if we knock, the door will not be opened to us." See how by repeating the same phrase he commends the mercy of God to the righteous and sinners alike, saying, "Everyone who seeks, whether righteous or sinner, ought not to hesitate to ask, should not fail to seek or cease to knock, because certainly nobody will be spurned except whoever hesitated to ask from God, neglected to seek or ceased to knock." That we may know the kindness of God, let us say about God what Christ said about us. Earlier he said, "Love your enemies,"[8] and other things of this sort and added, "For if you love those who love you, what reward have you? . . . Do not even the Gentiles do the same?"[9] Therefore let us say this about God: if God heard and helped only his righteous friends, what praise for kindness would he deserve? Do not people, evil though they may be, listen to their friends who ask them something and offer them some gifts of kindness? Do you see that when the Lord said, "Be merciful, even as your Father is merciful"[10] and "He makes his sun rise on the evil and on the good, and sends rain on the just and on the unjust,"[11] he wanted to show the mercy of God, namely, that his goodness has been prepared for the righteous and sinners alike. Nor is it even believable that he would enjoin a work of kindness on people who were constituted in evil but would himself not do it, even though he is good. Therefore whoever does not have righteousness either to believe in the heavenly kingdom or to be strong enough to do righteousness either certainly has not asked faithfully or has not sought it with zeal and labor or not knocked with good works. Consequently, it is not the hard-heartedness of God the giver but the fault of the individual who neglected to pray.

[6]See 1 Cor 5:1-5. [7]Rev 3:20. [8]Mt 5:44. [9]Mt 5:46-47. [10]Lk 6:36. [11]Mt 5:45.

[9]"Or what man of you, if his son asks him for bread, will give him a stone? [10]Or if he asks for a fish, will give him a serpent?"

See how he inclines us to hope in divine goodness, lest someone by chance ponder his sins and think of how great a difference there is between God and humankind and so not even begin to ask because he does not hope to obtain. Consequently he introduced a comparison with parents and children so that even if we despair because of our sins we might hope because of the fatherly truth and kindness of God. "Bread" is a word that refers to the knowledge of God the Father. The "stone" is every lie and whatever has in itself the power to cause someone to stumble in his mind. Therefore the prophet says to the righteous, "On their hands they will bear you up, lest you dash your foot against a stone."[12] Every righteous person is guarded by the angels lest by chance the foot of his lifestyle run into an opportunity for stumbling. We can understand "fish" to be a word standing for Christ, but the "serpent" would be the devil. Therefore, to obtain what we desire, these two things belong together: one is that we ask in prayer, seek with zeal and knock with our works; the other is the bread or fish that we are seeking. But if you seek those things that do not see you free (that is, carnal things, which harm your soul as a stone or serpent would), he will not give them to you, even if you pray, because he is a kindly father. Otherwise, if he gives you harmful things when you ask for them, he is not your father but your enemy.

[11]"If you then, who are evil, know how to give good gifts to your children, how much more will your Father who is in heaven give good things to those who ask him!"

It is not that they were wicked apostles, but rather that all people seem wicked in comparison with God, who alone is good, just as in comparison with snow or the sun every clean thing appears dirty and every bright thing dark. And because all parents (except for God) are evil, if a parent suffers an injury today from his child, at once his love is turned into hatred and perhaps he grows angry at him and punishes him. The parent does not grow angry at his child because he sinned against God when he injured his parent, but he grows angry because his child hurt him. Otherwise, if the injured parent had grown angry not because of his injury but because of his child's sin, he would grow equally angry at every sin of his children. But now they grieve and rage whenever they themselves are injured, but they do not care at all if their children sin against God. But whenever God has been offended by a person, he does not grow angry because he was despised by a person, although he himself is God, but because the individual offending God hurts his soul. Therefore he does not grow angry about his own injury but grieves for the human loss. And if he chastises, it is not to avenge his injury but to correct him for his salvation. Hear him as he says though the prophet, "If his children forsake my law . . . then I will punish their transgression with the rod . . . but I will not remove from him my steadfast love, or be false to my faithfulness."[13] Because he does not give everything to those who ask, but gives only good things, so he says, "How much more will your Father who is in heaven give . . . to those who ask him!" but adds, "to those who ask him for good things."

[12]"So whatever you wish that men would do to you, do so to them."

Because prayer must be kept holy, he had earlier commanded not to judge those who sin

[12]Ps 91:12. [13]Ps 89:30, 32-33.

against us, and so out of necessity he departed from the order of his discourse and introduced some other things such as, "Why do you see the speck that is in your brother's eye?" and "Do not give dogs what is holy," and the other things that follow. Now he returns to the commandment that he had begun with and says, "Whatever you wish that people would do to you, so do to them." That is to say, "Not only do I command you, 'Judge not that you be not judged,' a situation that everybody wants to have happen to themselves (namely, that they are not judged by others whenever they have harmed them), but also 'Whatever you wish that people do to you, do so to them,' and then you can pray and get what you wish. For whatever things the Law and the Prophets have commanded here and there in all the Scriptures are summed up in this comprehensive commandment, just as the countless branches of a tree derive from one root."

[13]***"Enter by the narrow gate."***

This third consequence pertains to the third act of righteousness (fasting) and is a part of the teaching given concerning fasting so that the discourse can be arranged as follows: "But when you fast, anoint your head and wash your face, that your fasting may not be seen by men but by your Father who is in secret; and your Father who sees in secret will reward you in secret. Enter by the narrow gate."[14] This is because every entrance of righteousness into eternal life is narrow for the person living in the flesh because of the adversity of the fleshly nature. But it is not as narrow and laborious as fasts undertaken sincerely.

Listen so that you may know. All passions are called and are "fleshly" because they are moved by the spirit of the flesh—whether it is anger, arrogance, envy, greed or vainglory. Nonetheless, there are mainly three passions that are particularly natural to, intimate with, and characteristic of the flesh: food and drink, then love of a man for a woman and of a woman for a man, and then sleep—because without these passions the very nature of the flesh cannot exist. They are, as it were, parts of and additions to the fleshly nature, for it is not the need of the fleshly nature that urges on all the other aforementioned passions, but it is the presumption of the spirit of the flesh that does so, but in the case of the last three passions (food, love and sleep) the need of the fleshly nature urges them on. Therefore it is also more difficult to cut off from the fleshly nature these passions than the rest of the passions. For it is a great toil to cut off those other passions through the wrestling of the heart, but for the last three passions it is not only a labor undertaking through the wrestling of the heart to cut them off but also a matter of destroying and wearing down and killing the very carnal nature and to cut off its very existence, as if someone were to cut off one of the limbs of his own body. Therefore, if these three passions are natural and intimate with and characteristic of the fleshly nature, the refraining of no other passion so hallows the body as the refraining from these, so that one becomes a chaste individual, engaged in fasting and persevering in vigils. And none of those other passions so steeps the body in iniquity as these passions so that someone becomes a fornicator or glutton or one given over to sleep. So also the apostle says, "Every other sin which a man commits is outside the body; but the immoral man sins against his own body,"[15] because the passion of the flesh[16] for fornication comes from the very nature of the flesh. And the Lord in the Gospel set forth a rich banqueter, next to whom the poor Lazarus was placed. And Abraham does not say to him,

[14]Mt 6:17-18; 7:13; the author adds the words "in secret" at the end of the first sentence. [15]1 Cor 6:18. [16]Alternate reading: "passion of the body" or "the bodily passion."

"son, remember that you did this and that in your life and now are in anguish," but "you in your lifetime received your good things."[17] And everywhere the Lord in the Gospel commands us to watch diligently. Therefore, because of all the acts of righteousness, but especially because of the most laborious act of fasting, he says, "Enter by the narrow gate," and so on.

The gate of damnation is the devil, through which one enters into hell, but the gate of life is Christ, through which one enters into the heavenly realms, as it is written: "This is the gate of the Lord; the righteous shall enter through it."[18] The devil is said to be a broad gate, not because he has been enlarged by the greatness of his power but rather because he has grown large by the license of his maddened arrogance. The Lord said such a thing: "Blessed are the poor in spirit."[19] One is poor in spirit who presents himself as of little account, although he is great. But the wealthy in spirit is one who presents himself as great, although he is of little account, just as the devil does, who was puffed up by the arrogance of his mind and, when he was a servant of God in heaven, took it on himself to go beyond the heavens against God, as though he were God. Christ is called the narrow gate not because he is little due to the smallness of his power but rather because he was reckoned as such by reason of his humility, as he testifies about himself: "I am gentle and lowly in heart."[20] Or does not he seem to you to be broad in his power but narrowly confined because of his humility since, although he was the Lord of majesty, he wished to appear as a human being in this age and since he closed himself up inside the narrow confines of a virgin's womb when the whole world could not take hold of him?

And it can be understood that the devil is the wide gate and Christ the narrow gate for another reason: the devil receives those who are wrapped up in all sins and bearing the whole bundle of the world, and he leads them to death, but Christ does not welcome anyone except those who have removed themselves from all sins and put down every burden of the world and become light and spiritual so that they may leave the world as they entered it. Moreover the devil is called "wide" because all things are without any law, as far as he is concerned, but Christ is called "narrow" because all things are under the plan of the Law, as far as he is concerned. Whatever has been released to be without the Law is broad, but whatever is under the Law is always narrow.

Every iniquity is the road to destruction. It is called roomy because it is not confined within the rule of truth and discipline but spread out through the various forms of fleshly pleasures. Those who walk on it do not do what they ought, but they pursue whatever pleases them. Their will is their own law, and they are not under the Law, but the Law is under them. The road of life is every righteous act. It is said to be narrow because it is bounded by the rule of truth and discipline, and those who walk on it do not do whatever delights them but whatever they ought to do, since the Law is not their will, nor is the Law under them, but they are under the Law.

One must consider, however, that a road leads to a gate and unless someone walks on a road he cannot arrive at a gate. So also those who do righteousness are the only ones who can know Christ and enter through him. But whoever does not walk on the road of righteousness cannot truly know Christ, although many who are not even walking by righteousness seem to know Christ. But if you were not and are not on the road of righteousness and yet think you know Christ, you are lying. Just as someone who has heard that honey is sweet, although he has not tasted it, recognizes indeed the word *honey* but does not know the pleasure of its nature, so also whoever hears

[17]Lk 16:25. [18]Ps 118:20. [19]Mt 5:3. [20]Mt 11:29.

that Christ is the Son of God but has not made use of his righteousness knows only the name of Christ but does not know the grace of his nature. So the prophet did not say, "Hear and see that the Lord is good," but "Taste and see."[21] Therefore, whenever we hear something about Christ, we learn only the name of Christ, as we have said, but whenever we do an act of his righteousness, we taste Christ himself. Likewise, no one runs into the hands of the devil except whoever walks on the path of sinners. Do you wish not to run into the devil? Turn from the road that leads to him, and the devil will have no power over you. But if you should walk on the path that leads to him, now you would not reckon your loss to be the devil's fault as if he had dragged you to himself but as your fault because you went to him. The gate does not lead to the path, does it? Instead the path leads to the gate. So the devil cannot lead people to sins, but sins must first lead people to the devil.

Do you see, then, that this road of destruction is as harmful as it is broad? And thus not only do the willing run into it but also the unwilling. And it is difficult for someone born in this world not to run into it for a little while. And because it seems broad from a far off and so even infants see it before they can see or understand the way of life, whenever someone enters it, it leads him just as he wishes, and it does not confine him in any part, with the consequence that he delights to walk on it. They indeed walk on it, rejoicing, laughing, not only eating and drinking but even devouring and getting drunk. The wealthy walk on it, and so do liars, perjurers, robbers, and those who make themselves rich. They walk on it with their wives—but not only they who have wives but also those who commit fornication or adultery. They do not know the meaning of suffering. And who would not be delighted to walk on it, at least as far as the flesh is concerned?

But this narrow road of righteousness is discerned, first, with difficulty, and thus whoever wants to enter it must wander a little ways on that broad path until he first considers and finds it at some time. And once he has entered it, he does not do whatever he wants. He is hemmed in on every side so that he regrets having entered it. Here walk the sad, grieving and fasting; even if they eat or drink, nonetheless they do not eat and drink without fear of the Law. Even if they are wealthy, they walk as paupers, because they are not rich for their own benefit but for others'. They do not touch other people's property but dispense their own. The chaste walk here, even if with their wives, but not dispersing their love without fear of the Law. Here too walk the blasphemed, the injured and the robbed. And who would not regret entering this road, at least as far as the flesh is concerned? If you wonder that I said that no one does not regret having entered it, listen to the prophet who says, "But as for me, my feet had almost stumbled, my steps had well nigh slipped. For I was envious of the arrogant, when I saw the prosperity of the wicked."[22] Therefore when people see this troubled and narrow road, many depart from it, and some of them do so from the beginning and do not draw near to it or even wish to see it. Some sinners, however, wish to see it and draw near to it, but when they consider its narrowness and its labors, they withdraw from it. Others are a little bolder and enter it, but later, when they cannot endure its labors and narrowness, again return and depart from it.

Moreover, that other road is called broad for this reason: everything that exists—wives, children, parents, friends, gold, silver, clothing, house, possessions, all types of good foods and drinks, all sorts of skills, all types of businesses, military service, public offices, and whatever else there is in this world that is a delight to see or hear or smell or taste or touch—is a path of

[21] Ps 34:8. [22] Ps 73:2-3.

destruction. It is not because all who employ these things sin but because all those things force one to sin. But the road of eternal life is narrow because there is only one type of thing there, that is, the abstinence from all things. Whoever separates himself from all those things is saved. We do not say that all who are amid those things perish, but all who separate themselves from those things will be saved. But they separate themselves not in body but in soul, not in space but by their act. For although he is in the world, he who does not make use of the world does not seem to be in the world.

The Nineteenth Homily: On Matthew 7

15"Beware of false prophets, who come to you in sheep's clothing but inwardly are ravenous wolves. 16You will know them by their fruits."

Earlier the Lord commanded his apostles not to give alms before others in order to be seen by them, as the hypocrites do, and not to pray in order to be seen by others, as the hypocrites do, and not to fast before others and show themselves off, as the hypocrites do. He also taught them not to behave in this way and instructed them that it is possible even to give alms, pray and fast in a hypocritical manner. Therefore, as if speaking to ones who already knew that all these things could be done hypocritically, he says, "Beware of false prophets, who come to you in sheep's clothing but inwardly are ravenous wolves."

What is the sheep's clothing? It is the outward appearance of a feigned religion. Feigned almsgiving is sheep's clothing, not the action of a sheep. Feigned prayer is sheep's clothing, not the action of a sheep. And so are the other forms of piety with which the ravenous wolves clothe themselves. Nothing so wipes out good as a feigned good. For one flees from and is wary of a manifest evil as an evil, but one is not wary of an evil concealed under the guise of good, as long as it is not recognized as such, but welcomes it as a good, and thus it is conjoined with the good and obliterates the good. It is in this way that the servants of the devil most wickedly corrupt Christianity when they pass themselves off as Christians. It is about them that Christ warns his disciples—and us even more so through them—when he says, "Beware of false prophets," since the ability to discern evil is a great power for humankind[1] to have, and to know whom to flee is the firm safeguard of salvation.

To be sure, heresy is a dangerous matter but also very useful. It is dangerous because many are seduced by it and perish, but it is useful because the faithful are tested by it and separated from the unbelievers. Whoever murmurs about the danger of testing must murmur about the reward of passing the test. One cannot find rest in any matter unless labor has preceded it. How much all the more in spiritual matters that there can be no approval unless testing has preceded it!

"Beware of false prophets."

First one ought to know that there are altogether false Christians. Nothing destroys Christian people as these do, because people count as Christians whomever they see being called Christians. If it is agreed that there are false Christians, then either he is a false Christian or you are. If you are not, then he is; if you are, then he is not; if he is, then why do you think him to be a Christian when Christ gave you a commandment about him? It is because he whom God does not confess to be his child is not a Christian. How then can you think of him as your brother?

But perhaps you will say, "How can I say that he is not a Christian when I see him

Nineteenth Homily [1]Alternate reading: "for a good man [person]."

confessing Christ, having an altar, offering the sacrifice of the bread and wine, baptizing, reading the Scriptures of the saints, and having every order of the priesthood?" O wise person, if he did not confess Christ, his heathenness would be clear, and if you were deceived by him, it would be sheer madness by which you were deceived. But now it is due to your negligence if you are deceived by one who confesses Christ but not in the way that Christ commanded. Whoever falls into a hidden pit is said to be negligent because he did not carefully look ahead, but whoever falls into an open pit is not said to be negligent but crazy. But as for the things that you said about his imitation of the ecclesiastical mysteries, listen to this response. Because a monkey has the same limbs as a human being and by them imitates a human being, it does not mean that he should be called a human being for that reason, does it? So also every heresy of the church has and imitates the mysteries, but they are not churches.

Moreover, because the Lord knew that they were not openly heathen but hidden under the name Christian, he did not say, "Look at them" but "Beware of them." To look is simply to see, but to beware is to consider cautiously. Wherever an object is certain and beyond doubt, it is looked at, but wherever it is uncertain and under doubt, one must beware. Therefore, because Christ knew that in them there is something that would seem to be something different to different people—to some it would look like something brought down from above but to others it would look like something closed inside—he said, "Beware," so that you may know not to pay attention by means of bodily sight but by spiritual vigilance. If you look at them from a bodily point of view, you cannot recognize them, because they have the outward forms of Christianity.

O humans subject to suffering, how can you see lies that are covered by a veil of truth? Therefore first pay attention to good works. If we do the works of righteousness and are not deceived by any error, we will perceive every error. For the very fact that makes us not recognize the error of another compels us to err. Whoever does not recognize the lie of another person does not understand his own truthfulness. Therefore, as long as we are doing good works, the very light of righteousness will open the truth in front of our eyes. So also sins make the senses of sinners grow dark so that they do not see the lie but fall into it. See from the beginning, when error was sown into the faith of people, the error of the devil did not make people evil, but evil people adopted the diabolical error for themselves. If error had made people evil, the fault would have been God's, who made people to be so constructed so as to be seduced by errors. But now the fault is humankind's, which voluntarily chose error because errors cannot prevail in humankind unless sin has preceded them. First humankind is blinded by very many sins and so is deceived by the deception of the devil and falls into death. Just as night cannot prevail as long as the sun remains but occupies the world as soon as it has gone to the west, so as long as the light of righteousness is in a human being, the darkness of error does not lay hold of him. Therefore one must keep watch with good works because error does not beget sins, but sins error. As Wisdom says, wickedness drags a person to error.[2]

Beware, just as he admonishes, beware, as if the devil were introducing heresies against God's will—although it is not against God's will but with God's permission. If the Gentiles had not believed in Christ, we would understand the power of the devil, who does not allow the Gentiles to believe. If the devil had any power, he would not have allowed them to believe from the beginning, but now ever

[2]A loose paraphrase of Prov 13:6.

since all the Gentiles have come to faith but afterwards heresies arose among the believers, it is clear that it was not the power of the devil but the permission of God that caused it. And why does he admonish as if he did not want this to take place? It is because he does not want to have his servants without judgment that he sent them testing. But because he does not want them to perish by their ignorance, so he warns them. Consequently he sends testing so that the evil are not crowned with the good, but he admonishes them so that the good do not perish with the evil.

"Beware of false prophets."

It was written, "All the prophets and the law prophesied until John,"[3] not because there would not be any prophets after John, for there were Agabus, Silas, and many others, but because after him there would not be any prophecy about Christ. Therefore, after John's prophecy about the coming Christ ceased, there have been and are prophets, but not such people as those who prophesied about Christ but who have interpreted those things that were prophesied about Christ in times of old, namely, the teachers of the church. But all Christians are also called prophets, who are anointed into the kingdom, priesthood and prophetic office. Indeed, no one can interpret the meaning of the prophets unless he has the spirit of prophecy. But we have said this to show that the prophets about whom Christ is speaking are called teachers. Therefore, because the Lord knew that there would be false teachers of various heresies against the true teachers and that the former would confuse the prophetic and apostolic Scriptures with their perverse interpretation, he warned the teachers of all the churches through his apostles, "Beware of false prophets."

And if by chance some heretical teacher should say, "He did not call *us* false prophets, but rather the teachers of the Gentiles and Jews," so he went on to say, "who come to you in sheep's clothing." Although he spoke those things concerning the Jewish false apostles and prophets, nonetheless he spoke about those Jews who would believe in Christ but speak perverse things as an evil spirit suggested to them and would speak in order to corrupt Christians. The apostle Paul diligently warns in every epistle of his about being wary of them. The heretics are now the offspring of these false teachers. The sheep are properly called Christians, but the sheep's clothing is a type of Christianity. Do you see that Christ is speaking about fleeing from heretical Christians who seem outwardly to be Christians in form but inwardly are heathen by the way their confession functions? And the heretics are much more dangerous than the Jews of Paul's letters because the latter were rejected and pointed out by the apostles and wandered erratically outside the assembly of Christians, but heretics secretly corrupted some people who were not cautious, all the while being established as Christians and having their own churches. And what shall I say? They even rule churches and openly subvert them with all liberty and have so multiplied that Christians seem to have wandered rather than they. And how can they not be dangerous or how can they persuade many?

Furthermore, do not let a heretic say that Christ is speaking about true Christian teachers who indeed are not Christians but sinners. Every Christian who commits a sin is called a false Christian and truly is such because a Christian who commits a sin and does not repent of the sin is a false Christian. Nonetheless, so that you can know that he is not talking about Christian sinners but about heretical teachers he not only said, "Who come to you in sheep's clothing," but added, "Inwardly they

[3]Mt 11:13.

are ravenous wolves." Christian teachers, even if they have been servants and are called servants of the flesh because they have been overcome by the flesh, nonetheless do not intend to destroy Christians and, consequently, are not called ravenous wolves. Thus you see that he is clearly talking about heretical teachers who have undertaken the forms of Christians with the intention of tearing Christians to pieces with the iniquitous bite of seduction, as much as the devil can help them. Concerning such wolves the apostle said to the Ephesians, "I know that after I leave, savage wolves will come in among you and will not spare the flock. Even from your own number men will arise and distort the truth in order to draw away disciples after them."[4]

Hear, therefore, you who have been taught by the heretics and think that you are wise, and baptized by them and think that you have been made a Christian. Look, what are the heretical teachers called by Christ? Devourers. Therefore, if you have been educated by heretics, you have been snatched by them and not educated and grazed. For it is the nature of wolves to devour, not to save.

16"You will know them by their fruits."

The fruit of a person is the confession of his faith and the deed of his manner of living. Thus if you see a Christian, consider at once if his confession agrees with the Scriptures; if so, he is a true Christian. But if it is not as Christ commanded, he is a false Christian. So also when John wrote his epistle about heretics, he did not say, "If someone comes to you not having the name of Christ, do not even greet him," but "If anyone comes to you and does not bring this doctrine."[5] He did not refer the proof of Christianity to the name of Christ but to the confession, because it is not the name of Christ alone that makes a Christian but also the truth of Christ, since many walk in the name of Christ but few walk in his truth.

Then look. A sheep does not ever chase after a wolf, does it? No, but rather a wolf chases after a sheep. So also Cain persecuted Abel, not Abel Cain. So Ishmael persecuted Isaac, not Isaac Ishmael. So also Esau persecuted Jacob, not Jacob Esau. The Jews persecuted Christ, not Christ the Jews. Heretics persecute Christians, not Christians the heretics. Therefore, "you will know them by their fruits." If someone covers a wolf with a sheep's fleece, how would you recognize him except through his voice or action? A sheep leans back and bleats, but a wolf turns his head to the air against the heavens and howls. Therefore whoever emits a voice of humility and confession is a sheep, but whoever shamefully howls against God in opposition to the truth with all sorts of blasphemies is a wolf, as the prophet says about them: "Loftily they threaten oppression. They set their mouths against the heavens."[6] A sheep eats grass, but the wolf delights in meat. Whoever you see gathering the flowery grass of righteousness from the meadows of the Scriptures is a sheep, but whoever you see rejoicing in the blood of persecution is a wolf.

Furthermore, consider whether the virtues that he does are useful or not. Those that are wondrously done are useful and are profitable for salvation, such as healing the sick and other things of this kind that Christ did. But those things that they cause those who see them to admire them but have no usefulness, such as flying through the air (as the devil urged the Lord to do) or to make statues to walk or to be joined to a flame and not burned (and other such things as Simon[7] did), are empty. For the full works are from God because he is full, but the empty works are of the devil, just as he is empty and vain. That some miraculous deeds

[4]Acts 20:29-30, New International Version. [5]2 Jn 10. [6]Ps 73:8-9. [7]Simon the Magician (Acts 8), who was considered to be the spiritual father of all heretics.

are done by God and some by the devil, Nicodemus shows. He did not say, "No one can do signs unless God is with him," but "No one can do *these* signs that you do, unless God is with him."[8] And then true and false prophets are discerned by this criterion alone, whether they do useful or useless signs.

But now because it will happen that power is given to the devil to do even good things to some extent, we ought to consider another criterion: if the sign is necessary for the time or not. If Christ was doing miracles for the sake of strengthening the unbelievers and not merely for the sake of those whom he was healing, he was able to heal them in faith but not in a sign. It is clear that now since there are no unbelievers, there is no need to do miracles. Therefore, if he does a useless sign, he is a false prophet because he does not do this to build up someone else in the faith but to show off by means of his feat.

"Are grapes gathered from thorns, or figs from thistles?"

A grape contains the mystery of Christ in itself. As a cluster hangs with many individual grapes in itself, with the wood holding them together, so also Christ holds the many faithful together through the wood of the cross. Likewise, just as a fig tree holds many individual fruits enclosed under one covering, so also one church holds many faithful people by the sweet embrace of love. And in the fig tree there are these signs of love in its sweetness and signs of unity in the conjoining of the individual fruits, as it is written: "God gives the desolate a home to dwell in."[9] In a grape there is a sign of patience because it is sent to the winepress; there is a sign of joy in hope, because "wine [gladdens] the heart of man";[10] there is a sign of sincerity because it is not mixed with water, and it is a sweet delight. Concerning these things it has been written, "But the fruit of the Spirit is love, joy, peace, patience, kindness, goodness, faithfulness, gentleness, self-control; against such there is no law."[11]

The thorns, however, are the heretics, as the discourse above ["beware of false prophets"] shows. Therefore the thorns and thistle cannot bear churchly fruit. But what do they produce? Wounds, tribulations and other evils. Just as a thorn or thistle has sharp prickly points wherever you look, so also from whatever vantage point you look at the servants of the devil, they are full of evil. If he speaks, he speaks in trickery. If he is silent, he plots evil. If he is angry, he rages. If he acts patiently, he awaits the time to harm and considers the opportunity for when he can harm. If he does evil, he does not blush. If he does well, he does so out of vainglory because of other people. How can he produce good fruit when his root is the devil? Under a good tree both wild beasts and animals may rest, but no animal can rest under thorns except for snakes. Thus both good and evil people can have peace and maintain it next to righteous people, but nobody can have peace next to unbelievers or find rest in them, except for the serpents, that is, the demons who have their dwellings in their hearts. None of their fruits are useful; they have no refreshing shade in them. And it is true that he called all the wicked heretics thorns and thistles. Nonetheless, because the Lord knew that this heresy would prevail beyond all others, he called them thistles, as if they were professors of the Trinity and carrying a triangular impiety in their unbelief.[12]

18"A sound tree cannot bear evil fruit, nor can a bad tree bear good fruit."

[8]Jn 3:2. [9]Ps 68:6. [10]Ps 104:15. [11]Gal 5:22-23. [12]The author may be showing his anti-Trinitarian colors by making a play on words with *tribulus* ("thistle"), which begins, as does *Trinitas*, with *tri-*, the Latin prefix for "three."

He did not say that a bad tree cannot become good or that a good tree cannot become bad. Otherwise whoever is evil could blame God for the fact that he is evil, and whoever is good could credit God for the fact that he is good. But now he says that an evil person cannot bear good fruit, that is, as long as he is evil. But if he becomes good, he can, so that everyone owes it to his will and not to his nature that he is bad or good. For if he was willing to do good works but could not produce them, nature is to blame, but if he could and did not want to do so, then his will and not nature is to blame.

Therefore the servant of God cannot do evil, and if it seems to you sometimes that he does evil, consider carefully his evil action and you will find him inwardly to be good. For even what seems evil is good when done out of a good intention because a good intention excuses an evil act, but an evil act does not condemn a good intention. You saw that Moses committed murder, but he did not do so to avenge his own injury but that of the servants of God. You saw Jacob speaking one thing with his tongue but intending another in his heart when he said to Esau, "To see your face is like seeing the face of God,"[13] not to deceive him but to restrain him.

Similarly, an evil person cannot do good, and if he seems to you to do good, consider carefully that good deed, and you will find it inwardly to be evil. For whatever happens from a bad intention, even if it is good, is evil, for a good work cannot excuse an evil intention, but an evil intention condemns a good work. If you see a humble or gentle unbeliever, know that he is crafty in his heart. The prophet says about such people, "His words were softer than oil, yet they were drawn swords."[14] If you see him doing good works, understand that he does them to please others. The Lord says about them, "They do everything to be seen by men."[15] Therefore just as all the works, even the bad ones, of good people are good, so all the works, even the good ones, of evil people are evil. Thus if you see someone who appears good but does not worship God in truth, do not believe your eyes and say that he is worthy of a good life, but believe God more than yourself, since he said, "nor can a bad tree bear good fruit." But if you call him good, you make Christ to be a liar. You see things that are on the face, but God sees what is in the heart.

Just as in a garden there are many trees that produce useless fruit or while in the woods one does not find a tree producing good fruit, but if they do produce fruit, they produce tasteless or bitter fruit, so in the church, which is the garden of Christ (as Solomon says: "A garden locked is my sister, my bride, a garden locked, a fountain sealed. Your shoots are an orchard of pomegranates with all choicest fruits."[16]), there are many evil people. But in the churches of the heretics, which are desolate woods, there is no good person because, even if someone is good, he is good in order to please other people and not God.

I have said these things in accordance with the faith, but listen to how these things accord with reason. Whoever does something has a reason for doing it; nobody does anything without a reason. Whoever fights does so for booty or the glory of victory; whoever sails does so out of necessity or profit. Just as nothing can be born without a root, so nothing can take place without a cause. Thus whoever does good does so either because of a reward in the kingdom of heaven or because of the sentence of punishment. I ask you then: why does an unbeliever do anything good? Because of the sentence of punishment, you say. But he does not fear God. How can he fear God so as not to sin in his actions when he does not fear God so as not to sin in faith, given that it is worse to believe badly than to behave badly? Well, he does it with the hope of a reward, you say. But

[13]Gen 33:10. [14]Ps 55:21. [15]See Mt 6:2, 5, 16. [16]Song 4:12-13.

he does not hope in God if he does not care whether he believes lies or the truth, since it is better to believe well than to behave well, since faith without works is something, even if it is dead, but a work without faith is nothing.

Therefore, why does he do the good? It is to be seen by people and praised by them—and so his good is evil. For if without labor a person could do good in this world, it could be believed that an unbeliever could do good for the sake of good itself, since it is good to do good. But now since it is so contrary to the nature of people living in the flesh to do good, and it is difficult for them to do so and well nigh impossible, with the result that not even those great saints have been able to fulfill what is good, how can an unbeliever do good with such great exertion when he does not have the hope of reward before his eyes? Who would undertake such a dangerous contest when he does not hope to obtain a prize for it? Well, what then? Without a doubt he hopes for something, and so does a good deed. What is it? It is to buy vainglory from people. For the desire for vainglory gives much power for people to labor, and, if I can speak plainly, the desire for vainglory gives more power to a hypocrite than the hope of the kingdom of heaven gives to the faithful. And this is the reason: the nature of the flesh fights against the hope of the heavenly kingdom, but the desire for vainglory comes from the flesh, and so the nature of the flesh agrees with it.[17] Therefore he says, "Every tree that does not bear good fruit," because also a bad tree seems to produce righteousness but not a good kind or one that is useful. For if someone acts righteously for God's sake, God brings about the righteousness, but if he does it for the sake of vainglory, the devil does that good and delights in it. Therefore how do you think that the false Christians, whom God promises to send to hell, will share in your glory?

[21]"Not every one who says to me, 'Lord, Lord,' shall enter the kingdom of heaven, but he who does the will of my Father who is in heaven."

With these words he clearly shows that the false prophets about whom he had said we should beware of are none other than false Christians and false preachers of Christians. For before the Gentiles or Jews come to faith, they do not say to Christ, "Lord, Lord," but only those among the Jews and Gentiles who appear to have come to faith in Christ but have become false preachers, since they live and preach contrary to the will of God and the command of Christ. Again, because he taught that one can distinguish false prophets from true ones by their fruits, here he teaches more clearly what those fruits are by which the honorable and dishonorable teachers are distinguished. Whoever only says to Christ, "Lord, Lord," and does not do the will of God is dishonorable, but whoever both says to Christ, "Lord, Lord," and does the will of God is alone worthy of honor. The Lord teaches what the will of God is: "For this is the will of my Father, that every one who sees the Son and believes in him should have eternal life."[18] Therefore doing the will of God consists of believing in Christ. Likewise, when the Jews asked him elsewhere, "What must we do, to be doing the works of God?"[19] he answered them, "This is the work of God, that you believe in him whom he has sent."[20]

A statement of faith points to both a confession and an act. Therefore whoever confesses Christ as he himself taught believes in Christ, but whoever does not confess him in the way that he taught does not believe in him. And if he lives as Christ commanded, he believes in Christ; but whoever does not live as he commanded does not believe in Christ. To believe Christ is to obey Christ. But whoever does not confess him or does not walk accord-

[17]Alternate reading: "it consists of the nature of the flesh." [18]Jn 6:40. [19]Jn 6:28. [20]Jn 6:29.

ing to his word listens to Christ and yet does not believe—and for that reason neither the one who fails to confess him nor the one who fails to live according to his word will enter into the kingdom of heaven.

22“*On that day many will say to me, ‘Lord, Lord, did we not prophesy in your name?’*”

On what day? It will be on the day when he comes in his majesty and separates them one from another, as a shepherd divides his flock, when nobody dares to defend himself with a talkative wrangling of speeches or lies or dares to contradict the truth, because then the worldly things and vainglory will no longer be desired, but rather punishment and the flame of judgment will be feared. It will be on that day when no mouth will speak and no work will be hidden (as happens in this time), but on the contrary, the works of every person will speak and their mouths will keep quiet—not as when a person is interrogated and his conscience is not seen, but rather every conscience will be torn to shreds and every person confounded, as the apostle says: “Their conscience also bears witness and their conflicting thoughts accuse or perhaps excuse them.”[21] It will be on that day when nobody will excuse sinners, but everyone will accuse them, nor will anyone intervene on behalf of another, but they will each stand in fear there, because in that judgment there will not be any people to serve as flattering witnesses, but the truthful angels will not judge those who show favoritism, but the just God will judge them. “For he will render to every man according to his works.”[22] How rightly he captured the voice of people in fear and distress when he quotes them as saying, “Lord, Lord.” It will not be enough for them to say “Lord” once, because the need caused by their fear will compel them.

“Did we not prophesy in your name?”

Consider that they say, “In your name,” not “in your spirit,” because many who do not have the spirit of Christ walk in the name of Christ in order to deceive others.

Christians must be recognized not by the name of Christ but by the spirit of Christ. Therefore false Christians prophesy in the name of Christ but in the spirit of the devil, such as diviners do. But they are recognized because the devil now and then tells the truth, but the Holy Spirit never lies now and then. We grant that the devil now and then tells the truth so that he can commend his lie by the occasional truth. If he never told the truth, his seductive power would never be able to be enough to lead people into temptation.

“And [did we not] cast out demons in your name?”

They cast out demons in the name of Christ, though they have the spirit of the enemy. But they do not so much as cast them out but appear to do so, as the devils collude with them—and consequently they always cast them out and yet never heal them. The demons always cry aloud before them, as if they were being chastised, but they never retreat from them, as if they were afraid.

“And [did we not] do many mighty works in your name?”

They also do many powerful things according to those things that we have spoken of: not useful and necessary things but useless and pointless things. Therefore, in all their cases their fruits are all torn to pieces by the commandment of Christ to see if their manner of living is good and their confession true. But if their confession does not agree with their man-

---

[21]Rom 2:15. [22]Rom 2:6.

ner of living or vice versa, then they are false Christians.

[23]***"And then will I declare to them, 'I never knew you; depart from me, you evildoers.'"***

"Then" means up until then I will sustain them because a great delay ought to precede a great wrath and a grand delay makes the judgment of God to be all the more just and the destruction of sinners all the more fair. This statement accords with the idea that God does not know sinners because they are not worthy to be known by God, just as the apostle also says: "The Lord knows those who are his."[23] It is not that he does not know who they are but that he does not recognize them as his own; thus, those who perish were not his. Or how would God recognize you when you do not want to recognize him? Just as all people naturally know God, but they seem not to really know him because they do not worship him worthily, as servants respect their master or a created item its maker (and nature, not the will, causes one to know him), so also God naturally knows all people, but he seems not to really know them because he does not love them as a creator loves his creation or as a master loves his own servants. And it is owing to his nature and not his will to know them because every evil is foreign to God. But Christ swears not to commend his own truthfulness but to condemn their unbelief. Christ would not lie, if he had not sworn, but they are all the more confounded by his firmer response since whoever is a liar does not think that anyone tells the truth, not even God. Whoever is deceived by the seduction of the devil and does not lie (though his intention is to lie) never ceases to lie, not even after death. Death, to be sure, separates the soul from the body, but it does not change the intention of the soul. Do you wish to know why I say this? Consider that even after their death they lie: "Lord, we did such and such in your name." Of course, they knew in their heart that they had never loved Christ or done his will. But they think that just as they deceived other people in this life, so also there they can deceive God. So he does not say to them, "Depart from me, you who were evildoers," but "you evildoers," because the wicked do not fail to be wicked not even after death, because, even if they cannot sin, they still have the intention to sin.

The Twentieth Homily: On Matthew 7

[24]***"Every one then who hears these words of mine and does them will be like a wise man who built his house upon the rock."***

Often we are astonished that people, either enticed by promises or broken by terrors or overcome by the persuasions of false teachers, abandon the truth of the faith and pass over to the lie of unbelief. But if we carefully understood at least this one sentence of Christ and remembered it, we would never be amazed at the loss of such people. How could one who never stood in Christ remain with Christ? Or how can truth lay hold of one who never laid hold of truth? Or how could righteousness preserve one who never preserved righteousness?

"Every one then who hears these words of mine and does them."

What words? The words that we said above, namely, that whoever wishes to be a true Christian must not only not kill but also not get angry without reason; not only must he not commit perjury but must not swear at all; not only must not commit fornication but must not lust with his eye; not only must not strike but must not strike back when struck; not only must not steal other people's property

[23]2 Tim 2:19.

but must also give up his own property when compelled; must not only love his friends sincerely but even his enemies. He must give alms but not in front of others; he must persist in prayer but by entering into his room; he must frequently fast but not with sadness; he must not judge his brother who sins but forgive him out of consideration of his own weakness; he must not give that which is holy to dogs or cast pearls before swine. Let him ask, seek, knock and receive. Let him beware of false prophets. Therefore whoever builds himself with such commandments, how can it happen that he will be broken by temptations and fall?

Or in contrast, how can one stand when struck by temptation when he has not bound himself to the foundation of any righteousness? Who ever kept those commandments and fell? We blame God because he did not keep him safe from harm. But if the might of the devil prevails against those in whom the righteousness of Christ is not found, God must be praised rather than blamed when they are destroyed, because only those who despise the commandments of Christ perish.

"[He] will be like a wise man."

He did not say, he "will be deemed a wise person" but he "will be like a wise person." Therefore the person who is likened is different from the person to whom the other is likened. Therefore the person who is being likened is the individual in question; the one to whom he is being likened is Christ. Christ, you see, is the wise man who built his house, that is, the church, on a rock, that is, on the strength of faith. For also the strength of faith is called a rock, for which reason Simon was called Peter,[1] to whom the Lord said, "You are Peter, and on this rock I will build my church, and the powers of death shall not prevail against it."[2]

Who then is the foolish man? The devil, concerning whom Jeremiah says, "Like the partridge that gathers a brood which she did not hatch, so is he who gets riches but not by right; in the midst of his days they will leave him, and at his end he will be a fool."[3] Therefore the devil is a foolish man who built his house on sand. His house consisted of all the Gentiles before Christ. Just as the saints were made the house of Christ, so also the impious are the house of the enemy. But they were built on sand, that is, the inconstancy of unbelief. If constancy of the faith is called a rock, the inconstancy of unbelief (that is, idolatry) is rightly called sand, since idolatry has always been scattered through the various forms of worship of idols. Or certainly he built on sand, that is, on carnal people and unbelievers. Such people are thus called sand, not soil, because soil produces fruit, but sand remains sterile.

There is a second reason for this comparison: because soil has been united and drawn together, but the grains of sand do not come together, nor do they stick to one another; so also all the unbelievers, who are under the sway of the devil, are not united, nor do they know one wise thing, but they are scattered through various demons, with one person saying one thing and another person saying another thing. So also the dogmas of the philosophers teach us, which always contradict themselves. In this way exists the treachery of the heretics, who never know one thing but have as many opinions as teachers. Therefore all the people of the devil are likened to sand. But the people of God are not only united like soil, which can be broken up even if it has been packed together, but they are drawn together and indissoluble like a rock.

Third, the people of the devil cannot be counted, just like sand, but few are the elect chosen by God out of the many.

Rain, however, is teaching, because just as rain waters the earth so that it bears fruit, so

Twentieth Homily [1]Peter means "Rock Man." [2]Mt 16:18. [3]Jer 17:11.

teaching waters a person so that he works righteousness. God says through Isaiah about the teaching that would be removed from the Jews: "I will also command the clouds that they rain no rain upon it."[4] The prophets and apostles are called clouds, because just as clouds carry rain and pour it on the soil, so also the prophets and apostles receive words from God and pour them out on the soil of people's mind. There are clouds that are stirred up by the Holy Spirit, and there are clouds that are stirred up by the spirit of the power of the air, as the prophet says: "Dark waters in the clouds of the air."[5] The clouds that are set in motion by the Holy Spirit bear glistening water, that is, true and holy doctrine. But the clouds set in motion by the spirit of the power of the air bear dark water, which does not illuminate the minds of those who receive it but makes them grow dark.

The winds are partly bad and partly good; those that make up the bad part of the winds are the unclean spirits that breathe into the hearts of people; those that make up the good part of the winds are the spirits of various virtues or angels, who work invisibly in the senses of humankind and lead them to good. And see how this accords with matters. It is the nature of rain to soften and loosen up the soil, but it is the nature of winds to press hard with power. Thus the clouds of the wicked soften people with their false doctrine and promises and loosen them with flattering and persuasions, but the devil enters into their hearts like a wind and invisibly presses them hard to consent to their lies or forces them into other sins. So also in a good way the holy clouds persuade people of the teaching of righteousness and soothe them rationally, but the Holy Spirit or the angels, like favorable winds, making them favorable in their hearts, cause people to acquiesce to the truth. Just as it is not possible for the ground to produce fruit from rain alone unless a wind blows over it, so it is not possible for doctrine alone to correct a person, unless the Holy Spirit also works together in his heart.

The rivers are partly bad and partly good. Those that make up the bad part are full of an individual's unclean spirit and are built on wordiness, such as the philosophers of various schools, the orators, grammarians, and all the rest who are not wise according to God;[6] from their belly flow rivers of dead water.[7] Those rivers that make up the good part are the evangelists, the teachers of the people, and the rest of those who are wise according to God; from their belly flow rivers of living water. Therefore neither the rains of false doctrine destroys the church, which Christ as a wise man built on a rock, nor does the wind of the devil strike hard against it, nor does the force of violent floods move it. For although the church is humbled because of testing, nonetheless it cannot perish because of its faith in Christ.

Nor does the fact that some from the church fall mitigate this fact, for they never were Christians. Not all who were of Israel were Israelites. So not all who are called Christians are also of Christ. One must look at the works of Christians and not their names. The apostle says, "The Lord knows those who are his. Let every one who names the name of the Lord depart from iniquity."[8] Therefore whoever departs from iniquity is of Christ, not one who idly names the name of Christ. Such people were not even built on the rock of faith, as we will show below.

The rain, that is, the teaching of truth through the prophetic and apostolic clouds, fell against the house that the foolish man built on the sand, that is, against the Gentiles and all ungodly who form the house of the devil. The winds blew, that is, the spiritual

[4]Is 5:6. [5]Ps 18:11 (trans. Kellerman). [6]Alternate reading: "and the rest who are teachers of worldly wisdom." [7]Alternate reading: "flow rivers of lying doctrine." [8]2 Tim 2:19.

graces or the angels who work invisibly and lead one to faith in the truth. The floods came, that is, the four Evangelists or other wise ones, and dashed on that house, and so the house of the devil fell and the house of Christ was erected with spiritual tools. And do not marvel that the Gentiles who come to faith are said to have fallen. Indeed, they fell as far as the devil was concerned so that they might rise to Christ. Behold, as long as anyone walks in sins, he stands as far as the devil is concerned, but he lies flat as far as Christ is concerned. But once he is converted to righteousness, in the devil's opinion he falls, but in Christ's he arises. The prophet says about those who have been freed by Christ: "He ascended on high, leading captivity captive."[9] Again, the Lord says, "When a strong man, fully armed, guards his own palace, his goods are in peace; but when one stronger than he assails him and overcomes him, he takes away his armor,"[10] namely, ungodly people whom the devil had built into a house for himself. Therefore, if in the language of the prophecy they are called captives with regard to the devil, they have been transformed into the freedom of faith with regard to Christ. If in Christ's language they are said to have been snatched away, those who have arisen in faith are consequently also said to have fallen with regards to their earlier state.

[27]***"And great was the fall of it."***

That is, when the idols in all the world were destroyed, the lies in all the earth were overcome and errors were removed, because all the world has fallen in the devil's opinion, but it has risen to Christ. Therefore the wise king has destroyed with the spiritual arms of his saints the house that the foolish man built on sand, but the foolish devil will never be able to destroy with the lying arguments of his servants the house that the wise Christ built on a rock. Therefore every Christian who builds himself on the rock (i.e., Christ) is like the wise man Christ. Whoever hears the words of Christ and does them is the person who builds himself on the rock of Christ. For Christ is love, and whoever builds himself in love builds himself on the rock Christ. Whoever builds himself in gentleness builds himself on the rock Christ, for Christ is gentleness. Whoever builds himself in chastity builds himself on the rock Christ, for Christ is chastity. Whoever builds himself in mercy builds himself on the solid rock Christ, for Christ is mercy. And whoever builds himself in any kind of goodness whatsoever is shown to have built himself on the rock Christ, because Christ is every good thing. He is like Christ because just as no adversity can destroy the church of Christ built on the rock, so no adversity can destroy such a Christian who builds himself on Christ, as Paul says: "Who shall separate us from the love of Christ? Shall tribulation or distress?"[11]

Every Christian who builds himself on the sand is like the foolish devil. Whoever hears the words of Christ and does not do them builds on the sand, for the words that are not turned into works are sand that is scattered. Just as the grains of sand do not come together as one or adhere to one another but are always separate, so the words that are heard and not turned into one lump of righteousness by works are separate and scattered. And so they become like sand, which never is joined together in itself. Therefore every Christian who believes in Christ because he has only heard his words and does not strengthen himself in good works in Christ builds himself on sand. But also whoever does evil works builds on sand. The sand is all evil, as we said above, and whoever builds on earthly goods builds himself on sand. He is like the foolish devil, because

[9]Ps 68:18 (trans. Kellerman). [10]Lk 11:21-22. [11]Rom 8:35.

just as the house of the devil (that is, idolatry) was destroyed by Christ through the works of his servants and of his graces, so also the evil person must be destroyed today or tomorrow by the devil through the works of his servants or of demons or of ungodly people, and these are the sort of people who, as we noted above, fall from the church inasmuch as they did not build themselves on the rock but rather on sand.

"And great was the fall of it."

How great? Just as a house that has a strong foundation will not suffer great ruin if some part of the wall or roof falls, because it can be repaired again, but if its foundation has experienced destruction, then its ruin is great because the whole house comes down, so also if a Christian either fornicates or commits adultery or commits homicide, he has indeed fallen, but nonetheless his fall is not great because he can arise again by repentance, just as David did. But if he experienced something in the foundation of his faith, that is, if he lies and goes over to the Gentiles or heretics, then his ruin is great because he falls completely and entirely.

28*And when Jesus finished these sayings, the crowds were astonished at his teaching.*

When someone's mind has been pleased in a rational manner, it generates praise, but when one's mind has been overcome, it generates astonishment. We are astonished at whatever we cannot adequately praise. Nonetheless, their astonishment pertains more to Christ's glory than to their own faith. For they did not marvel as ones who believed in Christ, but they marveled because they had heard blameless discourses. But if they had believed in Christ, they would not have marveled but rather believed. For every word or deed that overwhelms the person doing or speaking it stirs up astonishment as, for example, if a person should say or do something that exceeds the bounds of his nature. But even though whatever God says or does is great, nonetheless it is less than the full power of God. Therefore we should not be astonished at whatever we heard was done or said by God, because all those things are less than the power of God.

Nonetheless, the people were hearing with silence and seriousness, and by their astonishment they gained something by his words since, even if astonishment does not arise from faith, it still is an invitation to faith. Whoever is astonished at the words of teaching, even though he does not yet believe, he still stands on the very threshold of belief so that he may believe. It was the crowds that were astonished; that is to say, it was the common people.

The Pharisees were not there, nor were the princes of the people or the high priests, who have the habit of listening not out of eagerness for learning but for contradicting, not so as to obtain some salvation but so as to find some lie. And so the simple people were listening with simplicity of heart. If some of the leaders had been present, they would doubtlessly have troubled the silence and earnestness of the people with their own contradictory words, as had been their habit, because where knowledge abounds, malice is even stronger. For whoever had hastened to be first finds it difficult to be content with second place.

29*For he taught them as one who had authority.*

Every teacher is a servant of the Law because he cannot add anything beyond the Law from his own judgment nor remove anything according to his own understanding, but he preaches only what is contained in the Law. The human mind cannot even show him to be wrong, that is, do something outside of what is right, such as showing something perverse or evil, because it is divine wisdom that has suggested it. So Moses and Solomon say, "You shall not add to the word which I command you, nor take from it."[12] Whoever dares to do this thinks that he is wiser than God and begins to be a false witness because he says that which neither ear has heard nor eye seen. But Christ is the Lord of the Law and can take something away from the Law, which he had commanded due to the needs of the time. For example, because of the hardness of the heart it had been commanded that one ought to give a certificate of divorce. Since the Lord had the power, he removed that commandment when he said, "What therefore God has joined together, let not man put asunder."[13] Moreover, he also adds what previously had rarely been commanded because of the weakness of humankind, as for example, "You have heard that it was said to the men of old, 'You shall not kill,' but I say to you, 'Do not be angry.' "[14] Therefore they were astonished because he was not simply teaching what had been commanded, as if he were a servant of the Law and under its power, but he was adding to what had already been said, as if he was the lord of the Law and had the power. This is clear when he said, "You have heard that it was said to the men of old . . . but I say to you."[15]

The Twenty-First Homily: On Matthew 8

[1]***When he came down from the mountain, great crowds followed him.***

Note that only the disciples are said to have ascended toward Jesus, but when Jesus came down from the mountain, crowds followed him, and quite great crowds at that. The mountain is the height of virtue, the pinnacle of the church, where the crowds cannot draw near to Christ, either because they are weighed down by sins or burdened with worldly cares. They can neither imitate Christ nor listen to the noble discourses that are spoken on the mountain, but only the disciples can, who have been freed from the passions of vices and have not been burdened by worldly cares. For that reason—because they are light and unencumbered—they can draw near to Christ, since they have become his imitators in all things that they may be able to hear his more noble discourses. And yet, when he descended from the heights of godliness to more humble ground because the weakness of those who could not follow him on the mountain, then great crowds followed him.

[2]***And behold, a leper came to him.***

One ought to know that Luke and Mark begin with the curing of a demon-possessed individual and, in the second place, the freeing of a woman from the bodily ailment of fever, on the grounds that God cares more for the soul than for the salvation of the flesh.[1] This is, first, because the soul is nobler than the flesh. The soul can live without the flesh, but the flesh cannot live without the soul. Second, it is because in every sin the soul sins first and then the flesh does. For the flesh never can sin unless the soul is first overcome. To be sure, the flesh can first have an evil longing, but it cannot sin unless the soul agrees to it, since the flesh is under the power of the soul, not the soul under the power of the flesh. Therefore it was necessary that the soul, which had fallen earlier, also rise again before the flesh. Thereupon the soul freed from the power of the devil can free its flesh from sin, whereas the flesh healed from its weakness cannot free the soul from sin but rather overcomes it, since the safety of the flesh always fights against the discipline of righteousness.

[12]The quotation is Deut 4:2; Deut 12:32 and Prov 30:6 express similar thoughts. [13]Mt 19:6. [14]Mt 5:21-22; the RSV has been modified slightly to reflect the author's abridgment of the quotation. [15]See Mt 5:21-22. **Twenty-First Homily** [1]These are the first miracles that occur in their books (Lk 4; Mk 1).

Here, however, Matthew begins with the cleansing of the leper as a representation of the healing of the flesh. What does this mean? Does he overlook the reasoning of the other Evangelists? No, but he makes it all the more clear. Whereas they began with the curing of the demon-possessed man as a representation of the healing of the soul, Matthew began with Christ teaching on the mountain for the salvation of the soul—something the other Evangelists did not do. For just as the flight of an unclean spirit frees the soul from the power of sin (which takes place by the devil's instigation), so also the word of teaching breaks the working of the devil and frees the soul from error, sin and other evils that had arisen at the devil's instigation. The individual whose body is vexed by the devil is not the only person to suffer at the devil's hands, but everyone who does the will of the devil will be vexed by him even worse.

He makes the leprous individual to reveal a secret of the healing of the flesh. Leprosy, after all, is a fleshly affliction. To keep people from saying to themselves, "His words are great and fearsome, but his works are nothing; speaking grandly is nothing great, but doing something is worth much," he healed the leper so that Christ could add authority to his previous words by the miracle of cleansing him, with the result that he would be astounding in his words and even more astounding in his deeds.

Behold, the leper runs to meet him as he comes down the mountain, as if the leper had already been prepared for it. And perhaps it was for this very reason that he descended, namely, to cleanse the leper. The sin of our souls is leprosy. Therefore the Lord descended from the heights of the sky, as from a lofty mountain, to cleanse the leprosy of our sins. Why do you think that the leper did not climb the mountain with all the rest in order to hear his divine discourse? It was because he was weighed down by his leprosy and was bearing the weight of his sins; he did not have the strength to climb. Or did you not hear the prophet who said that those who ascend to the mountain of the church ought to be light? He says, "Who shall ascend the hill of the Lord? And who shall stand in his holy place? He who has clean hands and a pure heart."[2] So whoever walks in evil cannot ascend to the church, which is called the mountain of God, nor can he hear spiritual teaching. And if he comes, he comes with the body but does not ascend with the soul. But whoever does not come with a pure heart derives no benefit from his coming in the body. Even if he hears spiritual teaching, he does not understand it because his understanding has been corrupted by the leprosy of carnal vices. Nobody can taste the savor of good things as long as he delights in bad things. As long as evil delights him, good cannot delight him. But good begins to please him the moment that evil begins to displease him.

And knelt before him.

A perfect prayer is faith and confession, as the apostle says: "For man believes with his heart and so is justified, and he confesses with his lips and so is saved."[3] Thus the leprous man fulfilled the work of faith by praying, and he fulfilled the work of confession by his words: "Lord, if you will, you can make me clean." He did not ask him as a craftsman, but he worshiped him as God. He brought spiritual wages to a spiritual doctor. For all doctors are pleased by money, but Christ is pleased by prayer alone. Truly, nothing we offer is more worthy than faithful prayer. Whatever else we offer comes from our possessions, but prayer comes from us ourselves.

"Lord, if you will, you can make me clean."

[2]Ps 24:3-4. [3]Rom 10:10.

When he said, "If you will," he did not doubt about the willingness of Christ, which is ready for every good, but this remark indicates his uncertainty about what Christ's will would decide. Because Christ is good, he does not want to give anything harmful, even if asked. Nor does bodily health benefit all. Therefore, because the leper did not know whether that cure would benefit him, so he was uncertain about his will, although he knew that it was ready for every good. It is indeed the mark of a believer to believe in the goodness of God's mercy, but it is not given to a human being, not even a believer, to know the decisions of his mercy, since it is well known that not even the apostle was able to know them when he asked the Lord three times that the thorn in the flesh (the messenger of Satan) leave him. The thorn had been given to him so that he would not become proud; for this reason he was told, "My grace is sufficient for you, for my power is made perfect in weakness."[4]

And it is as if he said, "I believe that you desire everything that is good, but I do not know if what I desire is good for me. Nonetheless, I do not doubt, but rather I believe that if it is good for me, you also will it." This talk showed that he did not doubt about the mercy of God but did not know the decisions his mercy would make.

[3]***And he stretched out his hand and touched him.***

Because it had been written in the Law that whoever touched a leper would be unclean until evening, he touched the leper, on the grounds that he was not a servant of the Law but its master. For a law is subordinate to the lawgiver, not the lawgiver to the law. What shall we say? Did he break the Law? No. He broke the letter of the Law, to be sure, but he did not break its intention but rather added dignity to it. If the Law had been able to bring it about so that leprosy would not render the one touching it unclean, he would never have ordered people not to touch leprosy. Consequently, he gave the order not to touch leprosy because he could not bring it about that leprosy would not render the one touching it unclean. Therefore, whoever touched leprosy and was not rendered unclean by the leprosy did not act contrary to the Law but did more than what the Law demanded: he not only was not rendered unclean by the leprosy but even cleansed the leprosy. Nor is it even believable that he who cleansed leprosy could be said to be rendered unclean by leprosy. The Law did not forbid the touching of leprosy so that the lepers could not be healed, but rather so that those who touch leprosy would not share in their uncleanness. Therefore whoever touched leprosy and did not share in its uncleanness but in addition cleansed the leprosy did more than what the Law wanted.

Thus he touched the leprosy and broke the letter of the Law so that now not the leprosy of the body but the leprosy of the soul might be put to flight. One must pity the weakness of the body and not hate it, but one must not pity the weakness of the soul but rather hate it, because the weakness of the body does not lie in our power so that it may not come on us or withdraw from us, but the weakness of the soul lies in our power, so that it may not come on us or withdraw from us. The weakness of the body lays hold of us, and it is not held onto by us, but the weakness of the soul does not lay hold of us, but it is held onto by us. Thus the weakness of the body must be pitied but the weakness of the soul hated. Therefore he abrogated the law, not the righteousness of the Law—not the law that he wrote in people's hearts when he created them but that which he wrote in the book when the people had worshiped the calf. It was not that

[4]2 Cor 12:9.

law about which it is written, "The law of the Lord is perfect, reviving the soul,"[5] but that about which it is written, "For the law brings wrath, but where there is no law there is no transgression."[6] How then did it deserve to be kept when sins were what had instigated it? Quite rightly he calmly abrogated what he had spoken angrily. If the Law had not been abolished, the spiritual leper could never have been healed, because everyone who lives under the Law is a leper.

Saying, "I will; be clean." And immediately his leprosy was cleansed.

The leprosy departed not because it was touched but because it was ordered, in order to show that he did not touch him because the leprosy was fleeing, but he did it to break the Law. Otherwise it would have been enough for him to speak to the leprosy. But not even his words were necessary, but only his will. Therefore his will was done for the sake of the leper, but his words were spoken for the sake of the spectators. For if Christ had silently healed him when so many people were standing around him, who could have known by whose power he had been healed? Therefore he said, "I will; be clean," so that all may know that he was healed by Christ's power, who had given the command of healing. The "I will" that he spoke is an indication of his will and points back to the "if you will" that the leper had spoken. But the "be clean" is the commandment of power and pertains to the "you can" that the leper had said.

4And Jesus said to him, "See that you say nothing to anyone; but go, show yourself to the priest, and offer the gift that Moses commanded, for a proof to the people."

Do not understand this to mean that Moses commanded it as a proof to them but rather as "Go and offer the gift as proof to the people." He did not say, "Go, show yourself to the priests, and say nothing to anyone," but "First say nothing to anyone, and go, show yourself." He is not ordering him always to be silent but only until he can show himself to the priests, lest by chance if he were first to announce it to someone, the priests would hear from the grapevine and out of their hatred and hostility to Christ drive him out of the people as a leper, since they do not receive him as having been cleansed and have the pretext of his being a leper. Therefore he orders him to offer the sacrifices so that if they wish to expel him afterwards he can say to them, "You received the gifts from one who was cleansed; how can you expel me as if I were a leper? If I were still a leper, you should not have taken the gifts as from a cleansed man, but if I have been made clean, you ought not to drive me out as a leper." The same thing would happen in either case.

All the works of healing done by Christ have within themselves prefigurements of the hidden dispositions of God. Therefore his corporeal acts of healing were advantageous to them then and to us now, but his spiritual acts perhaps are advantageous to us only. Thus this leper who drew near to be healed after having already been prepared after the words of teaching exemplifies the Jewish people—standing down below because they were the crowd, but hearing the word then that had been spoken above and believing it, worshiping and embracing. As for everyone who worships the word of God, because he thinks that it is also divine, and embraces it with the longing of his heart, the word of God also touches his soul. Nor is it possible for the soul that embraces the word not to be touched by the word, but as soon as the word touches the soul, it cleanses it from the leprosy of unbelief, as it is written: "You are already made clean

[5]Ps 19:7. [6]Rom 4:15.

by the word which I have spoken to you."[7] And Peter in the Acts of the Apostles says, he "cleansed their hearts by faith."[8] For this reason, the people who had spent their life under an austere law and had not yet experienced grace believed firmly in his power according to the tradition of their ancestors, but they doubted about mercy, saying, "If you will, you can make me clean." For the law taught well enough the power of God, but it did not teach clearly enough his mercy. For this reason, the Lord fulfilled the Law for the one who knew the power of Christ according to the Law, which he had given, that he might recognize the mercy of his grace, saying, "I will; be clean," and he commanded him to offer sacrifices as Moses had commanded.

What were those sacrifices? A pair of turtledoves or two young pigeons. All righteousness consists of these two things: refraining from evil things and doing good things. Therefore, through the turtledove he orders the people to offer to God holiness of life by abstaining from evil things once they have been cleansed from unbelief. The spiritual chastity of the soul is abstinence from evils, so that it does not come together with an alien spirit or take the seed of its inspiration and so bear works similar to an evil spirit. By the pigeon he symbolizes every good work that arises out of love, since love produces every good work. Therefore whoever loves his neighbor as himself removes nothing good from his neighbor, just as he does not remove anything good from himself. Therefore whenever someone has fulfilled these two requirements of righteousness, refraining from all evil (which is chastity) and doing every good deed (which is love), clearly such a person has been cleansed from the leprosy of unbelief. Thus a people who have been cleansed and are offering such sacrifices to God have become a witness against unbelieving priests who drive away the author of the Law while they boast in the letter of the Law, because he purifies people from sins, which the Law could not purify them from.

And if you have embraced the word of God with the affection of your heart, the word has also no less touched your soul because it loves those who love it, as Solomon says in Proverbs,[9] and the word cleanses you from every leprosy of unbelief. But as soon as it has cleansed you, it orders you to show yourself as clean to the priests, chastising you from every participation in an evil work and unfolding your love to all through good works, so that through these sacrifices the priests may recognize you to be cleansed when they see that you are not doing to another what you do not wish to experience, but you are also doing to all what you wish to have done to you. If you do not offer to God the sacrifices of these forms of righteousness, it is clear to all that you have not been cleansed but still remain in your earlier unbelief.

The Twenty-Second Homily: On Matthew 8

5As he entered Capernaum, a centurion came forward to him, beseeching him 6and saying, "Lord, my servant is lying paralyzed at home, in terrible distress."

After the Lord taught the people on the mountain and cleansed the leper at the foot of the mountain, he later came to Capernaum to reveal a mystery: after the cleansing of the Jews, he is coming to the Gentiles. And behold, a certain centurion approached and beseeched him. The centurion was the firstfruit of the Gentiles; in comparison with his faith all the faith of the Jews would be found to be unbelief. This man had neither heard Christ when he was teaching, nor had he seen the leper cleansed, but only having heard of the

[7]Jn 15:3. [8]Acts 15:9. [9]Prov 8:17.

cleansing of the leper he believed more than he heard. The leper had brought himself saying, "If you will, you can make me clean." To be sure, these are the words of faith, albeit not a great one, because such words could be said to holy people, such as Elisha, who had cleansed a leper not with his hands but by his command.[1] But the centurion not only confessed the potency of his power but also recognized the very nature of his divinity. He did not ask him as a saint with a physical body but as God who was present everywhere when he said, "Say the word, and my servant will be healed." He addressed him as one who had the ability to give orders to the diseases of people who were absent.

This centurion portrayed the Gentiles of the future, who had not read any Law or Prophets about Christ or seen Christ as he was doing miracles, but in their hearts they perceived the righteousness of the Law that they had not read in the books and saw Christ with their mind, though they had not seen him with their eyes, thereby showing in themselves that the Scriptures were written for the impediment of sinners, not for the need of the saints, since the Scriptures are not necessary for the faithful, as the apostle says: "The law is not laid down for the just but for the lawless."[2] Nature itself is humankind's teacher of all righteousness, and the creation of all things is the Scripture about God that cannot be falsified,[3] because nothing has been created in the world through God is not most clearly shown. Thus the elements of all objects in this age admonish people of the power of God, but on the last day they will be condemned by their own judgment.

One must know that Luke portrays Christ being asked by the centurion through the priests, while Matthew portrays him being asked by the centurion himself. There are different kinds of explanations but just one meaning of it. Inasmuch as he set forth his request through the priests, he showed that every petition of the people ought to be sent to Christ through priests. But inasmuch as he explained his situation, he who asks Christ through the priests rightly seems himself to be asking. But since in Luke he obtained because the priests interceded on his behalf while in Mathew Christ promised while he himself was asking, it is clear that in Luke he did not obtain it through favoritism shown to the priests but rather because of the faith of the centurion himself, so that we may know that in every case it is not the merits of those interceding that are regarded but rather the faith of those who humbly seek.

"Lord, my servant is lying paralyzed at home, in terrible distress."

What do we first admire in the centurion? His humility or faith or wisdom or kindness? His humility because he did not think that he was worthy to welcome Christ into his home. His faith, because he believed that Christ could do what he was asking. His wisdom, because without anyone pointing it out to him he saw clearly the divine treasure hidden in the field—not by the acuity of his eyes but by that of a pure mind. His kindness, because he so diligently hastened for the health of a slave, counting his death to be not a loss of money but of health. I think that that centurion thought that there was no difference between servant and master, knowing that there are various rankings in this age among them, but still there is only one nature between the two. Thus he honored the image of God more in a fellow human being than he despised the work of captivity in a servant, because God did not so ordain it when he created according to

Twenty-Second Homily [1]See 2 Kings 5. [2]1 Tim 1:9. [3]For "that cannot be falsified" some read "ineffable," others "infallible." However, I have assumed that the neologism *infalsabilis* (and hence the *lectio difficilior*) is probably the correct word.

his righteousness, but he accepted it when he permitted it because of humankind's sins. For if you as a master put value on your slave, God has planted his Spirit in him. Therefore, to the degree that the Spirit of God is greater than the value of a human being, to that degree that which is loved in a slave is greater than that which is despised about him. See to it then that God does not settle accounts with you mercilessly on account of his Spirit once you have abused a slave without the fear of God because you want to get your money's worth.

Let slaves also hear this and understand. Just as masters have something to imitate in the centurion because of his mercy, so also slaves have something to imitate in the servant because of his sincerity. But do you think that he was such a lad so as to be loved by his master? Measure the faithfulness of the slave by the love of the master. It was not even possible for him to have obtained such great love of his master for himself unless his good character had won it. Therefore masters owe love to their slaves because of the shared nature, but slaves owe their masters respect because of the divine ordinance. And Christ is loved by masters in their slaves, and Christ is revered by slaves in their masters.

"In terrible distress."

Even if he was not really in terrible distress, nonetheless his master thought him to be in terrible distress because he loved him so. For everyone loves someone; even if he is only moderately under the weather, he thinks that he is in worse condition than he is. But see the wisdom of the centurion and his faith. See his faith because he did not say, "Come and save him," since he knew that Christ was present in every place, even though he was standing there. For although Christ seemed to be in the world because of the incarnation in the flesh, nonetheless the world was in Christ according to the essence of his deity. See his wisdom because he did not say, "At least while you stand here, heal him." For he knew that he was mighty to do anything, wise to understand and merciful to listen. Thus he only explained the weakness but left the remedy of healing to the power of his mercy. With a medical doctor, however, it is necessary only to explain the affliction, and he will know what it is or how he will treat it.

7And he said to him, "I will come and heal him."

He promised to go for many reasons, even though he was not asked to do so. First, to awaken his faith, he wanted him to answer what he did. Unless he had said, "I will come and heal him," he would never have replied,

8"Lord, I am not worthy to have you come under my roof; but only say the word, and my servant will be healed."

It was with this plan in mind that, as the Canaanite woman cried out, "My daughter is severely possessed by a demon,"[4] he answered that he would not do anything, saying, "It is not fair to take the children's bread and throw it to the dogs,"[5] so that she could be provoked to reply, "Yes, Lord, yet even the dogs eat the crumbs that fall from their masters' table."[6] So also he answered him what he did not want him to do so that he could hear what he wanted.

Second, because the petition of the centurion was for a slave, so he intended to go in order to teach us not to curry favor with the mighty and despise the lowly but to honor rich and poor alike. If you honor a rich person, you honor him because of who he is, but if you honor a poor person, you honor him because

[4]Mt 15:22. [5]Mt 15:26. [6]Mt 15:27.

of who Christ is. Therefore, also in one passage, when a ruler demanded on behalf of his son, he did not say, "I will come and heal him," but what did he say? "Go; your son will live."[7] In that passage, he did not want to go, even though he was asked, lest it appear that he favored the ruler, but here he promised to go, though he was not asked to do so, lest it appear that he despised the lowliness of the slave. Thus he despised the one whom regal honor had elevated but honored the one whom his status as a slave had made low.

[8]*But the centurion answered him, "Lord, I am not worthy to have you come under my roof."*

I owe you honor, not an insult, for your merciful act of kindness. It is enough for me that you will heal my servant. Why then would you suffer the insult of coming under the roof of an unworthy house? You suffer the insult of coming into this world, but you bore it for the sake of the common salvation of all humankind. Why will you suffer an additional insult by entering my house just to heal one slave?

"But only say the word, and my servant will be healed."

He knew that ministering angels stood by invisibly, who would do every word of his. But even if the angels should be remiss in their duties, nonetheless diseases and spirits of afflictions would be expelled by his living commandments, since every word of his is living power.

[9]*"For I am a man under authority."*

See how he portrayed a representation of the Father and the Son in himself, as the Spirit suggested to him? In order to confess the power of Christ was it not enough for him only to say, "For I am a man . . . with soldiers under me; and I say to one, 'Go,' and he goes, and to another, 'Come,' and he comes"? This is because also Christ has angels under him, to whom he gives the command of going and returning. Why then was it necessary to add, "I am a man under authority," unless it was to show in himself the honor of Christ most fully? That is to say, "I am under the authority of another, but nonetheless I have the power to order those who are under me. I am not prevented from ordering those who are lower in rank because I myself am under those higher in rank, but I am ordered by those under whom I am, but I give orders to those who are under me. So also you are under the authority of the Father, inasmuch as you are a man, but you have the power to give orders to your angels, and you are not prevented from giving orders to those below you because you have one who is above you. For as a man you are ordered by the Father as one who is lesser, but you order the angels as one who is greater."

But perhaps a heretic says, wishing to show that the Father and the Son are one or equal, "One should not understand this passage in that way, but rather as follows:[8] 'If I who am placed under authority can give orders to those who are under my power, how much more you, who are under no one's authority, can order those whom you have under your power?'" But the text does not fit such a perverse interpretation.[9] He did not say, "If I am a man under authority," but rather, "For I am a man under authority." By comparing himself and Christ he did not point out the difference but rather showed the similarity.[10] Notice then how this Gentile, rustic soldier knew the mystery of the truth, and yet Christians[11] who carry around the Scriptures in their mouth deny the truth. It is not because the mysteries of the truth are

[7]Jn 4:50. [8]This sentence was excised by Manhusius for doctrinal reasons. Here the author's Arianism is blatant. [9]Alternate reading: "The text most elegantly fits this interpretation." [10]The previous two sentences were excised by Manhusius for doctrinal reasons. [11]Alternate reading: "heretics."

obscure or deep that all do not know them but because their hearts are perverse and the spirit of truth does not rest in them; therefore truth flees from them. But whoever is right in heart so that the spirit of truth rests in him cannot be far off from the truth. It is written, "Wisdom will not enter a deceitful soul."[12]

But someone will say, "Are you all righteous and upright who think that you are in the truth?" Not all, but many who are in the truth of the faith are wicked—which is bad enough, but there is no upright individual among those in error. It is one thing for many to be evil; it is quite a different matter for nobody to be good. Wherever some are evil and others good, the difference lies in humankind; but where all are altogether evil, the wickedness lies in the heresy. For weeds grow spontaneously in the middle of a wheat field, but wheat does not spontaneously grow among weeds.

10When Jesus heard him, he marveled, and said to those who followed him, "Truly, I say to you, not even in Israel have I found such faith."

Andrew believed, but John had already pointed out Jesus to him and said, "Behold, the Lamb of God, who takes away the sin of the world!"[13] Peter believed, but Andrew was telling him the good news and saying, "We have found the Messiah."[14] Philip believed, but by reading the Scriptures, as he told Nathanael, "We have found him of whom Moses in the law and also the prophets wrote, Jesus of Nazareth."[15] As for Nathanael, unless he had heard Christ say, "When you were under the fig tree, I saw you,"[16] he never would have replied, "Rabbi, you are the Son of God! You are the King of Israel!"[17] He first received the proof of his divinity and so offered the confession of faith.

Or if we did not dare to think him to be more faithful than the apostles, so the witness of Christ must be understood to mean that each and every good item in a person is praised according to the condition of that individual. For example, if a farmer speaks something wisely, he is wisely praised as a philosopher all the more. A farmer is praised more for a modest discourse of wisdom than a philosopher is for a great discourse because it is great for a farmer to say something wise, but it is not astonishing for a philosopher to say something wise. Or if a child says something profound, we say, "The child is very wise," but if a grown-up person says something wise, he is not praised as wise—not because the child knew more than the grown-up, but he seems to be wiser than the grown-up in comparison with his age. So also in the case of the centurion it was said, "Not even in Israel have I found such faith," not because not even the apostles had such faith.

The Twenty-Third[1] Homily: On Matthew 10[2]

At that time Jesus said to his disciples:

16"Behold, I send you out as sheep in the midst of wolves."

Every evil that happens unexpectedly is very serious, but whatever is anticipated before it happens is found to be more bearable after it happens. So our Lord, knowing beforehand the coming persecutions, warns his apostles ahead of time, saying, "Behold, I send you out

[12]Wis 1:4. [13]Jn 1:29. [14]Jn 1:41. [15]Jn 1:45. [16]Jn 1:48. [17]Jn 1:49. **Twenty-Third Homily** [1]The twenty-third homily in PG 56:754-756 is a sermon of Chromatius of Aquileia and is omitted here. However, because it was included in some manuscripts as a part of the anonymous *Incomplete Commentary*, it can be found in the appendix in the second volume. Instead, I have renumbered the twenty-fourth homily as the twenty-third homily, and all other homilies have been reduced by one number until the twenty-eighth homily, which contains new material not found in PG 56 but discovered by Étaix. Beginning with the twenty-ninth homily, the numbering of the homilies will accord with that found in PG 56. [2]Mt 9 and the beginning of Mt 10, as well as the last half of Mt 8, are missing.

as sheep in the midst of wolves," so that when that danger occurred, they would not shrink back in fear as of something new, but they might accept it all the more bravely on the grounds that it was already known.

"Behold, I"—who set the limits for day and night, and never has one defied my limits and crossed into the boundaries of the other. "Behold, I"—who enclose the boisterous sea in its shores, like a cave confines a wild beast, and who bound it with my command like a chain that cannot be broken. Thus, he said, "Behold, I send you," so that they might not fear the greatness of the danger while they are considering the power of the one who sent them.

"As sheep."

I am not insulting human nature but enjoining a work of sheep-like forbearance. Servants do not get indignant at being called sheep when they know that their Lord bore the name Lamb. "Behold, the Lamb of God, who takes away the sin of the world!"[3] And how, he asks, is it advantageous for us to be sheep against wolves? The gentleness of sheep cannot resist the cruelty of wolves. The cruelty of wolves does not know how to soften, unless the grace of Christ should cause what nature itself says cannot be done. It is not your power or skill that is highly regarded or praised in you, but it is the power of my name that is perceived so that it is glorified through you, seeing that the glory of God is more powerful than the nature of anything.

"As sheep."

When wolves begin to nip at you, do not resist them or yelp, for you know that unless you are robbed others will not be clothed; that is, unless you die, others will not live. Do not fear this present biting. When the age of the resurrection comes, another fleece—that of immortality—shall appear over you. As long as the heathen wolves persist because of the devil's instigation, offer your back to them to nip on. But when those wolves have become lambs through your patience, offer them as sheep the milk of doctrine. It is clear that he called them sheep because of their gentleness, but he calls those who do not fear God wolves because of their cruelty.

But let us see why he said that they were "as sheep," while the others were not "as wolves" but "wolves." If he had called them sheep only because of their gentleness, since they were human beings by nature but sheep in their gentleness, he would have called the others "as wolves" because even if in their cruelty they were like wolves, they nonetheless were still humans in nature like those who were called "as sheep." Therefore I think that he called some "as sheep" while he called the others not "as wolves" but fully "wolves" for the following reason: a follower of God, though he is good, nonetheless has something evil in himself as far as his flesh is concerned insofar as he is human; he is called a sheep because he is good, but he is called "as a sheep" because he is not fully good. But whoever does not know God cannot have anything good in himself; therefore he is called a wolf, not "as a wolf," because he has nothing good in himself since he does not know God. The reason is that all people are evil according to the nature of the flesh and as the apostle says, "We were by nature children of wrath,"[4] but we were made good by the fear of God. Although we are made good through the fear of God, nonetheless something of the evil nature remains in human nature. Therefore, if the nature of the flesh is forced to be evil, the fear of God partly restrains a person from evil. But nature compels a person who does not know God (or one who knows him but does not fear him) to do evil,

[3]Jn 1:29. [4]Eph 2:3.

and the fear of God does not restrain him from evil, and so there cannot be anything good in them, except by chance if they do something to please other people, since such an action is not itself good but evil, as far as God is concerned. "Whatever does not proceed from faith is sin."[5] Thus the saints are called "as sheep," but the evil people are not called "as wolves" but fully "wolves."

Nor let it disturb you that even Christ is called "as a sheep," not "a sheep," although he is altogether good. In that place the character of Christ was not compared with the character of a sheep, but the death of Christ was compared with the death of a sheep. So at length he adds, "Like a sheep that before its shearers is dumb, so he opened not his mouth."[6] For a sheep, when it is led to slaughter, does not emit any sound. But in this passage the character of the apostles was compared with the conduct of sheep. It was not their being sent that was compared with sheep being sent; that is to say, the apostles are called "as sheep," but the way that they are being sent is not called the way that sheep are sent. For sheep are not ever sent to wolves, nor does anyone compare something that is possible with something that is impossible. Therefore, elsewhere he was called a lamb, not "like a lamb."

"So be wise as serpents,"

that is, in understanding deceit,

"and innocent as doves,"

that is, in forgiving injuries.

I do not want you to always be like doves, lest you be deceived and fall into a trap because of your excessive simple-mindedness. I do not want you to always be like serpents, lest you poor forth venom against someone from your heart, but I want you to change according to the time, character and conduct. Be serpents, so that you are not arrested. If you are arrested, be doves so that you do not bite. As long as a person is a heathen, there is a serpent in him because his wrath is like that of the serpent that separated humankind from God. But when he is converted to faith, the serpent recedes and the Spirit enters into him, who came down from heaven in the form of a dove and became a dove. Therefore against unbelievers be serpents because a serpent does not harm another serpent, but among the faithful be doves, so as to offer kisses of love as doves do to one another. In short, be wise as serpents in order to understand and avoid evil. And be as innocent as doves so as not to do any evil. Understanding evil is praiseworthy, but doing it is blamable. And it is not he who understands evil that does evil, but rather the one who does evil.

17"Beware of men; for they will deliver you up to councils."

Because he had said earlier, "Be wise as serpents and innocent as doves," now he shows the reason for each and why he wants them to be as wise as serpents and innocent as doves. They are to be wise as serpents to beware of people who will deliver them to the councils. It is the nature of a serpent to be wary of people. Thus the apostle admonishes us, "Conduct yourselves wisely,"[7] "because the days are evil."[8] Why then does he want them to be innocent? So that they may not remember the evil against their betrayers but love their enemies and do good to those who persecute them according to the command of God's Christ,[9] because we are not only harmed by unjust enemies when we are hurt by them, but we also benefit, since the constancy of our kindness is not defeated by their intentions and does not retreat by their malice, because it is the nature

[5]Rom 14:23. [6]Is 53:7; cf. Acts 8:32. [7]Col 4:5. [8]Eph 5:16. [9]Mt 5:44.

of a dove always to remain in innocence even to the point of death. Therefore it is also said about Job's endurance, "He still holds fast his integrity."[10]

"Beware of men; for they will deliver you up to councils and flog you in their synagogues, ***[18]and you will be dragged before governors and kings for my sake, to bear testimony before them and the Gentiles."***

So he said, "Beware of people," as you would beware of the very worst evils and evils worse than all evils. For if he did not say this to accuse people, it would have been enough for him to say, "Beware, they will deliver you." But now he adds, "Beware of people," wishing to show that humankind is the very worst evil beyond all evils. For if you want to compare humankind with beasts, you would find humankind to be worse. Although a beast may be cruel, nonetheless its cruelty can be avoided because it is irrational. But because humankind is cruel and rational, its cruelty is not easily avoided. If you compare a person with a snake, you will find him to be worse because even if a serpent has malice, it nonetheless fears people. Thus it bites if it can do so without being seen, but it flees if it cannot. But a human being has the malice of a serpent and yet is not afraid as a serpent is. Thus as long as he does not have the opportunity, he lies hidden like a serpent, but if someone finds him, he rushes at him like a beast. Moreover, if a snake is provoked, it turns vicious, but if it has not been provoked, it silently goes its way. And in brief, every beast has one evil that is characteristic of it, but a human being has all evils inside of himself. Finally, an evil human is worse than the devil himself. If a devil ever should see a just person, he does not dare to approach him, but although an evil person sees a holy one, he not only does not fear him but despises him all the more. For the devil does not offer power to humankind, but humankind to the devil, inasmuch as an evil person is the weapon of the devil. Just as a person cannot do anything against an enemy without weapons, so the devil cannot prevail at all against the saints without the help of a human being.

"They will deliver you up to councils and flog you in their synagogues."

They will flog you in the synagogues for the greater praise of God. Where prayers and praises take place, where readings or sacrifices occur, there they punished the apostles as if they were offering to God a sacrifice, but in reality the torture of the apostles was the sacrifice of God—not availing as a reward to the Jews but as a crown for the apostles—while also being the downfall of the Jews. But as to the fact that he says that they will stand before kings and rulers and they are not to think of what they ought to say, this is what he says in John: "But when the Counselor comes, whom I shall send to you from the Father, even the Spirit of truth, who proceeds from the Father, he will bear witness to me; and you also are witnesses, because you have been with me from the beginning."[11] Consequently, when the apostles are accused and give their reply, the truth of Christ is proclaimed in each and every court, the perfidy of the Jews is shown and the mystery of godliness is revealed to the Gentiles or at least to those who believe for their salvation.

When the apostles heard that they were being ordered to stand before kings and judges, they could have said to Christ, "You yourself know that scholars are in charge of their judges. How then can we fishermen, and uneducated at that, give witness before them? You did not teach us from the very beginning to speak but to believe; finally, when you

[10]Job 2:3. [11]Jn 15:26-27.

gather us as disciples, you did not find us reading philosophical books on the Capitoline[12] but casting nets into the sea. Nor did you say, 'Come, I will make you my advocates,' but 'Follow me, and I will make you fishers of men.'[13] You chose our consciences, not our eloquence." So Christ said,

[19]"*When they deliver you up, do not be anxious how you are to speak or what you are to say.*"

"The cause is mine. God does not need human help. So only offer yourself to me, and I will give you the meaning." For the thing to worry about before the judgment is not preparing for the case but despairing of God, for it is easy to despair of God in those circumstances where there is time for reflection. For example, if you are about to make a journey because of some undertaking, you consider the nature of the undertaking and the length of the journey, and you prepare your expenses accordingly. Or if you intend to build a home, you consider the nature of the building and prepare corresponding tools. But in a law court how can a defense be prepared? You do not know what the accusation will be like, do you? Not at all, since in such a court the judges do not speak by their own power, but the devil speaks through the judges.

Therefore, if a person does not know not only what another person will think but also what he is thinking now, how can he know the counsel of the enemy? Nobody knows the thoughts of a person except the spirit that is in him.[14] Therefore, if you speak by your own power, you will answer their words, but if the Spirit of God speaks, you will answer their thoughts. Therefore allow God to speak in your case, since he knows the conscience of your accuser. It is not possible to offer arms against an enemy like a king sending his soldiers into war. Therefore whoever worries about what to say hopes in his own wisdom, which is the primary cause of his downfall. For in persecutions one does not seek the power of God unless faith has already been present.

To the great consolation of the apostles he did not say, "The Spirit of your Father, who is speaking *in you*," but

[20]"*the Spirit of your Father [is] speaking*"

to show that not only then but also not even now do they do or say anything without the Spirit of God. It is as if to say to them, "It is a great thing that you believe in me or confess me to be true. You see me hungering and believe that I am the bread of heaven. You see me thirsting and believe that I am the font of water springing to eternal life. How is it that your human reason, which sees one thing and believes and confesses another? Therefore, if my grace works in you now when there is no danger, how much more it will be with you when persecution comes? For whoever sustains you in peacetime will help you all the more in time of war."

[21]"*Brother will deliver up brother to death.*"

The apostles heard this so that they would not think that it was by chance that they were delivered to the councils and flogged in the synagogues. At that time, for example, nobody will be a patron who can help; nobody will be a friend who can forgive; nobody will be a friend so as to take pity on them. So says the Lord: let nobody hope in patrons, friends or parents, when even brother delivers up brother to death, and the parent his child, and a child his parent. See then what sort of fire of persecution will burn then so that nature will not spare its very self. How then will you seek to rely completely on patrons or friends, when you see that the ties of brotherhood and par-

[12]The schools of philosophy were located on the Capitoline hill in Constantinople. [13]Mt 4:19. [14]See 1 Cor 2:11.

enthood have lost their power? For if friendship fails where it is most natural, how will it be found where it is not based on natural ties?

Therefore is it not remarkable enough if a brother delivers up a brother to death? Cain killed Abel his brother because he envied his sacrifice,[15] and Esau persecuted Jacob over the stolen blessing.[16] But who ever heard that a parent would deliver up his child to death simply for his faith in Christ, when there was no other injury? It is because the conflict stirred up by the enemy is more powerful than the ties of nature. The love of the flesh is corruptible. Every friendship in this world is false, unless it is bound by the bond of the fear of God. There is no trustworthiness among the servants of the devil. The devil does not beget, nor is he begotten. If he is not begotten, he does not know how to preserve the rights of kinship, since he has no close kin. Carnal-minded people hate not because the tribe of Christians is detestable but because it is divine. More people by far have been joined together and made dearer by being close kin, but a more blessed change results in a good hatred.

[22]*"And you will be hated by all for my name's sake."*

That is, by all the unbelievers—not only your enemies but also your friends; not only by strangers but even by parents; not only by parents or brothers but even your very parents. O inestimable blaze of the devil's madness, which not even the tenderness of parenthood can extinguish! The persecution, which burns beyond natural bounds and contrary to them, clearly shows the wise that it is not anger over some faults that happened that produces such hatred as usually happens among humans, but rather it is the envy of the devil over Christ that produces them.

"But he who endures to the end will be saved."

This is because many can begin, but few can finish. There is always delight in the beginning but testing at the end. Nobody can persevere to the end except one who was made to be of God for the sake of God alone. Everything that is done for the flesh pertains to the body, just as also the flesh itself is transitory. But whatever is done for God is eternal, just as God is eternal. The heart that has a good faith has a good outcome, because it is not a good and glorious thing to begin but to end. For whatever one begins, it is often the pleasure of the body that does so; but whatever one ends, it is the power of the soul that does so. Often the desire of the flesh begins something good but does not finish it except by the grace of God. Therefore when you are converted to God and begin to serve God and to do works of righteousness, do not ever remember your deeds, but think of your end because the recollection of past goods produces boasting, but recollection of the end produces fear, since "he who endures to the end will be saved."

Thus[17] the apostle said, "Brethren, I do not consider that I have made it my own; but one thing I do, forgetting what lies behind and straining forward to what lies ahead, I press on toward the goal for the prize of the upward call of God in Christ Jesus. Let those of us who are mature be thus minded."[18]

[23]*"When they persecute you in one town, flee to the next."*

Knowing the weakness of human nature in temptations he says, "When they persecute you in one town, flee to the next." For I do not despise the timid, nor do I choose only the brave, because God does not want the power of people but their will. For he who flees and

[15]Gen 4. [16]Gen 27. [17]The material from here to the end of this homily is found not in PG 56, the primary text for this translation, but in fragments discovered by Raymond Étaix and published in 1974. See Étaix 278-81. [18]Phil 3:13-15.

he who is powerful are dissimilar, but they are equal in will. For just as the one suffered so that he could be seen to not love himself more than God, so also the other fled so that he would not be overcome in grief and lose the treasure of Christianity. But he gives this order not so that it may be a sin to stay but so that it may not be a sin to flee. But he took into consideration human weakness, while he did not exclude the power of a more ready faith. We say this because we often read that the servants of God have stood in the face of the danger of testing, as in the Acts of the Apostles, when after Stephen's murder "a great persecution arose against the church in Jerusalem; and they were all scattered throughout the region of Judea and Samaria, except the apostles,"[19] who stayed in Jerusalem. But we say this to console those Christians who flee because indeed it is the mark of a strong faith to stay, but it is the mark of great humility to flee.

And just as if they were saying to him, "How long can we flee? For a long flight is more burdensome than a quick death," our Lord consoled them and said, "You will not have gone through all the towns of Israel, before the Son of man comes." But if we understand this to be said only about the apostles, it does not make sense because the apostles died long before Christ's return. But all the things that are said to the apostles also seem to be said to those who would soon thereafter believe through them up until the end of the world. For they were the twelve heads of the coming Christianity. And just as whatever you put in your mouth is scattered abroad through all the limbs of the body, so also what was said to the apostles pertains to the whole fullness of the Christian body. For the Lord knew that their knowledge would lay hold of all the cities so that the towns of Israel are understood to be all the countries of the whole earth, and (as Isaiah attests) all the parts of the world would belong to Mount Zion.[20]

And because around the time of the end a much greater persecution would be stirred up by the godless than ever had been, so he said, "You will not have gone through all the towns of Israel before the Son of man comes," indicating that although that latest persecution will have been stirred up, it cannot happen that this world will stand until the saints who are fleeing go around all the cities of Christians. That is to say, even though Satan rages and occupies the whole world as far as he is concerned, nonetheless there are more places of refuge for the fleeing saints than dangers caused by the godless who are persecuting them.

Or this is what he intended to say: "Truly I say to you that I will not allow you to endure the trouble of persecution for as long as you in flight can go through all the towns of Israel. But I will quickly come and give you peace after calming down the persecution." And you have this declared symbolically[21] when the apostles were tossed about in the middle of the sea by the waves as the wind blew against them. For just as there Jesus did not wait until those in danger had sailed the whole sea, but immediately he came to them walking on the water and gave them calm,[22] so also when his apostles suffered some persecutions and fled from city to city, Jesus never waited as long as they in flight went through the many towns, but immediately he came to them and gave them peace by treading the waves of their testing under their feet. But Jesus came to his disciples who were suffering some persecution—not in person so that he could be seen by face as before but as it befits God to come, working invisibly and snatching them away so that his coming could be understood in deeds, as he says to Paul: "But rise and stand

[19]Acts 8:1. [20]See Is 4:5; 2:3. [21]I followed the manuscripts' reading *in mysterio* instead of Étaix's emendation, *in ministerio*. [22]See Mt 14:24-33.

upon your feet; for I have appeared to you for this purpose, to appoint you to serve and bear witness to the things in which you have seen me and to those in which I will appear to you, delivering you from the people and from the Gentiles—to whom I send you."[23]

For example, when Peter was imprisoned by Herod and released by an angel, "he went to the house of Mary . . . where many were gathered together and were praying"[24] for him, and when he had spoken, "he departed and went to another place."[25] Note the flight of the apostle from city to city, when the swift coming of Christ is explained to him a little later when "Herod put on his royal robes, took his seat upon the throne, and made an oration to them. And the people shouted, 'The voice of a god, and not of man!' Immediately an angel of the Lord smote him, because he did not give God the glory; and he was eaten by worms and died."[26] When the persecutor was struck down in this way, peace came for Peter, who had been enduring persecution. The apostle indicates the same thing when he says, "God is faithful, and he will not let you be tempted beyond your strength, but with the temptation will also provide the way of escape, that you may be able to endure it,"[27] because "he will never permit the righteous to be moved."[28] And the histories of the ancestors in each and every persecution bear out this fact.

24"A disciple is not above his teacher."

Now he begins to console them in their coming sufferings by his own example.

"A disciple is not above his teacher nor a servant above his master. . . . 25If they have called the master of the house Beelzebul, how much more will they malign those of his household."

It is a natural thing that, if we suffer injury for God at the hands of some unworthy people, we are angry and hurt. But if we hear that some famous person has suffered similar things, we are refreshed, and the conceit of our indignation is mitigated. For we say, "If that person who is more famous than I suffered such things, clearly I ought not to feel any grief over my injury." And so the injury of one consoles the grief of another, as if the latter is vindicated if the former has suffered an injury. How much more were the disciples comforted in their sufferings when they were disciples and servants, recalling Christ their Lord and teacher who suffered such things or worse. It is as if he had said, "Every injury is like the character of the person who suffers the injury. For if a modest injury happens to a great person, it is a great injury. But if a great injury happens to a modest individual, it seems modest. So also even if you suffer more than I do, then you ought to grieve less. Why then do you think that you are offended as if you were suffering something great, when you see me to have suffered such things so that none of the saints can boast that he has suffered anything new or great?"

26"So have no fear of them."

If a soldier were to fear war, he would never enjoy victory. But if a farmer fled work, he would never gather the fruits of the earth. If a merchant feared the dangers of the land or sea, he would never gather the profits of commerce. So also if the servants of God fear the danger of testing and remain idle, they will never find the crown of approval. For there can never be a victory without a fight, so there can also not be a battle without labor and danger. Then if it must be thought to be labor, it will obtain living fruit. For every labor does not have grief, if it has fruit.

---

[23]Acts 26:16-17. [24]Acts 12:12. [25]Acts 12:17. [26]Acts 12:21-23. [27]1 Cor 10:13. [28]Ps 55:22.

The Twenty-Fourth[1] Homily: On Matthew 10

At that time Jesus said to his disciples:

26"Nothing is covered that will not be revealed, or hidden that will not be known."

Now he announces to them that their preaching would make progress because their preaching would have a glorious outcome. "Behold, I am light hidden in darkness, God veiled in man, nobility in humility. Then just as this mystery was hidden from the ages but now will be revealed to all by you, to fulfill the prophetic word that said of me, '[The sun's] rising is from the end of the heavens, and its circuit to the end of them; and there is nothing hid from its heat.'[2] Just as there is no place where the sun does not appear or its heat is not felt, so there is no place where Christ will not be known or his divinity understood, so that the whole human race will be divided into two parts that the believers may deservedly be crowned and the unbelievers punished without excuse. And although people will hate you now and then as their enemies, afterwards they will come to know you and embrace you as the founders of their salvation. Now and then they will abhor you as evildoers, but later they will revere you as saints. Now and then they will persecute you as persecutors, but later all people will adore you in their churches as gods. Remember the past and take comfort about the future, remembering when iniquity ruled over the righteousness of the Lord, when shadowy lies covered up the truth for a long time and when innocence has been long cloaked under the reputation of crime. Moses was hidden in Egypt and was said to be son of an Egyptian woman.[3] He fled as if he were a murderer, and he became a shepherd as if he were a despicable hired hand. Was his holiness never revealed, and was his innocence never crowned? Note that he who had been a shepherd of irrational sheep became the leader of a glorious people. He left Egypt as a murderer but returned as a judge of the saints—not as a child of an Egyptian woman but as a child of God. Egypt lost it own advantage: it could not make Moses its own by raising him well, when he had belonged to another by virtue of his being born more nobly. He who as a captive had feared Pharaoh the king later punished him with ten plagues as if Pharaoh were a guilty slave because 'nothing is covered that will not be revealed.' Joseph lived in obscurity in Egypt, being accused of adultery, though he preserved a loyal chastity.[4] Was not his innocence shown? Was not his chastity rewarded several times over? He had been thrown in jail as a criminal but released as a prophet. By the punishment of one child the whole world was flogged with hunger. And him whom the priest Potiphar had condemned as an adulterer with his wife he later made his own honored son-in-law in his own house.[5] Three children were hidden in Babylon and were accused of despising the king; it was ordered that the furnace for their destruction be heated seven times hotter than normal, not because such a great fire was necessary to burn the nature of their flesh but because the wrath of the maddened king suggested the idea. And what did the fire in its furnace, stirred on by the spirit of madness, correct? The heat of its power was lost, and it burned in appearance only, so that the corrupt fire showed their incorruptible integrity and the ardent flame showed their even more ardent faith, as the flame cried out, not by its voice but by its very nature that 'Nothing hidden will not be known.' But endure the harmful entrance so that you may have a glorious exit, on the grounds that you have a glorious consolation."

Twenty-Fourth Homily [1]The twenty-fifth homily in PG 56, as noted at the beginning of the twenty-third homily. [2]Ps 19:6. [3]Ex 2. [4]Gen 39. [5]Gen 41.

[27]***"What I tell you in the dark, utter in the light; and what you hear whispered, proclaim upon the housetops."***

What does it mean, "What I tell you in the dark, utter in the light"? Again he calls the Jewish people "darkness," as it is written, "The light shines in the darkness, and the darkness has not overcome it."[6] And so they are understood to be darkness because they could not know the true light. Therefore whatever the Lord said among the Jews he announced that it should be revealed in the church. For the light is understood as the Christian people, as the apostle says: "For once you were darkness, but now you are light in the Lord; walk as children of light."[7]

Or "What I tell you in the dark, utter in the light" can be understood in this way: "What I now tell you in the secret form of parables, tell openly." Whatever is hidden in a secret is placed in the dark, as it were. Thus also when Moses went up the mountain to receive the Law, as the Scripture says, "Moses entered the cloud,"[8] showing that the Law that was given and placed under a secret would be obscure, as under a very dark cloud. But whatever is said most clearly is said in the light.

What does it mean, "What you hear whispered, proclaim on the housetops"? That is, whatever you alone hear secretly, preach before all, and do not hide a word from anyone, just like someone standing on top of the housetops and shouting.

What is it that the apostles heard secretly? "A sower went out to sow his seed; and . . . some fell along the path . . . and some fell on the rock . . . and some fell among thorns . . . and some fell into good soil."[9] "All this Jesus said to the crowds in parables; indeed he said nothing to them without a parable."[10] "Then the disciples came and said to him, 'Tell us the parable.'[11] And he answered them, 'To you it has been given to know the secrets of the kingdom of heaven, but to them it has been given in parables.'[12] . . . Because seeing they do not see, and hearing they do not hear."[13]

What do we conclude then? That which was entrusted to the apostles alone in secret at that time now is daily told to all nations in the midst of the church as the Gospels recount them and the apostles proclaim them. Therefore, "What I tell you in the dark, utter in the light" means "What I say to you in secret, preach openly before all," just as when the Lord called his disciples to the side and said to them, " 'But who do you say that I am?' Simon Peter replied, 'You are the Christ, the Son of the living God.' "[14] "But he charged and commanded them to tell this to no one, saying, 'The Son of man must . . . be killed, and on the third day be raised.' "[15] This was because, if he had been clearly known to be the Son of God, nobody would have dared to raise a hand against him, and so he would not have been crucified or risen from the dead. Moreover, the reign of the underworld would still be on earth, and the power of the devil would still hold the whole world. After our Lord rose from the dead, Peter began to preach to all what he had heard in secret: "The God of our fathers glorified his servant Jesus, whom you delivered up and denied in the presence of Pilate, when he had decided to release him. But you denied the Holy and Righteous One, and asked for a murderer to be granted to you, and killed the Author of life."[16] Therefore, "whatever you hear whispered, proclaim on the housetops."

[28]***"And do not fear those who kill the body."***

That is, "Do not refrain from speaking freely what you have heard because of fear of death;

[6]Jn 1:5. [7]Eph 5:8. [8]Ex 24:18. [9]Lk 8:5-8. [10]Mt 13:34. [11]Mt 13:10; the author has paraphrased the disciples' request and thus their question differs from the RSV translation of this verse. [12]Mt 13:11; where the RSV translates "it has not been given," the author reads "it has been given in parables." [13]Mt 13:13. [14]Mt 16:15-16. [15]Lk 9:21-22. [16]Acts 3:13-15.

do not refrain from preaching faithfully in all matters what you alone heard whispered." Thus by these words he shows that not only is he a traitor to the truth who goes beyond the bounds of truth and openly speaks a lie instead of the truth, but so also is he who does not freely proclaim the truth that he ought to proclaim or does not freely defend the truth that he ought to. For just as a priest is obligated to preach freely the truth that he has heard from God, so also a lay person is obligated to defend faithfully the truth that he has heard from the priests and that has been proven in the Scriptures. But if he does not do this, he is a traitor to the truth. "For man believes with his heart and so is justified, and he confesses with his lips and so is saved."[17]

We have said these things because many Christians think that it is a sin to openly go beyond the truth, but do not think that it is a sin to keep quiet about the truth before unbelievers and for that reason many are found to be indicted under that charge. So it is appropriate for us to speak openly because the present instruction says nothing about a truth that is being denied but about a truth that is not being freely proclaimed, since he says, "What I tell you in the dark, utter in the light . . . and do not fear those who kill the body," which otherwise might give you grounds to say less in the light what you have heard in the dark.

Look how he is not only a transgressor of the truth who openly denies the truth, but so also is he who keeps silent about the truth out of fear of those who can kill the body. And what will I say? People keep quiet about the truth because of their fear of death, and because of their wretched belly and their hope for vain honor they keep silent about the truth in the presence of unbelievers. For example, people come to the banquet of godless priests and flee to the patronage of evil heretics. A sermon on faith takes place; that godless priest or patron blasphemes your truth as a lie and your faith as treachery so that he can either seduce or wound your conscience and make it weak, even if he cannot fully succeed. But even though you do not openly deny the truth, nonetheless you do not strive with his person, since you eat his bread—all so that you do not lose the hope of your patronage or greed. You keep silent about the truth, which you ought to freely defend, and you obscure the truth in the sight of its enemies so that by your silence it seems that what is true is really false. And how is it that you are not a traitor to the truth?

But perhaps you say, "If I keep silent about the truth before its adversaries, I am not agreeing to their lie, am I?" Tell me, if some prince of the emperor saw the Roman state being besieged by the enemy and neglected to defend it, although he could free it, will not he appear to have betrayed that which he could have freed, if he wanted to? So also when you saw that truth is being attacked by the ungodly and could have defended it, if you had wanted to speak, you silently besieged it by the fact that you consented to its being besieged. And if it is ungodly to keep silent about the truth out of fear for those who kill the body, as the present Scripture passage attests, how is it not a greater act of ungodliness to keep silent about the truth for the sake of your wretched belly and the hope of vain honor—and to make gratitude for bread and honor greater than the glory of the truth of God?

"And do not fear those who kill the body,"

because, even if the body is not killed by the ungodly for God's sake, it will die a little later by itself because of its nature. Therefore, if you are killed in the body by ungodly people, you do not lose anything except the delay of death, so that the body that was going to die a little later dies a little sooner. Put more accurately,

[17]Rom 10:10.

you do not even lose the delay of death. If it is true that not even a leaf falls from a tree without the command of God and that the days given to us to live are numbered, we ought to believe that we will not die before that day, nor can we live beyond it. Nonetheless, let us grant that whoever dies for God dies ahead of that day. Therefore, if we are going to die a little later for nothing, that is, without the trouble of someone murdering us, without any inducement from God being offered, why do we not die a little early with glory for God's cause, so that what is going to be necessary may be voluntary and so that we may offer to God as a sacrifice what can be repaid for the debt owed by you?

"Do not fear those who kill the body."

The substance of a person is not the body but the soul. God made the soul alone in his image and loved it; for the soul's sake he made the world. The enemy is jealous of the soul and persecutes it; because of it also the Son of God came into the world. The body is the clothing of the soul, as the apostle says: "For while we are still in this tent, we sigh with anxiety; not that we would be unclothed, but that we would be further clothed, so that what is mortal may be swallowed up by life."[18] Therefore, just as if someone in a rage tears clothing that had been worn by people, an individual senses the inflictor of the injury, but he does not suffer any loss in his nature, so if the body that has been worn by the soul is killed by the ungodly, the soul indeed feels the pain of the murder but does not suffer the loss of its nature.

But we have a proof of this matter in our limbs of which we can speak. Just as when the nails clothe the tips of the fingers they hurt the body when they are injured, but once they have been cut off, they are found to have none of the body's ability to feel in themselves, but a new set of nails grows by its very nature with the result that nature seems to have sustained no loss, so the soul feels pain as long as the body is being killed, but once it has been killed, there is no feeling or pain of the soul to be found in the body, but a second time it will reweave a more glorious body over the soul at an opportune time, so that the soul seems to have endured no loss but merely has claimed to.

But I will say what I really feel: not only was the flesh created to clothe the soul but rather to tempt it. The flesh, like a homegrown and natural enemy, was joined to the soul. As long as the soul is besieged by the flesh, it does not win or receive the prize from God. Paul attests to this hidden truth when he says, "For the desires of the flesh are against the Spirit, and the desires of the Spirit are against the flesh."[19] Therefore, if the flesh, the enemy of the soul, is a temptation, what wise person does not understand that the killing of the body ought to be hoped for rather than feared? Thus a corruptible nature was created in you; thence a time has been reckoned for putting aside the body so that you, a human being, are not sparing your body, which will die anyway, but you are comparing the life that remains to you with the destruction you deserve.

Look, if you receive on loan, say, a cow or a horse, do you not diligently work your work through it? You say to yourself, "Today or tomorrow it must be taken from me because it is not mine." Why do you who were born in a corruptible body not use your temporary body for the advantage of your soul, when you knew that a little later it has to be taken from you since it is not yours? What then is that foolishness of yours, to hate what is ours and to love what is not? Or to be eager to preserve what we cannot and to neglect what we will have forever?

"Do not fear those who kill the body."

[18]2 Cor 5:4. [19]Gal 5:17.

What is the fear of death? It is not the pain of departing from the body but the despair about the life after death. Whoever does not think that he will live after death fears death. Do you wish to know this? Note how people often suffer dire pain in sickness and do not die; often they have a little weariness and they die; and yet they were more satisfied to endure dire pain and not die. Do you see then that it is not the pain of death but death itself that is feared? Just as the fear of death works all evils, so despising death produces all good things.

Whoever fears dying, that is, whoever does not hope to live after death, neither gives alms nor is constant in prayer nor fasts often nor endures poverty nor bears reproach nor is content to suffer the loss of his wealth nor endures any bodily injury for God's sake. But he thinks that his life is profitable if he happily enjoys the goods of this world, and he thinks that his life has suffered loss if he is kept from those goods. Why? It is because he does not hope for any reward for his labors in the resurrection. But whoever is not afraid to die, that is, whoever hopes for life after death, gladly endures for God's sake all the things that we just mentioned because he awaits without doubt a reward many times over for his labors. Therefore he is a perfect disciple of Christ who endures all these things or was prepared to do so.

Therefore the Lord commands us, "Do not fear those who kill the body," not because it is necessary for every disciple of Christ to be killed, but he said it so that he does not have to give a commandment about all those things that we mentioned above, going through them one at a time. Instead, he said in summary, "Do not fear those who kill the body," because those who are not afraid to be killed despise all the more the other adversities of the flesh that take place before death. Because all the adversities of the flesh that take place before death are more bearable than death. Whoever then does not fear what is more burdensome despises all the more whatever is lighter. But how will someone endure death when he was not prepared to suffer for God's sake the other troubles that take place before death?

But consider that something in nature caused us to fear the evils of the flesh or to love good things—not so that we fear the evils of the flesh that we fear, but so that we may understand through our fear of evils befalling the flesh that we ought to fear spiritual evils even more. For example, you know that it is bad to suffer pain in the flesh. By this fact you understand that it is worse to suffer pain in the soul. You know that it is bad to be accused before people; by this you understand that it is worse to be accused before angels. Just as angels are better than human beings, so their accusation is worse than that of people. For the grief and shame of the body come to an end or are released along with the body, but the soul's grief and shame always rush headlong with the soul into punishment.

This also happens not so that you may love the good things of the flesh, which you do love, but so you that can understand through those good things that you should love spiritual goods more. For example, you know that it is good to rejoice in the flesh; by this you understand that the joy of the soul is greater. The joy of the flesh ends with the flesh, but the joy of the soul continues as long as the soul does. You know that it is good to boast on earth; understand by this that it is better to boast in heaven. As the heaven is brighter than the earth, so its glory is greater than the earth's. But it gives a little taste, as it were, in the world from the great treasury of goods or evils, so that we, from that little taste of evils or good things, may know the fullness of them.

"Do not fear those who kill the body but . . . rather fear him who can destroy both soul and body in hell."

What are you saying? The soul will perish?

Was it not created to be immortal? By "death" is meant not only the obliteration of the body but also punishment is called death. Thus also Paul says, "By my pride in you which I have in Christ Jesus our Lord, I die every day!"[20] And John in his Apocalypse says, "Blessed and holy is he who shares in the first resurrection! Over such the second death has no power."[21] The second death is fire and sulfur. You see then that by the damnation of the soul he does not mean the very break-up of the soul but rather the torture of hell, which is the second death.

And what follows is as a response to someone if he should happen to say, "Why was so much leeway given to evil people to have the power to harm saints contrary to the will of God?" That is not the case at all; nothing can happen against God's will.

[29]*"Are not two sparrows sold for a penny? And not one of them will fall to the ground without your Father's will."*

It is as if to say: "Therefore, if sparrows (whom God made for human use) have been placed under the will of God and not in human beings' power, how much more are not you under God's will, even when you are under other people's power? If a sparrow does not die or fall by chance because of the fact that it is God's creation, how much more does a just person not lie under fate because he is the image of God! But such a person either is handed over by God and dies or he is freed by God and escapes. If in the case of sparrows nothing is done without reason, though the price for two of them is a penny, how much more nothing is done among you without me, since your price is my blood. If sparrows are regarded like this, how must children be regarded? So you ought not to fear people because they have no power over you, but God does."

The godless are able to harm the saints not when the godless want to but only when God grants them a time to harm them so that he can provide his saints with a crown. Pilate said to Jesus, " 'Do you not know that I have power to release you, and power to crucify you?' Jesus answered him, 'You would have no power over me unless it had been given you from above.' "[22] Therefore, how is it wise not to fear the one who gives power but rather to fear him who received it? Whoever gives power gives it whenever he wants, but whoever receives it does not receive it whenever he wants. Therefore, if you have not been handed over, you are fearing without good reason, and if you have been handed over, you still are fearing without good reason. Since God is the one who sets us free, nobody can harm you, even if he wants to. Do you not know how Pilate wanted to release Christ but could not because God had handed him over to him?

[30]*"But even the hairs of your head are all numbered."*

How does it help us to have all our hairs numbered if we die? They were numbered so that we may live forever. God would not number anything in order to find out its number, would he, when, as Wisdom says, he created everything by weight, number and measure?[23] But he numbered them so that he may not lose anything of them, as the prophet says: "How precious to me are your thoughts, O God! How vast is the sum of them! If I would count them, they are more than the sand."[24] Those who are counted are not diminished but multiplied. Do you wish to know what honor it is to be counted? Consider how the shepherd did not stop running through the wilderness until he found that sheep and returned it to its pristine number.[25] He thought that he had none of

[20]1 Cor 15:31. [21]Rev 20:6. [22]Jn 19:10-11. [23]Wis 11:20. [24]Ps 139:17-18; the archaic language of the RSV has been updated. [25]Mt 18:12-13.

them if one was missing from his number. But those who will perish are not numbered. So the Lord says, "The hairs of your head are all numbered." But why would sinners be numbered when they are thought to be nothing? God numbers that which he wants to possess, but what he does not want to have, why would he number it? So sinners are not counted so that he does not perceive every one of them who perishes, nor does God care about them since they are not numbered, as it is written; "All the nations are as nothing before him."[26]

Are sparrows better then than sinners? No, but they are alike. God did not say that sparrows do not fall, but they do not fall without the will of God, for it is the will of God that they are rescued and go on to be enjoyed by people, since sparrows were created for this purpose. So it is the will of God that an individual who lived without the law of God also perishes without the law and that God not regard one who did not regard God. Truly in this regard a human sinner is worse than an animal because even if an animal does not glorify him, it does not exacerbate him, but an evil person not only does not glorify God but moreover exacerbates him.

How valuable it is to be counted is shown also in the book of Numbers,[27] because those who are elect and chosen are counted by Moses by God's command. The women among them are not counted. The women are understood to represent softness, which is a corruption of the body. But every man who is soft in mind, lax in faith and corrupt in deeds is a man in his body but understood to be a woman and so is not numbered among the saints. But if a woman has a holy virility, even though she is a woman in body, she is a man in spirit and is numbered among the saints. At that time, because the woman represented the flesh, she was driven out, but now because we are dealing with reality, the effeminate mind is not counted. At that time those subject to slavery were excluded, but here a slavish manner of living is excluded. He is not a slave who is a slave of people, but who is a slave to his sin. Therefore, if a free person does evil works, he is a slave of the devil; if a slave does good works, he is a child of God. Therefore a servile soul is not counted. Also a worldly Egyptian is not numbered. Therefore whoever loves the world rejoices in worldly business. He is saddened because of the passing business of the world but does not rejoice because of God. He who is an Egyptian in his soul is not counted. But if an Egyptian loves heavenly things, he is a Hebrew. Moreover, children are not counted. He who is a child in his manner of thinking is perfect in evil, but whoever is a child in evil is perfect in his manner of thinking. Whoever reaches the fullness of the stature of Christ, even if he is a child, is counted, just as Daniel was. And whoever goes out to war against foreigners, that is, whoever can fight against unclean spirits and destroy the camps of carnal desires, he alone is numbered.

But not even all who have spiritual goodness have the goodness of an Israelite. For also the Gentiles have the goodness of the soul, grammar, oratory and philosophy, but it is not the goodness of the Israelite because it is not done for God's sake but for the sake of much glory. But it is a good thing belonging to the Israelites, if one's mind sees God as the apostles' minds did. To them he said, "Even the hairs of your head are all numbered." Spiritually speaking, the hairs are the refined thoughts of the soul and the countless thoughts of the saints, who go forth from the spirit of Christ as from their head. But if a righteous person hands himself over under the sway of love, that love cuts off his hairs and removes the strength that he has in his hair, just as Delilah did to Samson's hair.[28] For every power of theirs has not been put in their body or in riches but in

[26]Is 40:17. [27]Num 3; 26. [28]Judg 16.

their spiritual powers. And nothing so cuts off the power of their hair as does bodily pleasure. Therefore, if he loses the power of his hair, foreigners, that is, unclean spirits, seize him and bind him with chains of various desires and blind the eyes of his heart so that he cannot see the light, that is, the way of truth so as to be able to leave, so that in him the Scripture is fulfilled, "Let them be blotted out of the book of the living; let them not be enrolled among the righteous."[29]

32"So every one who acknowledges me before men, I also will acknowledge before my Father who is in heaven; 33but whoever denies me before men, I also will deny before my Father who is in heaven."

And because he had commanded something impossible, as far as the flesh's nature is concerned, he now sets forth both a penalty and a reward so that the strength of the soul may be helped now by fear of punishment, now by desire for reward. Note the reward: "Every one who acknowledges me before people, I also will acknowledge before my Father." But he tells the reward first and then the punishment, because our merciful God is more ready to reward the good than to punish the unworthy.

See how much greater is God's reward than our righteousness and how more dire is punishment than our sin. If you confess Christ before people, you confess that you can offer nothing to God. But if he confesses you before God, he confesses that he can make you immortal. If you deny Christ before people, you cannot harm Christ by denying him. But if Christ denies you before God, he who can destroy you in eternal fire denies you. Who is so blockheaded that he does not desire to have Christ attest to his righteousness? Therefore, if it is a great thing to be a witness of Christ, how much greater is it to have Christ as your witness?

Consider this, finally, lest even faithful Christians should say, "If the distress of persecution comes, I will suffer punishment in front of others for my denial, but in my heart I will hold to the truth of Christ." Therefore he does not say, "Whoever acknowledges me in his heart," but "before people," because whoever does not confess before people it does not help at all to believe in Christ in his heart because it cannot happen that he who denies with his mouth will believe in his heart. The root of a confession is the faith of the heart, but confession is the fruit of faith. Therefore, just as a root must produce branches or leaves as long as it is living, but if it fails to, without doubt you understand that its root has dried up in the ground, so as long as the faith of the heart is sincere, it always engenders confession in the mouth, but if there is no confession of the mouth, understand without a doubt that the faith of the heart has long dried out. So the apostle says, "For man believes with his heart and so is justified, and he confesses with his lips and so is saved."[30]

Therefore the confession of the mouth has no power without the faith of the heart, and the faith of the heart has no power without the confession of the mouth. But if it is advantageous to you to believe in the heart and not to confess before people, then is it also advantageous for an unbeliever to confess Christ hypocritically, even if he does not believe it in his heart? But if it does not help anyone who confesses without faith, neither does it benefit you to believe without confessing. If it is enough for Christ, who knows all things, even if you do not confess him before people, then let it also be enough for you that Christ knows you, even if he does not confess you before people. But if his mere knowledge of you is not enough, then neither is your faith enough for him. For if the faith of your heart were enough for you, God would have created you with only a heart. But now God

[29]Ps 69:28. [30]Rom 10:10.

has created you with a mouth so that you may believe with your heart and confess with your mouth. Not only with the mouth but also with the five senses of the body. If either a heart or mouth had been sufficient, the prophet would also say, "Praise the Lord with the lyre," that is, "Say a psalm to him on one or two strings," but now he says, "Make melody to him with the harp of ten strings!"[31] That is because a human being, who is a harp, has ten sounds, five carnal and five spiritual.

We must confess Christ with all of them. If one of the senses is missing, it is not a perfect confession. Therefore, if someone should say to you, "Do not eat meat sacrificed to idols, but only look at the idols to see how beautiful they are," if you look at them as you were invited to do, you denied Christ with your eyes—you sin not because looking at idols is anything but because you look when invited to do so. But if you do not look with your eyes, you confessed Christ. Thus, it is written, "Turn my eyes from looking at vanities."[32] But if he says to you, "I do not want you to look at idols but only listen to how that Gentile blasphemes Christ in order to glorify the gods," if you listen to him, you deny Christ with your ears. If he says to you, "I do not want you to hear any blasphemy against Christ, but only see how incense is offered to the gods; just stand here and smell the incense," if you smell it, you offend Christ with your sense of smell. Again, if he said to you, "Do not eat meat with your teeth; only pretend that you are eating from meat sacrificed to idols," if you pretend to do so, you have denied Christ with your sense of taste. If you do not pretend to do so, you confessed Christ as Eleazar did in the book of Maccabees,[33] who did not want to eat mutton that was being passed off as pork. If he says, "I do not want you to eat from sacrificed meat but only touch the idol with your hand or hold the thurible," if you touch it or hold it, you have denied Christ with your sense of touch. But if you do not, you have confessed Christ with your sense of touch, as it is written: "If there is wrong in my hands."[34] God created all the members of your soul or body not only for your use but also for his glory.

The Twenty-Fifth[1] Homily: On Matthew 10 and 11

At that time Jesus said to his disciples:

[34]***"Do not think that I have come to bring peace on earth; I have not come to bring peace, but a sword."***

When the Lord said, "Whoever acknowledges me before people," and so forth, he spoke to the apostles as they were thinking and saying to themselves, "Up until now we have lived under tyrants and Gentile rule, and now we have hoped that peace will come to us; and how can he promise persecutions and judgments to come?" So he answered them, "Do not think that I have come to bring peace on earth." There is a good peace and an evil peace. The good peace exists among good people who are faithful and righteous, so that there is one harmony of life among whom there is the offering of one faith. For faith is born through the word of God and is preserved by peace and nurtured by love, as the apostle says; "faith working through love."[2] But a faith that does not have love cannot bear any fruit of good work. Therefore, if the faithful have separated themselves by some disagreement, that is an evil disharmony, as the Lord says: "No house divided against itself will stand."[3] If the brotherhood is divided, it is consumed by itself, as the apostle says: "But if you bite and devour one another take heed that you are not consumed by one another."[4]

[31]Ps 33:2. [32]Ps 119:37. [33]2 Macc 6. [34]Ps 7:3. **Twenty-Fifth Homily** [1]The twenty-sixth homily in PG 56. [2]Gal 5:6. [3]Mt 12:25. [4]Gal 5:15.

But there is an evil peace between unbelievers and the unrighteous, so that there is one agreement to do evil for those who have one evil intention. For unbelief and wickedness arise out of some suggestion of the devil but are preserved by peace. If then unbelievers and the unrighteous are divided from one another on a certain occasion, this is a good disharmony, because just as faith and righteousness stand when the good are at peace, unbelief and unrighteousness lie fallen, but when disharmony comes, faith and righteousness fall, but unbelief and unrighteousness arise again. So when the unrighteous are at peace, both unrighteousness and unbelief stand, but faith and righteousness lie fallen. But when harmony comes, unbelief and unrighteousness fall, but faith and righteousness arise.

Therefore the Lord sent a good division on earth in order to break up an evil alliance. All people, good and bad alike, were under evil; that is to say, those who loved evil were under evil, and those who were good were standing under evil because of their ignorance. All were enclosed and held together under the one house of unbelief, as it were. So the Lord sent a sword of separation among them, that is, the word of truth, about which the apostle says, "The word of God is living and active, sharper than any two-edged sword, piercing to the division of soul and spirit, of joints and marrow, and discerning the thoughts and intentions of the heart."[5] That sword is sharpened on two sides—on one side to cut the good from error, on the other to remove the evil from their excuses, so that ignorance may not ruin the good or excuse the evil and so that the good may know the truth and be saved with justice and righteousness as they follow the truth, while the evil may learn the truth, withdraw from it and be punished with justice and righteousness.

Therefore the Lord separated the good from the evil with this sword so that the good separated from evil might arise and the evil separated from the good might fall. For as long as good is mixed, it lies together with evil and is death because good cannot be joined together with evil. But once it has been separated from evil, it then arises and lives because good begins to be separated from evil. Likewise, as long as evil too is mixed with the good, it stands and lives because it oppresses the good under itself. But once it becomes separated from the good, then it falls and dies because once it has been manifested it can no longer oppress good under itself. So also as long as believers are joined with the unbelievers, they lie fallen and are dead because believers cannot be mixed with unbelievers. But when they have been separated from unbelievers, then they arise again and live because then believers begin to be mixed with believers. Again, as long as unbelievers are mixed with believers, they stand and live because they hold believers under their own unbelief. But if they are separated from believers, they fall and die because open unbelievers can no longer destroy believers. Every evil matter seems to stand and live as long as it can harm something good. But when it becomes clear, it can no longer harm but lies dead. But every dead item, even if it is evil, is nonetheless like an item that is not dead.

Why then do unbelievers, once separated from believers, break some of the believers with fear and corrupt others with a promise? This situation does not intend to ruin the good but rather to glorify those who remain in the good, since one who is broken by fear or corrupted by a promise never was truly good. Then truly the unbelievers are said to destroy believers, whenever the believers are joined with unbelievers through ignorance of the truth. Faith is not corrupted by enticements or persecutions but rather purified by them.

[5] Heb 4:12.

O marvelous power of the sword that separates! Not only cannot an alliance of strangers (whom a voluntary friendship has joined) resist it, but not even the impetuous love of the carnal nature can. And so it not only separates those who were joined together in love and separated by nature, but it even separates those whom the needs of the flesh had joined together in sweet bonds. Thus he says,

[35]*"For I have come to set a man against his father."*

We must note that those who are separated are the believers and that they are separated from the unbelievers. How does he show this? When he says,

[37]*"He who loves father or mother more than me is not worthy of me."*

Whoever loves his parent more than God remains with his parent. But whoever loves God more than his parent withdraws from his parent in faith, not his body. But we have said that those whom Christ separates are believers so that we may know that believers always withdraw from unbelievers, not unbelievers from believers, because the devil always desires that his unbelievers be with believers so that the unbelievers may be mixed with the believers and corrupt them. And Christ always hastens to separate believers from unbelievers so that the believers may not come together with unbelievers and be corrupted by them. And everywhere in the Scriptures one reads that a separation was made between the good and the evil, always the good withdrew from the evil and not the evil from the good. When the Jews were in exile, God did not say to the Assyrians through the prophet, "Depart, depart from the midst of my people," but he said to the people, "Depart, depart, go out thence, touch no unclean thing,"[6] because evil makes good share its iniquity, but good does not make evil share its iniquity. For example, put dirt in flour; the flour does not dirty the dirt, but the dirt dirties the flour. Again, put vinegar in wine. The wine does not spoil the vinegar, but the vinegar spoils the wine. Nothing can even be corrupted by anything else when it has been naturally corrupted by itself.

Therefore when the unbelievers say, "You departed from us, we did not depart from you," believe it, for it is true. Good always flees evil, but evil does not flee even before good. Again he says, "Look, the heretical priest desires to pray with the faithful and bless the faithful." Believe him, for it is true. He knows how to make the one given the blessing to share his guilt and not how to sanctify the one receiving the blessing. If he who gives the blessing knew how to sanctify the one he blessed, he would have been asked and would not himself have asked. But now because he makes the one blessed by him to share his guilt, he does not wait to be asked, but he himself seeks someone to destroy. See, the unbelieving lay person wants to receive a blessing from the faithful, not so that he can be sanctified by receiving the blessing but so that you can lose what you gave and that you may perish for having given that which is holy to the dogs.

He did not say that he would separate child from parent but "against his parent," because he does not mandate a physical separation but a spiritual one. Whoever is separated physically is separated from his parent but is not against him. But whoever is separated spiritually, he is with his parent in body but against his parent in the faith. For whoever is far away from his parent is not against him by back talking, flattering and arguing. One cannot believe that he is ordering us to leave our parent when he had said, "Honor your father and your mother."[7] Therefore, if you have an unbelieving

[6]Is 52:11. [7]Ex 20:12.

parent, obey him, and you will find the reward for your respect, and he will have his own condemnation for his unbelief. And so he did not say, "Whoever loves his parent is not worthy of me," but he said, "He who loves son or daughter more than me is not worthy of me." Just as it is one's duty to love parents after God, so it is a breach of duty to love them more than God. Therefore, if you have an unbelieving parent, obey him. But if he wants to plunge you into the same pit of unbelief in which he is, then love God more than your parent, because he is not the parent of your soul but of your flesh. But only God is the Father of all holy souls. Render to each person what belongs to him. Offer the obedience of the flesh to your parents in the flesh, but offer holiness of the soul to your spiritual parents.

And truly there is nothing that we ought to love more than God. Friends leave, parents fail, but Christ alone never leaves or fails at any time as long as we ourselves want to be with him. When we leave this world, every soul returns to its place, and nobody remembers the emotions of the flesh once the flesh has left—the parent does not remember his child nor the child his parent. Everything that we received from the earth will be released to the earth, and we will have nobody with us except our works; if they are good, they will redound to our glory; if they are bad, they will redound to our punishment.

38"And he who does not take his cross and follow me is not worthy of me."

One bears his cross, if he was prepared for every danger for God's sake, even to the point of death, rather than leave Christ. Even if such a person escapes a cross by God's mercy, he nonetheless is daily crucified as far as his intention is concerned. So even if he suffers no such thing, he nonetheless receives its reward. The will is rewarded, not the deed, because the will comes from our will, but the deed is accomplished by the grace of God.

39"He who finds his life will lose it."

It is better to die for God and to live forever than to live for yourself and to die forever. If he died for us, when he was not able to die unless he wanted to, how much more ought we to die for him, since we are mortal, even if we do not want to be? If the Lord died for his servants and this without a reward, it is more just that a servant should die for his Lord—especially when this is rewarded.

40"He who receives you receives me."

Because the apostles and other Christians, living among the persecutions of the Jews and Gentiles, considered it necessary sometimes to turn aside and flee dangers from one city to the next, following Christ's command, so he gave his honor to them—nay, he puts himself among them—so that he might encourage the whole Christian nation to help them. He reckons that what was given to them was received by himself, so that he will say to those who welcomed them on the last day, "Come, O blessed of my Father, inherit the kingdom prepared for you from the foundation of the world; for I was hungry and you gave me food."[8] "As you did it to one of the least of these my brethren, you did it to me."[9] For if someone does something for the least people in the church, he does it for Christ; how much more does he who welcomes the apostles receive Christ, since he bears the other desires of Christ in his body?

41"He who receives a prophet because he is a prophet shall receive a prophet's reward, and he who receives a righteous man because he is

[8]Mt 25:34-35. [9]Mt 25:40.

a righteous man shall receive a righteous man's reward."

Prophets are understood to be the teachers, as we explained earlier; the righteous are all the Christians. By the word *prophet* he wanted to indicate all preachers of Christ, but by the word *righteous man* he wanted to indicate every Christian because it does not happen only to teachers that they wander from city to city because of persecution, but to all perfect Christians who believe in Christ.

"In the name of a prophet,"[10]

that is, "as a prophet of Christ."

"In the name of a righteous man,"[11]

that is, "as a righteous servant of Christ." For a good work to have a reward these two things must happen: they must receive a Christian and must welcome him because he is a Christian, whether a priest or a lay person. But if someone either does not welcome a Christian or indeed welcomes him but not as a Christian, he does not receive the reward of a Christian.

But what does it mean that "he who receives a prophet because he is a prophet shall receive a prophet's reward, and he who receives a righteous man because he is a righteous man shall receive a righteous man's reward"? It means that he who takes in a refugee for God's sake has the same reward as the refugee. The two are made equal: he who works for God and he who refreshes one who works for God. For example, you received a priest; then you have the reward of a priest. You received a righteous lay person; you have the reward of a righteous lay person. He who is not a Christian but receives a Christian does not have the reward of that Christian because if he receives a Christian, nonetheless he did not receive him as a Christian or for the sake of Christ's honor but as anybody. How would somebody who does not know Christ understand to receive a Christian for Christ's sake? And how would someone who does not believe the truth welcome a confessor of the truth for the truth's sake? Therefore he does not receive him in the name of Christ as a Christian but as other Gentiles welcome travelers because of their humanity and not for Christ's sake.

But we said that whether or not he received a Christian (whether priest or lay) he does not have a reward because he did not receive him as a priest or a lay person. So we must understand that such a person receiving the priest does not have the reward of a priest and such a person receiving a Christian does not have the reward of a Christian. Otherwise he has a reward for this reason alone: that he did a good work, although he did not do it for Christ. Because whoever does not welcome a prophet as a prophet does not have a prophet's reward, but he has some reward. Daniel attests to this: "Let my counsel be acceptable to you; redeem your sins with alms."[12] Therefore, if that idolatrous king could redeem his sins with alms, who does not benefit from almsgiving? But listen to the mystery that Peter explained to Clement. If a believer does a good work, it both benefits him here, since it frees him from evil deeds, and it benefits him in the age to come so that he can perceive the kingdom of heaven. But it benefits him more there than here. But if an unbeliever does a good work, his work benefits him here, and here God gives him blessings for his work. But in the age to come his work does not benefit him at all. For he is not put among the rest of the faithful because of his work—and rightly so because he did his good deed because he was moved by natural goodness and not for God's sake.

[10]This is a literal rendering of the Latin rather than the RSV, but as the author makes clear, the RSV has captured the meaning of the Greek phrase that the Latin has rendered literally. [11]See the previous footnote. [12]Dan 4:27; the quotation after the semicolon is Kellerman's translation, and it varies significantly from the RSV.

Therefore he receives the reward of his work in his body, not in his soul.[13]

But if a Christian gives to him who is not of Christ, he does not have a great reward because he did not give it either to a Christian or one who was as a Christian, as Tobit says: "Place your bread on the grave of the righteous, but give none to sinners."[14] Again, Wisdom says, "Give to the good man, but do not help the sinner."[15] Nonetheless, because it is written, "Do good to all men, and especially to those who are of the household of faith,"[16] whoever gives to an unbeliever has, to be sure, a modest reward, while he who gives to a believer has a double reward: first, because he is a creation of God; second, because he is a servant of God. But whoever gives to an unbeliever has one reward because he is a creation of God, but in his will he is opposed to God. But if a Christian welcomes in the name of Christ not a Christian but an unbeliever, he will nevertheless have his appointed reward because inasmuch as he received the non-Christian, he did so thinking he was a Christian.

42*"And whoever gives to one of these little ones even a cup of cold water because he is a disciple, truly, I say to you, he shall not lose his reward."*

His reward will not perish. Because he had earlier said, "He who receives a prophet because he is a prophet shall receive a prophet's reward, and he who receives a righteous man because he is a righteous man shall receive a righteous man's reward," here he piles up the reward of those who welcome them and speaks more fully beyond measure: "This is what I mean: whoever offers cold water to one of the very little ones who are neither prophets nor righteous men but simply believers in me—that is, I am not talking about those who have lavishly entertained them but about those who offer at least some cold water to them—his reward will not perish." The little ones in the church are those who have a little righteousness or a little faith.

And see how appropriately he speaks of the little ones. He does not say, "Whoever receives one of the little ones," as when he spoke about the prophets and righteous people, because the little ones among the Christian people do not have a need to be welcomed. They do not flee as refugees because of persecution and are not eager to undergo any trouble caused by persecution but stumble at once. Therefore elsewhere he also says concerning them, "And alas for those who are with child and for those who give suck in those days!"[17] But it is characteristic of prophets and righteous people to flee as refugees from city to city because of persecution. He commands us to welcome them, but he commands us to give to the little ones, lest by chance they stumble because of their trivial need. Thus, he did not say, "Whoever causes one of the great ones to sin," but "one of these little ones,"[18] because the great are not caused to stumble, but the little are. Truly he is a just judge. He who established a penalty for an idle word rightly also gave a reward for cold water.

Earlier he prudently added, "because he is a disciple," knowing that if someone did not give in the name of Christ, he does not have a reward. He said cold water so that he might not impose the labor of heating it. It is not because that which he gives is something that he has a reward but because of the fact that he for whom he gives it is great.

But what if someone wanted to give and could not? It is not fair for a bountiful will to be confined according to one's modest circumstances, is it? It is better, then, for the work to be revealed in accordance with the will than for the bountiful will to be confined according to the work. How then does it comfort all the poor people who want to show kindness,

[13]Pseudo-Clement *The Clementine Homilies* 11:25; cf. ANF 8:289-90. [14]Tob 4:17. [15]Sir 12:7. [16]Gal 6:10. [17]Mt 24:19. [18]Mt 18:6.

other than to show that those who do not want to show kindness have no excuse? For I think that he who established a reward for cold water will also give a reward to the mere willingness without any deed.

11:1 And[19] when Jesus had finished instructing his twelve disciples, he went on from there to teach and preach in their cities.

When Christ sent his disciples to preach, he armed them with spiritual commandments as with celestial arms. For they could not be light commandments with which they were being sent as sheep to conquer wolves. So he says, "When Jesus had finished instructing his disciples," he went out to preach so that the teacher might not be lazy while the disciples labored. For he had not ordained them to be substitutes of his work but his assistants. And so as the hired hands were hastening, it was necessary for the head of the household to hasten even more. For among worldly people whoever is greater or more famous also has lesser or subordinate people by him—indeed, they fulfill everything whatsoever that is necessary—but the dignitary only is in charge of the commands and has no concern about any labor. But among spiritual people this is not the case, but whoever is greater has greater labor. So while the apostles were preaching, Christ labored all the more. For he had sent them as the sun sends his rays, as a rose sends the aromas of its fragrance, as a fire scatters its sparks, so that just as a sun appears in its rays and a rose is perceived in its aromas and a fire is viewed by its sparks, so the power of Christ might be known in their virtues. For who would not praise the knowledge of the teacher if he saw his students well instructed, or who would not admire his power when he considers their great works? Therefore Christ was doing miracles, and so were his disciples, and amid so many workers of miracles the great fame of their great powers grew so that John, sitting in prison, heard of the works of Christ.

The Twenty-Sixth[1] Homily: On Matthew 11

2 Now when John heard in prison about the deeds of the Christ, he sent word by his disciples 3 and said to him, "Are you he who is to come, or shall we look for another?"

John was in appearance a man but in grace an angel, because there was no flesh in him but only in his appearance. He was held in jail in his body, but his soul was in heaven. And what Herod did to him to punish him he welcomed as an act of kindness. And so he enjoyed his mercy as God's mercy, because it is the saints' true joy to leave the world. Just as if in the case of a person hastening to something that he desires, if another person did not know his plans and forced him with evil intention to go where he wanted to go, so I think, when a wicked person wants to kill a righteous one, he kills one eager to die. Just as a servant rejoices to appear before his lord's face after he has fulfilled the task of a work assigned to him, so also John rejoiced to go to him after the mystery of the preaching entrusted to him had been completed. And not only was he not sad about his death, but he thought that any delay of his life was punishment.

Do you want to know what is beyond human nature? Having been cast into prison, he was not worried about his own danger but was thinking of the salvation of others, that is, of his disciples. Therefore he sent them to Christ and asked, "Are you he who is to come, or shall we look for another?" At first glance John seems to do something strange. He had said

[19]The material from here to the end of this homily is found not in PG 56, the primary text for this translation, but it is the second fragment found in Étaix 281. **Twenty-Sixth Homily** [1]The twenty-seventh homily in PG 56.

to Jesus, who was coming to be baptized by him, "I need to be baptized by you, and do you come to me?"[2] When he came amid countless people, John pointed to him and said, "Behold, the Lamb of God, who takes away the sin of the world!"[3] And what is more, while John was still in the womb, before he was born, he not only recognized him but also by his spiritual leaping he made his mother to be a prophetess. But now John asks as if he did not know the answer, "Are you he who is to come, or shall we look for another?" But John in prison knew that he would soon die and wanted to join his disciples to Christ, just as if a prudent dying parent were to entrust his children to a faithful tutor. He wanted to see the full faith of his disciples while he was still alive, and he wanted to see them without any doubt believing in Christ. Just as if a dying parent sees his children adorned with good character and perfect in all wisdom, he dies without a worry, fearing nothing further for his children, so also John wanted to see his disciples perfect in Christ so that he could die a more pleasant death. But not like a parent entrusting his children did he entrust them to Christ as a tutor, but rather as pedagogue entrusting another person's children, whom for a while he had received in order to educate them, he wanted to return them to Christ as to their own parent, after they had been educated. So he asked through his disciples not so that he might receive a reply in turn and hear from Christ and learn, but so that his disciples who had been sent might see his works with their eyes and believe.

"Are you he who is to come, or shall we look for another?"

When he says, "Are you he who is to come, or shall we look for another?" he shows that there are two people who are to come, Christ and Antichrist, about whom also the Lord elsewhere indicates, saying, "I have come in my Father's name, and you do not receive me; if another comes in his own name, him you will receive."[4] This means that whoever does not receive Christ waits for Antichrist to come. Christ understood John's intention; the king noticed the plan of his own prince; the Lord understood the speech of his servant. What the Spirit had spoken in John God understood, as the apostle says: "He who searches the hearts of men knows what is the mind of the Spirit."[5] Therefore a spiritual individual easily understands a spiritual person. But a carnal person does not understand a spiritual one, though a carnal person is understood by a spiritual person because "the spiritual man judges all things, but is himself to be judged by no one."[6] This is because a carnal individual speaks according to the flesh and always understands according to the flesh, but a spiritual individual speaks according to his heart and understands his thoughts.

Consider, finally, how the words and their meaning are alike. Just as John at first glance asked Christ through his disciples, "Are you he who is to come, or shall we look for another?" but really says this to his disciples, "Go, see and believe, because there is not another who was to come other than myself," so also Christ at first glance told John in reply,

4"Go and tell John what you hear and see: 5the blind receive their sight . . . and the deaf hear . . . 6And blessed is he who takes no offense at me."

But in reality he was saying this to John's disciples: "Look, see and learn that the blind see, the deaf hear, and you are blessed if you take no offense in me."

What does the phrase "what you hear and see" mean? The Lord knew that the disciples were coming from John, as Luke says, at that

[2]Mt 3:14. [3]Jn 1:29. [4]Jn 5:43. [5]Rom 8:27. [6]1 Cor 2:15.

hour when he was preparing a suitable banquet for many, good guests, so that even if Christ kept silent, his works would speak about him.[7] For those who had been healed were giving thanks, and some were saying, "We never saw anything like this!"[8] while others were saying, "God has visited his people!"[9] and still others said, "Glory to God who had given such authority to men."[10] The disciples in this way were feeding their eyes and their ears as they saw miracles of healing and heard voices of those giving thanks, or as they saw his miracles and heard his teaching or saw the healings of the sick and heard the confessions of the demons who were being cast out. O the mercy of Christ! He did all things so that he might win the souls of a few people because in God's eyes one just person is better than a whole world full of sinners.

[7]As they went away, Jesus began to speak to the crowds concerning John.

How well he began to praise John as his disciples went away! Not as some flatterers who freely praise a person to his face or when they see his trusty friends or his servants whom they believe will tell him what they hear. That person is a fool who is glad when praised to his face. But when a wise person is praised to his face, he is scourged in his heart. There are two reasons why you ought not to praise a person to his face. First, if you think him to be a wise person, he will receive the praise sternly. And why do you cause trouble to him by your praises? But if you think him to be a fool, he ought not to be extolled. Why do you nurture his folly with your praises? Do not we say that a fool is one who wants to be praised to his face? For all people want to be praised. And so let us do good that we may obtain praise from him, as the apostle says: "If there is any excellence, if there is anything worthy of praise, think about these things . . . and the God of peace will be with you."[11] For whoever wishes to be praised because of evil people is vain, but whoever praises a person before his servants, the one to blame is not the person being praised but the one praising. For he praises him before them not so that he may commend his good opinion to people but so that the one being praised can hear that he praised him.

"What did you go out into the wilderness to behold?"

They did not go out into the desert to see John, nor was John in the desert but in prison. But he refers to the past, when the people often went into the desert to see John, since he was still in the desert then.

"A reed shaken by the wind?"

A reed is empty and has no power, and so whatever wind blows on it bends it every which way. So also is a carnal and profane person in whom there is no marrow of faith and in whom there is no power of truth found in him; whatever temptation comes on him bends him. For when God wanted to show Job in what kind of people the devil rests, he introduced the dragon as a figure of the devil, and when he had said many things about him said among other things, "Under the lotus plants he lies, in the covert of the reeds and in the marsh."[12] A reed is hollow, but a papyrus plant[13] is very light and supple. So every carnal person, hollow in faith and light in understanding and supple in his passions, is a reed and papyrus plant. Because John up to that time had given much testimony about Christ in various ways, as we read at the beginning of the Evangelist John, but later sent his disciples to Jesus

[7]Lk 7:18-23. [8]Mk 2:12. [9]Lk 7:16. [10]Mt 9:8; the author writes this as a direct quotation but the RSV as an indirect quotation. [11]Phil 4:8-9. [12]Job 40:21. [13]For "marsh" the author uses "papyrus plant," which would make up much of the marsh vegetation along the Nile.

and asked him, saying, "Are you he who is to come, or shall we look for another?" perhaps it seemed strange to the people who were there at the time and an indication of a lightweight individual that earlier he had preached to all as if he knew, but now he asked as if he did not know if Jesus was the one or somebody else. Therefore Jesus did not explain John's reasoning but his honor, and he announced his grace that John was such and such so that Jesus' proclamation of John's honor might remove any suspicion of fickleness from him. It was also so that, when the disciples had passed along the explanation, those who deserved to have the spirit of God might be understood to be worthy and faithful, because they examined the depths of God.

8"*Why then did you go out? To see a man clothed in soft raiment?*"

That is to say, a friend of the world who enjoys its goods. Did you not see that his clothing was of camel's hair and a leather belt was around his loins? His food was locusts and wild honey so that he could despise the world along with its goods, as his very manner of life bore witness. To be sure, he stood in the world. But as to the fact that he entered the world, he entered it not so that he could remain in the world but so that he could rob the world. That is to say, although he was indeed born in the world, he did not enter into any goods of this world. As to the fact that he was born in the world, he did not remain sinning in the world, but, converting sinners to righteousness, he freed them from the world. That world shows many delights to seduce people. Just as if an evil person sees that some orphan has his parent's wealth, he often takes him to lunch, gives him now and then some splendid garment, speaks to him sweet flattery until he takes away his resources, so also the devil sees people have a heavenly treasure inside of them, namely, the immortal soul created by God, a heavenly wisdom placed in an earthly coffer, and so the devil shows him gold and silver and decorations much to be desired, costly items of clothing and delicious foods and glorious offices of state. He does this so that by subjugating him through this to his own pleasures, he may take away the salvation of his soul and destroy the grace of his heart.

9"*Why then did you go out? To see a prophet? Yes, I tell you, and more than a prophet.*"

It is the task of a prophet to preach about Christ. It was not the task of the prophet while still in the womb to recognize God in the womb while he was in the womb, was it? It is the task of a prophet to accept the prophecy as a reward for his manner of life and faith. It was not the task of a prophet to receive the prophecy before he became a prophet and receive grace before he became a man, was it? It is the task of a prophet to receive honor from God. It was not the task of a prophet to give the honor of baptism to God, was it? It is the task of a prophet to proclaim a word about Christ before the time. It is not the task of a prophet to point out Christ with his finger face to face, is it? It is the task of a prophet to prophesy about God. It is not the task of a prophet for God to prophesy about him, saying, "Behold, I send my messenger before your face,"[14] is it?

10"*This is he of whom it is written, 'Behold, I send my messenger[15] before your face, who shall prepare your way before you.'*"[16]

Now he begins to say for what reasons the blessed prophet John was greater than a prophet, who deserved to have such a person

[14]Lk 7:27; cf. Mt 11:10; the archaic language of the RSV has been updated. [15]In Latin, "angel." The Greek word that lies behind the Latin translation means "messenger," whether it is a human being or an angelic one, although in Christian literature the latter sense predominates. [16]The archaic language of the RSV has been updated, not only here but wherever this quotation is used throughout this passage.

praising him. And John indeed had testified about Christ, "Behold, the Lamb of God, who takes away the sin of the world!"[17] But John received more from Christ than he gave him. When John glorified Christ, he gave him human praise, but when Christ did so, he gave John divine glory. For John showed him to be the lamb, but he proclaimed John to be an angel. John praised less in Christ than was there. For not only did he take away the sins of the world, but also he gave eternal life to the world. But Christ raised him up higher than he seemed to be so that he who was a human being was said to be an angel.

"Behold, I send my messenger before your face."

Listen now and understand his honor. I think, if it is not too audacious to say, that John is more glorious than if he had been an angel in name and nature because he was a human being and called an angel because of the just deserts of his virtue. For an angel, as far as the fact that he is an angel is concerned, is not so much a reward for his virtue as the quality of his nature. But John is remarkable, since he entered angelic holiness while in human nature and obtained by the grace of God what human nature did not have.

Behold, all the prophets sent before the face of Christ are also called angels, as it is written: "You who received the law as delivered by angels and did not keep it."[18] And how did it happen that it was only said about John as a proof of a unique grace that "I send my messenger before your face"? All the prophets were sent before the face of Christ, but only John was sent before the face of Christ so that he would come at almost the same time as Christ himself. As John was closer in time to Christ than the other prophets, so his righteousness was closer to Christ's than theirs. Many stars precede the rising of the sun, announcing its coming, but none of them deserved the name of lightbearer except for the one that precedes it with its light; so all the prophets precede the face of Christ, announcing his arrival, but only John is called his forerunner because not only did he announce his coming but also showed him with his own finger: "Behold, the lamb of God."[19] All the prophets attested that he was coming, but only John showed that he had now come. Therefore the other prophets were sent to announce his arrival, but John was sent to prepare his road.

It is one thing to announce his coming and another to prepare his way. A sermon of preaching was entrusted to them announcing his arrival, but the work of correcting humanity was instructed to the one preparing his way, just as his angel: "And he will turn the hearts of fathers" to their Lord.[20] Therefore John corrected humanity so that Christ could receive it. John cleansed so that Christ could sanctify; John prepared so that Christ could dwell there.

There is another reason why he is greater than the prophets.

11"Truly, I say to you, among those born of women there has risen no one greater than John the Baptist."

Concerning what prophet was a prophecy given? All the prophets prophesied about Christ, but no prophecy was given about them. But not only did John prophesy about Christ, but other prophets prophesied about him. Who said, "The voice of one crying in the wilderness"?[21] For all were bearers of the word, but John was the voice that was able to make the desert like a cultivated field. Just as the voice is closer to the word but is not the word, so John was closer to Christ but was not Christ. Which of the prophets could make a prophet, even though he was a prophet? Elijah,

[17]Jn 1:29. [18]Acts 7:53. [19]Jn 1:29. [20]Mal 4:6. [21]Lk 3:4; cf. Is 40:3.

to be sure, anointed Elisha to be a prophet, but nonetheless he did not give him the grace of prophecy.[22] But while John was still in the womb of his mother, he gave his mother the knowledge that divinity had entered the room, and she opened his mouth in a word of confession, so that she recognized the honor of the person she did not see and said, "And why is this granted me, that the mother of my Lord should come to me?"[23] For because Christ was in his mother's womb he could not ordain John who was in his mother's womb as his forerunner—and even if he could, he could not do it in such a way so that all could hear—so he made Mary to greet Elizabeth, so that his speech might proceed from the womb of his mother where the Lord was dwelling and, entering in the ears of Elizabeth, descend to John and there anoint him as a prophet. For just as his mother attests, as soon as the voice of greeting entered the ears of Elizabeth, at once the boy leaped and prophesied, not by his voice but by his movement.

Notice that he did not say "among those born from women," but "among those born of women." It is one thing to be born of a woman and quite another to be born from a woman. Whoever is born of a woman indeed was born in a woman and has his beginning from a woman and did not exist before the woman did. But whoever was born from a woman was not even born in a woman. Behold, Christ was born from a woman. In common parlance, he was born of a woman, and yet he was born in a woman although he existed before the woman did. Therefore he did not say "among those born from women," so that he would not include himself with them. Indeed, Scripture does not say that John is greater than all the saints but that the other saints are not greater than John. He made him equal with them; he did not put him ahead of them. But since there is a great depth to righteousness that nobody can be perfect in it except for God alone, I think that all the saints are mutually inferior or superior to themselves. From this fact we understand that whoever does not hold himself to be greater is greater than all. At last the word that follows indicates this: "Yet he who is least in the kingdom of heaven is greater than he." But who is both lesser and greater? Christ, who is younger in body but greater in spirit. See how he is greater than all the saints if he thinks that Jesus Christ is earlier, since he lives and reigns with the Father and the Holy Spirit forever and ever. Amen.

12 ***"From[24] the days of John the Baptist until now the kingdom of heaven has suffered violence."***

How? Because the grace of God is greater in people than their will is. But when a person who has been established in his free will hastens, labors and conquers, he enters into the kingdom of heaven as a reward for his merit, and so he does not do violence to the heavenly kingdom. But when an abundance of divine grace presses the soul more than the soul presses it, he enters the kingdom of heaven not so much by the intention of his soul hastening there as by the power of grace that compels him, and so the kingdom of heaven suffers violence because grace is not given as a reward for his labor, but he is snatched there free of charge. As long as God called people to the kingdom, few entered it, and it stood vacant. This is not to the disgrace of God who created it but to the shame of people who did not want to come to the kingdom. But afterwards he sent to lead them in this way: not only by word but also by deed, and more by grace than by his voice. It was not because of

[22]1 Kings 19. [23]Lk 1:43. [24]The material from here to the end of this homily is not found in PG 56, the primary text for this translation, but in the third fragment listed in Étaix 281-85.

some need that he led them, but so that no human being could boast that he had been saved by his own merit. For this is indicated by that parable where the head of the household sent to call his friends to dinner, and when they made excuses for various reasons he said, "Go out . . . and bring in the . . . maimed and . . . lame."[25] You see then that after the invited people did not come, he later ordered them to bring in people, not to invite them. For truly if God were abandoning us to the desires of our heart, none of us would vie for life. If he were to look at the merit of our heart or labor, he would not be able to find anybody whom he could save. But he visibly calls us through the Scriptures, but he stirs up in us invisibly a desire for the kingdom of heaven, so that there may not be any boasting of those people who come, but rather of God who leads us, as also Paul says: "So it depends not upon man's will or exertion, but upon God's mercy."[26]

Therefore previously, unless someone hastened and knocked, he did not come to the kingdom of heaven, and so few people came. But afterwards almost even those who did not want it (so to say) were invited and brought in by the grace of God, and nobody was left behind in perdition except for him who clearly opposed God, saying, "I want to belong to the devil, not God." And if a person opposes God, ask Job, and you will hear: "They say to God, 'Depart from us! We do not desire the knowledge of your ways.'"[27] You see then how the kingdom of God suffers violence and how they take it by force. For it is one thing to suffer violence, another to take it by force. They do violence to it when they enter contrary to their merit; they take it by force when they enter actively, not as much as human beings can come, but as much as God can lead them. The kingdom becomes booty, not a reward, as it were.

It is one thing to enter the kingdom and another to receive the glory of the kingdom. To enter the kingdom is to believe in Christ, for Christ is the kingdom. Therefore many people are indeed in the kingdom, but few accept the glory of the kingdom. Just as he was teaching that the person who did not have a wedding garment and was reclining at the wedding banquet was dragged outside by his feet.[28] Thus, many enter into the kingdom, but one who is worthy of the kingdom remains. For without a verdict of righteousness we are led in, but we are kept in the kingdom with a verdict of righteousness. For all of us are led in so that we may not have the excuse of ignorance, but we are not all kept there, so that the honor of the kingdom may not be dirtied by the unworthy. You see then that John is great. In his time such grace was poured out on earth and—something that never occurred during the days of all the prophets—he was made a minister of this grace at his time.

[13]***"For all the prophets and the law prophesied until John."***

Therefore John is the end of the promise. But if John is the end of the promise, he is also the beginning of blessing. For whatever good things have been promised to this age up until the time of John were indeed promised. But since then they are no longer future things that are being promised, but the things that have been promised are being fulfilled. Up until John there was hope, but since then the substance has begun to exist. Therefore there is not a little glory to the man[29] . . . who became the beginning[30] of all good things; he understands and judges and confesses him to be righteous, if faithful people justified the wisdom of God both while John fasted and Christ ate. But God is in no way pleasing to an

[25]Lk 14:21. [26]Rom 9:16. [27]Job 21:14; the archaic language of the RSV has been updated. [28]See Mt 22:11-13. [29]Two manuscripts leave a half-line blank; probably something is missing here. [30]This word is missing but has been suggested by Étaix.

unbelieving person. If he does something well, he does not understand that he has benefited him; but if he punishes him, he murmurs about his cruelty.

[20]Then he began to upbraid the cities where most of his mighty works had been done, because they did not repent. [21]"Woe to you, Chorazin!"[31]

Bethsaida is "home of the hunters" and Capernaum is "field of exhortation."[32] Then when John was in prison, as if he had been placed in the grave, he sent to Christ, saying, "Are you he who is to come, or shall we look for another?"[33] Considering how the course of John's life had already been fulfilled, but his work had not greatly had the benefit of converting the Jews, Christ made a speech both in praise of John and against the incorrigible hard-heartedness of the Jews. They had not wept in repentance over their sins when John lamented, that is, with the sadness of his anger, nor did the heavenly joys of the wedding feast dance and leap about in their mind by their faith and good works as Christ sang to them. Therefore, moved by that opportunity for such words, "he began to upbraid the cities where most of his mighty works had been done, because they did not repent." Just as it often happens among people, some who are moved by certain causes pursue other causes because of the likeness of their very causes. But there is a difference because the cause itself draws a person to say or do some such thing, but a cause does not draw Christ, but rather Christ drew the cause into the middle so that he might have an opportunity to speak about such things.

Consider, Christians, that some miracles were done in Chorazin, some in Bethsaida, some in Capernaum, but all have been done among us Christians. Perhaps Bethsaida did not know about the things done in Chorazin, and perhaps Capernaum did not know about what was done in Bethsaida. But Christians have learned whatever Christ has done, since the gospel teaches all things. Therefore, if Christ grieves over those cities because they did not repent, although they did not see all the miracles of Christ, how do you think that he daily grieves over us Christians who daily read and hear about his acts of power in the church and yet nonetheless do not repent of our sins? If Christ had come at the time of the Sodomites and shown such things, perhaps they would have been converted; because they did not hear the just man Lot, they were burned with fire and brimstone. Such torments await us who despise Christ!

And see that he did not say, "Then he upbraided the cities," but "Then he began to upbraid the cities." Therefore if he began then, he also is upbraiding such places up to now. And as often as the word *upbraid* is read in the church, he upbraids those who are like them in the church. Therefore woe to you Christians to whom daily the holy Scriptures are shouted, and you, as deaf vipers, stopping up your ears, do not hear their voices! Woe to you Manicheans, from whom the blood of Christ will be required, because it was poured out in vain for you! Woe to you who overturn the order of things to a different configuration than God arranged when you say, "So God created the world so that we may possess it with many riches; he made many good things in the world so that we can enjoy them," which is not true! But these things were made so that we could be tempted in them. Therefore the world pertains to the corruption of those who are not wise but to the testing of those who are wise. How then is God to have mercy on you when he does not see his image in you? For a person is the image of God, so that his soul may not serve the flesh in fleshly matters but so that his flesh could serve the soul in spiritual mat-

[31]A lacuna of up to one full line occurs here. [32]Étaix suggests that this sentence is a gloss and not part of the text. [33]Mt 11:3.

ters. For even the wise of the Gentiles knew this, that whoever lives in carnal delights or trespasses, his flesh does not serve the soul but the soul the flesh.

Some say, "We are embarrassed to confess our sins." Tell me, what is worse: to do evil or to say it? Therefore if you were not ashamed to do evil before the sight of God, how are you embarrassed to say it before the sight of another human being? You did not fear to stir up God to wrath, and yet you hesitate to turn him to mercy? Others say, "Let it go; we still need greater wealth," clearly fearing that after their repentance of unjust acts they will return and become paupers. O mortal, consider all the generations. Who was converted to God and returned to the disgrace of poverty? "The young lions suffer want and hunger; but those who seek the Lord lack no good thing."[34] But suppose that you are going to be poor, nonetheless what do you choose: to be poor for a while or for eternity in hell? Yet others say, "What will we leave our children?" But what will you do for your soul when you do not have a child? See how you benefit your parent because you left behind the wealth he had gathered up for you with iniquity. So also your child will help you if you get rid of the wealth for him that you have gathered with iniquity.

The Twenty-Seventh[1] Homily: On Matthew 11

[25]At that time Jesus declared, "I thank you, Father, Lord of heaven and earth, that you have hidden these things from the wise and understanding and revealed them to babes."[2]

After he rebuked the cities, or rather their citizens, because they had been so often sown with doctrine but never sprouted with faith since they received the power and miracles of Christ not as acts of spiritual edification but as carnal entertainment, he says to them in reply, as if in the context of the disciples explaining their mission, as Luke states: "I thank you, Father, Lord of heaven and earth."[3] One must consider that Luke introduces this context in this manner: "In that same hour he rejoiced in the Holy Spirit and said, 'I thank you, Father.'"[4] But Matthew puts it in this way: "At that time Jesus declared." Just as people coming from various paths hasten to one dwelling, so also the Evangelists speaking from different occasions enter into one meaning. Therefore Luke introduces it in this way: after the disciples returned and gave thanks and said, "Lord, even the demons are subject to us in your name,"[5] and as Christ saw the gratitude of the disciples, how they were faithful in fulfilling the mystery entrusted to them and how they were devout in their giving thanks, he "rejoiced . . . and said, 'I thank you, Father.'" But after Matthew showed the implacable spirits of the Jews and their hardened minds, which so many miracles could not bend to faith, he answered, stirred up by the persuasion of his disciples and hearing their good curses, to whose good news he responded. Or alternatively, it was because he was compelled to do so by the hardness of the Jews. Therefore he gives thanks because the uneducated and simple people have been enlightened, who impute to their Creator whatever good they do. But he gives thanks not only because the little ones have been illuminated but also because the literate and wise of the Jews have been blinded and everyone else who imputes every grace of God to themselves.

"I thank you, Father, Lord of heaven and earth, that you have hidden these things from the wise and understanding and revealed them to babes." The understanding of those words

[34]Ps 34:10. **Twenty-Seventh Homily** [1]The twenty-eighth homily in PG 56. [2]The archaic language of the RSV has been updated not only here but wherever this quotation is used throughout this passage. [3]Lk 10:21; the archaic language of the RSV has been updated. [4]Lk 10:21; the archaic language of the RSV has been updated. [5]Lk 10:17; the archaic language of the RSV has been updated.

is in accordance with the intention of Christ, who is speaking in this place. After he rebuked the unbelieving cities, he took the opportunity from their unbelief and introduced into their midst the just arrangement of God and spoke a prayer of thanksgiving. This was because it pleased God to reject the Jews who were given the eloquence of God more than wise people, although they were foolish (truly wisdom is not knowing the eloquence of God but living according to the eloquence of God), and it pleased God to welcome the Gentiles, because they were babes in their knowledge of God and babes through ignorance and not arrogance. You can extend the matter you are treating to any persons you wish because God always hides the mystery of the truth from all wise people, who are wise according to the understanding of the flesh and not according to the spirit of the heart, and he reveals it to the babes who are babes in malice.

Who are the wise? The ancient philosophers and orators, who are quite keen in natural wisdom by their training in literature and strive to inquire about the nature of God—not desiring to find God but desiring to argue lofty matters. They have been defeated in their talents and fail in their speech. At last they confessed that they could not find anything more than that God is unknowable. And why then did you labor so much, if you are as ignorant after you made your inquiry as before you did? Just as one who takes it on himself to sail across an unnavigable sea must return by the same path by which he entered, so also they began in ignorance and end in ignorance.

O wise person (or rather a fool)! God is invisible, and who can see him unless he sees himself? Keep then the commandments of God and sanctify your heart so that God may dwell in you and you may see God. Or rather you will not see, but God who is in you will see you. God is incomprehensible. Who can understand him unless he understands himself? Then keep the commandments of God and sanctify your heart so that God may dwell in you, and daily you will find God more and more. Then you will not find God, but God will find you.

Who are the babes? They are Christians who cannot think more about Christ other than what they see in him and cannot believe more about him other than what they hear in the books about him. That is the nature of infants: when they see something, their simple mind can consider nothing more about it than what their eyes see; and what they hear from someone they understand nothing more fully in the sermons of someone explaining it to them, nor can they discuss the matter they have heard but believe whatever they hear. If it is something good, they rejoice wholeheartedly; if it is something bad, they are sad. So also if the unbelievers hear Christ saying, "I am not alone, but the Father who sent me is with me," they cannot understand it, since they think that God the Father and Son are not one. If he were one, he would never have said, "I am not alone." Whoever is one is also alone, but whoever is not alone is not one either.[6]

If we see Christ hanging on the cross, we cannot understand of our own strength that he who is hanging there is a mere human being. For we do not see that the majesty of God has withdrawn from the body, nor do we hear this. But perhaps you will say, "How then did he cry aloud on the cross, 'My God, my God, why have you forsaken me?'"[7] if his body had not been abandoned? And did you not hear how he said to the thief, "Truly, I say to you, today you will be with me in Paradise"?[8] How could a mere human being, who complained that he had been abandoned, offer to lead anyone to Paradise? Therefore the Son cried out to the

[6]The three previous sentences were excised by Manhusius for doctrinal reasons. [7]Mt 27:46; cf. Ps 22:1; the archaic language of the RSV has been updated. [8]Lk 23:43.

Father in order to prove to people that he was suffering in the weakness of his body, not in order to show that his body had been abandoned by his divinity.

Again, who are the wise, from whom the mystery of Christ is hidden? The priests, scribes and Pharisees, who met in the temple and said, " 'How long will you keep us in suspense? If you are the Christ, tell us plainly.' Jesus answered them, 'I told you, and you do not believe. The works that I do in my Father's name, they bear witness to me.' "[9] "The Jews took up stones again to stone him . . . [saying] 'It is not for a good work that we stone you but for blasphemy; because you, being a man, make yourself God.' "[10] Who are the babes to whom he is revealed? Those whom the Lord asks saying, "But who do you say that I am?"[11] They said in reply, "You are the Christ, the Son of the living God."[12]

Therefore, if fishermen and uneducated people found as they daily handled nets in their hands what the Jews who daily meditated on the Law of God could not find, so you too should never discuss the counsels of God or what he did in his works or in what way he made it, but give thanks for however he wanted to ordain his creation and let the very nature of God be enough of a witness to you that God does not do anything without reason or without justice. ("Yea, Father, for such was your gracious will"[13] does not indicate by what reason it so pleased him, but Christ only thanked his Father that it did please him.) God did not create you for you to discuss these matters with him but for you to honor him. Nor did he want you to be a judge of his deeds but a servant of his precepts. It is the responsibility of a master to provide all things that pertain to the usefulness of a servant. But it is the task of a good servant to work faithfully and not discuss the deeds of his master.

[27]***"All things have been delivered to me by my Father."***

By whom were they delivered to him, if the Father and the Son are one? Or why did he not have it unless they had been given him, if he was equal in all things to his Father? For the meaning of "delivered over" excludes the notion of unity as much as equality. For neither the one who accepts is one with the giver, nor is he who accepts what is given equal to the one who gave it. These things were delivered to him in accordance with the statement that he "for a little while was made lower than the angels."[14] For according to that statement that "he did not count equality with God a thing to be grasped,"[15] God was one and equal with him, who delivered all things to him.

"All things have been delivered to me,"

whether heavenly, earthly or under the earth. Heavenly things have been delivered so that never again will there be anything rebelling and so that none of the heavenly beings will say, "I will ascend above the heights of the clouds, I will make myself like the Most High."[16] Earthly things have been delivered so that people may leave behind their idols and sins and believe in me and obey my commandments. Things under the earth have been delivered so that they may be called to live, "that at [my] name every knee should bow, in heaven and on earth and under the earth."[17] Heavenly things have been delivered so they may help earthly things; earthly things so that people may become imitators of heavenly things; things under the earth so that they may not longer be of benefit to besiege humankind but to test the saints.

And see that he did not say, "All people have been delivered to me," as if he were speaking

[9]Jn 10:24. [10]Jn 10:31, 33. [11]Mt 16:15. [12]Mt 16:16. [13]The archaic language of the RSV has been updated. [14]Heb 2:9. [15]Phil 2:6. [16]Is 14:14. [17]Phil 2:10.

only of people who would believe in him. But he is speaking also about all things, which would be converted to his glory, although they were hostile to him because of the devil's corrupting them. For example, all things have been handed over to him—heaven and earth, sun, moon, stars, air and fire, waters, rivers, hell and death, so that nobody may think any longer that all these things are gods or unbegotten, as the devil suggests, but that all people may know and confess that they are works of Christ, as the Holy Spirit teaches. Therefore they were not delivered to him so that now they might become Christ's by nature, which they always had been, but so that they could be believed to be his and now converted to his glory, just as God always was in existence for humankind, but up until then he had not been known. But now they have been delivered to him absolutely so that they might recognize him as their creator God, as it is written, "Since you have given him power over all flesh, to give eternal life to all whom you have given him. And this is eternal life, that they know you the only true God, and Jesus Christ whom you have sent."[18]

It is as if to say, "Life and death have been delivered to me so that life might not be an occasion for people to sin or death a punishment, but so that those who live would gain the profit of righteousness by living well and those who die would live better as they reign with me in heaven. Riches and wealth have been delivered to me. Up until now, poverty has forced people to blaspheme and persuaded them to commit theft, while riches have puffed up people and given them the power to hurt others. But now they have been given to me so that poverty may profit to the glory of God, provided that it is endured magnanimously, and wealth may profit to the glory of God, provided that it is dispensed mercifully. Slaves and kings have been delivered to me so that slaves may not be ashamed of their servitude but boast in me, their Lord, and kings may not vaunt themselves in their power but bend their knees to me."

"And no one knows the Son except the Father, and no one knows the Father except the Son and anyone to whom the Son chooses to reveal him."

So we must understand that nobody can know either of them by his own power, unless the Son reveals the Father or the Father the Son. For Christ said about the person of the Father that nobody knows the Father unless the Son reveals him. But concerning the person of the Son he did not say, "Unless the Father reveals him," because he had already said earlier, "I thank you, Father, Lord of heaven and earth, that you have hidden these things from the wise and understanding and revealed them to babes,"[19] namely, "those things that had been revealed about me at my coming." For he said to Peter, when he confessed about him, "For flesh and blood has not revealed this to you, but my Father who is in heaven."[20] And Isaiah said, "I am the LORD, your Holy One, the Creator of Israel, your King."[21] Or certainly it is so according to the fullness of the Father that nobody knows the Father except the Son. And according to the fullness of the Son nobody knows the Son except the Father, because a creature that is easily comprehended cannot comprehend an incomprehensible nature. This is because even if the Son reveals something about the Father or the Father about the Son, he nonetheless does not reveal the whole truth but only as much as he to whom it is being revealed can understand. Or certainly it is understood from the words that precede: "All things have

[18]Jn 17:2-3; the archaic language of the RSV has been updated. [19]Mt 11:25; the archaic language of the RSV has been updated. [20]Mt 16:17. [21]Is 43:15.

been delivered to me by my Father."

It is also understood from the words that follow.

[28]"*Come to me, all who labor and are heavy laden.*"

I think that according to this nobody recognizes the Son according to which all things have been delivered to him, "that at the name of Jesus every knee should bow, in heaven and on earth and under the earth, and every tongue confess that Jesus Christ is Lord, to the glory of God the Father."[22] Moreover, nobody knew all the things that would take place. And because of this nobody recognized the Father whereby he decided to give salvation to all through his Son. Thus the apostle said, "The revelation of the mystery which was kept secret for long ages but is now disclosed."[23]

"Come to me, all who labor and are heavy laden."

Who are those who labor? Those who do the righteousness of the Law. And who are the heavy laden? The Jews, on whom Moses imposed such commandments of the Law after they made an idol of the calf, from which they could never extricate themselves. Peter says about them, "Now therefore why do you make trial of God by putting a yoke upon the neck of the disciples which neither our fathers nor we have been able to bear? But we believe that we shall be saved through the grace of the Lord Jesus."[24] So he said, "All who labor," that is, "You who strive to be righteous and cannot because while you cannot fulfill the command of the Law, it makes your conscience guilty." And among the Jews, the Law (that is, the Decalogue) that they received before their lapse into idolatry was light and righteous, but without grace it was found to be burdensome. Without the aid of grace all righteousness is burdensome to people because the Law is a bare command, but grace is the power of God. Law is written in a book, but grace is planted in the heart. So the Law is an unbearable weight, but grace is the delight of the heart, as the Lord says through Solomon, "Come to me, you who desire me. . . . For the remembrance of me is sweeter than honey."[25]

Therefore, the Law is not only so heavy because it orders serious commandments of strict observance but also because it orders it to be done and does not offer any help to do it. Nor is grace light only for the reason that it sets forth easy commandments, but also because grace itself works the power in us to do what it orders to be done. Behold, the Law commands, "You shall love your neighbor as yourself and hate your enemy."[26] But grace orders, "Love your enemies." But is not the commandment of grace harder than that of the Law? And yet nonetheless it is easier for us to fulfill these impossible things through grace than it was for the Jews to fulfill those possible things through the Law, because in the grace of God we can do all, but without the grace we can do nothing, as the apostle says: "I can do all things in him who strengthens me."[27]

But I say moreover: even if someone fulfills all righteousness of the Law and indeed lives in it, he still is not justified. Thus the Lord said to the young man, "Do this, and you will live."[28] He did not say, "And you will be righteous," because the Law commands refraining from evil deeds, such as 'You shall not murder" and the like. It does not enjoin a work of righteousness, as grace does, so as not to become angry without a reason and not to lust. But whoever restrains himself from evil deeds is innocent, to be sure, but he is not righteous unless he also fulfills the work of righteousness.

[22]Phil 2:10-11. [23]Rom 16:25-26. [24]Acts 15:10-11. [25]Sir 24:19-20. [26]Lev 19:18; the author adds, "and hate your enemy." [27]Phil 4:13. [28]Lk 10:28.

To be sure, he will not die, but neither will he have glory. For that reason the apostle who was a son of Abraham and had spent his life in the Law without reproach said, "We ourselves, who are Jews by birth and not Gentile sinners, yet who know that a man is not justified by works of the law but through faith in Jesus Christ, even we have believed in Christ Jesus, in order to be justified by faith in Christ."[29] But everyone who strives to act righteously and is not justified labors in his work because he does not enjoy the fruit of his labor, while he who strives and is justified does not labor but delights in his work because he enjoys the fruit of his work.

Moreover, who does not know that the righteousness of the Law is less than that of grace? For example, "you shall not murder, you shall not commit adultery"—this is easier than not getting angry or not lusting. Many, even those who do not fear God, restrain themselves from murder and adultery. But scarcely even spiritual people restrain themselves from anger or lust. Nonetheless the Law is found to be more difficult and burdensome because it seeks works, not the will. But though the righteousness of grace may be greater, it is still found to be easier because it seeks the will, not the works. For example, if someone was not angry but struck someone with a rod in order to discipline him and by accident killed him, as sometimes happens, he is innocent as far as grace is concerned since it looks at the will, not the deed, but he is guilty as far as the Law is concerned because it demands works. Again, if a virgin was pressed into prostitution in time of persecution, under the Law she is rejected as being no longer a virgin, but under grace she is welcomed as a virgin because it does not search after the works but the will. Do you see that the Law is unjust and burdensome? So Christ urged people to leave from under the weight of the Jewish law and to come to the delightful grace, saying, "Come to me, all who labor and are heavy laden, and I will give you rest," that is, "I will refresh you."

And see how he says, "Why do you labor?" Who is it that labors? It is he who hastens to fulfill righteousness and does not prevail. But whoever does not wish to act righteously does not labor under the weight of the Law. For example, if you see some weighty bundle before you, if you try to raise it above yourself and cannot, you labor, but if you do not try, you do not feel any labor under the weight. Therefore Christ does not call to himself those who did not want to behave righteously at all, but those who hastened and who labored and could not prevail. He calls by those words of his those Christians burdened by the weight of sins to the rest that comes from repentance. Do you think that sinners of this world do not labor? Indeed, they have greater labors and worries than the servants of God do, as the prophet says: "Sorrow and misfortune is on their paths and they do not know the way of peace."[30] Again, Solomon says in the persona of sinners repenting, "So it was we who strayed from the way of truth, and the light of righteousness did not shine on us, and the sun did not rise upon us. We took our fill of the paths of lawlessness and destruction, and we journeyed through trackless deserts, but the way of the Lord we have not known. What has our arrogance profited us? And what good has our boasted wealth brought us? All those things have vanished like a shadow."[31] Therefore they labor much and are worn away in the world, but they do not perceive their labor, for the spirit that seduces them delights in evil. For just as Christ delights in spirit in those who take the yoke of Christ, so that they do not grow weary in good works, so also the devil delights in those who take the yoke of the devil on themselves,

[29]Gal 2:15-16. [30]Ps 14:3 (trans. Kellerman). The Septuagint and Vulgate translations of this verse include substantially more material, including the words the author cites here, than does the Masoretic Text or the RSV. [31]Wis 5:6-9.

and the devil deceives them so that they do not ever depart from the evil of the ungodly until they die.

Therefore the righteous Christ says,

[30]"For my yoke is easy, and my burden is light."

Although sinners are not burdened in their body nor do they labor, nonetheless their souls are weighed down and labor, as the prophet says about the burden of sin: "For my iniquities have gone over my head; they weigh like a burden too heavy for me."[32] And again Zechariah writes that iniquity was seated over a talent of lead.[33]

[29]"Take my yoke upon you, and learn from me; for I am gentle and lowly in heart, and you will find rest for your souls."

O most heavy weight, that comforts instead those who carry it! The weight of earthly lords wears away little by little the strength of their servants, but the weight of Christ rather helps the one carrying it because we do not carry grace, but grace carries us. Nor were we given to grace in order to help it, but grace was given to us to help us.

[30]"For my yoke is easy, and my burden is light."

"Take my yoke and learn from me" means "From my yoke (because it is easy) and from my burden (because it is light) accept the proof that I am gentle and humble of heart." Consequently, also the prophet says about Christ, "O taste and see that the LORD is good!"[34] To the inexperienced the righteousness of Christ is heavy, but to the experienced it is easy. Therefore the Law was harsh because whatever it commanded it commanded in its wrath after the Israelites had made the idol—not so that the Law could save them but rather punish them for the hardness of their heart. But Christ is gentle because whatever he commands he does because of his mercy, not to punish but to save. Moreover, the Law is haughty. It forbids everyone but the high priest to approach the holy place. It further forbids menstruating women or a man with an emission of semen to enter the temple. It forbids a one-eyed man or a leper or someone deformed in any limb to carry out the priesthood. Do you see how arrogant the Law is? But Christ was humble, since he sought nothing else other than a pure faith and a clean conscience.

"And you will find rest for your souls."

He did not say, "You will find rest" and then say no more, but added, "for your souls," because the commandments of Christ are a rest for souls, not bodies, in this world. Even if they labor and are sad in body, their souls rest and rejoice in their spirit and in hope. So elsewhere he says, "I have said this to you, that in me you may have peace. In the world you have tribulation; but be of good cheer, I have overcome the world."[35]

[32]Ps 38:4. [33]Zech 5:7. [34]Ps 34:8. [35]Jn 16:33.

Scripture Index

OLD TESTAMENT

Genesis
1:11, *137*
3:17, *138*
3:19, *136*
4, *178*
12:1, *3*
15:9, *2*
20:7, *2*
22:18, *2*
27, *178*
27:43-44, *4*
28:17, *30*
32:30, *129*
33:10, *157*
38:27-30, *5*
39, *181*
41, *181*
41:51, *18*

Exodus
1:9-10, *6*
2, *181*
3:7, *6*
4:22, *30*
5:1, *63*
6:23, *7*
20:5, *16*
20:12, *191*
20:13, *96*
21:27, *99*
23:15, *38*, *127*
24:18, *182*

Leviticus
19:18, *207*

Numbers
1:7, *7*
2:3, *7*
3, *187*
12:11, *99*
24:17, *32*
26, *187*

Deuteronomy
4:2, *165*
12:32, *165*
32:7, *145*

Joshua
2, *9*
6, *9*

Judges
16, *187*

Ruth
1:16-17, *10*

2 Samuel
3, *12*

1 Kings
18:27, *121*
19, *200*

2 Kings
5, *170*
24, *20*

1 Chronicles
3, *12*
6, *7*

2 Chronicles
16:7-9, *15*
19:2-3, *15*
21–26, *16*
22:2, *15*
24:20, *17*
25, *17*
25:15, *17*
25:16, *17*
32, *19*

Job
2:3, *176*
21:14, *201*
38:11, *25*
40:21, *197*

Psalms
4:4, *99*, *120*
7:3, *3*, *189*
7:4, *107*
8:3, *59*
14:3, *208*
18:11, *162*
18:30, *73*
19:6, *181*
19:7, *168*
22:1, *204*
24:3-4, *166*
24:7, *59*
26:2-3, *52*
27:8, *129*
27:13, *3*, *75*, *86*
28:2, *119*
33:2, *189*
33:14, *87*
34:8, *151*, *209*
34:10, *203*
34:13, *87*
37:3, *135*
37:9-11, *50*
38:4, *209*
38:6-7, *101*
41:1, *84*
44:18-19, *75*
46:4, *129*
49:1, *94*
50:21, *54*
51:5, *25*
51:7, *49*
51:17, *49*, *127*
54:6, *7*
55:21, *157*
55:22, *180*
63:1, *63*
66:10, *52*, *61*
66:12, *61*
66:18, *3*
68:6, *156*
68:15, *84*
68:16, *84*
68:18, *163*
68:26, *119*
69:28, *188*
73:2-3, *151*
73:8-9, *155*
77:10, *2*, *39*
80:1, *68*
87:2, *91*
87:3, *91*
89:19, *14*
89:30, *148*
89:32-33, *148*
89:38, *14*
91:9, *68*
91:12, *148*
94:12, *53*
95:11, *8*
104:15, *127*, *156*
107:18, *81*
118:20, *30*, *150*
119:19, *131*
119:37, *189*
119:70, *84*

119:98-100, *22*
119:105, *91*
122:7, *91*
132:11, *2*
135:6, *123*
139:17-18, *186*
140:5, *115*
141:2, *38*

Proverbs
5:15, *12*
8:15, *69*
8:17, *169*
9:1, *30*
13:6, *153*
18:12, *71*
25:21-22, *100*
30:6, *165*
30:7-8, *97*

Song of Solomon
1:6, *48*
4:12-13, *157*
5:2, *120*

Isaiah
1:16, *48*, *130*
1:16-17, *48*
2:3, *69*, *179*
4:4, *61*
4:5, *179*
5:6, *162*
7:1-7, *18*
8:4, *31*
14, *56*
14:13, *56*
14:14, *205*
19:1, *39*, *42*
26:10, *50*
37, *18*
40:3, *199*
40:9, *83*
40:17, *187*
43:15, *206*
49:2, *6*
52:11, *191*
53:7, *175*
53:8, *2*
53:9, *131*
60:6-7, *38*
60:10, *91*

Jeremiah
1:18, *50*
17:11, *161*

Ezekiel
9:4, *85*

Daniel
2:34-35, *91*
4:27, *193*
5, *97*

Micah
5:2, *35*

Zechariah
3:7, *77*
5:7, *209*

Malachi
4:6, *199*

APOCRYPHA

1 Esdras
3:17–4:11, *22*
4, *22*
4:60, *22*

Tobit
3:17, *73*
4:17, *194*
8:7, *25*
12:12, *118*

Wisdom of Solomon
1:4, *173*
5:6-9, *208*
11:20, *186*

Sirach
1:26, *146*
2:1, *53*
3:6, *11*
4:17, *52*
6:37, *146*
12:7, *194*
18:23, *127*
19:22, *146*
23:9, *105*
23:11, *105*
24, *59*
24:19-20, *207*
24:45, *59*
26:9, *26*
35:17, *41*

Bel and the Dragon
1:33-37, *67*

2 Maccabees
6, *189*

NEW TESTAMENT

Matthew
2:3, *42*
2:8, *40*
2:20, *42*
3:2, *55*, *76*
3:11, *55*
3:14, *196*
4:19, *177*
5:3, *150*
5:8, *133*
5:14, *74*
5:16, *113*, *117*
5:21, *45*, *46*
5:21-22, *128*, *165*
5:27, *45*
5:27-28, *46*, *128*
5:33, *45*
5:33-34, *46*, *128*
5:38, *45*, *46*
5:38-39, *128*
5:39-40, *88*
5:43, *45*
5:43-44, *46*, *128*
5:44, *147*, *175*
5:45, *147*
5:46-47, *45*, *147*
6:1, *128*
6:2, *157*
6:2-4, *131*
6:5, *157*
6:12, *87*
6:12-13, *139*
6:16, *157*
6:17-18, *149*
6:19, *131*
6:20-21, *133*
6:22, *102*
7:1, *138*
7:1-2, *140*
7:13, *149*
9:8, *197*
9:29, *82*
10:23, *4*
10:29-30, *73*
11:3, *202*
11:7-8, *45*
11:10, *198*
11:13, *154*
11:25, *206*
11:29, *150*
12:25, *189*
12:34, *48*
12:36, *97*
13:10, *182*
13:11, *182*
13:13, *182*
13:29-30, *115*
13:34, *182*
13:40-41, *122*
14:24-33, *179*
14:36, *82*
15:22, *171*
15:26, *171*
15:27, *171*
16:15, *205*
16:15-16, *182*

16:16, *205*
16:17, *206*
16:18, *161*
17:5, *60*
17:21, *127*
18:3, *84*
18:6, *194*
18:12-13, *186*
19:6, *165*
20:16, *55*
21, *30*
21:43, *122*
22:11-13, *201*
23:33, *48*
24:19, *194*
25:21, *95*
25:34-35, *192*
25:40, *130*, *192*
26:7, *130*
26:39, *4*
27:46, *204*

Mark
1, *165*
2:12, *197*
10:5, *74*
14:3, *130*

Luke
1:13, *28*
1:38, *43*
1:43, *200*
1:48, *29*, *42*
2:10, *3*
2:14, *34*
3:4, *199*
4, *165*
4:23, *141*
4:30, *67*
6:27, *86*
6:36, *86*, *147*
6:37, *138*, *139*
6:37-38, *140*
7, *130*
7:1-10, *12*
7:16, *197*
7:18-23, *197*
7:21, *82*
7:27, *198*
7:37-41, *130*
8:5-8, *182*
9:21-22, *182*
10:17, *203*
10:21, *4*, *203*
10:28, *207*
11:21-22, *163*
12:7, *46*
12:32-33, *134*
12:35-36, *134*
12:45-46, *14*
12:50, *61*
14:11, *72*
14:21, *201*
16:24, *85*
16:25, *150*
19:8, *99*
23:43, *204*
24:25, *60*, *98*

John
1:5, *182*
1:14, *2*
1:29, *55*, *75*, *173*, *174*, *196*, *199*
1:31, *50*
1:41, *173*
1:41-42, *61*
1:45, *173*
1:45-46, *43*
1:46, *43*
1:48, *173*
1:49, *173*
2:19, *30*
3:2, *156*
3:5-6, *1*
3:26, *56*
4:24, *28*
4:50, *172*
5:43, *196*
6:28, *158*
6:29, *158*
6:40, *158*
6:41, *36*
6:42, *24*
6:63, *28*
7:1, *36*
7:13, *36*
7:37, *86*
8:31, *36*
8:34, *93*
8:48, *36*
10:24, *205*
10:31, *205*
10:33, *205*
12:1-4, *130*
12:11, *36*
13:35, *79*
14:9, *87*
15:3, *51*, *61*, *169*
15:12, *78*
15:26-27, *176*
16:33, *209*
17:2-3, *206*
19:10-11, *186*

Acts
1:1, *57*
1:5, *61*
3:13-15, *182*
4:20, *77*
4:32, *120*
7:53, *199*
7:56, *58*
8, *155*
8:1, *179*
8:32, *175*
10, *12*
12:12, *180*
12:17, *180*
12:21-23, *180*
15:9, *169*
15:10-11, *207*
19:3-5, *51*
20:29-30, *155*
26:16-17, *180*

Romans
2:6, *54*, *159*
2:14, *81*
2:15, *159*
2:15-16, *54*
2:24, *92*
4:15, *168*
6:7, *61*
7:8-9, *5*
7:24, *75*
7:25, *102*
8:7, *96*, *101*
8:9, *8*, *51*
8:14, *62*
8:27, *196*
8:35, *163*
9:16, *201*
10:10, *166*, *183*, *188*
11:25, *5*
11:25-26, *5*
12:1, *20*
12:12, *129*
12:19, *4*
13:10, *84*
14:23, *175*
16:25-26, *207*

1 Corinthians
2:11, *177*
2:15, *196*
3:12, *38*
4:4, *72*
5:1-5, *147*
6:18, *80*, *149*
10:13, *125*, *180*
15:25, *30*
15:31, *186*
15:51, *5*
16:2, *127*

2 Corinthians
5:4, *184*
12:9, *167*

Galatians
2:14-15, *36*
2:15-16, *208*
3:1, *97*

4:4, *3*
5:6, *189*
5:15, *189*
5:17, *101, 133, 184*
5:22-23, *156*
6:2, *104*
6:10, *194*

Ephesians
2:1, *102*
2:3, *174*
2:13, *47*
2:14, *5, 87*
2:19, *91*
4:29, *97*
5:8, *122, 182*
5:16, *175*
5:26, *51*
6:12, *122*
6:16, *6*

Philippians
2:6, *205*
2:10, *205*
2:10-11, *207*
2:15-16, *91*
3:12, *72*
3:13-15, *178*
3:20, *46, 83*
4:8-9, *197*
4:13, *207*

Colossians
2:18-19, *102*
3:5, *8*
4:5, *175*

1 Thessalonians
4:10-11, *72*

1 Timothy
1:9, *170*
4:5, *144*
4:12, *83*
4:13, *30*
5:6, *26*
5:11-12, *71*
6:8, *9*
6:8-9, *80*
6:8-10, *72*
6:17-18, *109*

2 Timothy
1:13, *14*
2:2, *35*
2:17, *14*
2:19, *160, 162*
2:23, *14*
3:12, *62*

Hebrews
2:9, *205*
4:12, *190*

1 Peter
4:8, *100*
5:3, *14*

1 John
2:15, *8*
3:15, *96*

2 John
10, *155*

Revelation
2–3, *12*
3:20, *147*
5:8, *118*
20:6, *186*